4/12

GREAT DEBATES
AT THE
UNITED NATIONS

GREAT DEBATES AT THE UNITED NATIONS

An Encyclopedia of Fifty Key Issues
1945–2000

ROBERT F. GORMAN

Greenwood Press
Westport, Connecticut • London

341.23
G

Library of Congress Cataloging-in-Publication Data

Gorman, Robert F.
    Great debates at the United Nations : an encyclopedia of fifty key issues 1945–2000 /
Robert F. Gorman.
        p.   cm.
    Includes bibliographical references and index.
    ISBN 0–313–31386–5 (alk. paper)
    1. United Nations—Encyclopedias.   I. Title.
KZ4968.G67   2001
341.23—dc21   00–057652

British Library Cataloguing in Publication Data is available.

Library of Congress Catalog Card Number: 00–057652
ISBN: 0–313–31386–5

First published in 2001

Greenwood Press, 88 Post Road West, Westport, CT 06881
An imprint of Greenwood Publishing Group, Inc.
www.greenwood.com

Printed in the United States of America

∞™

The paper used in this book complies with the
Permanent Paper Standard issued by the National
Information Standards Organization (Z39.48–1984).

10 9 8 7 6 5 4 3 2 1

Contents

Preface

This reference work summarizes and explains fifty United Nations (UN) debates. The entries are presented in rough chronological order based on the time when they first appeared on the UN agenda or, in some cases, when, though having previously appeared on the agenda in some form, they gained more prominent notice. Thus, a reader seeking to get a sense for the historical flow of UN debates may productively begin with the first entry on disarmament and read straight through until the last entry, which deals with the Kosovo issue. Such an approach will allow the reader to view the changing panorama of UN debate through time. Each entry may be consulted on its own, however, since all entries include a discussion of the significance of the issue, its historical background, the history of the UN debate itself, and a discussion of the outcome of the debate. Suggestions for further reading provide additional sources on the history of the subject or contrasting evaluations of the issue.

Some of these debates concern issues that are quite specific and admissible of concrete solutions. Other issues are perennial in nature, appearing periodically or even annually in some cases. Many of the issues are closely interrelated. Lessons learned by member states in one situation are sometimes applied to later similar situations. The issues vary in terms of their historical complexity and their development. Whatever the case, each entry seeks to explain some of the background factors that led to the emergence of the issue, to review the historical dimensions and developments of the debate, and to explain its later or ongoing significance.

Debates at the United Nations begin when issues of concern to states or other international bodies are brought to its attention, usually through the office of the secretary-general. The secretary-general is the keeper of the agenda of the main UN organs, especially the Security Council and the General Assembly. When emergency issues or conflicts occur any member state may ask that a meeting of the Security Council be convened to address them. Once a matter has been considered by the Security Council, it determines whether further meetings are necessary, although subsequent requests by governments for additional meetings may always be made. Governments may also request that the secretary-general inscribe less pressing issues of international significance on the agenda of the General Assembly. Such requests may be made by individual governments or by groups of states, or by UN committees, specialized agencies, conferences, or other bodies. The secretary-general keeps track of all such requests and, at the beginning of each annual session of the General Assembly, he submits a report to the General Committee of the General Assembly. The General Committee decides how to allocate the various issues and agenda items and makes recommendations to the General Assembly, which ultimately determines its own agenda.

UN debates are marked both by public statements and formal arguments that appear in the official records of the United Nations and by a great deal of private lobbying, discussion, and maneuvering, as governments seek to hammer out acceptable and viable proposals. More often than not, the critical decisions are made behind closed doors, at private gatherings, or even at social functions rather than on the actual floor of the General Assembly, the Security Council, or other UN bodies. This is especially true of the decision-making process in major UN conferences. Usually, meetings of member states among themselves and with UN officials responsible for conference planning are held long before a UN conference is to meet. Typically, not only the agenda of the meeting is discussed, but also proposed draft texts of a conference declaration and/or program of action will be largely negotiated even before the conference meets. Sometimes such draft texts are produced by a small and fairly like-minded group of governmental, UN, and nongovernmental agency elites seeking to promote a particular agenda or cause that would otherwise meet stiff opposition if proposed before national legislative bodies. In such cases, draft texts will usually excite opposition when they are further deliberated at the conference itself, where all governments will have a say, rather than in working groups or preparatory committees, which normally consist of smaller groups of state representatives. The conferences themselves usually consist of a parade of formal speeches and the eventual and often, but not always, predictable adoption of the text of the declaration and program of action as negotiated before the opening gavel. Sometimes, when differences are unresolved by the time of the conference, as they were at the Cairo Population Conference in 1994 or the International Women's Conference in Beijing in 1995, they must be hammered out at the conference itself, either in smaller working groups or in executive sessions. For some debates, such as those giving rise to the UN Law of the Sea Treaty, annual sessions over several years may be necessary to win broad acceptance of a potential treaty or conference resolution.

Because so much of UN debate is informal and goes unrecorded in UN documents, students of UN debates must rely to some extent on the actual position papers and statements of individual governments to identify points of contention and of potential agreement between or among governments. It is also helpful to know that a country's position in a debate may be in part a reflection of bloc politics. Countries of the former East bloc, for instance, had a very high percentage of agreement on issues debated before the United Nations. Members of the Group of Seven are often in agreement on political and economic issues. Members of the Africa Caucus share many similar concerns, as do countries in the Islamic Conference or the Asia Group. Members of the European Union group are fairly like-minded.

On any particular issue, these bloc alignments may do very little to predict the position of a particular country. In the Law of the Sea debate, for instance, Zambia as a copper-producing landlocked state had different interests from Chad, which, though African and landlocked, possessed no mineral resources to be potentially threatened by a glut on international markets owing to sea-based production. Similarly, Angola, Zambia's neighbor to the west, is a coastal state with substantial fishery resources. Angola's concerns moved along different lines than those of Zambia. On any given UN issue, then, bloc affiliation is important to know but not necessarily decisive in explaining a particular country's policies.

The public statements of governments in UN debates are sometimes affected by the emotion of the moment or by rhetoric calculated to be heard by domestic constituencies. This has long been a criticism of public and multilateral diplomacy. A foreign minister or UN delegate ultimately represents a government that seeks either to be reelected or at least to be respected by its domestic constituencies or public. As such, a little grandstanding and overblown rhetoric are to be expected. But, in the United Nations, as in traditional negotiating contexts, the most effective diplomacy is not conducted under the glare of the camera and the blare of the open microphone but through confidential and private discussions and caucuses.

Adding to the difficulty of UN debates is the fact of cultural and linguistic diversity. Although English is widely spoken by most diplomats representing their countries before UN bodies, it is not universally spoken. Thus, the United Nations has made provision for its debates to be translated simultaneously into each of its six working languages: English, French, Russian, Chinese, Spanish, and Arabic. This is a burden rarely encountered in national decision-making bodies. Although a complication, linguistic diversity rarely inhibits UN debates. Occasional misunderstandings may arise over a mistranslation or misinterpretation, but these are rarely a major hindrance.

UN debates reflect, ultimately, the positions staked out on important international issues by the governments of particular states. As the governments representing states change owing to political trends, revolutions and coups d'état, one can expect some, if not many, of the positions held to change as well. There is nothing static about UN debates. The issues change, and so do the arguments and the players articulating the arguments. Governments, in turn, are affected by public opinion, even in nondemocratic states. Their publicly stated positions on debates in UN forums will be scrutinized by the political opposition at home. Governments are lobbied by private groups, organizations and enterprises as well. At the United Nations alone, hundreds of nongovernmental organizations (NGOs) enjoy various levels of consultative status with the Economic and Social Council (ECOSOC) and the UN General Assembly. NGOs have been routinely invited to participate as observers and in some cases as active participants in the deliberations of international conferences. They are a source of potential information to governments and international bureaucrats, as well as being advocates of particular causes. They can levy pressure on governments not only privately but through the media. They have no direct capacity in the United Nations to dictate the outcome of a debate among governments, but they can help to shape the broad outlines of such debates and make public their specific views on important international issues. Thus, groups such as Amnesty International, the Lawyers Committee for Human Rights, Greenpeace, Oxford Committee for Famine Relief (OXFAM), Caritas International, Cooperative for Assistance and Relief Everywhere (CARE), World Vision, the Red Cross, and many others are in a position to influence, if not to dictate, the outcome of UN debates.

Ultimately, UN debates are moved by the decisions and interests of member states who seek to protect and defend their own national interests, as they define them, while advancing international cooperation when this is to their mutual advantage. Politics within and between governments drives the debates at the United Nations. To fully understand UN debates, then, one must know a great deal about the domestic debates within various countries regarding international issues of concern to them. One must understand the psychology, the attitudes, and views that prevail in the thinking of the dominant political parties and leaders of each country participating in the UN debate. One must know how each UN delegation views the world and the United Nations itself and who it considers to be its current or potential allies and opponents in articulating its positions on any particular agenda topic. In short, one must know something about the international politics of the issue under consideration. In the entries that follow, information is provided to help a student understand how many important UN issues have evolved, how interested governments have differed, and how the debate has progressed. This general knowledge, however, is only a beginning. A full understanding of a specific country's position on any of the great debates summarized in this encyclopedia requires further research into that country's domestic situation and foreign policy outlook. Cross-references to related subjects follow the entries; each subject is followed by the debate number since chapters are arranged chronologically rather than alphabetically. A bibliography of sources is provided at the end of each entry to offer additional resources that may be consulted to help in this process, and a bibliographic essay at the end of the book provides further suggestions for the reader seeking information on the policies of particular countries.

The appendixes include a chart on the structure of the UN system; a list of UN member states by year of their entry into the United Nations; and lists of UN General Assembly Special and Emergency Sessions, of UN World Years, of UN Peacekeeping Operations, of Secretaries-General of the United Nations, and of Presidents of the UN General Assembly. A sample Security Council Resolution (242) and General Assembly Resolution (377) are provided to serve as examples of both the form and content of such resolutions. Finally, a copy of the UN Charter is found in Appendix 9, so that the reader may reference various remarks referring to the Charter in the entries.

Acronyms

ABM	antiballistic missile
AEC	Atomic Energy Commission
AIDS	acquired immunodeficiency syndrome
ANC	African National Congress (South Africa)
CARE	Cooperative for Assistance and Relief Everywhere
CFCs	Chlorofluorocarbons
CIAV	International Commission for Support and Verification
CSCE	Conference on Security and Cooperation in Europe
DHA	Department of Humanitarian Affairs
EC	European Community
ECOMOG	ECOWAS Military Observer Group
ECOSOC	Economic and Social Council
ECOWAS	Economic Council of West African States
EEC	European Economic Community
EPTA	Expanded Program of Technical Assistance
EU	European Union
EXCOM	Executive Committee of the UNHCR
FAA	Angolan Armed Forces
FAO	Food and Agriculture Organization
FMLN	Frente Farabundo Marti para la Liberación Nacional (El Salvador)
FNLA	National Front for the Liberation of Angola
FRELIMO	Front for the Liberation of Mozambique
FRETILIN	Frente Revolucionária Timor Leste Independente (East Timor)
FRY	Federal Republic of Yugoslavia

FUNCINPEC	National United Front for an Independent, Neutral, Peaceful, and Cooperative Cambodia
FYROM	Former Yugoslav Republic of Macedonia
GAOR	General Assembly Official Records
GATT	General Agreement on Tariffs and Trade
GEMS	Global Environmental Monitoring System
GIS	Group of Interested States (Disarmament)
GNP	gross national product
HIPCs	heavily indebted poor countries
HIV	human immunodeficiency virus
IAEA	International Atomic Energy Agency
IBRD	International Bank for Reconstruction and Development
ICAO	International Civil Aviation Organization
ICARA	International Conference on Assistance to Refugees in Africa
ICEM	Intergovernmental Committee for European Migration
ICJ	International Court of Justice
ICRC	International Committee of the Red Cross
IDA	International Development Association
IFAD	International Fund for Agricultural Development
IFC	International Finance Corporation
IFOR	Implementation Force
IFRC	International Federation of Red Cross and Red Crescent Societies
IGCR	Intergovernmental Committee for Refugees
IGOs	intergovernmental organizations
ILO	International Labor Organization
IMCO	International Maritime Consultative Organization
IMF	International Monetary Fund
INCB	International Narcotics Control Board
INF	intermediate-range nuclear force
INSTRAW	International Research and Training Institute for the Advancement of Women
INTERFET	International Force in East Timor
INTERPOL	International Police Organization
IOM	International Organization for Migration
IPDC	International Program for the Development of Communication
IRO	International Refugee Organization
ISA	International Seabed Authority

KFOR	International Force in Kosovo
KLA	Kosovo Liberation Army
KPNLF	Khmer People's National Liberation Front (Cambodia)
LDCs	less-developed countries
MFN	most-favored nation (trade clause)
MICIVIH	International Civilian Mission to Haiti
MIGA	Multilateral Investment Guarantee Agency
MINUGUA	United Nations Verification Mission in Guatemala
MINURCA	United Nations Mission in Central African Republic
MINURSO	United Nations Mission for the Referendum in the Western Sahara
MIPONUH	United Nations Civilian Police Mission in Haiti
MNF	Multinational Force (Haiti)
MONUA	United Nations Observer Mission in Angola
MONUC	United Nations Observer Mission in the Democratic Republic of the Congo
MPLA	Popular Movement for the Liberation of Angola
MSAs	most seriously affected countries
NATO	North Atlantic Treaty Organization
NBC	nuclear, bacteriological, and chemical
NGOs	nongovernmental organizations
NICs	newly industrializing countries
NIEO	New International Economic Order
NIIO	New International Information Order
NPT	Non-proliferation Treaty
OAS	Organization of American States
OAU	Organization of African Unity
OEOA	Office of Emergency Operations in Africa
OIC	Organization of the Islamic Conference
OIHP	International Office of Public Health
ONUC	United Nations Operation in the Congo
ONUCA	United Nations Observer Group in Central America
ONUMOZ	United Nations Operation in Mozambique
ONUSAL	United Nations Observer Mission in El Salvador
ONUVEH	United Nations Observer Group for the Verification of the Elections in Haiti
ONUVEN	United Nations Observer Mission for the Verification of Elections in Nicaragua
OPEC	Organization of Petroleum Exporting Countries

OSCE	Organization for Security and Cooperation in Europe
OXFAM	Oxford Committee for Famine Relief
PAHO	Pan-American Health Organization
PCNB	Permanent Central Narcotics Board
PDK	Party of Democratic Kampuchea (Cambodia)
PLO	Palestine Liberation Organization
POWs	prisoners of war
PRC	People's Republic of China
RENAMO	Mozambican National Resistance
ROC	Republic of China
RPF	Rwandan Patriotic Front
SALT	Strategic Arms Limitation Talks
SDRs	special drawing rights
SNA	Somali National Alliance
SNC	Supreme National Council
SNM	Somali National Movement
SPM	Somali Patriotic Movement
START	Strategic Arms Reduction Talks
SUNFED	Special United Nations Fund for Economic Development
SWAPO	Southwest Africa People's Organization
TNCs	transnational corporations
UN	United Nations
UNAMET	United Nations Assessment Mission in East Timor
UNAMIC	United Nations Advance Mission in Cambodia
UNAMIR	United Nations Assistance Mission for Rwanda
UNAMSIL	United Nations in Sierra Leone
UNASOG	United Nations Aozou Strip Observer Group
UNAVEM	United Nations Angola Verification Mission
UNCED	United Nations Conference on Environment and Development
UNCHS	United Nations Centre for Human Settlements
UNCIP	United Nations Commission for India and Pakistan
UNCND	United Nations Commission for Narcotic Drugs
UNCPSG	United Nations Civilian Police Support Group (Croatia)
UNCRO	United Nations Confidence Restoration Operation in Croatia
UNCTAD	United Nations Conference on Trade and Development
UNDCP	United Nations Drug Control Program
UNDOF	United Nations Disengagement Observer Force

UNDP	United Nations Development Program
UNEF	United Nations Emergency Force
UNEP	United Nations Environment Program
UNESCO	United Nations Educational, Scientific, and Cultural Organization
UNFDAC	United Nations Fund for Drug Abuse Control
UNFICYP	United Nations Peacekeeping Force in Cyprus
UNFPA	United Nations Fund for Population Activities
UNGOMAP	United Nations Good Offices Mission in Afghanistan and Pakistan
UNHCHR	United Nations High Commissioner for Human Rights
UNHCR	United Nations High Commissioner for Refugees
UNICEF	United Nations Children's Fund (formerly United Nations International Children's Emergency Fund)
UNIDO	United Nations Industrial Development Organization
UNIFEM	United Nations Voluntary Fund for the Decade on Women
UNIFIL	United Nations Interim Force in Lebanon
UNIIMOG	United Nations Iran-Iraq Military Observer Group
UNIKOM	United Nations Iraq-Kuwait Observer Mission
UNIN	United Nations Institute for Namibia
UNIPOM	United Nations India-Pakistan Observation Mission
UNITA	National Union for the Total Independence of Angola
UNITAF	Unified Task Force (Somalia)
UNKRA	United Nations Korean Reconstruction Agency
UNMIBH	United Nations Mission in Bosnia and Herzegovina
UNMIH	United Nations Mission in Haiti
UNMIK	United Nations Interim Administration Mission in Kosovo
UNMOGIP	United Nations Military Observer Group in India and Pakistan
UNMOP	United Nations Mission of Observers in Prevlaka (Croatia)
UNMOT	United Nations Mission of Observers in Tajikistan
UNMOVIC	United Nations Monitoring, Verification, and Inspection Commission
UNOCA	United Nations Office for the Coordination of Humanitarian Assistance to Afghanistan
UNOCHA	United Nations Office for Coordination of Humanitarian Affairs
UNOGIL	United Nations Observer Group in Lebanon
UNOMIG	United Nations Observer Mission in Georgia
UNOMIL	United Nations Observer Mission in Liberia

UNOMSA	United Nations Observer Mission in South Africa
UNOMSIL	United Nations Observer Mission in Sierra Leone
UNOMUR	United Nations Observer Mission Uganda-Rwanda
UNOSOM	United Nations Operation in Somalia
UNPAs	United Nations protected areas
UNPREDEP	United Nations Preventive Deployment Force (Macedonia)
UNPROFOR	United Nations Protection Force (Balkans)
UNRRA	United Nations Relief and Rehabilitation Administration
UNRWA	United Nations Relief and Works Agency for Palestine
UNSCOM	United Nations Special Commission (Nuclear Inspection Team)
UNSMIH	United Nations Support Mission in Haiti
UNTAC	United Nations Transitional Authority in Cambodia
UNTAES	United Nations Transitional Administration for Eastern Slavonia, Baranja and Western Sirmium (Croatia)
UNTAET	United Nations Transitional Administration in East Timor
UNTAG	United Nations Transition Assistance Group
UNTEA	United Nations Temporary Executive Authority (West Irian)
UNTMIH	United Nations Transition Mission in Haiti
UNTSO	United Nations Truce Supervision Organization
UNYOM	United Nations Yemen Observation Mission
USC	United Somali Congress
WFP	World Food Program
WHO	World Health Organization
WSLF	Western Somali Liberation Front
WTO	World Trade Organization
ZANU	Zimbabwe African National Union
ZAPU	Zimbabwe African People's Union

Timeline of Important Events

1941 (June)   Inter-Allied Declaration recognizes a need for freedom and peaceful cooperation among nations.

1941 (Aug.)   The Atlantic Charter enunciates principles for international security.

1942 (Jan.)   Twenty-six countries sign a Declaration by the United Nations.

1943 (Nov.)   United Nations Relief and Rehabilitation Administration (UNRRA) begins work.

1944 (July)   Bretton Woods Conference meets to discuss reorganization of the international monetary system.

1944 (Aug.–Oct.)   Great powers meet at Dumbarton Oaks to negotiate principles of a new post-war intergovernmental organization.

1945 (Feb.)   Yalta meetings of the Big Three powers lead to refinements of proposed UN security system and UN membership.

1945 (Feb.–Mar.)   Latin American States meet to discuss great power proposals for the United Nations at the Mexico City Conference on Problems of Peace and War.

1945 (Apr.–June)   UN Conference meets in San Francisco; produces the UN Charter, which is signed by fifty nations on 26 June.

1946 (Jan.–Feb.)   The UN General Assembly meets for the first time in London; establishes the Atomic Energy Commission (AEC).

1946 (Feb.)   First International Court of Justice (ICJ) judges are elected.

1946 (Dec.)   United Nations International Children's Emergency Fund (UNICEF)—later renamed the UN Children's Fund—is established by General Assembly; incorporation of Southwest Africa (Namibia) into South Africa is rejected;

	constitution of the International Refugee Organization (IRO) is approved.
1947 (Nov.)	World Bank brought into relation with the United Nations; General Assembly approves partition of Palestine.
1948 (Jan.)	Kashmir dispute between India and Pakistan reaches Security Council agenda.
1948 (May)	Palestine Mandate of the United Kingdom is terminated; Israel proclaims independence and receives recognition by the United States; war in Palestine intensifies.
1948 (July)	Security Council orders cease-fire in Palestine; World Health Organization (WHO) is brought into relation with the United Nations.
1948 (Nov.)	General Assembly approves creation of UN Relief for Palestine Refugees.
1948 (Dec.)	General Assembly approves Genocide Convention; adopts Universal Declaration of Human Rights.
1949 (Feb.–July)	Egypt-Israel, Lebanon-Israel, Jordan-Israel, and Syria-Israel, armistices take effect in Middle East, ending hostilities.
1949 (July)	Atomic Energy Commission suspends work.
1949 (Dec.)	General Assembly establishes Office of the High Commissioner for Refugees (UNHCR) and the United Nations Relief and Works Agency for Palestine (UNRWA).
1950 (Jan.)	Soviet Union withdraws from Security Council to protest UN refusal to seat the Communist government of China.
1950 (Mar.)	ICJ upholds necessity of Security Council recommendations (subject to veto) for admission of member states to the United Nations.
1950 (June)	North Korean invasion of South Korea prompts Security Council to call upon members to resist aggression and provide the Republic of Korea with military assistance.
1950 (July)	Security Council establishes a unified command to oppose aggression in Korea.
1950 (Aug.)	Soviet Union resumes participation in Security Council meetings.
1950 (Nov.)	Uniting for Peace Resolution is adopted by the General Assembly; General Assembly considers question of aggression and duties of states to end hostilities.
1950 (Dec.)	General Assembly establishes the UN Korean Relief and Reconstruction Agency; calls upon South Africa to refrain

from implementing Group Areas Act; adopts statute of the UNHCR.

1951 (Jan.)	UNHCR commences operations in Geneva; UN Genocide Convention enters into force.
1951 (July)	UN Conference on the Status of Refugees and Stateless Persons is held; cease-fire talks on Korea begin.
1952 (Jan.)	General Assembly establishes Disarmament Commission to replace AEC.
1952 (Dec.)	General Assembly establishes a Commission on the Racial Situation (apartheid) in the Union of South Africa and a fifteen-member Special Committee for the Study of the Question of Aggression.
1953 (July)	Korean War ends with armistice.
1954 (Aug.–Sept.)	UN World Population Conference meets in Rome.
1954 (Dec.)	Draft Statute of the International Atomic Energy Agency (IAEA) is approved by the General Assembly.
1955 (Dec.)	Crisis over admission of new UN members resolved with package deal, as sixteen new membership applications are approved.
1956 (Oct.)	Hungarian Question placed on agenda of Security Council; Israeli invasion of Egypt, followed by UK/French intervention in the Suez Crisis.
1956 (Nov.)	General Assembly special sessions on the Suez Crisis and the Hungarian Situation; General Assembly deploys emergency force to Suez.
1957 (July)	IAEA formally comes into being.
1958 (Feb.–Apr.)	United Nations Law of the Sea Conference is held.
1958 (June)	Security Council establishes United Nations Observer Group in Lebanon (UNOGIL).
1958 (Aug.)	General Assembly holds special emergency session on Lebanon.
1960 (Mar.–Apr.)	Second United Nations Conference on the Law of the Sea is held.
1960 (July)	Congo Crisis erupts; United Nations Operation in the Congo (ONUC) begins.
1960 (Aug.)	ONUC forces enter Katanga.
1960 (Sept.)	Decolonization efforts in Africa succeed as sixteen countries achieve independence; proposals for independence and development of Africa submitted to General Assembly by the United States; Soviet Union submits troika pro-

posal for reorganization of the UN Secretary-General Office.

1960 (Dec.)	General Assembly adopts Declaration on Granting of Independence to Colonial Peoples; establishes UN Capital Development Fund.
1961 (Mar.)	Single Convention of World Drug Control is adopted after ten years of preparation.
1961 (Sept.)	Dag Hammarskjöld killed in plane crash en route to talks in Katanga.
1961 (Dec.)	UN financial crisis deepens as members fall in arrears on payments for ONUC and United Nations Emergency Force (UNEF) operations; General Assembly seeks ICJ Advisory Opinion as to whether peacekeeping operations may be assessed on members.
1962 (Feb.)	General Assembly takes up the question of independence of Southern Rhodesia.
1962 (June)	General Assembly deplores movement toward white minority rule in Southern Rhodesia.
1962 (July)	ICJ decides that peacekeeping expenses may be assessed as regular obligations upon member states.
1962 (Dec.)	General Assembly endorses ICJ Advisory Opinion concerning assessment of peacekeeping expenses.
1963 (Jan.)	World Food Programme (WFP) commences operations; ONUC establishes control in Katanga.
1963 (May–June)	General Assembly holds special session on UN financial problems.
1963 (June)	Security Council endorses deployment of UN Yemen Observer Mission.
1963 (Aug.)	General Assembly calls for embargo on arms sales to South Africa.
1963 (Oct.)	General Assembly appoints a special mission to investigate situation in South Vietnam.
1963 (Dec.)	Security Council takes up the Cyprus situation.
1964 (Mar.)	Security Council deploys the United Nations Forces in Cyprus (UNFICYP).
1964 (Mar.–June)	United Nations Conference on Trade and Development (UNCTAD) meets for the first time.
1964 (June)	Military phase of ONUC ends in Congo.
1964 (Aug.)	Security Council meets at U.S. request to consider Gulf of Tonkin incident off shores of Vietnam.

1964 (Nov.)	Decision taken to hold Nineteenth UN General Assembly Session as a "no vote" session in order to prevent a confrontation over crisis in budget arrears.
1965 (Jan.–Feb.)	"No-vote" session of General Assembly continues.
1965 (Apr.–May)	UN Security Council deliberates on crisis in the Dominican Republic; calls for a cease-fire.
1965 (Aug.)	United States notifies United Nations that it will not insist on application of Article 19, thus ending the budget standoff; General Assembly resumes regular voting procedures; funding for peacekeeping expenses is placed on a voluntary footing.
1965 (Sept.)	India-Pakistan conflict erupts; draws Security Council attention; United Nations India-Pakistan Observation Mission (UNIPOM) is deployed.
1965 (Nov.)	Security Council condemns unilateral declaration of independence of Ian Smith regime in Southern Rhodesia; General Assembly takes up debate on the Nuclear Non-Proliferation Treaty; General Assembly establishes the United Nations Development Program (UNDP).
1965 (Dec.)	General Assembly proposes establishment of the UN Capital Development Fund.
1966 (Feb.)	At U.S. request, Security Council meets to discuss Vietnam situation, but indecision leads to no action.
1966 (July)	ICJ rules that Ethiopia and Liberia have no standing to sue on behalf of Southwest Africa (Namibia), causing controversy.
1966 (Oct.)	General Assembly revokes South African Mandate over Southwest Africa (Namibia), placing it under the direct authority of the United Nations.
1966 (Nov.)	General Assembly decides to establish the United Nations Industrial Development Organization (UNIDO).
1966 (Dec.)	Security Council invokes Chapter VII to impose compulsory economic sanctions against Southern Rhodesia; General Assembly adopts two human rights covenants, one governing civil and political rights, the other economic, social, and cultural rights.
1967 (May)	Gamal Abdel Nasser calls for United Nations to withdraw UNEF forces from along Sinai border.
1967 (June)	War breaks out as Israel attacks Arab neighbors; cease-fire achieved.
1967 (Nov.)	Security Council passes famous "land for peace" Resolution 242.

1968 (Mar.)	International Narcotics Control Board comes into being.
1968 (June)	General Assembly approves the Treaty on the Non-Proliferation of Nuclear Weapons.
1968 (Aug.)	Soviet intervention in Czechoslovakia excites Security Council discussion, but Soviet Union vetoes any action.
1968 (Sept.)	General Assembly recommends Latin American Nuclear Free Zone Treaty.
1969 (Jan.)	Convention on Elimination of All Forms of Racial Discrimination comes into force.
1970 (Sept.)	Security Council debates problem of aircraft hijacking.
1971 (May)	Crisis in East Pakistan leads to huge refugee flows into India.
1971 (Oct.)	General Assembly votes to recognize and seat representatives of the People's Republic of China in the United Nations and to expel representatives of the Republic of China from UN organizations.
1971 (Dec.)	Crisis in East Pakistan intensifies; General Assembly establishes the UN Disaster Relief Organization.
1972 (June)	First UN Conference on the Human Environment is held in Stockholm.
1972 (Sept.)	Secretary-General Waldheim asks the General Assembly to discuss the issue of terrorism as part of its agenda.
1972 (Dec.)	General Assembly establishes the UN University.
1973 (May)	UN Fund for Population Activities is established.
1973 (Oct.)	Yom Kippur War breaks out in Middle East as Israel is attacked by Arab neighbors; Security Council deploys UNEF II.
1973 (Dec.)	First Session of the UN Conference on the Law of the Sea meets in New York.
1974 (May)	Security Council establishes the UN Disengagement Observer Force to patrol Israeli-Syrian border in aftermath of Yom Kippur War.
1974 (May–June)	General Assembly holds a special session on raw materials and development; issues a Declaration on the Establishment of a New International Economic Order.
1974 (June–Aug.)	Law of the Sea Conference continues at Caracas, Venezuela.
1974 (July)	Fighting breaks out in Cyprus as Turkish forces invade; Security Council calls for cease-fire.
1974 (Nov.)	World Food Conference is held in Rome.

1974 (Dec.)	General Assembly approves a definition of "aggression"; establishes the UN World Food Council; establishes an Information and Research Center on Transnational Corporations.
1975 (Mar.)	First Session of Commission for Transnational Corporations is held; Law of the Sea Conference resumes in Geneva.
1975 (June–July)	World Conference of the International Women's Year meets in Mexico City and adopts World Plan of Action; General Assembly responds in following year with establishment of the United Nations Voluntary Fund for the Decade on Women (UNIFEM) and of the UN International Research and Training Institute for the Advancement of Women (INSTRAW).
1975 (Nov.)	General Assembly votes to equate Zionism with racism.
1975 (Dec.)	General Assembly condemns corrupt practices of transnational corporations; deplores Indonesian intervention into East Timor.
1976 (Jan.)	International Convention on Economic, Social and Cultural Rights enters into force; Committee on the Elimination of Racial Discrimination is formed under terms of the International Convention on the Elimination of All Forms of Racial Discrimination.
1976 (Mar.)	International Covenant on Civil and Political Rights enters into force.
1976 (Mar.–May)	Fourth Session of the UN Conference on the Law of the Sea meets.
1976 (Apr.)	Security Council calls upon Indonesia to withdraw forces from East Timor.
1976 (May–June)	Habitat Conference on Human Settlements meets in Vancouver, Canada.
1976 (June)	UN Food Conference at Rome establishes the International Fund for Agricultural Development (IFAD); South Africa condemned by Security Council for actions taken in Soweto riots.
1976 (Aug.–Sept.)	Fifth Session of the UN Conference on the Law of the Sea meets.
1976 (Nov.)	General Assembly adopts ten antiapartheid resolutions.
1977 (Mar.)	UN hosts a Conference on Water Resources in Mar del Plata, Argentina.
1977 (May–July)	Sixth Session of the UN Conference on the Law of the Sea meets.

1977 (Aug.)	Joint UN/Organization of African Unity (OAU) World Conference for Action against Apartheid is held in Lagos, Nigeria; UN Conference on Desertification is held in Nairobi, Kenya.
1977 (Nov.)	UN General Assembly condemns acts of aerial hijacking; Security Council imposes mandatory arms embargo against South Africa under Chapter VII of the UN Charter.
1978 (Mar.)	Security Council calls for Israeli withdrawal from Lebanon; establishes the United Nations Interim Force in Lebanon (UNIFIL) to monitor situation.
1978 (Mar.–May)	Seventh Session of the UN Conference on the Law of the Sea meets.
1978 (Apr.)	General Assembly holds Eighth and Ninth Special Sessions on Lebanon and Namibia.
1978 (May)	Security Council calls for withdrawal of South African Forces from Angola.
1978 (May–July)	General Assembly holds Tenth Special Session on Disarmament.
1978 (Aug.)	Proposal for establishment of the United Nations Transition Assistance Group (UNTAG) to assist in peaceful settlement of the Namibia dispute is considered by the Security Council.
1978 (Aug.–Sept.)	Seventh Session of the UN Conference on the Law of the Sea resumes.
1978 (Sept.)	Security Council considers question of political repression in Nicaragua.
1978 (Oct.)	New UN Disarmament Commission comes into being.
1978 (Dec.)	General Assembly rejects internal settlement reached in Rhodesia (Zimbabwe); calls for comprehensive settlement involving exiled resistance groups.
1979 (Jan.–Apr.)	UN Law of the Sea Conference continues in Eighth Session.
1979 (Apr.)	Security Council declares elections in Rhodesia (Zimbabwe) null and void.
1979 (July–Aug.)	Eighth Session of the UN Law of the Sea Conference resumes.
1979 (Sept.)	UN Economic Commission endorses financial assistance to Nicaragua in wake of downfall of the Somoza regime.
1979 (Nov.)	Refugee situation in Southeast Asia prompts international pledging conference and proposals for coping with boat people.

1979 (Nov.–Dec.)	Security Council calls upon Iran to release detained U.S. diplomats in Teheran; litigation begins in ICJ leading to decision calling for release of hostages.
1979 (Dec.)	General Assembly approves Outer Space Treaty on Activities of States on the Moon and Other Celestial Bodies and adopts International Convention on the Elimination of All Forms of Discrimination against Women; UN Security Council terminates sanctions against Southern Rhodesia, as Britain resumes full authority in preparation for free and fair elections; Soviet Union intervenes in Afghanistan.
1980 (Jan.)	Security Council calls for special session of the General Assembly as Soviet Union vetoes resolution calling for withdrawal of foreign forces; General Assembly special session on Afghanistan calls for immediate withdrawal of all foreign troops from Afghanistan.
1980 (Mar.–Apr.)	Ninth Session of the UN Conference on the Law of the Sea meets.
1980 (Apr.–May)	UN Conference on the International Code of Conduct on the Transfer of Technology fails to adopt code.
1980 (June)	Security Council condemns South African intervention in Angola.
1980 (July)	Second World Conference on Women meets at Copenhagen, Denmark; General Assembly holds Seventh Emergency Special Session on the question of Palestine.
1980 (July–Aug.)	Ninth Session of the UN Conference on the Law of the Sea resumes.
1980 (Aug.–Sept.)	General Assembly holds Eleventh Special Session on global economic matters and development.
1980 (Sept.)	Iran-Iraq War commences; Security Council calls for peaceful settlement.
1980 (Dec.)	General Assembly adopts recommendation approving United Nations Educational, Scientific, and Cultural Organization (UNESCO) efforts to establish a New International Information Order.
1981 (Mar.–Apr.)	Tenth Session of the UN Conference on the Law of the Sea meets.
1981 (Apr.)	International Conference on Assistance to Refugees in Africa (ICARA I) is held in Geneva.
1981 (July)	International Conference on Kampuchea (Cambodia) calls for a comprehensive political settlement.

1981 (Aug.)	Tenth Session of the UN Conference on the Law of the Sea resumes; UN Conference on New and Renewable Sources of Energy is held.
1981 (Sept.)	UN Conference on Least Developed Countries adopts proposals; General Assembly holds Eighth Emergency Special Session on Namibia.
1981 (Dec.)	General Assembly asserts the right to development as inalienable.
1982 (Jan.–Feb.)	General Assembly holds Ninth Emergency Special Session on the Middle East situation.
1982 (Mar.–Apr.)	Eleventh Session of the UN Conference on the Law of the Sea meets; adopts draft Convention on the Law of the Sea.
1982 (Apr.)	Security Council takes up the Falkland Islands question and calls for withdrawal of Argentine forces; United States vetoes draft Security Council resolution on the use of force in Central America.
1982 (June–Sept.)	Security Council addresses intensified conflict in Lebanon.
1982 (July-Aug.)	UN World Assembly on Aging meets.
1982 (Dec.)	UN Law of the Sea Treaty is signed.
1983 (May)	Security Council calls upon Contadora group to continue search for peaceful solution to the conflicts in Central America.
1983 (Aug.)	United Nations sponsors International Conference on Palestine.
1983 (Oct.)	United States vetoes draft Security Council resolution deploring armed intervention in Grenada.
1983 (Nov.)	General Assembly calls for immediate withdrawal of foreign forces from Grenada; condemns acts of aggression against Central American countries; Security Council declares Turkish Cypriot declaration of independence invalid.
1984 (Mar.)	UN secretary-general sends group of experts to investigate use of chemical weapons in the Iran-Iraq conflict.
1984 (Apr.)	Nicaragua files complaint against United States with the ICJ.
1984 (May)	ICJ calls upon the United States to refrain from mining of Nicaraguan harbors.
1984 (July)	Second International Conference on Assistance to Refugees in Africa (ICARA II) is held in Geneva.
1984 (Aug.)	UN Population Conference is held in Mexico City.

1984 (Dec.)	General Assembly adopts the Declaration on the Critical Economic Situation in Africa; calls for immediate and long-term relief and development responses; adopts the Convention against Torture and Other Cruel Inhuman or Degrading Treatment and Punishment; approves UNIDO as a specialized agency; proposes a draft Convention against Traffic in Narcotic Drugs and Psychotropic Substances; establishes an Office of Emergency Operations in Africa (OEOA).
1985 (Mar.)	United Nations sponsors the International Conference on the Emergency Situation in Africa to mobilize aid.
1985 (May)	Security Council debates the Central American question.
1985 (July)	Third World Conference on Women adopts Forward-looking Strategies at Nairobi, Kenya; UN Development Fund for Women established within UNDP.
1985 (Aug.)	Security Council condemns South Africa's repressive acts under the state of emergency.
1985 (Dec.)	General Assembly condemns acts of terrorism as criminal; General Assembly establishes the "Group of 18" to review UN administrative and financial affairs and seek needed reforms.
1986 (Feb.–Apr.)	First part of UN Disarmament Conference is held.
1986 (May–June)	General Assembly holds Thirteenth Special Session; adopts program of action for economic recovery in Africa.
1986 (June)	ICJ rules that U.S. activities in and against Nicaragua constitute a breach of international law.
1986 (June–Aug.)	Second part of UN Disarmament Conference is held.
1986 (Aug.)	Group of 18 on UN reform submits seventy-one recommendations for improving the United Nations.
1986 (Dec.)	General Assembly approves Group of 18 recommendations for UN reform.
1987 (Feb.–Mar.)	Under sponsorship of the UN secretary-general, negotiations for resolution of the Afghanistan situation make significant progress.
1987 (May)	Security Council condemns repeated use of chemical weapons in the Iran-Iraq War.
1987 (June)	International Conference on Drug Abuse and Illicit Trafficking meets in Vienna; Convention against Torture enters into force.
1987 (Aug.)	Esquipulas II agreement on peace in Central America is reached.

1987 (Aug.–Sept.)   International Conference on the Relationship between Disarmament and Development meets in New York.

1987 (Oct.)   General Assembly holds special meeting on war against acquired immunodeficiency syndrome (AIDS).

1987 (Dec.)   General Assembly calls for renewed cooperation in establishing a new world information and communication order.

1988 (Apr.)   Afghanistan peace agreement signed in Geneva.

1988 (May)   Security Council establishes United Nations Good Offices Mission in Afghanistan and Pakistan (UNGOMAP).

1988 (Aug.)   Agreement on Southwest Africa (Namibian) situation is reached; Security Council establishes United Nations Iran-Iraq Military Observer Group (UNIIMOG) to monitor border and cease-fire.

1988 (Dec.)   Angola and Cuba agree to withdrawal of Cuban troops as prelude to settlement of Namibia dispute; Security Council authorizes formation of the United Nations Angola Verification Mission (UNAVEM).

1989 (Jan.)   Montreal Protocol of 1987 on Substances that Deplete the Ozone Layer enters into force; UNAVEM forces arrive in Angola; Security Council authorizes deployment of UNTAG forces in Namibia.

1989 (Feb.)   Soviet Union completes withdrawal of forces from Afghanistan.

1989 (Mar.)   Conference on Saving the Ozone Layer meets in London.

1989 (Apr.)   UNTAG forces commence operations in Namibia.

1989 (May)   International Conference on Central American Refugees is held in Guatemala City; adopts a declaration and program of action.

1989 (June)   International Conference on Indochinese Refugees meets in Geneva; adopts a comprehensive plan of action.

1989 (July)   Security Council establishes the United Nations Observer Mission for the Verification of Elections in Nicaragua (ONUVEN).

1989 (Aug.)   International Commission for Support and Verification (CIAV) is established, beginning joint UN/Organization of American States (OAS) verification of collection of arms and demobilization of the Nicaraguan resistance.

1989 (Nov.)   UNTAG supervises free and fair elections in Namibia; Security Council establishes the United Nations Observer Group in Central America (ONUCA) to verify Esquipulas

	peace accords; General Assembly adopts Declaration on the Rights of the Child.
1989 (Dec.)	U.S. intervention in Panama draws criticism from the General Assembly.
1990 (Jan.)	Nearly sixty countries sign UN Convention on the Rights of the Child.
1990 (Feb.)	Security Council nears agreement on the Cambodian peace accord; United Nations monitors free and fair elections in Nicaragua.
1990 (Mar.)	Haiti requests UN help in organizing elections; UNTAG forces leave Namibia on successful completion of elections and mission.
1990 (Aug.)	UN Security Council condemns Iraqi invasion of Kuwait, passes a series of resolutions imposing economic sanctions, freezing Iraqi assets of foreign accounts, denying legality of the annexation of Kuwait, and imposing a naval blockade; Security Council permanent members reach final agreement on terms of a comprehensive settlement of the Cambodia situation.
1990 (Sept.)	UN Convention on the Rights of the Child enters into force; World Summit for Children meets; Security Council imposes restrictions on air flights into Iraq.
1990 (Oct.)	United Nations recognizes reunification of Germany and consolidation of two German UN seats into one.
1990 (Nov.)	UN Convention against Illicit Traffic in Narcotic Drugs and Psychotropic Substances enters into force; Paris Conference on Cambodia leads to peace agreement and to terms of a United Nations Transitional Authority in Cambodia (UNTAC); Security Council authorizes member states to use all necessary means to uphold past resolutions concerning Iraq's invasion of Kuwait and to force Iraq's compliance after 15 January 1991.
1990 (Dec.)	United Nations Observer Group for the Verification of the Elections in Haiti (ONUVEH) monitors presidential election; General Assembly initiates negotiations of a climate convention.
1991 (Jan.)	ONUVEH monitors legislative and local elections in Haiti.
1991 (Feb.)	UNIIMOG forces along Iran-Iraq border depart on completion of mission; U.S.-led forces evict Iraq from Kuwait, as retreating Iraqi forces start oil well fires.
1991 (Mar.)	Security Council sets terms for Iraq's surrender.

1991 (Apr.)	Security Council establishes sweeping terms of peace with Iraq and deploys the United Nations Iraq-Kuwait Observer Mission (UNIKOM) to patrol border; Security Council establishes the United Nations Mission for the Referendum in the Western Sahara (MINURSO).
1991 (May)	Security Council authorizes formation of the United Nations Observer Mission in El Salvador (ONUSAL) to monitor elections; UNAVEM II mission is authorized to succeed UNAVEM I in Angola.
1991 (June)	First chemical weapons and nuclear weapons inspection missions commence in Iraq.
1991 (July)	ONUSAL begins operations in El Salvador.
1991 (Aug.)	First biological weapons inspection team is deployed in Iraq.
1991 (Sept.)	Special Emergency Program for the Horn of Africa is launched to offer relief; peace agreement for El Salvador is reached in New York.
1991 (Oct.)	October coup in Haiti prompts Security Council demand for restoration of the legitimate government; Security Council authorizes deployment of the United Nations Advance Mission in Cambodia (UNAMIC) to pave the way for UN administration of the transition to democracy as Cambodian factions sign peace agreement in Paris.
1991 (Dec.)	General Assembly calls for creation of a universal registry of conventional arms; revokes 1975 resolution equating Zionism with racism; creates the UN Emergency Relief Coordinator to ensure rapid response to humanitarian crises; El Salvador peace agreement ends twelve years of civil war.
1992 (Jan.)	United Nations Observer Group in Central America (ONUCA) forces depart Central America on successful completion of mission; Security Council places arms embargo on Somalia as crisis there deepens; acknowledges that end of Cold War promises new opportunities for international peacekeeping.
1992 (Mar.)	Security Council authorizes deployment of the United Nations Protection Force (UNPROFOR) to ensure delivery of humanitarian assistance in the former Yugoslavia; United Nations Transitional Authority in Cambodia (UNTAC) replaces UNAMIC to pave the way for refugee repatriation, rehabilitation, and elections in Cambodia.
1992 (Apr.)	Security Council establishes the UN Operation in Somalia to ensure safe delivery of humanitarian aid.

1992 (May)	Security Council imposes economic sanctions on Yugoslavia, as Bosnia war deepens.
1992 (June)	United Nations Conference on Environment and Development (UNCED) meets in Rio de Janeiro, Brazil, produces the Rio Declaration of Principles and Agenda 21; UN fact-finding teams sent to Nagorno-Karabakh and Moldova; United Nations begins emergency humanitarian airlift to Sarajevo.
1992 (July)	Security Council authorizes deployment of the United Nations Observer Mission in South Africa (UNOMSA) to assist in peaceful transition from white minority to majority rule; Transnational Corporations and Management Division of UN Department of Economic and Social Development issues report describing transnational corporations (TNCs) as "engines of growth," signaling new UN attitude toward TNCs.
1992 (Aug.)	UN Commission on Human Rights condemns ethnic cleansing operations in the former Yugoslavia.
1992 (Sept.)	Security Council informs Federal Republic of Yugoslavia (Serbia and Montenegro) that it may not automatically continue membership in United Nations under Yugoslavia's seat and must apply for membership; UN good offices mission sent to Georgia; UN fact-finding team dispatched to Uzbekistan and Tajikistan.
1992 (Oct.)	Security Council assumes control of Iraqi assets frozen on foreign accounts to compensate victims of Iraqi aggression and to defray costs of UN activities related to Iraq.
1992 (Nov.)	Security Council authorizes use of all necessary means to ensure delivery of relief supplies to Somalia under the Unified Task Force (UNITAF) headed by the United States as Operation Restore Hope.
1992 (Dec.)	Security Council authorizes deployment of the United Nations Operation in Mozambique (ONUMOZ) to implement Rome peace accords and pave the way for elections; calls for closure of detention camps in Bosnia.
1993 (Jan.)	Chemical Weapons Convention is signed in Paris.
1993 (Feb.)	Economic and Social Council creates the Commission on Sustainable Development.
1993 (Mar.)	UNOSOM II takes over from UNITAF; presses for disarmament of Somalia factions.
1993 (Apr.)	Security Council demands immediate cessation of hostilities in Nagorno-Karabakh.

1993 (May)	Security Council establishes International Tribunal for War Crimes committed in the former Yugoslavia.
1993 (June)	UN peacekeepers killed in Somalia; World Conference on Human Rights meets in Vienna and recommends creation of a new UN High Commissioner for Human Rights; UN Security Council endorses results of Cambodian election; United Nations Observer Mission Uganda-Rwanda (UNOMUR) is deployed to prevent arms flows across border; Security Council imposes sanctions on Haiti.
1993 (Aug.)	New UN assistant secretary-general post to oversee the Office for Inspections and Investigations is created to enhance UN reform efforts; Security Council authorizes deployment of United Nations Observer Mission in Georgia (UNOMIG) to monitor civil war.
1993 (Sept.)	Security Council establishes United Nations Observer Mission in Liberia (UNOMIL) to monitor civil war; creates UN Mission in Haiti; UNTAC is terminated upon successful mission in Cambodia.
1993 (Oct.)	Security Council lifts sanctions on South Africa; United Nations Assistance Mission for Rwanda (UNAMIR) established to monitor situation in Rwanda.
1994 (Feb.)	Security Council authorizes creation of a civilian police component for ONUMOZ; North Atlantic Treaty Organization (NATO) air strikes taken to halt Serb attacks on Sarajevo.
1994 (Mar.)	Security Council calls upon Democratic Republic of Korea to allow nuclear inspections by the International Atomic Energy Agency (IAEA); UN Conference on Straddling Fish Stocks is held in New York.
1994 (Apr.)	Slaughter of Tutsis begins in Rwanda; South African elections lead to a peaceful transition to majority rule under President Nelson Mandela.
1994 (Apr.–May)	World Conference on Small Island States is held in Bridgetown, Barbados.
1994 (May)	World Conference on Natural Disaster Reduction meets in Yokohama, Japan.
1994 (May–June)	Security Council deploys the United Nations Aozou Strip Observer Group (UNASOG) to the Libya/Chad border.
1994 (June)	Security authorizes deployment of French troops in Rwanda (Operation Turquoise) to establish safe areas and promote relief assistance; flows of Hutu refugees inundate neighboring Tanzania and Zaire; UN Convention to Combat Desertification is concluded at Paris.

1994 (July)	International Law Commission adopts draft Statute of the International Criminal Court.
1994 (Sept.)	International Conference on Population and Development meets in Cairo and produces a program of action; UNOMUR mission is terminated along Uganda/Rwanda border.
1994 (Nov.)	Security Council establishes an International Tribunal for War Crimes in Rwanda; UN Law of the Sea Treaty enters into force.
1994 (Dec.)	ONUMOZ forces in Mozambique are terminated after successful election process; Security Council deploys the United Nations Mission of Observers in Tajikistan (UNMOT).
1995 (Jan.)	World Trade Organization (WTO) is established.
1995 (Feb.)	UNAVEM III replaces UNAVEM II in Angola following Lusaka Protocol.
1995 (Mar.)	UNOSOM II forces leave Somalia after failed effort to resolve civil war; Security Council deploys the United Nations Confidence Restoration Operation in Croatia (UNCRO) and the United Nations Preventive Deployment Force (UNPREDEP) in the Former Yugoslavia Republic of Macedonia.
1995 (Apr.)	ONUSAL forces leave El Salvador on successful completion of elections.
1995 (June)	The African Nuclear-Weapon-Free Zone Treaty is adopted in Addis Ababa by the OAU.
1995 (Aug.)	Treaty on Straddling Fish Stocks and Highly Migratory Fish Stocks is adopted at New York.
1995 (Sept.)	Fourth World Conference on Women meets in Beijing, China.
1995 (Oct.)	International Conference on Families meets in New York.
1995 (Nov.)	World Ministerial Conference on Organized Transnational Crime meets in Naples.
1995 (Dec.)	UN Conference on Straddling Fish Stocks and Highly Migratory Fish Stocks concludes work on Treaty; UNPROFOR is terminated after Dayton Accords as an International Force (IFOR) is deployed to implement peace deal in Bosnia and a new United Nations Mission in Bosnia and Herzegovina (UNMIBH) is established to support civil administration and relief activities.
1996 (Jan.)	Security Council deploys the United Nations Transitional Administration for Eastern Slavonia, Baranja and Western

	Sirmium (UNTAES) in Croatia and the UNCRO is terminated.
1996 (Mar.)	World Summit for Social Development meets in Copenhagen, Denmark; Security Council terminates UNAMIR force in Rwanda.
1996 (June)	Habitat II City Summit to Forge the Future of Human Settlements in an Urbanizing World meets in Istanbul, Turkey; Security Council replaces UNMIH, which is followed by deployment of the United Nations Support Mission in Haiti (UNSMIH) in July.
1996 (Sept.)	General Assembly adopts the Comprehensive Nuclear-Test-Ban Treaty.
1996 (Aug.)	Abuja II Agreement is reached, leading to new hope for settlement of Liberian civil war.
1996 (Oct.)	International Convention on Nuclear Safety enters into force.
1996 (Nov.)	World Food Conference meets in Rome; UN humanitarian activities in Zaire intensify as security situation deteriorates.
1996 (Dec.)	Security Council approves oil-for-food program allowing Iraq to sell oil to meet humanitarian food needs.
1997 (Jan.–May)	UN Verification Mission in Guatemala is deployed.
1997 (Feb.)	Security Council calls for a negotiated solution to the Zaire conflict.
1997 (Mar.)	Security Council determines that situation in Albania constitutes a threat to international peace and security.
1997 (Apr.)	Chemical Weapons Convention enters into force.
1997 (June)	UNAVEM III is terminated in Angola and the United Nations Observer Mission in Angola (MONUA) is established to monitor deteriorating situation; Earth Summit +5 meets in New York to review progress on UNCED's Agenda 21.
1997 (July)	Secretary-general announces sweeping reform proposals for UN management, leadership, and organization; UNSMIH is terminated in Haiti and is followed in August by deployment of the United Nations Transition Mission in Haiti (UNTMIH).
1997 (Sept.)	UNOMIL force in Liberia is terminated after successful elections.
1997 (Oct.)	International Conference on Child Labor meets in Oslo; produces global strategy for elimination of child labor.

1997 (Nov.)	UNTMIH is terminated and followed in December by deployment of the United Nations Civilian Police Mission in Haiti (MIPONUH).
1997 (Dec.)	Third Climate Change Conference meets in Kyoto to finalize amendments and a Protocol to the Convention on Climate Change; General Assembly adopts the International Convention for the Suppression of Terrorist Bombings.
1998 (Jan.)	UNTAES force in Croatia is terminated.
1998 (Feb.)	Secretary-General Kofi Annan's visit to Baghdad defuses crisis over United Nations Special Commission (UNSCOM) rights to undertake nuclear, bacteriological, and chemical weapons inspections.
1998 (Mar.)	Security Council authorizes deployment of the United Nations Mission in Central African Republic (MINURCA).
1998 (Apr.)	UN Preparatory Committee on the Establishment of an International Criminal Court produces a Draft Statute.
1998 (June)	General Assembly holds a special session on Countering the World Drug Problem; Security Council expresses concern over breakdown in mediation efforts in the Ethiopian-Eritrean conflict.
1998 (July)	Security Council authorizes deployment of the United Nations Observer Mission in Sierra Leone (UNOMSIL); UN Diplomatic Conference in Rome establishes a permanent International Criminal Court.
1998 (Sept.)	International Criminal Tribunal for Rwanda issues first ever judgment by an international court for the crime of genocide; Security Council, acting under Chapter VII, demands all parties in Kosovo to cease hostilities and maintain a cease-fire.
1998 (Dec.)	The United States and United Kingdom unleash bombing attacks on Iraq after months of tense standoff over the issue of UNSCOM inspections, sparking controversy on the Security Council.
1999 (Jan.–Feb.)	Talks on resolution of East Timor situation make dramatic progress.
1999 (Feb.)	UNPREDEP is terminated after Chinese veto of extension of its mandate; MONUA operation in Angola formally expires.
1999 (Mar.)	Ottawa Treaty on the Prohibition of the Use, Stockpiling, Production and Transfer of Anti-personnel Mines and on Their Destruction enters into force; NATO begins war against Serbia with intense bombing campaign; huge

	flows of Kosovar Albanian refugees begin to flee into neighboring countries.
1999 (Apr.)	Effort by Russia to stop bombing in Kosovo is voted down in UN Security Council.
1999 (Apr.–May)	Security Council demands cessation of hostilities in Democratic Republic of the Congo (Zaire) and withdrawal of foreign forces; humanitarian aid for 850,000 Kosovo refugees floods into neighboring countries.
1999 (May)	President Slobodan Milosevic is indicted for war crimes by the prosecutor of the International Criminal Tribunal for the Former Yugoslavia.
1999 (June)	Security Council establishes the United Nations Mission in Kosovo (UNMIK) to help restore civil administration and provide basis for economic recovery; establishes United Nations Advance Mission in East Timor (UNAMET) to organize a popular consultation to determine future status of the area as an independent state or a part of Indonesia.
1999 (July)	Exodus of Serbian Kosovar suggests difficulties in implementation of effective peace and security efforts.
1999 (Aug.)	UN reform initiative results in first written guidelines for UN employees to ensure greater openness with new media; popular consultation in East Timor discovers overwhelming support for independence.
1999 (Sept.)	Following UNAMET-sponsored consultation, Indonesian-backed forces undertake a campaign of genocide in East Timor, prompting huge refugee flows; Security Council authorizes deployment of an International Force in East Timor (INTERFET) to stop the fighting and bloodshed.
1999 (Oct.)	War in Chechnya resumes, leading to refugee flows and war-related miseries; Security Council establishes the United Nations Transitional Administration in East Timor (UNTAET) to guide East Timor's transition to full independence; Security Council establishes United Nations Mission in Sierra Leone (UNAMSIL) to disarm, demobilize, and reintegrate contending forces.
1999 (Nov.)	Impasse in the U.S. Congress over contributions to the United Nations is broken, clearing the way for U.S. payment of arrears; Security Council establishes the United Natons Observer Mission in the Democratic Republic of the Congo (MONUC).
1999 (Dec.)	Contingents of the UN Mission in Sierra Leone arrive in Freetown; UN human rights team visits East Timor, investigating possible crimes against humanitarian law; WTO meetings in Seattle evoke protests concerning effects of

globalization; Security Council establishes a new arms in-spections system for Iraq and promises possible end of sanctions if Iraq cooperates; United States pays first install-ment of back dues owed to United Nations, avoiding loss of its General Assembly vote; General Assembly adopts new treaty to stop flow of money to terrorist groups.

2000 (Jan.)   Kosovo is plagued by ongoing violence and instability.

2000 (Feb.)   Russian forces capture Chechen capital of Grozny, and badly divided rebels flee into southern mountains as charges of Russian human rights abuses in Chechnya mount; INTERFET hands over command of operations to UNTAET in East Timor; Security Council expands size of MONUC operation in the Congo; UNCTAD X meets in Bangkok, Thailand.

2000 (Mar.)   MIPONUH forces in Haiti hand over police administra-tion to the International Civilian Support Mission in Haiti; UNEP hosts Hague Conference on International Water-courses; Security Council establishes the United Nations Monitoring, Verification, and Inspection Commission (UNMOVIC) to replace UNSCOM duties in Iraq.

2000 (Apr.)   Security Council delegation visits Kosovo, appeals to eth-nic communities to shun violence; UN Conference on Crime and Justice meets in Vienna, Austria.

2000 (May)   Preparatory Committee for the World Conference on Rac-ism, Racial Discrimination, and Xenophobia and Related Intolerance meets in Geneva to plan 2001 Conference; NGOs meet at New York and adopt a Millennium Forum Declaration and Program of Action.

2000 (June)   UNGA holds Special Session on Women 2000: Gender Equality and Peace in New York and a Special Session on Social Development in Geneva.

2000 (July)   Security Council expresses concern about use of Afghan Territory to threaten neighboring states.

Introduction

HISTORICAL ROOTS OF THE UNITED NATIONS

The birth of the United Nations was preceded by nearly a century and a half of growing international activity among nations. The primary actors in international relations for many centuries, but especially after the Peace of Westphalia in 1648, which brought the Religious Wars of Europe to a close, were nation-states and the sovereign authorities within national boundaries who acted in the name of the state. The principle of national sovereignty, which was asserted at the Peace of Westphalia, implied that the government of a state had independent and exclusive control over its territory and population concerning not only questions of religion but also of the whole range of domestic legal issues pertaining to the maintenance of domestic order and prosperity. Moreover, each state could fashion its own foreign policy, and although in doing so they would need to accommodate other national powers and governments, they were free to enter into alliances, agreements, and treaties that would call for limitation and regulation of their behavior. Thus a system of international law would be necessary to govern interstate behavior, but no sovereign state could have treaty obligations forced upon it against its own will. International law, then, was conceived as a process of coordination and cooperation between and among states, not as a system of subordination in which states submitted to a higher power. The governments of states constituted the highest legal authority within their own territories, and no higher international authority could dictate to states their legal obligations. Rather, obligations flowed from the decisions made by the sovereign states themselves to voluntarily enter into agreements that suited their foreign and domestic needs.

Through diplomacy, then, governments could hope to advance their own national interests as well as the common interests of like-minded states. Ancient norms protecting the persons and legal immunities of diplomats were acknowledged as customary law and as a necessary precondition for the conduct of international relations. If one country expected its diplomats to be protected and their rights to be respected, then it would be necessary for that country to extend similar protection and respect to the diplomats of other countries. Much international law developed through custom and treaty by way of this reciprocal recognition of mutual obligations among nations. Moreover, governments could, during an era of land- and sea-based transportation, trade, and communication, rely on bilateral exchanges of diplomats to conduct their foreign relations. But during the eighteenth century, with the Industrial Revolution well under way in many European countries, and with the accompanying expansion of colonial and European trade, bilateral diplomatic approaches to the conduct of foreign relations became more cumbersome.

Added to the commercial and economic factors that complicated the traditional diplomatic system was the emergence in the early nineteenth century of Napoleonic Imperialism. Under Napoleon, French armies began a conquest of Europe, which threatened the independence of European states as well as the structure of the Westphalian state system itself. Defensive alliances were formed among European states to protect their independence from the imperial pretensions of France, and eventually they prevailed. Following the Napoleonic Wars, the governments of England, Prussia, Austria, and Russia joined in a collaborative effort to maintain the security of Europe in what came to be known as the Concert of Europe, which consisted of periodic international conferences held to manage questions of common concern to the security of European states. France was eventually readmitted to the process, the intense phase of which lasted into the 1820s. Moreover, the first modern intergovernmental organization, the Rhine River Commission, was established by the Congress of Vienna in 1815 to regulate commercial shipping and to resolve potential disputes between states that relied on the Rhine for commercial transport. Though very modest in its scope and purpose, the Rhine River Commission was motivated by a desire both to limit and control conflict among European states and to promote interstate trade and commerce.

In subsequent decades, European states continued a process of multilateral diplomacy and conferences in order to promote common interests and security, and as at the Berlin Conference in 1885, they even engaged in conference diplomacy to redraw the colonial map of Africa in an effort to avoid unnecessary conflict in the colonization of African territories. Throughout the nineteenth century, governments began to create more intergovernmental organizations (IGOs) to promote and facilitate international commerce and encourage harmonious resolution of disputes. After the Crimean War, the Congress of Paris in 1856 established a Danube River Commission to serve ends similar to those that earlier gave rise to the Rhine River Commission. In 1865, governments established the International

Telegraphic Union to regulate the use of new telegraphic technology. In 1873, the World Meteorological Organization was established to enhance the collection and sharing of global weather information, which had obvious implications for the safety of shipping and maritime commerce. In 1874, governments established a Universal Postal Union to harmonize and facilitate the international circulation of mail. About fifty IGOs had been established by governments when World War I broke out.

As in the nineteenth century, the outbreak of wars in the twentieth century stimulated the creation of many new IGOs as governments redoubled their efforts to devise ways in which to control future conflict and promote cooperative interstate relations. This was true both after World War I, which gave rise to the League of Nations, and after World War II, which gave rise to the United Nations. Increasingly, governments realized that it was necessary, with the growth of technology and with the increasingly destructive capacity of modern armies and weapons systems, to supplement their bilateral diplomatic efforts with multilateral initiatives to promote security and prosperity. Both the League of Nations and later the United Nations, and the host of related or specialized agencies that grew up around them, were devised by governments to meet certain collective security

The League of Nations at its opening session in Geneva on 15 November 1920. UN/DPI Photo by Jullien

needs or to promote specific functional ends related to the regulation of new technologies, commercial activities, or humanitarian needs. In creating such new organizations the governments did not give up their sovereignty but, rather, sought to coordinate their foreign relations in ways that would promote greater international stability and that would advance mutual prosperity.

The League of Nations was the first great global experiment dedicated to the maintenance of international peace. It embodied the principle of collective security and called upon states to renounce the use of force in resolving disputes and to agree to participate in the punishment of any aggressor state that used force against another member state. This principle of collective security was not new. Indeed, the ancient Greek city-states explicitly adopted and employed the principle in the Delphian League. During the Concert of Europe, collective security motivations guided European diplomacy. While the principle was not new, the League did represent the first effort to apply the principle globally. There were problems in how collective security theory worked in practice. One problem involved defining aggression. This was not so easy in complicated international disputes. Another problem is that although states might agree in principle not to use force, or agree to join in an obligatory military response to an aggressor, the real historical ties, friendships, and enmities that existed among states caused them to be less eager to join in a collective military action against a longtime ally. Even if an aggressor could be clearly identified, and even if the aggressor were not a close ally, concerns about involving one's military forces in a punitive war against the aggressor if one's own national security was not at stake caused governments to balk at the use of retaliatory force. This reluctance would inevitably grow if the country's government calculated that powerful allies of the aggressor might be provoked to support it if a collective security action were undertaken. The League of Nations Council faced such dilemmas in punishing Italy for its invasion of Ethiopia. Governments on the League Council could not agree to a military response, owing in part to fear about how Nazi Germany might respond. They did impose economic sanctions that hurt the Italian economy, but harsh sanctions were studiously avoided and the sanctions were eventually lifted. Moreover, Italy's invasion of Ethiopia was not reversed until the outbreak of World War II, which was itself a great indication that the collective security idea as practiced by the League was powerless to prevent great power war, although it successfully resolved numerous small power disputes.

The League was more successful in promoting functional cooperation among its member states. It developed a capacity to provide humanitarian relief to the Russian famine of the early 1920s. It developed a capacity to protect and advance the interests of refugees. The League cooperated with the International Labor Organization (ILO) to promote cooperation among labor unions, governments and businesses. It addressed the problem of trafficking in women and children and in narcotic drugs. The League encouraged the development of international law through registration of treaties and maintained close ties with an active Permanent Court of International Justice. It developed a mandate system for former colonies of the Axis powers in an effort to ensure the fair treatment of non-self-governing peoples. League bodies encouraged freedom of transit and communications, equitable international trade, and the control and prevention of disease. In all of these areas, the League of Nations established precedents for the later work of the United Nations.

THE GENESIS OF THE UNITED NATIONS

When World War II broke out, the League of Nations became essentially a holding operation. Its offices in Geneva, Switzerland, continued to function, but its mandate for collective security and economic and social cooperation had been rendered ineffectual by the war. Still, as the Allied powers cooperated to halt the aggression of Germany in Europe and of Japan in the Pacific, they also began discussions about the future shape of international relations in the postwar era. On 1 January 1942, the Declaration by the United Nations was issued by twenty-six countries that pledged to resist Axis aggression. The Declaration insisted that complete victory over the aggressive powers would be necessary to defend life, liberty, independence, religious freedom, human rights, and justice. In this Declaration, the Allies emphasized principles that would later be incorporated into the purposes and principles of the United Nations. As the war progressed the United States, Great Britain, and the Soviet Union held several wartime conferences at Dumbarton Oaks, Yalta, and Potsdam, at which they gradually hammered out an understanding of what a new global postwar organization would look like. In dealing with the all-important question of maintaining global peace and security, they decided that a Security Council was necessary and that it ought to operate largely on the consensus of the great powers. Thus, unlike the League Council where any member state could prevent League action by voting against collective security proposals, only the five permanent members of the UN Security Council would have the power of the veto. Joseph Stalin of the Soviet Union was especially insistent on this point, arguing at Dumbarton Oaks that this privilege of great power status ought to be unlimited. He feared that Soviet interests might be compromised on a body dominated by Western and non-Communist powers. Winston Churchill of Great Britain and President Franklin Roosevelt of the United States eventually agreed that a great power veto was probably necessary and ultimately saw the logic that ensuring great power agreement on the use of force would both guarantee a greater degree of success and avoid potentially dangerous Security Council actions where one great power was at odds with the majority. However, at

Great power representatives meet at Dumbarton Oaks to discuss the establishment
of the UN organization. UN/DPI Photo

the Yalta Conference of February 1945, the veto power was qualified. It
could only be employed on substantive matters, not procedural ones. This
would permit a great power to prevent enforcement action in cases of a
breach of or a threat to international peace and security or an act of aggression, but it could not be used to stop discussion of disputes involving great
powers. Stalin conceded to these limitations on the use of the veto in return
for British and American concessions allowing the Ukraine and
Byelorussia to be admitted as original members of the United Nations, despite the fact that they were under Soviet rule.

The dominance of the great powers on the Security Council, though resented by other governments, became a nonnegotiable feature of any postwar organization in the view of the great powers themselves. The great
powers also determined at Dumbarton Oaks that the United Nations
should have a General Assembly in which all member states would be represented, as well as a Secretariat and a Court. As the great powers later
sought the involvement of other countries, it became apparent that smaller
powers would demand a larger role for the General Assembly than initially
envisaged by the great powers. Latin American countries meeting in Mexico City in March 1945 insisted not only on expanded authority for the General Assembly but also for the International Court of Justice and for
regional organizations that might seek to deal with collective security is-

sues on their own terms. They also demanded guaranteed representation for Latin American countries on the Security Council.

Parallel negotiations on the establishment of a new international monetary system took place during World War II. The International Bank for Reconstruction and Development (World Bank) and International Monetary Fund (IMF), for instance, were established at the Bretton Woods Conference in 1944, and a year prior to that, governments had agreed to establish the Food and Agriculture Organization (FAO). The Allies also faced the growing problem of the massive displacement of populations owing to the devastation and destruction wrought by the war in Europe and the Pacific. To cope with this problem, they created the United Nations Relief and Rehabilitation Administration (UNRRA) in 1943. It served the needs of millions of displaced persons during World War II. Thus, whether in the context of meeting specific wartime needs or in planning for the structure of the postwar international system, governments made substantial progress in laying the foundation for the emergence of the United Nations even before World War II came to an end.

The UN Conference on International Organization met on 25 April 1945 in San Francisco. Delegations of fifty governments engaged in a series of debates over the structure and powers of the United Nations. The small states attacked the proposed veto power for permanent members as a violation of the sovereign equality of states, but the great powers held firm and all attempts to eliminate the veto failed. However, small powers did achieve some concessions. Regional organizations were permitted under Chapter VIII of the UN Charter to participate in collective security actions within their own regions under the oversight of the Security Council. In addition, a Trusteeship Council was established as a major organ of the United Nations to deal with the disposition of former League mandate territories that had yet to gain their independence as well as other territories placed under its authority. In addition, a Declaration Regarding Non-Self-Governing Territories was incorporated into the Charter at small power insistence and served as the tool whereby in subsequent decades the decolonization process could be overseen and promoted. In addition, the small powers lobbied for the elevation of the Economic and Social Council (ECOSOC) to the status of a major organ within the United Nations, although it would report to and act under the direction of the General Assembly. In turn, the ECOSOC was granted the power to call conferences, to coordinate UN relations with nongovernmental organizations (NGOs), and to coordinate the activities of all UN specialized agencies.

What emerged from San Francisco was a UN organization consisting of six major organs, including the General Assembly, the Security Council, the Economic and Social Council, the Trusteeship Council, the International Court of Justice, and the Secretariat. The General Assembly possessed the authority to discuss any matter under the competence of the United Na-

The Egyptian delegation signs the UN Charter at San Francisco on 26 June 1945.
UN/DPI Photo

tions as a whole, including peace and security matters, so long as it did not
make recommendations on matters actively under consideration by the Security Council. The Security Council was charged with primary responsibility for encouraging peaceful resolution of disputes and making
recommendations or decisions with regard to actions concerning breaches
or threats to international peace or with regard to punishing acts of aggression. In Chapter VII of the UN Charter, the Security Council was granted
the authority to impose economic sanctions against aggressor states or to
take military action against them. Whenever the Security Council decided
to employ economic or military sanctions, member states agreed to follow
its lead. Regional organizations were brought within the collective security
structure in Chapter VIII of the Charter.

Apart from attempting to maintain peace, control and resolve conflict,
and punish aggression, another major purpose of the United Nations was
to address and eliminate the underlying causes of conflict, which included
activities to promote economic development, to promote and respect human rights, to progressively develop international law, to encourage the
right of self-determination, and to meet social and humanitarian needs.
The UN General Assembly had the competence through its full or plenary

sessions and its main committees to discuss and make recommendations on all such matters. The First Committee of the General Assembly dealt with political questions, the Second Committee with economic issues, the Third Committee with social and humanitarian questions, the Fourth Committee with trusteeship matters, the Fifth Committee with budget and administrative questions, and the Sixth Committee with legal questions. In addition, ECOSOC could address all questions of an economic, social, or humanitarian nature and articulate agreements between the United Nations and specialized agencies operating under autonomous treaties or agreements established by governments, such as the World Bank, the IMF, the ILO, and others.

The UN Trusteeship Council, coupled with the ECOSOC and the General Assembly, shared the responsibility of promoting the progressive attainment of independence for peoples in non-self-governing territories. Agitation for independence and freedom of peoples was regarded as one potential major cause of conflict and threats to peace. The protection and promotion of human rights also fell in varying measures to the competence of the General Assembly, ECOSOC, and the Trusteeship Council. The International Court of Justice (ICJ), in turn, served as the chief judicial organ of the United Nations, and its Statute was annexed to the UN Charter. Because all member states of the United Nations were automatically members of the ICJ, and because many states were known to be reluctant to participate in any international court possessing a compulsory jurisdiction, member states were given the option under the ICJ Statute to recognize or to deny the Court's compulsory jurisdiction. The ICJ, then, served not only as a kind of constitutional court for the UN system to interpret the UN Charter where disputes arose over the proper authorities of the various organs but also as a means of legal resolution of disputes among member states who agreed to accept its jurisdiction and submit cases to it for adjudication. Finally, the UN Secretariat, although it would be independent of the control of any state, would serve at the disposal of governments in carrying out the wishes and directives of the various other organs of the United Nations. Thus, the tradition of an international civil service, begun so admirably under the League of Nations, continued in the form of the UN Secretariat, which was headed by the secretary-general who serves as the United Nations' chief administrative officer.

This institutional structure was directed toward the attainment of several main purposes and imbued with numerous and sometimes contradictory principles. The main purpose of the United Nations was to maintain international peace and security through peaceful measures and, where necessary, to undertake collective enforcement measures in cases of threats to peace, breaches of the peace, and acts of aggression. However, closely related to this main goal was a second purpose, namely, to achieve international cooperation in meeting economic, social, cultural, and humanitarian needs and in the promotion of human rights and fundamental freedoms, including the rights of self-determination and nondiscrimination. The first enumerated principle of the United Nations was that of the sovereign equality of all its members. This principle, however, remained in tension with the notions of promoting human rights and the self-determination of peoples, and it was qualified by the obligation member states accepted in regard to settling international disputes by peaceful means and without threatening international peace and security. Still, insofar as countries refrained from actions that threatened international peace and security, the Charter underscored that the United Nations could not interfere with matters falling within the domestic jurisdiction of a member state. The United Nations was firmly grounded, then, in recognition of the sovereignty and independence of its member states, who, in turn, acknowledged their duty to refrain from actions constituting a threat to international peace and security. Beyond that, governments could use the cooperative machinery of the United Nations as they saw fit to advance their national and common interests in harmonizing and facilitating their interrelations.

The UN Charter came into effect on 24 October 1945, and the General Assembly met for the first time in London on 10 January 1946, pending the relocation of UN headquarters to the United States, which took place shortly thereafter to temporary sites in New York until its current location in midtown Manhattan along the East River was secured and facilities completed in the early 1950s.

MAJOR DEBATES IN THE FIRST DECADE

UN activities during its first tenuous decade dealt largely with the terrible humanitarian and human rights consequences of World War II and with the deepening of the Cold War. As delegates debated the UN Charter in San Francisco, war continued in Europe and Asia, millions of people were displaced by the effects of war, and plans for the occupation of the Axis powers were already under way with the imminent conclusion of hostilities. From the outset the United Nations had to deal with the relocation and resettlement of the huge numbers of displaced persons. The United Nations Relief and Rehabilitation Administration (UNRRA) undertook this work until the creation of an International Refugee Organization in 1947, which, in turn, largely completed its work over the course of the next five years. Added to the compelling humanitarian needs of the displaced people, the world discovered to its shock and horror evidence of wartime atrocities of the Nazis, as advancing Allied forces liberated concentration and death camps during 1945. Concern about Nazi war crimes, including the execution of hostages by Axis powers, led to earlier warnings from Allied governments about action to bring war criminals to justice and, on 7 October 1942, to the creation of the UN Commission for the Investigation of

War Crimes. The Allies concluded a formal agreement on 8 August 1945 known as the London Charter that established the International Military Tribunal at Nuremberg for the trial and punishment of war criminals. The many references to human rights and fundamental freedoms contained in the UN Charter took on a new gravity in light not only of the pervasive commission of war crimes but of the grisly discovery of widespread crimes against humanity. Relatedly, under Article 48 of the Charter, ECOSOC established the UN Commission on Human Rights in February 1946, charging it with the task of developing proposals for the enactment of an International Bill of Human Rights and making proposals on the prevention of discrimination, the protection of minorities, and the status of women. Among its earliest efforts was the drafting of a Universal Declaration of Human Rights, which was approved by the UN General Assembly on 10 December 1948. A few days later, on 13 December, the Assembly also passed a resolution condemning genocide and calling upon ECOSOC to prepare a draft convention on genocide, a task that was completed two years later. The early steps taken in defense of human rights by the United Nations in its first few years of operation were to be followed in subsequent years and decades by a flood of human rights agreements and institutions.

The newly constructed UN Secretariat building rises above the East River in New York. UN/DPI Photo

But if human rights issues were of major concern to the United Nations in its early years, the problem of international conflict and the effective operation of the UN's collective security machinery also garnered substantial attention, especially with the bickering of the former Allies and deepening of the Cold War, which was marked by increasingly rancorous and ideologically rooted debate between the Soviet Union and the Western governments. The first complaint the Security Council heard originated with Iran, which charged Soviet troops stationed in Azerbaijan with fomenting civil war in Iran. Apart from a call for the two countries to continue negotiations, the Council could do little more. The matter was resolved with a withdrawal of Soviet troops from Iran's Azerbaijani region. A confrontation was avoided, but tensions along the borders of the Soviet Union and its East European satellite states continued for many years. In this climate, the hope that military cooperation among the great powers would provide a stable basis for UN peacemaking actions soon evaporated. Discussions to operationalize the Security Council's Military Staff Committee were marked by deep divisions and little agreement. As distrust between the Soviet Union and Western governments increased, so did confrontations in various parts of the world. With the exception of Austria, every country the Soviet Union occupied after World War II had a Communist regime installed under Soviet supervision. Refugees began fleeing from Eastern Europe. Winston Churchill announced that an Iron Curtain of political repression had descended over central Europe. Soviet occupation forces in East Germany prevented British, French, and American forces access by road to the portions of Berlin occupied by them after the war. The Berlin confrontation of 1948 led to an extended airlift to provide supplies to the besieged occupants of West Berlin. A Communist civil war in China began in 1946 and culminated in the victory of Mao Tse-tung's Communist Party in 1949. Ideological division and confrontational politics became the order of the day.

Added to the ideological tensions of the Cold War were major regional problems in the Indian subcontinent and the Middle East. The partition of British-occupied India into a Muslim state of Pakistan and a Hindu state of India saw considerable sectarian bloodshed and the displacement of 10 million people, as Muslims fled from India into Pakistan and Hindus from Pakistan to India. In the Middle East, the United Kingdom, unable to resolve the conflicting claims of Jews and Palestinians in its trust territory of Palestine, turned to the United Nations for help in 1947, and in May 1948 the UK mandate terminated. The Assembly decided to partition Palestine into a Jewish State and a Palestinian State. War broke out immediately upon the creation of the State of Israel, and after months of fighting, hundreds of thousands of Palestinians, on the wrong side of a losing war, found themselves as refugees without a state of their own. An angry Arab world agreed only to a temporary cease-fire in a conflict that would erupt into outright war on three subsequent occasions, deeply involving the United Nations as an agent of diplomacy and of peacekeeping.

The biggest challenge to the United Nations, however, came in the form of the Cold War. With the victory of Communist forces in mainland China in 1949, and deteriorating relations between the Soviet Union and Western governments, debates in the United Nations were often marked by shrill ideological denunciations. When the UN General Assembly refused to accept the credentials of the new Communist Chinese government, choosing instead to continue to acknowledge the Republic of China whose government had fled to Taiwan, the Soviet Union petulantly boycotted UN proceedings. Ironically, it was during this boycott that North Korea invaded South Korea, and what had been a Cold War of ideological confrontation became a hot war of open military hostilities. With the Soviet Union absent from Security Council discussions, Western governments condemned the invasion of South Korea and agreed under Article 39 to deploy UN forces to oppose the aggression. Before the Soviet Union returned to take its Security Council seat in August of 1950, UN forces had been authorized and were functioning under the UN flag, although the majority of the military force was American. With the Soviet return to the Council, no further consensus could be obtained in that body concerning the major issues of the Korean situation. On 3 November of the same year, the UN General Assembly, at the initiative of Western powers, passed the Uniting for Peace Resolution (see Appendix 8 for a text of this resolution), which gave the General Assembly the capacity to hold special emergency sessions and to make recommendations regarding threats to peace, breaches of the peace, and acts of aggression at such time as the Security Council failed to perform its primary function in the collective security arena. In addition, the resolution also requested governments to make available to either the Assembly or the Security Council specially trained forces for deployment in situations posing a threat to international peace and security as a partial remedy for the failure of governments to implement the Military Staff Committee provisions of the Charter. This innovation during the Korean War served as an expansion of General Assembly authority to act in the area of collective security, but unlike the Security Council, it could not undertake decisions binding on member states; rather, it could only recommend action to member states. Under Secretary-General Dag Hammarskjöld, General Assembly involvement in peacemaking situations would reach their zenith as the Security Council continued to be in the grip of Cold War stalemate.

Another issued that loomed ominously over the debates of the United Nations in its first decade was that of the nuclear arms race. The use by the United States of the atomic bomb on the Japanese cities of Hiroshima and Nagasaki served as a chilling symbol of the destructive power of this new weaponry and the need to curtail its usage. In January 1946, the UN General Assembly, only months after the atomic explosions that brought an end to the war in the Pacific, established an Atomic Energy Commission (AEC), which consisted of eleven members of the Security Council with the addition of Canada. This was effected by the very first resolution of the UN General Assembly. The Security Council also created a commission to deal with the question of conventional arms. Efforts to establish a coherent mechanism for the limitation and control of nuclear weaponry and to put the nuclear genie back into the bottle largely failed. The United States proposed in the Baruch Plan to internationalize the production and control of nuclear materials, the prohibition of nuclear weapons, complete with international inspections to ensure that nuclear energy would be used only for peaceful purposes. The Soviet Union, at the time well on its way to developing an atomic weapon of its own, lambasted the U.S. proposal as a means of freezing the American monopoly on nuclear technology. The plan was thus stillborn, and the nuclear arms race, which at that early date might have been avoided had superpower jealousy, rivalry, and distrust not been so great, instead escalated in subsequent years, with both the United States and the Soviet Union obtaining hydrogen bombs by the early 1950s. Although the two superpowers maintained a nuclear monopoly for a time, other countries opted to develop similar systems for their own national security, and the problem of nuclear proliferation emerged. Although very little progress was made in stopping the arms race, the UN Security Council and General Assembly routinely kept the matter of disarmament on their agendas. Security Council debates over disarmament made little progress owing to great power differences, and General Assembly activities could do little more than urge the nuclear powers to negotiate, to refrain from nuclear testing, and to limit their nuclear arsenals. It became clear that the United Nations could do little more than urge restraint and that bilateral nuclear arms control or disarmament measures would ultimately bear fruit only in the context of bilateral talks between the superpowers.

Approval of new members of the United Nations was another area in which the Cold War intruded at least for the first decade of the United Nations' existence. Apart from the original 51 member states, only 9 countries, including Afghanistan, Iceland, Sweden, Thailand, Pakistan, Yemen, Myanmar (then known as Burma), Israel, and Indonesia, were admitted to membership, none of which was a clear ally of either the West or East bloc. Bulgarian, Hungarian, Romanian, and Albanian applications for membership failed to gain majority approval in the Security Council owing to opposition from Western powers. The Soviet Union, on the other hand, vetoed the membership bids of Austria, Ceylon (Sri Lanka), Ireland, Italy, Japan, Jordan and Portugal for one reason or another but mainly because of their potential support for Western policies. In December 1955, both sides agreed to stop the charade, and sixteen new members were admitted in what was called a "package deal." Since that time the United Nations has routinely admitted member states, and membership currently stands at 185. Although the Cold War reared its head from time to time in subsequent years, as in Hungary in 1956, the problems associated with decolonization and economic development gradually began to ascend to the top of the UN agenda, especially as new states gained their independence in the late 1950s and early 1960s. Thus, the priorities of African and Asian countries and the issues most dear to developing countries began to compete for time and attention on the UN agenda.

EAST/WEST VERSUS NORTH/SOUTH: UN DEBATES FROM 1955 TO 1980

If the East/West dispute dominated UN debates during its first decade, the emergence of the developing world from colonial status to independent nationhood began to change the tone of UN debates. The emerging countries of the South, as early as the Conference of Non-Aligned Countries in Bandung, Indonesia, in 1955, served notice that they did not desire to become entangled in the East/West dispute. With Yugoslavia and India serving as the leaders of this movement, many newly independent countries gravitated to the nonaligned posture, although in reality many were heavily dependent on Western or East bloc military or economic aid.

Still, in the General Assembly and in ECOSOC, new emphases emerged on issues of most immediate concern to the countries of the Third World, most of which were located in the Southern Hemisphere. Thus, issues concerning decolonization, national self-determination, racial discrimination, apartheid, economic development, foreign assistance, and fair trade policies took prominent places on the UN agenda. The United States and the Western powers, which had controlled majorities in the UN General Assembly and ECOSOC, no longer exercised the same degree of influence over the voting behavior of member states. The newly independent countries favored the nonalignment principle as a rule, but a number of governments explicitly embraced or flirted with the socialist doctrines of the East bloc. Soviet foreign aid programs and foreign policy sought more aggressive ties with key countries in Africa, Asia, and the Americas. Wars of independence in southern Africa, the Vietnam War, and the Cuban revolution offered opportunities for the expansion of Soviet influence. Once quite isolated in the UN context, the Soviet Union made a bid to win friends and influence nations.

This was also the period known as peaceful coexistence, as the East and West settled down for what both thought would be a long struggle for international dominance in the economic and political spheres. Although the military forces of the United States and the Soviet Union were never directly engaged with each other during these decades of the Cold War, many opportunities arose for both sides to fight proxy wars through client states or rebel groups. Thus, while the United States deployed forces in Vietnam, the Soviet Union and China supplied military aid to the North Vietnamese Communist regime and to Viet Cong guerrilla forces in South Vietnam. The Soviet Union and China supported leftist independence movements in Rhodesia, Angola, Mozambique, and El Salvador. The United States tended to support authoritarian pro-Western governments in efforts to put down leftist rebellions. Thus, to a very large extent, the Cold War did in fact intrude on the political life of many newly independent countries of the Third World, making it difficult for them to claim that they were truly neutral or nonaligned.

From 1955 to 1980, the issues of East/West competition were inextricably intertwined with the new agenda of economic development and antiimperialism proclaimed by the growing number of developing countries that gained membership in the United Nations. Indeed, UN membership doubled from 76 members in 1956 to 154 members in 1980, with only the Federal Republic of Germany and the German Democratic Republic being clear members of the East and West blocs. Of the 77 new members during this period, 75 were countries of the developing world. The aims of the Non-Self-Governing Territory provisions of the UN Charter were largely realized during this twenty-five-year period. The next twenty-year period saw about 30 new members join the United Nations, and more than half of those were associated with the collapse of communism in Eastern Europe and the Soviet Union. With the tremendous growth in membership came pressure to expand the size of the Security Council and ECOSOC so that the voices of new members might be more broadly represented in the specialized bodies. In 1965 the Security Council was expanded from eleven seats to fifteen, so that the body consisted of five permanent members and ten nonpermanent members. Whereas before under a so-called gentlemen's agreement of 1946 two seats were given to Latin American states and one each to Western Europe, Eastern Europe, the British Commonwealth, and the Middle East, under the new arrangement, Latin America retained two seats, five seats were reserved for African and Asian countries, one for Eastern Europe, and two for Western Europe and other states. ECOSOC was also expanded in 1965 from eighteen to twenty-seven, and again from twenty-seven to fifty-four in 1973.

The new issues of interest to the South included not only the rapid decolonization of the world, which was largely achieved in these decades, but also the progressive economic development of the Third World where the problems of poverty, overpopulation, disease, and vulnerability to disaster were most evident. Calls for reform of international economic policies became annual mantras at UN General Assembly meetings. The developing country members began to collaborate in the "Geneva 77" process, which referred to the number of developing countries that first gathered to discuss developing country issues at the United Nations Conference on Trade and Development (UNCTAD) held in Geneva in 1964. In subsequent years, the Geneva 77 grew in membership to well over a hundred countries. Through this consultative process, the developing nations lobbied for preferential trade policies, transfers of wealth and technology to developing states, and the creation of new UN institutions and machinery to address the economic development needs of the Third World. By caucusing within the UN General Assembly, these countries exerted a major influence on agenda setting, on calling of international conferences, and on the establishment of budget priorities.

The influence of this group can be seen in its lobbying for the creation of the UNCTAD in 1964 to reform the General Agreement on Tariffs and Trade (GATT) policies requiring reciprocal reductions in tariffs between trade partners. Developing countries argued that this would condemn them to permanent status as agricultural economies, since their efforts to establish new industries would be undercut by reducing tariffs on imported manufactures at prices the new domestic industries could not hope to match. Only by protecting such infant industries from external competition could they hope to establish even a domestic market. Thus UNCTAD members successfully argued that developing countries should be given preferential trade status, whereby they could have access to wealthy countries' markets with lower tariffs but also be allowed to impose higher tariffs on wealthy country manufactured goods so as to protect domestic infant industries. Through the UNCTAD debates, developing countries eventually demanded that the entire international economic order be restructured to meet their needs. Thus, by the 1970s they were calling for the establishment of a New International Economic Order (NIEO), a very controversial set of measures that were strongly opposed by the United States and other Western capitalist governments. Among the reforms called for was the creation of transnational codes of conduct to regulate corporate investments, mandatory commodity indexation schemes, and mandatory transfer of technologies from wealthy countries to developing countries. A related set of demands took shape as governments of developing countries demanded that news reporters be registered and the transfer of information among and between countries be subjected to a greater degree of regulation as part of a New International Information Order. This initiative was strongly resisted by Western governments as an infringement on basic rights of free speech and freedom of the press. The NIEO and New Information Order demands by Third World countries gradually fizzled out as tough-minded, budget-conscious governments emerged in the United States and Europe during the 1980s. However, during the 1970s, the concept produced spirited debates about the inequalities of income distribution and wealth among nations. Generally, the Soviet Union and Communist countries supported the efforts of developing nations to advance these debates.

If the functionalist agenda of the UN General Assembly and ECOSOC took on more importance with the expansion of UN membership, issues relating to the United Nations' collective security functions continued to pose problems. Under Secretary-General Dag Hammarskjöld, peacekeeping forces were twice fielded and supervised under General Assembly authority. In 1956, in the wake of the settlement of the Suez Crisis, the United Nations Emergency Force (UNEF) was dispatched to the Middle East, and in 1960 the United Nations Operation in the Congo (ONUC) was deployed to quell violence and rebellion in the newly independent Congo. The Soviet Union regarded these actions as encroachments on Security Council authority, and owing to the fact that they were large and expensive operations of nearly $600 million, it refused to pay any share of the budget assessments for operations it opposed. This created a financial crisis, especially during the years 1963 and 1964, during which the Soviet Union fell in arrears on its payments and thus risked losing its vote in the General Assembly. During the 1964 session, no formal votes were taken so as to avoid a confrontation. In the following year, member states agreed that finances for peacekeeping would no longer be assessed as part of the regular budget but rather on an ad hoc and voluntary basis.

The Security Council reasserted its primary responsibility for matters related to keeping peace during this same period. In 1964, it deployed the United Nations Peacekeeping Forces in Cyprus (UNFICYP), which were funded by Cyprus, the states sending peacekeeping contingents and other voluntary contributions. In 1967, the Security Council passed the landmark Resolution 242 (see Appendix 8 for a text of the resolution), in which it established the land for peace principles that have subsequently guided efforts to resolve the Arab-Israeli dispute. Although no new peacekeeping forces were deployed after the 1967 Arab-Israeli war, the Security Council did authorize the deployment of a 7,000-member UNEF II force after the Yom Kippur War in October 1973 in the Sinai region. In 1974, a United Nations Disengagement Observer Force (UNDOF) was also authorized in the Golan Heights to separate Israeli and Syrian troops. When civil war struck Lebanon in 1978, the Security Council deployed the United Nations Interim Force in Lebanon (UNIFIL). The renewed Security Council activity occurred in part because of the growing realization that Cold War politics need not prevent the great powers from responsibly limiting tensions and conflict in the highly volatile Middle East. The early 1970s also marked the détente era, during which the superpowers sought to reduce tensions and promote cooperative relations.

The middle decades of the United Nations also saw the emergence of major international conferences to address such problems as world population growth, the environment, food production, human settlements, and the law of the sea. The first UN conference on population was actually held at Rome in 1954, and every ten years since then, including 1964 in Belgrade and 1974 in Bucharest, where governments first adopted a formal plan of action. Subsequent population conferences were held in 1984 at Mexico

City and 1994 in Cairo. Population is a sensitive issue for governments, and much heated debate occurred at the Bucharest, Mexico City and Cairo conferences. Some states view population as a major resource, whereas others, especially in the developed world, view population growth in poor countries as a major deterrent to development. Other issues surrounding family planning are highly sensitive to cultural variations and evoke heated debate. Generally, however, governments acknowledge that population growth issues are closely tied to economic development and the education and betterment of the lives of women. Related to the issue of population was the issue of human settlements, a question addressed in 1976 by the United Nations Conference on Human Settlements, known as Habitat, which was held in Vancouver, Canada, in 1976, which called upon governments to treat as a matter of priority the establishment of adequate shelter for all people.

The 1972 World Conference on the Human Environment in Stockholm represented another effort by governments to cope with an emerging global issue. Issues regarding pollution of the environment had been largely viewed as a problem in the wealthier industrialized countries, but by the 1970s evidence showed that the environments of Third World nations were also threatened. Moreover, while developed nations could afford to undertake expensive environmental protection measures, developing countries viewed such measures as expensive intrusions on their efforts to promote wider economic growth. Would they be required to forego development in order to ensure a clean environment? This was one of the central fault lines in the debate, as the impact of environmental policies on development became a major bone of contention. The Stockholm Conference produced a declaration and plan of action for international efforts to protect the environment, and upon its recommendation, the UN General Assembly approved the establishment of the United Nations Environment Program (UNEP) to coordinate international environmental programming.

The 1974 World Food Conference at Rome took up similar issues as governments grappled with the problem of inequitable food production and distribution around the world. Developing means of improving food production, responding to emergency food needs, and encouraging a reduction in chronic malnutrition were major topics of discussion. Growing out of the conference was a greater degree of international coordination of food-related agencies of the UN system through a World Food Council. The International Fund for Agricultural Development (IFAD) was established by the UN General Assembly in 1977 upon the recommendation of the Rome Conference.

The United Nations has also been heavily involved in sponsoring conferences on the Law of the Sea. The first such conference was held in 1958 to review the rules of territorial jurisdiction claimed by coastal states in their territorial waters and continental shelves. A total of eighty-six countries participated in that conference in order to harmonize increasingly conflicting state claims to jurisdiction on the seas, but despite progress, many problems persisted even after a second conference held in 1960. The discovery of potentially enormous wealth in the form of deep seabed mineral nodules during the late 1950s raised issues concerning potential claims to mineral rights in international waters. In 1973, the UN General Assembly called for a third and much more ambitious Law of the Sea Conference to deal comprehensively with coastal jurisdiction claims, rights of innocent passage, fishing regulations in coastal waters, marine pollution, scientific research, dispute resolution mechanisms, and the establishment of a regime to govern the exploration and exploitation of deep seabed resources. Complicated compromises were made to incorporate the interests of the many different states participating in the negotiations, and in 1982, the conference approved the Law of the Sea Treaty, which comprehensively addressed all of these matters, although not without controversy, especially in regard to its deep seabed mining provisions.

Human rights issues were also affected by the emergence of new nations. The focus on civil and political rights upon which Western governments had insisted in contrast to the Communist nations gave way to an emphasis on collective rights and economic, social, and cultural rights. The emerging nations were especially jealous in guarding their sovereign prerogatives to control civil and political rights. African and Asian countries demanded that the right to self-determination be respected. They condemned white majority regimes and racist policies in Rhodesia and South Africa. The practice of apartheid in South Africa became a hot-button issue that evinced annual denunciations and condemnations. South African control of its former League mandate in Southwest Africa was formally revoked by the General Assembly under the new Third World majority, and the Southwest Africa People's Organization (SWAPO) was acknowledged as the sole legitimate representative of the Namibian people. Linking up with Arab country hostility toward the state of Israel, African countries and other members of the Geneva 77 voted in 1973 to equate Zionism with racism. This ideologically motivated rhetorical gesture evoked substantial opposition from Western governments. African countries generally supported the right of the Palestine Liberation Organization (PLO) to observer status at the United Nations just as Arab and Muslim countries joined African states in condemnation of South Africa.

Western governments' influence on the UN agenda declined significantly during the 1960s and 1970s. Still, these governments provided the vast majority of funding for UN operations. Their resentment grew as the developing countries commandeered the agenda of the United Nations during these decades and as the tone of UN debates grew more shrill, antiimperialistic, and anti-Western in tone. This resentment eventually provoked Western governments to reduce their reliance on UN bodies and to reemphasize bilateral political, economic, and military ties as the East and West dug in for a final confrontation that would culminate in the collapse of communism during the 1980s. Coupled with the tremendous instabilities, civil wars, and governmental coups d'état experienced in many developing countries of the Third World, the Soviet Union made its most determined effort, in cooperation with Cuba and other allies, to extend its influence in Africa, Asia, and Central America. Civil war, revolution, and refugee flows of major proportions occurred during the 1970s. The détente era of the early 1970s gave way to renewed hostilities and military confrontations between client states of the East and West. In December 1979, the Soviet Union invaded Afghanistan in a fateful move that contributed heavily to its own demise a decade later. The turbulent international politics of the 1960s and 1970s gave way to a final standoff in the East/West dispute during the 1980s, a decade during which the United Nations receded in importance before reemerging in the post–Cold War era as a refurbished and renewed player on the global stage.

TAKING STOCK OF THE CRISIS DECADE OF THE 1980s

UN debates do not take place in isolation from domestic reactions within countries to the international events of the day. Governments often use the United Nations as a forum for scoring rhetorical points meant more for domestic political consumption than as a means of advancing international cooperation. On the other hand, they are capable of quietly using UN institutions and machinery to achieve real diplomatic progress while publicly denouncing UN capacities and capabilities.

During the 1980s, international relations reached a critical juncture as major events were dictated by the major powers and as the influence of the Third World majority waned. During this time, the United Nations played a less central, though not unimportant, role in promoting international peace and security. In the United States and in Europe, conservative governments won decisive elections. They brought to government, on the one hand, a new fiscal conservatism that called for disciplined budgetary control and, on the other, a new patriotic fervor that called for "standing tall" in foreign affairs. In reaction to the massive Soviet buildup in nuclear and conventional arms, and the Soviet Union's more adventuresome foreign policy of the mid- to late 1970s, President Ronald Reagan of the United States urged a massive expansion in U.S. military and defense spending and enunciated a policy of support for "freedom fighters" anywhere in the world where they sought to overthrow Communist regimes. American aid to opposition forces in Afghanistan, Angola, and Nicaragua was instrumental in toppling Marxist governments or forcing concessions from them. The American intervention in Grenada emphasized the anti-Communist policies of the Reagan administration. In opposition to the Third World governments who had clamored for a New International Economic Order, Reagan and the new conservative governments in Europe countered with programs encouraging private initiative and free enterprise. Given that they contributed about 70 percent of the UN budget, Western governments demanded that the United Nations undertake extensive budgetary and bureaucratic reforms. Flexing their budgetary muscle, these governments demanded greater accountability on the part of the United Nations, more consensus in budget matters, substantial streamlining of overlapping UN bureaucracies, and substantial reductions in UN staffing. They withheld contributions to the UN budget until called-for reforms were initiated. Where UN agencies continued to pursue highly politicized and ideologically motivated agendas, as in the United Nations Educational, Scientific, and Cultural Organization (UNESCO), where a highly politicized secretariat and membership had promoted an anti-Israel and anti-Western agenda for years, including the New International Information Order (NIIO), some Western countries, including the United States and the United Kingdom, demonstrated their resolve by withdrawing completely from the organization.

As this new conservatism persisted throughout the 1980s, the tone of UN debates began to change. Third World countries, realizing that they now needed to compete for increasingly scarce foreign assistance, tempered their rhetoric. The rancorous NIEO debates of the 1970s were overtaken by a new and more sober attitude toward grappling with poverty within and among nations. Many developing countries, having experimented with a range of socialist economic policies that often led to large and ineffectual state-run institutions and stagnant economies, began gradually to implement domestic economic reforms emphasizing privatization. Fantastic economic growth among the export-led economies of Southeast Asia during the 1980s provided further evidence that economic development and free enterprise could well go hand in hand. Although painful transitions and slow progress were experienced by countries that chose the road to reform, many governments persisted along this track of reform well into the 1990s. In many cases, the economic reforms were matched by political reforms and the election of democratic governments. This process accelerated during the late 1980s, as it became clear that the Soviet Union and the Communist bloc were gradually imploding economically and disintegrating politically. The tides of history were changing, and many countries in the developing world sensed them. As Soviet aid dwindled in the face of its own economic paralysis, its military overextension, its increasingly expensive and ineffectual intervention into Afghanistan, and its incapacity to match U.S. and North Atlantic Treaty Organization (NATO) military spending, all eyes turned to the West for future economic security.

The United Nations was, to a large extent, sidelined as an immediate player in the drama of international confrontation and conflict during most of the 1980s. Not until the late 1980s was there adequate consensus on the Security Council to deploy UN peacekeeping forces or peace-monitoring groups. The inactivity from 1978 to 1988 was not for lack of conflicts. During this time Vietnam invaded Cambodia, China invaded Vietnam, the Soviet Union invaded Afghanistan, the United Kingdom and Argentina fought the Falkland Islands War, Uganda invaded Tanzania, provoking a counterinvasion by the latter, and Iran and Iraq fought the world's bloodiest war since Korea. Civil wars raged in Angola, Mozambique, Namibia, Ethiopia, Uganda, Sudan, Lebanon, Nicaragua, and El Salvador. In almost every case, direct or indirect great power involvement in these disputes prevented engagement of the United Nations. This does not mean that the United Nations was completely inactive. Secretary-General Javier Perez de Cuellar, for instance, was intimately involved through a special representative in negotiating an end to the war in Afghanistan, and UN forces continued to operate in the Middle East and elsewhere to provide stability in regions previously torn by strife. But as a general rule, effective engagement of the United Nations came only near the end of the wars of the 1980s, as the Soviet Union maneuvered to reduce its commitments abroad and focus on much-needed domestic reforms.

Thus in the late 1980s, a rash of UN peacekeeping activities became possible. After eight years of war, Iran and Iraq finally agreed to a cease-fire in 1988, which was monitored by the United Nations Iran-Iraq Military Observer Group (UNIIMOG). After successful negotiations between the Angolan government and rebel forces brokered by the United States, Cuba agreed to withdraw from Angola, permitting the United Nations to field the United Nations Angola Verification Mission (UNAVEM) to monitor Cuban troop withdrawal. Relatedly, this paved the way for a resolution of the Namibian question, as South Africa, after extensive U.S. diplomatic initiatives, agreed to withdraw from Namibia and permit the repatriation of Namibian refugees and elections. The United Nations Transition Assistance Group (UNTAG) was successfully deployed to oversee Namibia's transition to independent statehood. In Central America, after long years of civil war and efforts by states in the region to broker a peace in the region, the United Nations was able to deploy the United Nations Observer Group in Central America (ONUCA) to monitor arms flows, oversee the cease-fire, and demobilize Nicaraguan Contras. The United Nations also fielded a special United Nations Observer Mission for the Verification of Elections in Nicaragua (ONUVEN), which successfully monitored elections that saw opposition forces defeat the Sandinista government. Many of these successful regional peace agreements were possible because the Soviet Union was encouraging its former socialist clients to negotiate with the West, rather than providing them aid to prolong conflict with Western-backed forces. At the same time, aggressive diplomacy by the Reagan administration in southern Africa contributed to the negotiation break-throughs in that region.

During the 1980s, global conferences continued to meet and international agencies quietly continued to work in provision of economic, social, and humanitarian assistance. The number of refugees and displaced persons requiring assistance increased dramatically. Conferences on refugee problems in Africa and Central America produced greater global awareness to the connections between civil wars and humanitarian distress. Governments and international agencies cooperated during the mid-1980s to cope with the most extensive drought and famine ever to hit the continent of Africa. In Southeast Asia, Vietnam, which was in deep recession and considering the need for economic reform, began to negotiate seriously with neighboring countries and the international community to resolve the boat people problem. At the Second Geneva Conference on Indochinese Refugees, a comprehensive plan of action was adopted that eventually brought the Southeast Asian refugee situation to a close, paving the way for the later inclusion of Vietnam as a full member of the region.

Where the United Nations did not seem to be suited for advancement of U.S. and Western economic values, it was ignored in favor of regional collaboration and cooperation. The West European countries deepened their commitment to one another with the passage of the Single European Act and the intensification of the economic integration process. The dominant economic powers of the globe, the so-called Group of Seven, including France, the United Kingdom, Germany, Italy, Japan, Canada, and the United States, turned to periodic consultations among themselves to promote economic prosperity. Increasingly they spoke and acted with one voice in wider multilateral settings and in the United Nations, especially in calling for budgetary and bureaucratic reforms.

The international environment was in the process of change. Communism was on the wane, while capitalism was resurgent. The United States moved aggressively into a position of economic and political leadership. Regional conflicts and civil wars, once aggravated by Cold War divisions, began to admit of negotiation and resolution. The arms race of the 1980s stimulated the first real not just arms control but arms reductions and disarmament talks. After the monumental confrontations of the early 1980s, the world reaped the rewards of peace. Both superpowers seemed dedicated to peace abroad and, in the case of the Soviet Union, to economic reforms at home. However, the forces of change unleashed within the Communist world could not be contained within the framework of a reformed Communist structure. Powerless to stop democratic movements, Poland, and other East European countries, Mikhail Gorbachev stepped aside in 1989 and allowed the forces of change to unfold naturally. East Germans voted with their feet by flooding into West Germany, and the Berlin Wall came tumbling down. Gradually, the spirit of independence spread to the Soviet Union itself, as one former Soviet Republic after another began to agitate for independence. The genie was out of the bottle, and the reforms eventually precipitated the almost total collapse of communism, then the disintegration of the Soviet Union itself in the early 1990s. These developments gave rise to a great optimism that a New International Order, as President George Bush called it, would be possible in the wake of the demise of the Cold War. International cooperation would resuscitate long-dormant UN collective security provisions, and a new and expanding free enterprise would offer new hopes of global prosperity. The decade that began under the gloomy pall of renewed East/West conflict ended with bright new hopes for the world and for the role of the United Nations as the chief universal body of global cooperation.

OPPORTUNITIES AND CHALLENGES FOR THE UNITED NATIONS IN THE POST–COLD WAR PERIOD

Debates in the United Nations during the early 1990s reflected momentous events in international relations including, most significantly, the collapse of communism and the end of the East/West dispute. Progress toward peace and democratic rule in Central America, Southeast Asia, and southern Africa also took place. In the case of South Africa, a peaceful transition to black majority rule finally removed such perennial issues as apartheid from the UN agenda. These promising global and regional developments revived hopes that the United Nations' collective security and economic, social, and humanitarian goals could be more effectively attained. Indeed, as the Cold War diminished, allowing for regional resolution of conflicts that had been aggravated by ideologically motivated international interventions, many hoped that the United Nations could at long last focus on issues related to economic development, the building of civil society, and the attainment of greater prosperity.

The hope for a more effective United Nations was raised even further in light of the UN response to Iraqi aggression against Kuwait in 1990 and 1991. When Saddam Hussein invaded and subjugated Kuwait in August 1990, he violated the most basic principles of the UN Charter, to refrain from the use of force in resolving disputes with member nations and to respect their sovereign independence and territorial integrity. The United Nations condemned this aggression and called for the imposition of economic sanctions. In late November 1990, the Security Council authorized the use of military force. The Soviet Union, preoccupied with its own domestic problems, cooperated with the United States, the United Kingdom, and France to support the enforcement of the Security Council sanctions. China abstained but offered no resistance to the international consensus. The liberation of Kuwait that soon followed the offensive unleashed by the

The Forty-seventh Session of the General Assembly meets in New York in 1992.
UN/DPI Photo Milton Grant

UN coalition of forces symbolized a new capacity for cooperation and consensus on the UN Security Council. Soon that body was authorizing deployment of UN forces and observer missions at an unprecedented rate.

A United Nations Iraq-Kuwait Observer Mission (UNIKOM) was deployed to monitor the Iraq-Kuwait border situation after the Persian Gulf
War. In 1991 alone, UNAVEM II was deployed to monitor peace accords,
the United Nations Observer Mission in El Salvador (ONUSAL) was deployed to supervise a peace agreement, the UN Mission for the Referendum in the Western Sahara (MINURSO) was fielded to further a peace plan
aimed at a national referendum, and the United Nations Advance Mission
in Cambodia (UNAMIC) was sent to supervise a cease-fire pending the deployment of the United Nations Transitional Authority in Cambodia
(UNTAC) a year later. In 1992 additional UN forces or observer groups
were deployed in the Balkans, Somalia, Cambodia, Mozambique, and
South Africa. In 1993 additional United Nations peace missions were deployed in Haiti, Eritrea, Uganda-Rwanda, Liberia, Rwanda, and Georgia.
The resources and capacities of the United Nations were stretched and
sorely tested during this phase of enthusiasm for collective response to regional conflicts and civil wars. Some of the situations were admirably re-

solved. The biggest success stories were in Central America, Cambodia, and Mozambique. Elsewhere complications arose, and UN involvement was either indecisive or, as in the Balkans and Somalia, counterproductive. In the latter instances the UN forces and agencies were simultaneously responsible for the provision of security and humanitarian aid in a context of ongoing violence and civil war. Responding to this new wave of UN peacekeeping and peacemaking activity, Secretary-General Boutros Boutros-Ghali issued an important study, *An Agenda for Peace*, in 1992 in which he discussed the need for preventive diplomacy as well as peacekeeping, peacemaking, and peace-building activities. Clearly the United Nations was being engaged in many different and more complicated situations of conflict and conflict resolution, which, in turn, deeply enmeshed UN bodies in complicated humanitarian and security dilemmas.

Complex humanitarian emergencies in the Balkans, Somalia, and Rwanda and the surrounding Great Lakes region of Africa sorely tested UN capabilities. In the Balkans, a civil war of ethnic cleansing turned every UN effort to provide humanitarian assistance into a focal point for conflict. UN safe areas established to protect Bosnian Muslims from Serbian ethnic cleansing became military targets. Aid convoys were blocked and delayed and UN aid personnel subjected to harassment and gunfire. In Somalia, after a first successful phase in providing humanitarian food aid, the United Nations Operation in Somalia (UNOSOM) devolved into a guerrilla war scenario once UN forces attempted to actively disarm the warring factions. UN forces were subsequently ambushed and killed in the streets of Mogadishu, prompting a U.S. and then a full UN withdrawal. Smarting from the defeat in Somalia, President Bill Clinton of the United States and other UN powers stood by almost silently as extremist Rwandan Hutus unleashed a vicious genocide of Rwandan Tutsis and Hutu sympathizers in 1994. Not until after the genocide was complete, and Hutus began to flee from advancing Tutsi forces that eventually took over Rwanda, did the international community act decisively to respond to the human misery. But even then it failed to muzzle Hutu militants who ruled refugee camps with brutal impunity and later provoked a destabilizing civil war in the Congo/Zaire.

UN interventions in Haiti proved more successful, and though the ultimate resolution of regional conflicts in Afghanistan and Angola resisted resolution, the United Nations continued to serve as a mechanism through which conflicting parties negotiated. The mixed success of UN peacekeeping and peacemaking activities of the early 1990s suggested that it was not sufficiently well organized or prepared to meet the complicated and extensive needs posed by simultaneous complex emergencies in many parts of the globe. A noble effort to rapidly expand UN involvement was thus followed in the late 1990s by more caution as governments turned to their own regional resources to meet regional security needs.

The Bosnian war, for instance, was only resolved when the United States intervened to serve as the direct broker between the conflicting parties. Security in Bosnia is provided by NATO forces as well as by the International Force, which includes non-NATO forces, such as those from Russia. The United Nations was called upon through its specialized and humanitarian agencies to participate in the reconstruction of Bosnia but not in the provision of its security. Similarly, the outcome of the Kosovo Crisis of 1999 was ultimately determined by the deployment of NATO bombers and occupation forces, rather that a direct UN military involvement. As in Bosnia, the United Nations operates in a postconflict position of coordinating reconstruction of the country. Conflicts in West Africa have been largely handled by the Economic Council of West African States (ECOWAS) Military Observer Group (known as ECOMOG), which has been deployed in successive conflicts in Liberia, Sierra Leone, and Guinea-Bissau. UN involvement in the Congo and in East Timor in late 1999 holds out hope that member states have not ruled out new UN Security Council actions where circumstances permit, but the distinctive hallmark of international responses to conflict situations from 1995 to 2000 was avoiding direct UN action in favor of unilateral or regional initiatives.

The frustration with UN venues for dealing with international crises was further illustrated in the efforts to force Iraqi compliance with the provisions of the Persian Gulf War cease-fire resolution of the Security Council, which called upon Iraq to submit to nuclear inspections and destruction of its nuclear, bacteriological, and chemical weapons. The United States and the United Kingdom argued that they were authorized under earlier Security Council resolutions to take all necessary means, including bombing, to force Iraqi compliance, even in the absence of further Security Council approval. Iraq successfully defied all UN threats and U.S./UK retaliatory bombings and won increasing sympathy among UN members for an easing of the economic sanctions that continued long after the Persian Gulf War's end.

The optimism of the early 1990s had given way by the late 1990s to a more sober attitude regarding the capabilities of the UN system. The collapse of the Soviet Union in the early 1990s, in turn, placed even more pressure on the United Nations, as conflicts in the former Soviet Union emerged and as the assistance needs of these new republics became known. Soon these new countries were seeking multilateral assistance along with the long line of Third World nations still struggling to put their nations' economies on a firmer footing.

Apart from the issues of international peace and security, the United Nations and its member states have continued to cooperate toward the end of promoting international trade and economic development. Growing out of periodic consultations of the General Agreement on Tariffs and Trade, the World Trade Organization was established in the mid-1990s. Coupled with ongoing progress toward economic integration in the European Union, the promulgation of the North American Free Trade Agreement, and the conclusion of an economic union among Latin American states, momentum gathered in the 1990s toward greater global and regional economic cooperation. Related to the movement toward greater economic cooperation and free trade was growing concern about the state of the world's environment. The Rio Conference on the environment in 1992 illustrated that the developed world expected greater progress among developing countries in controlling pollution and other policies that degrade the environment, whereas developing countries expected considerable financial support from the wealthier nations to achieve sound environmental practices. With the global population continuing to grow adding to concern about the impact of increased industrialization on the environment, the Kyoto Treaty proposed a new global assault on pollution to control climate change. This controversial agreement required substantial reductions in greenhouse gas–producing emissions among industrialized countries. The expansion of the desertification problem in Africa and Asia and of deforestation, especially in tropical rainforest areas, also sparked concern and controversy among various countries. An increased awareness of the impact of economic activity on the environment was one of the major trends of the 1990s. All nations continued to place a priority on economic development, but many came to view the degradation of the environment as a major issue that will claim more time and attention in future debates.

Reform of the United Nations has been another underlying theme of debates during the 1990s that carried over from initial great power initiatives toward reform undertaken in the 1980s. The United Nations has undertaken ongoing reforms during the 1990s owing to constant financial pressures from major contributors and a desire to rationalize and improve UN institutional structures. By the late 1990s, the UN actually experienced zero budget growth years and deep cuts in staffing. Still, many members, including the United States, remained substantially in arrears, and regular budget deficits were covered by delayed reimbursements to governments for their contributions to peacekeeping and peacemaking operations. Among the important reforms were efforts in 1992 and again in 1997 to streamline UN coordination of refugee, disaster, and humanitarian assistance activities. The establishment of the Department of Humanitarian Affairs in 1992 and of the Office for Coordination of Humanitarian Affairs in 1997 represented efforts to grapple with the more complicated international conflicts that arose in the 1990s. The United Nations had been fashioned largely to deal with interstate conflicts and relations, rather than with domestic civil wars that threatened international peace and security. Most of the conflicts of the 1990s took the latter form, and devising effective coordination mechanisms between regional or UN security forces and humanitarian assistance agencies proved to be a difficult transition for UN agencies, NGOs, and governments alike.

Another area in which many governments called for reform was in the organization and work of the Security Council. Here, as from the very inception of the United Nations, most of the criticism came from smaller powers who continued to resent the permanent member veto power. Predictably, the permanent members themselves continue to be resistant to the idea of eliminating or circumscribing the use of the veto, and without the approval of their governments, no amendment to the UN Charter concerning the veto is possible. However, the idea of adding additional Security Council members or even additional permanent members without a veto power remains a possibility that would not excite great power opposition. Lengthy and difficult discussions about the resuscitation of the Military Staff Committee and the establishment of some kind of standing force that could be readily deployed by the Security Council to meet collective security needs have not produced a consensus. For this reason, the Security Council continues to rely on ad hoc arrangements to face each new situation that threatens international peace and security.

In the arena of human rights, governments held a major World Conference on Human Rights in Vienna in June 1993 that recommended the establishment of a new United Nations High Commissioner for Human Rights, a

The UN Security Council votes on the situation in Angola. UN/DPI Photo E. Schneider

position that was formally established by the UN General Assembly in December 1993. The World Conference on Human Rights was attended by 171 governments and over 800 NGOs, signifying the importance attached by them to the promotion and protection of human rights. A major theme of the conference was discussion about including as a human right the right to development. This debate, which had been initiated during the 1980s, proved to be controversial as some Western developed countries, including the United States insisted that inclusion of development as a basic human right, confused the very idea of a human right with complicated institutional and societal structures that are necessary to promote development. In relation to the advancement of human rights more generally, the conference called for human rights to be made a priority issue by governments. The sad fact was that human rights abuses in the conflicts of the 1990s continued to be routinely and sometimes grossly violated. The distance between the hoped-for aspirations for the protection and respect of human rights and the actual practice of many countries continued to be very wide, indeed. Recognizing this, the conference called for the establishment of an international criminal court to deal with gross violations of human rights in such areas as the former Yugoslavia. The UN Security Council had already a month previously established a special International Tribunal for the Prosecution of Persons Responsible for Serious Violations of International Humanitarian Law Committed in the Territory of the Former Yugoslavia Since 1991. In November 1994, the Security Council likewise established an International Tribunal for Rwanda, to investigate allegations against persons accused of committing genocide and other violations of international humanitarian law. Many countries, frustrated by the ad hoc nature of these tribunals, turned to the idea of creating a permanent international criminal court. In 1998, many governments signed a treaty establishing such a court, but important countries balked at joining such a body, in particular the United States, which feared that its military forces, widely engaged in a variety of peacemaking and peacekeeping missions throughout the globe, might be singled out by hostile governments for legal action under the new court's jurisdiction.

Related to the issue of violations of human rights is the issue of combatting terrorism. Here, too, governments have had difficulty in agreeing what constitutes terrorism. Government-sponsored support for terrorist training and activities remains a highly controversial issue in international relations. Terrorist bombings of U.S. embassies in Kenya and Tanzania in 1998, the American retaliations against alleged terrorist camps in Afghanistan, and a highly controversial attack on a pharmaceutical plant in Sudan illustrated the highly volatile nature of this issue.

Underlying much of the debate in the United Nations concerning the reform and streamlining of its organization and work is the perennial issue of national sovereignty. The UN Charter sanctions interference in the domestic affairs of a member state only when events taking place within its territory represent a threat to international peace and security. There has been a tendency, as in the UN response to the Kurdish crisis in Iraq in 1992, to the Somalia crisis where no effective central government existed in 1993, and to the Haiti situation where human rights violations committed by an unrecognized government fomented civil strife in 1995, to treat significant humanitarian upheavals and refugee problems within and between countries as a threat to international peace and security. Although the United Nations was not involved in the decision by NATO powers to bomb Serbia and Kosovo in 1998, NATO countries justified an otherwise clear violation of Serbian sovereignty by claiming that it was necessary to prevent a human rights and humanitarian crisis in the southern Balkans. The great suffering that was in part precipitated by the NATO bombings raised serious questions about how far this principle can be pursued, especially without explicit approval of the UN Security Council, where in this particular instance Russian and Chinese opposition would certainly have prevented any UN action.

Although many students of international relations applaud the notion that national sovereignty is waning and that global approaches to promotion of collective security and of human rights are long overdue, many governments are reluctant to undermine the notion of sovereignty, worrying that Kosovo-like actions could become common in a world where less than perfect governments and government opposition forces clash over political control of their nations. As the world embarks on a new century these concerns will no doubt continue to shape UN debates of the future.

FOR FURTHER READING

Alger, Chadwick. *The Future of the United Nations System: Potential for the Twenty-first Century*. Tokyo: United Nations University Press, 1998.

Alker, Hayward R., and Bruce Russett. *World Politics in the General Assembly*. New Haven, CT: Yale University Press, 1965.

Bailey, Sydney D. *The General Assembly of the United Nations: A Study of Procedure and Practice*. New York: Praeger, 1964.

———. *The Procedure of the UN Security Council*. Oxford: Oxford University Press, 1975.

Claude, Inis L., Jr. *Swords into Plowshares: The Problems and Progress of International Organization*. 4th ed. New York: Random House, 1984.

Durch, William J, ed. *The Evolution of UN Peacekeeping: Case Studies and Comparative Analysis*. New York: St. Martin's, 1993.

Goodrich, Leland, Edvard Hambro, and Patricia Anne Simons. *The Charter of the United Nations*. New York: Columbia University Press, 1969.

Hovet, Thomas, Jr. *Bloc Politics in the United Nations*. Cambridge, MA: Harvard University Press, 1960.

Mingst, Karen A., and Margaret P. Karns. *The United Nations in the Post–Cold War Era*. 2nd ed. Boulder, CO: Westview Press, 2000.

Northledge, F. S. *The League of Nations: Its Life and Times, 1920–1946.* New York: Holmes and Meier, 1986.

Rabkin, Jeremy. *Why Sovereignty Matters.* Washington, DC: American Enterprise Institute, 1998.

Urquhart, Brian. *A Life in Peace and War.* New York: W. W. Norton, 1991.

Weiss, Thomas G., David P. Forsythe, and Roger A. Coate. *The United Nations and Changing World Politics.* Boulder, CO: Westview Press, 1997.

Weiss, Thomas G., and Leon Gordenker. *NGOs, the UN, and Global Governance.* Boulder, CO: Lynne Rienner, 1996.

THE FIFTY GREAT DEBATES

Disarmament (1946)

SIGNIFICANCE OF THE ISSUE

From its inception a significant preoccupation of UN bodies has been the problem of armaments, arms races, and nuclear weapons development. Although most of the progress in actual arms control, arms reduction, and disarmament has followed bilateral and multilateral negotiations directly between governments, the UN system has always served both as a site of general discussion of these issues and as a means of enforcing many arms control and disarmament treaties. In the 1990s, with the end of the Cold War, the UN Disarmament Commission and the Conference of the Committee on Disarmament have undertaken a more central role in advancing negotiations among governments. The importance of the issue for the United Nations is seen in the fact that the very first resolution ever passed by the UN General Assembly established an Atomic Energy Commission (AEC). Moreover, in subsequent years it established three disarmament decades for the 1970s, 1980s, and 1990s, and it held three special sessions on the question of disarmament in 1978, 1982, and 1988.

BACKGROUND TO THE DEBATE

The idea of disarmament as a means for achieving peace is an ancient one hearkening back to Hebrew Scriptures, where, in the contemporaneous writings of the prophets Isaiah (2:4) and Micah (4:3–5), we find the verses: "He shall judge between many peoples and impose terms on strong and distant nations; They shall beat their swords into plowshares, and their spears into pruning hooks; One nation shall not raise the sword against another, nor shall they train for war again." This biblical prophecy has yet to be achieved in international relations, but the preamble of the UN Charter and its statement of principles and purposes reflect this ancient desire for controlling war. Unlike the Covenant of the League of Nations, however,

On a wintry day, the statue *Let Us Beat Swords into Ploughshares*, by Soviet sculptor Evgeny Vuchetich, symbolizes the hope of the United Nations as an agent of peace and disarmament. UN/DPI Photo M. Tzovaras

which placed a much more explicit emphasis on the need for disarmament in Article 8(1) where member states acknowledged that the maintenance of peace necessitated the "reduction of national armaments" and later that this reduction should be effected "to the lowest point consistent with national safety," the UN Charter does not explicitly mention disarmament as one of the organization's goals, purposes, or principles. Indeed, although inclusion of such language in the Charter was considered at Dumbarton Oaks, the great powers explicitly rejected such a formulation and ultimately decided that matters of disarmament should be left entirely to the future deliberations of the Security Council and General Assembly. This variance in approach was related to the different international security conditions prevailing before and after World War I and World War II. Despite efforts by the Interparliamentary Union in 1889 to launch a campaign against disarmament, and later Hague Conferences in 1899 and 1907, which called for limitations on armaments and a study of the question of disarmament, governments in Europe engaged in a furious arms race prior to the outbreak of World War I. Thus, members of the League of Nations believed it was necessary to curb weapons development for use on land, sea, and air, as they saw the arms race as one major cause of the war. A League Commission of Experts drew up lists of arms necessary for maintaining national defense with a view to limiting military expenditures by member states. Conferences in Washington and in London on the limitation of land and naval forces led to the signing of agreements in the 1920s and 1930s, but the realities of Japanese and German armament policies mooted such agreements in the long run. Indeed, framers of the UN Charter believed that one cause of World War II was the lack of military readiness by the non-Axis powers to resist Nazi and Japanese aggressions during the 1930s. In addition, the UN Charter, unlike the League Covenant, was promulgated while World War II was still being fought. Talk of specific disarmament proposals under such circumstances would have been premature. Moreover, some degree of armed force was anticipated by the very collective security provisions of the UN Charter, which would require great power cooperation and consensus to keep the peace. The availability of some level of arms would obviously be not only prudent but necessary to keep these Charter objectives.

All of these conflicting needs and circumstances led the great powers to emphasize the need for the regulation of arms, although the General Assembly may consider principles governing disarmament under Article 11, and in Article 47 the Charter mentions the Military Staff Committee's role in making recommendations to the Security Council on "possible disarmament." Apart from Article 11, which permits the General Assembly to consider and make recommendations on the regulation of arms and disarmament, the Charter, in Article 26, accords the Security Council, through its Military Staff Committee, which never fully got off the ground, the right to formulate plans on a system for the regulation of arms. Read in connection with Article 24, which confers on the Security Council primary responsibility for the maintenance of international peace and security, arms control and disarmament policymaking would appear to rest principally with the Security Council, with the General Assembly exercising an advisory role.

The notion that the Security Council and General Assembly could work out a system for arms control at their future leisure was rudely shaken even before the United Nations held its first session. With the advent of the atomic bomb, used by the United States against Japan to hasten the end of the war in the Pacific, the whole question of arms control took on a new urgency. The U.S. government, after consultations with other countries, decided to seek immediately means by which this new and awesomely destructive weapons technology could be placed under international control. In doing so, these countries turned to the United Nations.

HISTORY OF THE DEBATE

Realizing the destructive power and the potential for the spread of nuclear weapons–making technology, various governments, including the United States, the Soviet Union, the United Kingdom, and Canada, brought the issue of nuclear armaments to the General Assembly, which in the first resolution of its first session on 24 January 1946 established the United Nations Atomic Energy Commission (AEC) consisting of all UN Security Council members, plus Canada. Later in the same year, the United States proposed to the AEC a comprehensive plan for the international regulation of all aspects of nuclear weapons development from mining and processing of fissionable materials to ensure their exclusive use for peaceful purposes and for inspections to ensure that such materials could not be used for the production of weapons other than for use in research and development of nuclear technology. Bernard Baruch, who was the chairman of the U.S. Atomic Energy Commission, presented this plan, known as the Baruch Plan, to the AEC at its first meeting of 14 June 1946 and called for the creation of an international atomic development authority, which would exercise direct authority over the mining, processing, and production of nuclear materials in such a way as to lie beyond the veto powers of UN Security Council permanent members.

The Soviet Union, which already entertained hopes for developing its own atomic weapons capability, rejected the Baruch Plan, arguing that it was inconsistent with the UN Charter, with the role of the Security Council, and with the idea of national sovereignty. Soviet representative Andrei Gromyko countered on 19 June 1946 with a plan, known as the Gromyko Plan, that called for the universal prohibition of the use of atomic weapons, of their production or storage, and for the destruction of all atomic weapons regardless of the state of development. Because the Gromyko Plan contained no provision for inspections or guarantees, it was unacceptable to other members of the AEC, who distrusted Soviet motives. A modified version of the Baruch Plan known as the Lilienthal Plan also failed to win the support of the AEC in 1947. By 1949, the Soviet Union had developed its own atomic weapons, and the nuclear arms race was off and running. The tragic failure of the major powers to resolve the atomic weapons issue at the outset led to a tense and dangerous nuclear arms race in subsequent decades, especially during the Cold War, which entailed arduous subsequent negotiations on arms control, disarmament, and nonproliferation. These made progress in fits and starts, but significant progress in real disarmament was not made until the demise of the Cold War, and even then, the proliferation of nuclear capability in a number of countries, such as China, India, Iraq, North Korea, and Pakistan, that are reluctant to submit to international inspection continues to haunt international politics.

The Security Council on 13 February 1947, pursuant to a General Assembly resolution of 14 December 1946, established a second UN weapons control body known as the Commission for Conventional Armaments, which was composed of Security Council members. The deepening rift between the Soviet Union and the U.S.-led majority on the Security Council, which reflected overall developments in the Cold War, produced a complete stalemate in both UN commissions by 1950. By this time the Soviet Union had joined the United States as a nuclear power. Casting about for ways to restart negotiations, the General Assembly established a Committee of Twelve in 1950 to discuss the possible merger of the two UN commissions. This committee recommended such a merger, which was approved by the General Assembly on 11 January 1952, with the creation of the UN Disarmament Commission. Ominously, the Soviet Union tested a partial-hydrogen bomb in 1952, just a few months before the United States developed a thermonuclear weapon, and by 1953 both superpowers had successfully tested and exploded full hydrogen weapons, which were far more powerful and destructive than the first atomic bombs. Both countries set out to create effective delivery systems, first through intercontinental strategic bombers, then by intercontinental ballistic missiles. Each step further complicated the nuclear arms race, even as other countries became nuclear powers. By the late 1950s, the superpowers both possessed an intercontinental weapons delivery capability, and during the 1960s and 1970s, they developed submarine missile capacities and increased the quantity and quality of the nuclear missile arsenals.

Against the backdrop of the nuclear arms race, the United Nations served as a means of placing constant pressure on the superpowers, usually through the General Assembly, its First Committee on political affairs, and subsidiary bodies, including the Disarmament Commission, and, after 1984, through twice annual meetings of the UN Conference on Disarmament at Geneva. Through these bodies the United Nations has prodded the superpowers and other nations that attained nuclear power status to negotiate arms control and arms limitation agreements. In July 1957, the International Atomic Energy Agency (IAEA) was formally established in Vienna and brought into relationship with the United Nations as a specialized agency in November 1957. With headquarters in Vienna, it would later serve as a primary vehicle for inspections concerning the enforcement of treaties banning testing of nuclear weapons and ensuring the nonproliferation of nuclear weapons. In 1957 the General Assembly also expanded the Disarmament Commission beyond its membership of Canada and the Security Council members to include fourteen additional countries; and in 1958, it expanded membership to include all members of the United Nations, to emphasize the global impact of the arms race.

In the late 1950s, discussion in the UN Disarmament Commission centered on proposals to suspend nuclear weapons testing, to cease production of fissionable material, to reduce nuclear weapons stockpiles, to increase inspection capabilities, and to study ways to prevent the expansion of the arms race into outer space. Parallel regional negotiations were established in Europe with the creation of the Ten-Nation Committee composed of North Atlantic Treaty Organization (NATO) and Warsaw Treaty Organization (Warsaw Pact) states, but these negotiations collapsed in 1960 and were later reconstituted in 1962 as the Eighteen-Member Committee. The UN Disarmament Committee and the General Assembly constantly exhorted the major powers and the Eighteen-Member Committee to cease weapons testing in light of increasing and irrefutable evidence of the harmful effects of nuclear radiation caused by open-air testing. They also called upon them to refrain from the transfer of such weapons or technology to countries not possessing them, that is, to observe the principle of nonproliferation. The first arms control agreement to prohibit the spread of nuclear weapons, the Antarctic Treaty, was adopted in 1959 by more than twenty governments. A Partial Nuclear Test Ban Treaty was signed in 1963, with the subsequent approval and acclamation of the General Assembly, which welcomed it as a positive development. In the same year, the nuclear powers agreed to the Outer Space Treaty, which prohibited the stationing or deployment of nuclear weapons in outer space. Various regional initiatives to declare parts of the world nuclear free zones gained momentum in the 1960s. African states initiated a proposal to denuclearize Africa in 1960 in the General Assembly, which was followed up by Organization of African Unity (OAU) and General Assembly declarations calling for the denuclearization of Africa in 1964 and 1965. A Treaty on the Prohibition of Nuclear Weapons in Latin America was signed at Tlatelolco, Mexico, in 1967 and entered into force in 1968. A Treaty on the Prohibition of the Emplacement of Nuclear Weapons on the Seabed extended nonnuclear areas beyond Antarctica and outer space to the ocean seabeds in 1971. The South Pacific became a nuclear free zone much later in 1985 as a result of the South Pacific Nuclear Free Zone agreement.

The UN General Assembly turned its attention to calling for the passage of the Treaty on the Nonproliferation of Nuclear Weapons in 1966 and 1967, an agreement that was eventually signed in July 1968 and entered into force in 1970. It broadened the authority of the IAEA, concerning its safeguard and inspection powers.

During the 1970s, with a relaxation in tensions of the Cold War, considerable progress was made in direct bilateral negotiations between the superpowers and in the reinvigoration of regional negotiations initiated by the Helsinki Agreement of 1975 and the establishment of the Conference on Security and Cooperation in Europe. The Stockholm talks, otherwise known as the Conference on Disarmament, began in the aftermath of the Helsinki talks, as a means of developing confidence-building measures between NATO and Warsaw Pact members. In the meantime, the United States and the Soviet Union signed several arms control agreements in the early 1970s, including a Communications Link agreement (1971), a Nuclear War Risk

Reduction agreement (1971), and Antiballistic Missile Treaty (1972), and a Threshold Test Ban Treaty (1974). Additionally, the two superpowers initiated bilateral Strategic Arms Limitation Talks (SALT I) in 1972, which were followed in 1979 by a SALT II process.

In 1978, the UN General Assembly held its tenth special session, which was devoted to the question of disarmament. It produced a broad-scope Declaration on Disarmament and a Program of Action that called upon all states to cease the development production of nuclear weapons, to reduce their stockpiles of nuclear weapons, to cease the testing of nuclear weapons, to establish nuclear free zones, to minimize the danger of the proliferation of nuclear weapons, and to refrain from the production and use of bacteriological or chemical weapons. This session and its successors in 1982 and 1988, which failed to adopt consensus resolutions, served the purpose of raising international awareness on the need for arms control and disarmament talks and agreements. At the session the Disarmament Committee was enlarged from thirty-one to forty members.

In 1984, the General Assembly decided to convene in New York an International Conference on the Relationship between Disarmament and Development, which was postponed until September 1987. Concern about the link between disarmament and development had first been articulated in 1962 by the Economic and Social Council (ECOSOC), which had commissioned a study by a team of ten experts on the subject; the study concluded that substantial savings from disarmament could lead to "the improvement of world economic and social conditions . . . and be an unqualified blessing to mankind." Subsequent studies by the United Nations in 1971, 1978, and 1982 echoed the sentiments expressed in the earlier report. In a sense, the very language of the UN Charter intimates that the founding members of the United Nations recognized a link between disarmament and economic development. In Article 26, the Charter grants the Security Council primary authority in the area of disarmament "in order to promote the establishment and maintenance of international peace and security with the least diversion for armaments of the world's human and economic resources." This idea found more frequent and explicit expression with the enlargement of the United Nations during the 1960s, as developing states gained their independence. Thus, yet another reason was articulated by UN bodies as a justification to pursue arms control and disarmament agreements.

However, politics among the great powers dictated whether and when progress could be made on attaining such goals. In the 1980s, U.S. President Ronald Reagan proposed the commencement of Strategic Arms Reduction Talks (START I). These talks broke down over a variety of issues, but particularly the strategic defense initiative of the Reagan administration, by which the United States would have developed a capacity to defend itself against nuclear attack by development of space-based and ground-based antiballistic missile (ABM) capacities, in apparent violation of the 1972 ABM agreement. The talks were resurrected in 1985, and at a summit meeting in 1987 between Reagan and Soviet General Secretary Mikhail Gorbachev a treaty to eliminate intermediate-range nuclear force (INF) missiles in Europe was signed, marking the first real disarmament, as opposed to mere arms control, agreement between the superpowers. Under President George Bush, the START I talks produced an agreement with the Soviet Union in 1991 in which both parties agreed to reduce long-range missile forces by about a third. With the disintegration of the Soviet Union, protocols were subsequently reached with a number of former Soviet states to remove nuclear weapons from their territories. This was followed in 1993 by a START II agreement that would further reduce American and Russian nuclear missile arsenals. Success in the START I and II talks was directly related to improved East-West relations and the fall of communism in Eastern Europe and the Soviet Union.

The disintegration of the Soviet Union in the early 1990s was a mixed blessing, raising new concerns about the implementation of START provisions calling for the dismantling of nuclear missiles and warheads, as well as worries about proliferation of nuclear materials and technology. However, compared to the days when people worried about imminent nuclear annihilation, the 1990s brought a degree of hope and relief to the nuclear weapons dilemma, and the international community began to focus on how disarmament efforts could be expanded into new arenas.

OUTCOME OF THE DEBATE

During the 1990s, the General Assembly, through the increasingly active UN Disarmament Commission and the UN Conference on Disarmament, turned its attention to drafting and promoting several treaties including the Register of Conventional Arms (1992), whereby states supply information on their national arms import and export policies regarding tanks, armored combat vehicles, artillery, combat aircraft, warships, and missile systems. It also promoted a Convention on the Prohibition of the Development, Production, Stockpiling and Use of Chemical Weapons and on Their Destruction, also known simply as the Chemical Weapons Convention (1993), and the negotiation of a Comprehensive Nuclear Test Ban Treaty (1993).

The Security Council decided in 1992 that serious violations of the Nonproliferation Treaty might be brought to the attention of the Council for consideration. The Chemical Weapons Convention (which entered into force in 1997) and the Comprehensive Test Ban Treaty both incorporated similar provisions. The Security Council was heavily involved in the wake of the Persian Gulf War in monitoring Iraq's compliance with a promise to dismantle its nuclear, bacteriological, and chemical weapons making capacity, although Iraq successfully prevented the Council from conducting full and unfettered inspections of its facilities through the IAEA and the United Nations Special Commission (UNSCOM), much to the chagrin of the Council and of the United States and the United Kingdom, who engaged in retaliatory bombing against Iraq in 1998. The bombings brought to a standstill all inspection efforts by the United Nations in Iraq, indicating the fragility of the Security Council's and the great powers' capacities to enforce such matters in the face of a defiant and determined government. Iraq subsequently resisted effective UN inspection proposals, although hope for improvements in this area increased when Iraq cooperated with the formation of the United Nations Monitoring, Verification, and Inspection Commission (UNMOVIC), which replaced UNSCOM in March 2000.

Another issue of great concern during the 1990s, especially given the widespread outbreak of civil wars, the indiscriminate use of mines in those conflicts, and attendant with the great human suffering such weapons exact in civil war–prone areas, led to the negotiation in the mid-1990s of the Ottawa Convention, also known as the Convention on the Prohibition of the Use, Stockpiling, Production and Transfer of Anti-personnel Mines and on Their Destruction. This convention entered into force on 1 March 1999, although the United States refrained from signing or ratifying it. This treaty owed its existence in large measure to the lobbying efforts of nongovernmental organizations that had to deal on a daily basis with the devastating humanitarian effects of land mines.

The widespread violence associated with civil wars and with post–civil war recovery processes led Secretary-General Boutros Boutros-Ghali in his *Agenda for Peace* of 1992 to call countries affected by civil war to consider "practical disarmament" in dealing with small arms, demining, demobilization, and reintegration of armed forces into civil life and other rehabilitation activities. Secretary-General Kofi Annan continued to place an emphasis on these activities. The First Committee and the General Assembly in 1996 called for affected states to consolidate peace through practical disarmament measures, and in 1997 the Assembly established a Group of Interested States (GIS) to facilitate such measures, and it cooperates with the UN Secretariat's newly established Department of Disarmament Affairs to promote the establishment and coordination of concrete programs in countries devastated by civil wars. The Department also serves as the UN focal point for initiatives to coordinate efforts to control action on small arms. Switzerland offered to host a conference on that subject in the year 2000.

The great dilemma of nations in the post–World War II era has been that with very few exceptions, governments throughout the world have maintained armies and weapons systems as a means of promoting their national security. Even the few countries that have resisted this rely on powerful and friendly neighbors to protect their security. But wherever disputes arise among or even within states, one side's defense is considered an offensive threat by the other party. This has led not just to global nuclear arms races but to regional and even bilateral arms races among and between nations, to a proliferation of weapons development and trade in weapons, and to enormous expenditures on national defense and national security. Few countries can claim to be free of participation in the global arms bazaar, either as a seller, as a buyer, or as a middleman in arms transactions. The United Nations is not in a position to dictate to states how to resolve their security dilemmas and certainly not in a position to force them to disarm. However, it has proved over the years to be a venue in which governments can gather to chide each other and urge one another to find ways of controlling and, where possible, eliminating weapons that are most devastating and most destabilizing. This process of cooperation would be largely impossible were it not for the disarmament machinery of the United Nations and the increasingly large body of treaties is has promoted, welcomed, and often ends up enforcing when governments have gathered the wherewithal to place limits on or to eliminate various types of weaponry. Not all swords are likely ever to be beaten into plowshares, nor are all spears likely ever to be beaten into pruning hooks, but to the extent that humankind makes any progress in these areas, bodies such as the United Nations are likely to be crucial players in the process.

See also Nonproliferation of Nuclear Weapons (Debate 26); Terrorism (Debate 28); Third World Development Programming (Debate 25).

The UN Committee on World Disarmament Conference considers the organization of its work in New York on 1 April 1975. UN/DPI Photo Yutaka Nagata

FOR FURTHER READING

Arms Control and Disarmament Agreements: Texts and Histories of the Negotiations. Washington, DC: U.S. Government Printing Office, 1996.

Bennett, A. LeRoy. *International Organizations: Principles and Issues.* Englewood Cliffs, NJ: Prentice-Hall, 1995.

Goodrich, Leland, Edvard Hambro, and Anne P. Simons. *Charter of the United Nations: Commentary and Documents.* 3rd rev. ed. New York: Columbia University Press, 1969.

Osmañczyk, Edmund Jan. *Encyclopedia of the United Nations and International Agreements.* London: Taylor and Francis, 1985.

Sauer, Tom. *Nuclear Arms Control: Nuclear Deterrence in the Post–Cold War Period.* New York: St. Martin's, 1998.

SIPRI Yearbook 1999: Armaments and International Security. London: Oxford University Press, 1999.

UN Chronicle, 1991–1999.

UN Disarmament Yearbook. New York: UN Publications, 1997.

United Nations Office of Public Information. *Everyman's United Nations.* New York: 1968.

UN Yearbooks.

Status and Condition of Children (1946)

SIGNIFICANCE OF THE ISSUE

Coupled with its emphasis on humanitarian assistance and refugees, UN activity on behalf of children represents one of its earliest, longest, and most urgent initiatives. Although the United Nations acknowledges the primary right of parents in raising and educating children, conditions of war, natural disaster, and grinding poverty often leave parents and children alike in deplorable condition and in need of national and international protection and assistance. The vast majority of the world's victims of disaster, hunger, war, and abuse are children, today as in 1946 when the United Nations first decided to assist the needs of children in the wake of World War II.

BACKGROUND TO THE DEBATE

The care and education of children constitute the primary responsibility of parents and families. This principle is ancient and continues to be honored in human rights agreements in modern times. Thus national and international action on behalf of children should be regarded as exceptional and supplemental to the primary role of the parents in nurturing, rearing, and educating their children. In the twentieth century many governments undertook programs on behalf of the education of children, and this pattern continues to be widespread today. So although education of children still remains a parental responsibility, most governments offer educational opportunities through public school systems. In addition, when children become orphaned, governments have a responsibility to ensure that they are properly cared for, and in exceptional cases, where children are the subject of abuse within the home, governmental intervention is regarded as necessary. Governmental or even international intervention on behalf of children is also often necessary, especially in poor and developing countries, where natural disasters or war place children at the brink of starvation or expose

Education is one of the basic needs of children. Here schoolgirls gather in a reading class in Karachi, Pakistan. UN/DPI Photo John Isaac

them to death or mutilation. In such circumstances of grave emergency, parents are often no longer able to protect or provide for their children.

The first international efforts on behalf of children were conducted by the League of Nations, which undertook to control and eliminate the trafficking of women and children. In 1924, the League adopted a Geneva Declaration asserting the fundamental and universal principles of children's rights. The advent of World War II, with its destructive and genocidal consequences, left millions of children in desperate straits. Destitute and displaced families without homes, jobs, or means to feed themselves placed millions of children at risk by war's end. Tens of thousands of children were orphaned. Disease and malnutrition were widespread. At this juncture, it was meaningless to speak about children's rights; they needed emergency assistance just to live. It was in this context, during its first year of existence, that the UN General Assembly created the United Nations International Children's Emergency Fund (United Nations Children's Fund; UNICEF) on 11 December 1946.

HISTORY OF THE DEBATE

Although the United Nations Relief and Rehabilitation Administration (UNRRA) was hard at work meeting the needs of the war-displaced populations in Europe as early as 1943, the UN General Assembly believed that additional attention was needed to provide for the vulnerable condition of children in war-ravaged Europe. With the establishment of UNICEF in December 1946 the UN General Assembly promoted the provision of special emergency assistance to ensure adequate relief measures on behalf of children. UNICEF was intended at first to be a temporary measure in relief of children affected by the war until those needs were met. However, in 1952, the General Assembly decided to broaden UNICEF's mandate from emergency assistance to include not only material aid but technical assistance and programs to assist governments in the development of long-term child welfare programs in such areas as health and nutrition. It renamed UNICEF the United Nations Children's Fund, consistent with this effort to broaden its mandate from emergency aid to longer-range development programs on behalf of children. UNICEF was no longer considered a temporary body, and it began to function as an agency with ongoing authority in the area of children's social welfare policy, reporting to the Economic and Social Council (ECOSOC) and the General Assembly. It is governed by an Executive Board composed of forty-one UN member states chosen by ECOSOC and is funded primarily by voluntary contributions of governments, although other income is generated by its sale of holiday cards and special fund-raising campaigns. UNICEF from its early days has remained a staunch advocate of the social welfare needs and the rights of children.

In the late 1950s, ECOSOC prepared a draft Declaration on the Rights of the Child, which was unanimously approved by the General Assembly in 1959. This declaration consisted of nine principles that, though not legally binding, represented widespread international opinion. Children were not to be subjected to any form of discrimination. They were to enjoy special protection to ensure their physical, mental, moral, spiritual, and social development. They were entitled from birth to a name and a nationality and to benefit, together with their mothers, from adequate nutrition, housing, recreation, and medical services. Where handicapped, they were entitled to special programs of assistance. Parents were to provide for the child's upbringing, and where deprived of parents, children had a right to social care and support. The child had a right to an education, to priority protection and relief in times of emergency, and to be protected against all forms of neglect, cruelty, and exploitation. ECOSOC monitored the progress of nations in reflecting such principles in their national legislation.

During the 1960s, 1970s, and 1980s, UNICEF emerged as a major operational program for development assistance. With the growth of United Nations membership and the growing needs surrounding the provision by governments of basic social welfare programs, UNICEF collaborated extensively with other UN development organizations, including the United Nations Development Program (UNDP) and the World Health Organization (WHO) in providing technical and program support to governments. During these same decades, however, emergency assistance needs also grew, and UNICEF also collaborated with the United Nations High Commissioner for Refugees (UNHCR) and the World Food Program (WFP) in the provision of emergency assistance. In 1965 UNICEF received the Nobel Peace Prize for its work on behalf of children. By the late 1980s, UNICEF operated programs in about 120 countries. Its programs included child survival and development programs, provision of oral hydration technologies to prevent death owing to diarrheal diseases, as well as programs for water supply and sanitation, literacy, immunization, breast-feeding, nutrition, primary health care, and provision of basic drugs. During the 1980s, it also turned its attention to the growing problem of acquired immunodeficiency syndrome (AIDS) among children.

During the late 1980s, UNICEF was heavily engaged in the promotion of a Convention on the Rights of the Child, which was formally drafted by the UN Human Rights Commission in 1989. In that same year, the UN General Assembly adopted the Convention without vote. Building and expanding on the list of principles contained in the 1959 Declaration on the Rights of the Child, the Convention also established a Committee on the Rights of the Child to examine the progress made by states parties in achieving the realization of the obligations undertaken in the Convention. Governments party to the Convention are obliged to submit periodic reports on their progress in national legislation and action in defense of the rights of children. Within months, more than 60 governments had ratified the Convention, an unprecedented rate of ratification. It entered into force on 2 September 1990, less than a year after its adoption by the General Assembly. By 1995, virtually the entire UN membership of 185 governments had ratified the Convention.

Coupled with the entry into force of the Convention on the Rights of the Child, the United Nations held a World Summit for Children in September 1990, where it adopted the World Declaration and a Program of Action on the Survival, Protection and Development of Children, containing many goals and objectives for governmental action, including reductions in infant mortality rates, maternal mortality rates malnutrition rates, and progress in extending universal access to safe drinking water, sanitation, and education. The Summit was attended by 159 countries, and its Declaration and Program of Action were adopted unanimously by Summit representatives and later by the General Assembly.

OUTCOME OF THE DEBATE

In the realm of children's rights, a large degree of consensus has been exhibited by nations. The debates have typically led to consensus actions. In 1995, UNICEF reported that substantial progress had been made by governments in their efforts to implement the World Declaration and Program of Action on the Survival, Protection and Development of Children. Still, the battle had not been won. Millions of children throughout the developing world still face malnutrition, preventable disease, and poor sanitary conditions. They continue to be the majority of the refugees and starvation victims around the world. While international agencies such as UNICEF, the UNHCR and other UN specialized agencies such as the WHO have done much to reduce hunger and disease, the poor state of development in many countries leaves children vulnerable to disaster.

Children are also the main victims of war. By the mid-1990s, over forty wars, mainly civil wars, had killed 1.5 million children. Injuries and mutilations owing to mines or other devices disabled about 4 million children. Over 5 million were refugees, and well over 10 million left homeless. Clearly the ideals exhibited in the Convention on the Rights of the Child had not been realized in the actual practice of nations.

Concern about the condition and status of children has occupied UN attention since its earliest years. This concern continues to be a major one for United Nations agencies and governments alike as they struggle for peaceful solutions in an increasingly violent and unsafe world. The current situation suggests that the United Nations will need to continue focusing on the condition of children as a practical reality now that the legal status of children has been bolstered by human rights treaties. To accomplish this, governments and opposition groups alike in this new environment of epidemic civil conflict will need to learn how to practice what they preach. The United Nations will no doubt remain a venue in which pressure can be brought to bear on those governments that have difficulty matching their human rights rhetoric with their actual record.

See also Food Issues (Debate 32); Health (Debate 8); Human Rights (Debate 10); Refugees and Stateless Persons (Debate 4); Status of Women (Debate 33); Third World Development Programming (Debate 25).

FOR FURTHER READING

Black, Maggie. Children First: The Story of UNICEF, Past and Present. New York: Oxford University Press, 1996.
LeBlanc, Laurence J. The Convention on the Rights of the Child: United Nations Lawmaking on Human Rights. Lincoln: University of Nebraska Press, 1995.
UNICEF. State of the World's Children Report. New York: UNICEF, annual.
United Nations Office of Public Information. Everyman's United Nations. New York: United Nations, 1966.
UN Yearbooks, 1946–1995.

Southwest Africa (Namibia) Dispute (1946)

SIGNIFICANCE OF THE ISSUE

Like the dispute over Southern Rhodesia (see Debate 21), the dispute over Southwest Africa or Namibia, proved to be one of the most controversial and intransigent issues in the struggle for decolonization and national self-determination and in eliminating the practices of apartheid and racial discrimination. All of these related issues attracted significant attention in often very heated UN debates in the 1960s and throughout the 1970s and 1980s. A host of UN bodies, including the Security Council, the General Assembly, the Economic and Social Council (ECOSOC), the Trusteeship Council, and the International Court of Justice (ICJ), were engaged at one time or another in attempts to resolve the Namibia dispute and to deal with South African policies and control of the territory, which had been granted to it under a League mandate.

BACKGROUND TO THE DEBATE

The area now known as Namibia was first colonized by German settlers in the 1880s, although both English and German trading posts and missions had been established in different parts of the territory as early as 1802. In 1902, the German government made a determined effort to gain control over all of Namibia and in 1907 fully colonized the area. German responses to tribal rebellion were ferocious, including programs of extermination against belligerent groups. With the outbreak of World War I, troops from South Africa invaded Namibia in 1915. By the terms of the Treaty of Versailles (28 June 1919), which established the League of Nations, and a mandate system for territories seized from the vanquished Axis powers, Namibia, then called Southwest Africa, became a British protectorate administered by the Union of South Africa.

With the formation of the United Nations and its Trusteeship system, complications arose in the status of Namibia. The United Nations, on one hand, wanted to bring Namibia within the authority of the Trusteeship Council, which was created to supervise former League mandates as well as any other non-self-governing territories voluntarily submitted by member states. South Africa, on the other hand, had different ideas, namely, a desire to incorporate Southwest Africa into its own territory. This issue was first discussed in the General Assembly in 1946, when the South African application for incorporation of Namibia was rejected by the Assembly on 14 December. Nonetheless, South Africa began introducing objectionable policies, including apartheid, in the territory, which prompted the General Assembly in 1949 to seek an Advisory opinion from the ICJ regarding the legal status of the territory. The ICJ decided that the administration of the territory had not been affected by the extinction of the League of Nations, that the appropriate organs of the United Nations had assumed the supervisory functions of the League in relation to the territory, and that South Africa was not at liberty to change the status of the territory on its own. However, it also upheld South Africa's right not to submit the territory to the jurisdiction of the Trusteeship Council, which implied that the General Assembly would by default be the appropriate body to exercise supervisory functions.

HISTORY OF THE DEBATE

Although the General Assembly had weighed in from its first session on the issue of Namibia, most of the substantive action on the matter was decided by the ICJ. This pattern continued into the early 1960s, when, under increasing pressure from newly independent African states, the issue was once more joined in the legal setting, then eventually became a full-blown political matter fully within the hands of the General Assembly.

After the General Assembly urged member states in 1959 to take individual legal action against South Africa and its administration of Namibia, Ethiopia and Liberia pressed suit in the ICJ. In 1962, the Court ruled that it could exercise jurisdiction over the case, but in 1966, it decided, in a controversial decision decided by one vote, that Liberia and Ethiopia lacked standing to bring suit against South Africa. This decision marked a watershed in UN dealings on the matter of Namibia. The tactics now shifted from the courtroom to the General Assembly hall and the arena of politics.

African member states of the General Assembly reacted with anger to the ICJ ruling but took immediate steps to resolve the matter politically, having failed to do so juridically. On 27 October 1966, the General Assembly passed Resolution 2145 (XXI), stripping South Africa of its authority to administer the territory of Namibia and transferring administrative responsibilities to the General Assembly. The vote was 119 to 2 ¦South Africa and Portugal) with 3 abstentions (France, Malawi, and the United States). The Assembly also established a fourteen-member Ad Hoc Committee for South-West Africa (consisting of Canada, Czechoslovakia, Chile, Egypt, Ethiopia, Finland, Italy, Japan, Mexico, Nigeria, Pakistan, Senegal, the Soviet Union, and the United States) to consider practical matters concerning the administration of the territory. In May 1967, at its Fifth Special Session, held exclusively to deal with the Namibia question, the General Assembly established an eleven-member UN Council for Namibia, consisting of Chile, Colombia, Egypt, Guyana, India, Indonesia, Nigeria, Pakistan, Turkey, Yugoslavia, and Zambia, to assume direct administrative control over the territory in a vote of 82 to 2, with 30 abstentions. The office of UN Commissioner for Namibia was also established to serve as a liaison between the Council and the UN secretary-general. In June 1968, the United Nations officially changed the name of Southwest Africa to Namibia and again reiterated that South Africa's ongoing administration of the area was illegal.

The Security Council entered the fray in January of 1968, urging its members to ensure South African compliance with General Assembly resolutions. In 1969 the Security Council called upon South Africa to withdraw from Namibia. It refused to do so, and the Council subsequently called upon all states to discontinue dealings with South Africa in connection with its supposed administration of Namibia. In 1970 the Council requested an advisory opinion from the ICJ regarding the legal consequences of South Africa's continued administration of Namibia. The Court replied in 1971 that South Africa's continued administration of Namibia was illegal, that South Africa was obliged to withdraw immediately, and that all states were obliged to refrain from recognizing South Africa's illegal claims to authority in Namibia. In this ruling the Court essentially upheld the General Assembly's termination of South Africa's mandate authority over Namibia and declared South Africa's occupation of Namibia illegal, retroactive to the 1966 Assembly decision. The Council subsequently called on states to refrain from any action implying recognition of South Africa's claim to control Namibia.

The utter refusal of South Africa to comply with any and all UN pronouncements in this matter led to an increase in the resistance activities of the South West Africa People's Organization (SWAPO), which had been founded in 1959. In 1971 SWAPO was recognized by the Organization of African Unity (OAU) as the legitimate representative of the people of Namibia, and it campaigned extensively for international recognition, going so far as to host an international conference on Namibia in 1972. In 1973 the General Assembly, following suit with the OAU, recognized SWAPO as the legitimate representative of the Namibian people. An important step taken by the General Assembly in anticipating Namibia's independence was the creation in 1974 of the United Nations Institute for Namibia (UNIN), established in Lusaka, Zambia, where young Namibian refugees could receive training in law, management, teaching, and social services. When independence finally did arrive in 1990, many graduates of the Institute were available to serve their country. In 1976, the UN General Assembly Committee on Decolonization voted to officially support the armed struggle of SWAPO. Although this measure won 108 affirmative votes, the United States, the United Kingdom, France, the Federal Republic of Germany, Belgium, and Luxembourg opposed the measure, while a dozen countries abstained. The Assembly, to show its concern over the question, devoted its Ninth Special Session to the question of Namibia in 1978.

Pressure mounted with a decision in 1977 by the Security Council to impose a mandatory arms embargo on South Africa. Previous efforts to impose sanctions on South Africa had failed, owing to vetoes by France, the United Kingdom, and the United States. Their change of heart in 1977, coupled with an intensive diplomatic campaign to press for a negotiated set of principles that would guarantee Namibia's eventual independence, which was joined by Canada and the Federal Republic of Germany, in what was known as the Western Contact Group, put substantially more pressure on South Africa to reconsider its ongoing presence in Namibia. In 1978, both South Africa and SWAPO agreed to a proposal by the Contact Group for a cease-fire. The proposal also called for preparation for elections, the eventual release of Namibian political prisoners, the repatriation of refugees, and the creation of a United Nations Transition Assistance Group (UNTAG) to implement the plan. The deal was violated by South Africa, however, which held its own elections in Namibia later the same year, a move condemned by the General Assembly and the Security Council. The international community ignored the results of the election, considering them completely invalid, while the Western Contact Group pressed forward with efforts to gain South African compliance with the 1978 agreement. Western powers were often chided by the General Assembly, as, for example, when it accused several of them of collusion with South Africa in the nuclear field. However, serious negotiations with South Africa by the Contact Group continued, and increasingly the Frontline States of southern Africa (countries such as Angola, Botswana, Mozambique, Tanzania, Zambia, and Zimbabwe occupying territory in or near Southern Africa) also began to play a diplomatic role. These discussions promised the only real hope for progress.

The major breakthrough in the negotiations came with a development in neighboring Angola that at first appeared to threaten, rather than augur well for, a resolution of the Namibian problem. Part of South Africa's concern about withdrawing from Namibia had to do with the presence of socialist regimes in the neighboring countries of Angola and Mozambique, not to mention the socialist program of SWAPO's leaders and the presence of Cuban troops in Angola, where SWAPO guerrilla forces also maintained bases. The Cuban forces, in turn, were deployed to help the Angolan government fight against the South African–backed and pro-Western forces of the Jonas Savimbi's National Union for the Total Independence of Angola (UNITA). In 1983 South Africa invaded deep into Angola, arguing that Cuban support for SWAPO guerrillas compromised its security in Namibia. In 1984, the Security Council called for South Africa's immediate withdrawal, which South Africa rejected. However, a tortuous negotiation process was started, which would eventually lead not only to the withdrawal of South African forces from Angola but also to new progress on linking a phased Cuban withdrawal of forces from Angola with South African withdrawal from Namibia.

Serious discussion to that end was furthered mainly through the efforts of the United States acting as a mediator between the governments of Angola and South Africa. In July 1988, South Africa agreed to a proposal linking implementation of the Security Council resolution of 1978 (i.e., elections, South African withdrawal, etc.) with the withdrawal of Cuban forces from Angola. Negotiations then moved to Geneva in November 1988, where further progress on troop withdrawal schedules was achieved. On 1 April 1989, the first UNTAG forces were in position to monitor the transition of Namibia to independence. Although violations of the cease-fire occurred, once UNTAG was in position, demobilization of SWAPO forces began, and formal repatriation of refugees followed in sub-

Voters settle in for the long wait to cast their votes at a polling station in Tsumeb, Namibia, November 1989. UN/DPI Photo Milton Grant

sequent months as preparations for the elections began. Elections began in November as some forty parties vied for seats in the new Constituent Assembly of Namibia. SWAPO won less than the two-thirds necessary to dominate the Parliament and so needed to compromise with other parties to reach the needed majority. A democratic constitution was approved by the Constituent Assembly. Independence was finally achieved on 21 March 1990, and the following September, Namibia took a seat at the United Nations.

OUTCOME OF THE DEBATE

The patient efforts of U.S. negotiators, especially under President Ronald Reagan's policy of constructive engagement with South Africa, eventually bore fruit, despite the criticism aimed at the policy by SWAPO sympathizers and enemies of South Africa. As is often the case in difficult political circumstances, the rhetoric of public debate often stings, but the most productive negotiations are usually conducted behind the scenes. Such was the case in the successful, if exceedingly difficult, negotiations leading up to the independence of Namibia.

The United Nations played a useful role by keeping the constant pressure of world opinion on South African leaders. In establishing the UNIN, it helped to train a generation of civil servants to pave the way for the transition from white South African administration of the country to one in which black Namibians could fruitfully contribute to the building of their new country. The UNTAG operation paved the way for full, free, and fair elections in which an amazing 97 percent of the eligible electorate voted, after SWAPO soldiers had been demobilized and refugees in neighboring countries had returned home.

SWAPO, which won a majority, but not too commanding of a majority, decided to temper its socialist rhetoric and to work with smaller parties, thus giving the new democratic constitution time to set roots. The Frontline States played a useful role in moderating their stances toward South Africa at a critical stage of the negotiations, and some, such as Mozambique, had opted for direct relations with South Africa as early as 1984. These political shifts made it possible for South Africans to look to the north with less fear of being surrounded by Communist-backed socialist states. To this end, the reforms that were in progress in Eastern Europe and the Soviet Union also played a part in the decreasing of tensions in Southern Africa. Indeed, South Africa, which underwent substantial reforms at the same time as Namibia was achieving independence, eventually scrapped the apartheid system and had elections of its own that resulted in the peaceful downfall of white minority rule.

Namibia, in turn, has proved to be a stable country in the first decade of its existence, and it serves as a positive example of UN engagement over many decades in resolving a very bitter political controversy, through a persistent assertion of the rights to self-determination of peoples, coupled with timely and stubborn diplomatic engagement by the United States and other interested governments.

See also Apartheid (Debate 14); Decolonization (Debate 18); Mozambique Situation (Debate 47); Rhodesian Question (Debate 21).

FOR FURTHER READING

Grotpeter, John J. *Historical Dictionary of Namibia.* Metuchen, NJ: Scarecrow Press, 1994.

Hearn, Roger. *UN Peacekeeping in Action: The Namibian Experience.* Huntington, NY: Nova Science Publications, 1999.

Herbstein, Denis, and John Evenson. *The Devils Are Among Us: The War for Namibia.* London: Zed Books, 1989.

Kaela, Laurent C. W. *Question of Namibia.* New York: St. Martin's, 1996.

Katjavi, Peter H. *History of Resistance in Namibia.* Trenton, NJ: Africa World Press, 1990.

Osmañczyk, Edmund Jan. *Encyclopedia of the United Nations and International Agreements.* London: Taylor and Francis, 1985.

UN Chronicles, 1989–1990.

Von Glahn, Gerhardt. *Law among Nations: An Introduction to Public International Law.* 6th ed. New York: Macmillan, 1992.

Refugees and Stateless Persons (1946)

SIGNIFICANCE OF THE ISSUE

Taken up by the United Nations in its earliest years, the refugee problem in Europe after World War II encompassed nearly 30 million displaced persons, most of whom were successfully assisted or resettled. However, the spread of refugee problems throughout the world in subsequent decades led to an expanded protection and assistance role for UN humanitarian agencies, especially the United Nations High Commissioner for Refugees (UNHCR), which by the late 1990s commanded a budget of nearly $1 billion to assist and protect millions of refugees, making it one of the largest and most visible UN agencies.

BACKGROUND TO THE DEBATE

The international refugee problem began well before World War II, although that war gave added impetus to the search for solutions to the refugee problem. The first international efforts to assist and protect refugees and stateless persons came after World War I, when governments instituted visa and passport requirements to control the entry of aliens and the travel of citizens abroad, thereby regulating immigration and preventing free access and movement across international boundaries. However, the 1917 Bolshevik revolution in Russia and the unstable political situation surrounding the breakup of the Ottoman Empire after World War I led to large flows of refugees and displaced persons, who lacked legal documentation and in many cases were in desperate need of protection and assistance. Not possessing valid visas, they could not reside or travel legally outside of their country of nationality, nor could they return to their countries of origin without fear of persecution. Private agencies such as the Red Cross that provided assistance eventually appealed to the League of Nations to address the problem, and the League High Commissioner for Refugees Com-

Secretary-General Perez de Cuellar (center) makes an opening statement at the Second International Conference on Assistance to Refugees in Africa (ICARA II) at Geneva on 9 July 1984. UN/DPI Photo

ing from Russia was established in 1922, with Norwegian explorer and philanthropist Fridtjof Nansen at the helm. He developed the Nansen passport, which gave refugees greater mobility to find jobs and countries of settlement until they could repatriate safely to their homelands. The office was established as a temporary stopgap measure and was succeeded by several other temporary offices, including one to assist Jewish refugees from Germany in the late 1930s. The outbreak of World War II brought this first phase of international activity on behalf of refugees to a close.

World War II was disruptive to the war-affected populations also. The Allies began to refer to themselves as the "United Nations" as early as 1942. The twenty-six signatories to the Declaration of the United Nations included the United States, the United Kingdom, the Soviet Union, China, Australia, Belgium, Canada, Costa Rica, Cuba, Czechoslovakia, Dominican Republic, El Salvador, Greece, Guatemala, Haiti, Honduras, India, Luxembourg, Netherlands, New Zealand, Nicaragua, Norway, Panama, Poland, South Africa, and Yugoslavia. Acting together in 1943 they created a United Nations Relief and Rehabilitation Administration (UNRRA) to cope with the assistance needs of millions of war-displaced refugees and homeless persons, not only in Europe but in Africa and the Far East as well. UNRRA, which eventually resettled over a million refugees, gave way to the International Refugee Organization (IRO), which was given a five-year mandate by the UN General Assembly at its first session on 15 December 1946 to provide assistance and promote the repatriation or resettlement of the remaining displaced persons in Europe. The IRO presided over the successful repatriation or resettlement of over a million people during its five years of operation. However, the outbreak of the Cold War generated thousands of new refugees fleeing from Communist regimes in Eastern Europe. When the IRO was disbanded in February 1951, 400,000 refugees still required protection and assistance in Europe, and the newly created UNHCR, which was established by the UN General Assembly and became operational on 1 January 1951 as the IRO's successor, assumed responsibility for their legal protection. The creation of the UNHCR traces its roots to the debates surrounding state concern over how to handle the problem of refugees, displaced persons, and stateless persons, which had been a major preoccupation of the United Nations since its inception and the subject of the United Nations' second international conference in 1950.

HISTORY OF THE DEBATE

Debates over the negotiation of treaties and creation of international institutions to protect and assist refugees drew on the earlier experience of the League of Nations. Generally, governments viewed refugee situations as temporary problems that could be resolved in short order by the voluntary repatriation of refugees or by their settlement in the country of first asylum or resettlement to a third country. Governments acknowledged that any person who had a well-founded fear of persecution and who had escaped from or feared returning to their country of origin or nationality should be granted refugee status. Any person could seek asylum as a refugee, but governments would determine whether or not they qualified legally, and even then, no government had a responsibility to grant permanent asylum to any particular refugee or group of refugees. However, once refugee status was granted, no country could legally deport refugees to their home country where persecution was likely to occur. These legal norms were reflected in the practice of the IRO, in the Statute of the UNHCR, and in a 1951 Convention Relating to the Status of Refugees, which was the ultimate fruit of the 1947 UN Conference on Refugees. These legal instruments, together with the creation of the UNHCR in 1951, and prior to it, the United Nations Relief and Works Agency for Palestine (UNRWA) in 1949 to deal with Palestinian refugees from the 1948 Arab-Israeli War, provided cooperative mechanisms by which governments could protect and assist refugees. But such agencies and treaties were created under the mistaken assumption that refugee situations were temporary and localized. The 1951 UN Refugee Convention, for instance, only classified as refugees those persons who had fled from events prior to 1 January 1951 and allowed states to further limit their obligations to refugees fleeing events in Europe. The UNHCR Statute was broader, allowing that agency to deal with situations that would emerge at later times and in other places. But funding for the UNHCR was restricted to administrative expenses for the purpose of overseeing the legal protection of refugees. Resettlement programs and other operational activities were denied to the UNHCR, which was given an initial mandate of only three years.

The creation of the UNHCR in turn reflected the variable political interests of governments during the late 1940s. The United States, which had funded over 70 percent of the IRO budget and had accepted over a third of the refugees resettled during the IRO's tenure in the late 1940s, was anxious to avoid a new and expanded UN bureaucracy. It sought, therefore, to limit the UNHCR to the legal protection function and to minimize the expenses associated with resettlement of refugees. It favored leaving the resettlement and assistance process to other agencies. By contrast, West European countries had a different agenda. The refugees were residing in their territories and proving to be a lingering burden and concern. Thus the Europeans wanted generous and robust resettlement programs for the remaining refugees. In the meantime, with the deepening distrust surrounding the Cold War, the Soviet Union and Communist countries of Eastern Europe argued that no international agency for refugees should be created. They worried that such an agency might encourage migration from their territories, while repatriated refugees would prove a security risk. They refused to become members of the UNHCR and other refugee organizations, viewing them as political devices of the capitalist governments and as threats to their national interests. When the Soviet Union invaded Hungary to put down a liberalization movement in 1956, the UNHCR, together with the Intergovernmental Committee for European Migration (ICEM), which is now known as the International Organization for Migration (IOM), responded effectively with legal protection, assistance, and resettlement programs for Hungarian refugees fleeing the Communist crackdown. This event convinced the Western governments of the usefulness of the UNHCR while cementing the fears of Communist countries that it was a manipulative tool of Western imperialism. Not until the end of the Cold War in the early 1990s and the emergence of many refugee problems in the former Soviet Union and in Eastern Europe did those nations seek membership in the UNHCR.

In 1967, non-Communist governments enacted a Protocol to the 1951 Refugee Convention to eliminate the time and geographical restrictions placed on the acquisition of refugee status. In the ten years following the Hungarian invasion, refugee problems had emerged in Africa and Asia, and the UN General Assembly had gradually asked the UNHCR to extend its good offices to those non-European countries to protect and assist refugees. As the refugee problem gradually evolved into a global phenomenon, governments prudently determined that the scope of the UNHCR's legal and assistance functions should be broadened. Gradually, the UNHCR emerged as a major operational assistance agency. Governments of the Third World, increasingly flooded with refugees and overwhelmed by the economic burdens associated with the large influxes, either appealed for international aid, as in Africa, or, as in Southeast Asia, refused to accept boat people. Controversy attended many refugee situations. Southeast Asian countries took highly restrictive measures against the reception of Vietnamese and Cambodian refugees, viewing them as a potential security risk. The UNHCR and Western governments eventually convinced the countries of first asylum in Southeast Asia to accept the boat people temporarily, pending their orderly resettlement to third countries. The United States, France, Canada, and Australia eventually served as the major destinations for resettled Southeast Asian refugees. These and other countries also agreed to pay for the costs associated with the maintenance of the boat people in their countries of first asylum until they were resettled. This arrangement, which came to a controversial end in the early 1990s, eventually saw the resettlement of nearly 2 million Southeast Asian refugees.

Countries in Africa, however, which had provided generally hospitable asylum to refugees from neighboring countries, felt largely overlooked. Expensive resettlement programs in Southeast Asia commanded large sums of money, whereas meager resources were directed toward the assistance and maintenance of African refugees. Two international conferences in the early 1980s were held in Geneva in order to heighten international awareness of the refugee problem in Africa. These conferences on assistance to refugees in Africa did increase international attention to the specific needs of refugee-affected African nations, but only modest success was achieved in terms of increasing assistance levels.

Cold War competition, regional disputes, and civil wars occurred in almost every region of the globe during the 1970s and 1980s. In Central America, bloody civil wars in El Salvador and Nicaragua generated large refugee flows. Cuban refugees fled in several waves from the regime of Fidel Castro, beginning in the early 1960s but also in the 1970s and 1980s. The invasion of Afghanistan by the Soviet Union in 1979 precipitated a flow of 5 million refugees into neighboring Pakistan and Iran. Civil wars in Angola, Ethiopia, Mozambique, Sudan, and Zimbabwe (formerly Rhodesia) led to the displacement of millions from those countries. Controversy surrounded international responses to each of these situations. Cuban refugees won ready asylum in the United States, whereas Haitian refugees fleeing a non-Communist but authoritarian regime were turned away. Necessary humanitarian aid to Afghan refugees in Pakistan was accompanied by military assistance to Afghan guerrilla fighters in border camps, even though military combatants are not considered refugees. On the other hand, when international agencies attempted to move refugee camps in Honduras away from the border with El Salvador to ensure greater security, Salvadoran refugees and humanitarian advocacy groups opposed the move as violation of the refugees' rights. Even the resettlement policies of governments came under criticism. The United States, which accepted over a million Southeast Asians, maintained annual resettlement quotas of only a few thousand for Central American and African refugees during the 1980s, raising charges of racism and bias. All of this controversy should not be viewed as surprising. Refugees flee from highly intense political conflicts. They, and the groups that seek to assist them, often have strong political views. The more important point to be understood is that governments have made a substantial commitment over the decades to protect and assist refugees. These efforts, though not free of political controversy, represent a truly remarkable and sustained level of energy and attention.

Like all intergovernmental organizations (IGOs) the UNHCR takes its direction from and reports to an authorizing and monitoring body of member states. This body is known as the Executive Committee (EXCOM). In addition, like all specialized agencies, the UNHCR takes direction from and reports to the UN Economic and Social Council (ECOSOC) and the UN General Assembly. But the annual budgets and programs of the UNHCR are directly supervised by its member states. Governments debate and approve the UNHCR annual budget, which is supported by voluntary contributions made by the member states. The UNHCR may seek additional emergency funds as they are necessary but must otherwise tailor its programs to fit within budget limits established by the member states. The Executive Committee may call upon the High Commissioner to undertake new initiatives or reform the agency's structure. When the UNHCR responded poorly to the refugee emergency in Somalia in the early 1980s, for example, the EXCOM called upon it to develop an emergency unit to better anticipate and respond to refugee emergencies. Over the years, member states of the UNHCR have encouraged it to develop and deepen its ties with nongovernmental organizations (NGOs) as implementing partners. Indeed, among all UN agencies, the UNHCR has the most extensive contact with NGOs that often serve as the implementors of UNHCR refugee assistance, repatriation, and resettlement programs. The annual budget and policy debates of the EXCOM regular session usually held in October, and of the mini-EXCOM meeting held in the early winter months, offer an opportunity for governments to consider new programs and proposals from among their own membership and from the High Commissioner's Office.

With the emergence of many complex emergencies involving not only refugee flows but substantial internal displacement owing to civil wars, responses to refugee situations in the 1990s became much more complicated. For example, the UNHCR was named by the UN Security Council as the lead for provision of humanitarian assistance in the Bosnian civil war. This required a delicate political task of placating the warring Serbian, Croat, and Bosnian Muslim factions in order to ensure the protection and assistance of vulnerable populations. A UN Protection Force was deployed to protect humanitarian assistance efforts. But war continued, as did ethnic cleansing and displacement. Providing both military security and humanitarian aid during the midst of a civil war proved difficult. Similar lessons were learned in the UN response to the Somali civil war and famine of the early 1990s. Moreover, even when civil wars have been politically resolved and peace agreements reached—as, for example, they were in Mozambique and in Cambodia in the early 1990s—humanitarian aid must cope not only with repatriation of refugees but also with reconstruction and rehabilitation of destroyed infrastructure; housing and social services; mine clearance programs in cities, towns, and rural areas; demobilization of hostile forces; reconstitution of police forces; preparation for elections; provision of economic aid; transportation for returnees; and sometimes investigation of war crimes. Such multitask environments go beyond the capabilities of a single organization, such as the UNHCR, and call upon coordinated responses with other UN agencies such as the United Nations Children's Fund (UNICEF), the United Nations Development Program (UNDP), the World Food Program (WFP), the World Bank, and UN peacemaking and peacekeeping forces, as well as with the dozens of NGOs, notably the International Committee of the Red Cross (ICRC), among many others, that will become engaged. In Mozambique and Cambodia, such coordinated efforts were largely successful. In Somalia, Bosnia, and the Great Lakes region of Africa they were not.

To better coordinate this response to complex emergencies, and owing to the ever-present demand by governments for streamlined UN organization and budget reform, the Department of Humanitarian Affairs (DHA) was established in 1992, along with the position of emergency relief coordinator. However, in practice, the DHA proved unable to manage or displace the more well-entrenched and experienced agencies such as the UNHCR and UNDP, among others. Still, an Inter-Agency Steering Committee consisting of international humanitarian agencies and nongovernmental bodies met under DHA auspices and did provide a useful mechanism for sharing of information and stimulated some interagency coordination. In 1997, after a thorough review under Secretary-General Kofi Annan, the DHA was superseded by the UN Office for Coordination of Humanitarian Affairs, which represents the latest effort of the United Nations to provide greater central direction and coordination of international humanitarian aid in complex emergency situations.

OUTCOME OF THE DEBATE

With the collapse of communism, many hoped at long last that the world could solve the regional wars that had produced so many refugees in Asia, Africa, and Central America. This hope was short-lived, for although progress was made in solving conflicts and repatriating refugees in Mozambique, Cambodia, and Central America in the early 1990s, the emergence of civil wars and refugee flows in the newly independent republics of the former Soviet Union, and in Eastern Europe, especially in the Balkans, meant that new and bitter disputes would be unleashed between rival ethnic and religious communities. Thus, international aid had to be spread even more thinly across an increasingly large and complicated set of refugee problems. Civil war in Afghanistan precluded a full repatriation of refugees to that war-torn land. Vicious civil wars of ethnic cleansing rocked the Balkan States from Croatia and Bosnia to Kosovo. And while many African refugee situations admitted of resolution, civil war in Angola resisted resolution while new conflicts erupted in Liberia and Sierra Leone, and a terrible genocide in Rwanda produced great upheaval in the Great Lakes region of Africa and in the Congo. These conflicts sorely tested UN efforts to streamline and rationalize the coordination and funding of humanitarian responses to these exceedingly complex emergency situations. But they also illustrated that improved coordination would be essential to improved international responses to such emergencies.

If the international community has learned anything from its experience with refugees and humanitarian emergencies over the past fifty years, it is that particular refugee situations and humanitarian emergencies may be temporary but that as global phenomena they are not easily eradicated. Still, the persistence of UN assistance activity in this arena stands as a tribute to the equally tenacious humanitarian capacity of the United Nations and its member states.

See also Angola Situation (Debate 42); Balkan Civil Wars (Debate 45); Cambodia Situation (Debate 38); Central American Wars (Debate 37); Genocide (Debate 9); Human Rights (Debate 10); Hungarian Question (Debate 16); Kosovo Situation (Debate 50); Mozambique Situation (Debate 47); Rwandan Civil War (Debate 49); Soviet Invasion of Afghanistan (Debate 39); Status and Condition of Children (Debate 2).

FOR FURTHER READING

Allen, Tim, and Hubert Morsink. *When Refugees Go Home*. London: James Currey, 1994.

Carlin, James L. *The Refugee Connection: A Lifetime of Running a Lifeline*. New York: Macmillan, 1989.

Goodwin-Gill, Guy. *The Refugee in International Law*. Oxford: Clarendon Press, 1998.

Gorman, Robert F. *Historical Dictionary of Refugee and Disaster Relief Organizations*. 2nd ed. Lanham, MD: Scarecrow Press, 2000.

———. *Mitigating Misery: An Inquiry into the Political and Humanitarian Aspects of U.S. and Global Refugee Policy*. Lanham, MD: University Press of America, 1993.

Loescher, Gil. *Beyond Charity: International Cooperation and the Global Refugee Crisis.* New York: Oxford University Press, 1993.

Marrus, Michael R. *The Unwanted: European Refugees in the Twentieth Century.* New York: Oxford University Press, 1985.

United Nations High Commissioner for Refugees. *Refugees.* Geneva: UNHCR, published quarterly.

———. *The State of the World's Refugees.* Geneva: UNHCR, published every other year.

United States Committee for Refugees. *World Refugee Survey.* Washington, DC: USCR, published annually.

Zarjevski, Yéfime. *A Future Preserved: International Assistance to Refugees.* New York: Pergamon Press, 1988.

Zolberg, Aristide, Astri Suhrke, and Sergio Aguayo. *Escape from Violence: Conflict and the Refugee Crisis in the Developing World.* New York: Oxford University Press, 1989.

World Monetary System (1947)

SIGNIFICANCE OF THE ISSUE

The collapse of the pre–World War II monetary and trade system, coupled with the huge destructiveness of World War II, gave rise to the need for a complete rethinking and overhaul of the international monetary system. Even before the end of World War II and the formal establishment of the United Nations, forty-four governments gathered at Bretton Woods, New Hampshire, and agreed to the establishment of a monetary system that would guarantee the rapid restoration of the world economy. Aimed primarily at the resuscitation of war-torn Europe, the monetary system and its chief institutions, the World Bank and the International Monetary Fund (IMF), eventually turned their attention in the 1960s to fostering the economic development of the newly independent countries of the developing world. Subject to controversy from the beginning as capitalist-oriented institutions, these bodies have been the target of ongoing and often intense criticism from developing countries and left-wing intellectual circles for failing to take into account the humanitarian and environmental effects of their restrictive loan conditions. Nonetheless, governments continue to seek resources from these bodies, and the structural adjustments they have insisted upon, though painful, have often resulted in necessary and productive changes in national economic policies.

BACKGROUND TO THE DEBATE

International monetary policy has always been a very decentralized process where no single agency or institution is in charge but, rather, where a combination of national central banks and private banks, coupled with governmental policies and procedures, determines the flow of capital and the payment of international transactions. Before World War II, the British pound served as a kind of reserve currency, and gold was used to establish

Over forty nations meet at Bretton Woods, New Hampshire, to discuss monetary
stabilization and trade issues in July 1944. UN/DPI Photo

the value of currencies. Even before World War II, shortages of capital and
protectionist trade policies contributed to the global depression. World
War II was the quietus to the international monetary system, as virtually all
of the major powers in Europe faced economic ruin, destroyed infrastructure, and an immediate need for huge amounts of capital. The United States
alone had emerged from the war with its industrial sector largely intact and
humming away in a wartime production mode. Nearly 70 percent of the
world's gold reserves were held on American accounts.

   In 1944, at Bretton Woods, New Hampshire, forty-four countries met to
discuss how to structure the postwar international monetary and economic
system so as to ensure a stable flow of capital for reconstruction of
war-ravaged economies and national infrastructures. With whole cities
laying in ruin, roads and bridges destroyed, communications and transportation systems badly degraded, and industrial and energy facilities
badly damaged, there was a need for substantial liquidity in the international monetary system. In other words, countries needed a lot of cash and
quickly, in order to rebuild their nations and restore economic production.
The only country whose currency could function in this capacity was the
United States, with its massive gold reserves. Thus at Bretton Woods the
dollar was given a fixed value in gold (one ounce of gold was pegged at
$35), and all other currencies were valued in reference to the dollar at fixed
values. Such a system of fixed exchange rates would guarantee greater sta-

bility and predictability in international trade. Moreover, the U.S. dollar was backed by gold, and countries holding U.S. dollars could convert them on request into gold assets. This gave confidence in the use of the dollar as a means of international liquidity. In addition, two institutions were created at Bretton Woods in order to serve as mechanisms to stabilize monetary relations and ensure the broad distribution of capital to countries in desperate need of long-term loans for reconstruction and development. The IMF was created to help countries pay short-term balance of payments deficits, and the International Bank for Reconstruction and Development (IBRD), otherwise known as the World Bank, was established to provide long-term loans for productive purposes to enhance international trade and standards of living, to promote private foreign investment, and to provide technical assistance to countries regarding economic development. Because the IMF and World Bank were unable to make sufficient money available through their loan programs, the United States essentially became the world's banker by promoting the outflow of dollars into the international economy through aid programs, overseas military expenditures, and investments of American corporations. The United States alone could maintain balance of payments deficits serving in this capacity, and this was workable as long as other countries maintained confidence in the U.S. economy and the dollar—a situation that prevailed until the late 1950s, when U.S. gold reserves became badly depleted. By this time, however, the economies of Europe and Asia were back on their feet, and the Bretton Woods system had achieved its primary goals.

The World Bank and the IMF officially came into being in December 1945, even before the first meeting of the UN General Assembly, and they commenced operations in June 1946. Established originally as autonomous intergovernmental organizations, they were eventually drawn into relation with the United Nations on 15 November 1947 as both the Bank's Board of Governors and the UN General Assembly approved an agreement establishing formal relations. The Bank is in turn governed by its Board of Governors, on which all member states are represented. To be a member of the World Bank it is necessary to be a member of the IMF. Decisions regarding the approval of Bank loans are made on a weighted voting scale, with all states having 250 votes, with 1 additional vote for every share of the capital stock held. The Board of Governors meets annually, and the day-to-day operation of the Bank is conducted by a secretariat known as the Executive Directors, who in turn elect a president. The IMF is organized along similar lines. Both of these institutions have been consistently run by conservative, hard-nosed bankers who have managed Bank assets creatively to leverage large amounts of private bank resources to fund Bank loans to needy countries. However, from the outset, Communist nations refused to participate in these financial institutions, seeing them as tools of capitalist imperialism. This changed dramatically with the demise of communism in the early

1990s, as former Communist countries sought membership. By the late 1990s, membership in both the IMF and World Bank exceeded 180 member states, vindicating the wisdom of the initial founders of these institutions at Bretton Woods.

HISTORY OF THE DEBATE

When the World Bank and IMF joined the family of UN specialized agencies in 1947, it undertook to report to the UN General Assembly through the Economic and Social Council (ECOSOC), which, in turn, was authorized to provide coordination of the work of various agencies. During the first decade of operations, the Bank and the IMF operated largely unto themselves under the principles established at Bretton Woods. When European states ran large balance of payments deficits from 1945 to 1947, World Bank and IMF resources proved insufficient, and the United States, which had served as the primary architect of the monetary system, exercised leadership by promoting huge outflows of dollars to compensate. Since the dollar was a highly prized currency asset accepted by virtually all nations in settling of trade accounts, the system worked well until U.S. gold reserves became depleted during the late 1950s. By this time, the economies of Europe and Japan had completely recovered from the destruction of World War II and were becoming trade competitors with the United States. U.S. leadership in putting the international economic system on a stable footing was related in part to its concern about the vulnerability of Europe to Communist subversion and attack as the Cold War emerged in the late 1940s. But as its Allies recovered and began to compete with the United States in the trade sector, the United States began to take steps to reduce its vulnerability to large balance of payments deficits.

At the same time, however, the emergence of the developing nations onto the international scene created a new need for World Bank and IMF activity on their behalf. In 1956, the International Finance Corporation (IFC) was established as an affiliate of the IBRD and became a part of the World Bank structure. It was aimed principally at promoting the economic development of developing countries through promotion of private sector investment. In 1960, as a number of poorer nations gained independence, the World Bank added yet another affiliate, the International Development Association (IDA), which though legally a distinct body is governed by the same administrative and oversight bodies and is open to all members of the World Bank. The purpose of the IDA is to make available to the poorest countries loans free of interest and with long periods of repayment, initially fifty years, but later reduced to forty years, in order to promote economic development, improve productivity, and raise standards of living among the poorest nations.

While the institutional mechanisms of the Bretton Woods system continued to grow, the international community began to experience monetary instability during the 1960s. In 1969, the IMF created the first artificial international currency, the special drawing rights (SDRs), which functioned a little like a revolving credit card system, in an effort to supplement fund availability for countries seeking to cover short-term imbalances of their national accounts. In the meantime, the U.S. economy not only had been running large balance of payments deficits—now no longer to anyone's benefit—but also began to run trade deficits and unbalanced domestic budgets, as the administration of President Lyndon Johnson attempted to fight an expensive war in Vietnam and finance the Great Society, a huge new domestic spending program, without raising taxes. As pressure on the dollar increased, other governments refused to revalue their currencies. The fixed exchange rate system came under heavy pressure as well, and finally President Richard M. Nixon unilaterally renounced the convertibility of the dollar into gold and devalued the dollar. Further devaluation of the dollar followed as countries attempted to adjust to the new circumstances, which included an end to the fixed exchange rate system, as the value of currencies "floated" in relation to one another. This in turn increased the unpredictability of the international trade sector. The dollar remained a major reserve currency for settling international accounts, but it was now joined by other leading currencies, such as the British pound, the French and Swiss franc, the German deutschmark, and the Japanese yen, among others. The volume of SDRs also was substantially expanded to serve as a major reserve asset. Governmental leaders of these countries in turn began to meet regularly to ensure the stability of international currency markets.

Coupled with the monetary instability of the 1970s was the inflationary effect of increases in the price for oil and the incredible growth in the value of private capital on the accounts of hundreds of private banks and multinational corporations. While developing countries were adversely affected by the instability and the inflationary trends, international lending institutions, such as the World Bank affiliates, were able to leverage some of this private capital for development loans to developing countries. Private corporations also lent large sums to various developing nations as well. Unfortunately, several of the countries that received large loans on expectation of their future income as oil producers fell on hard times when the oil glut of the 1980s sent oil prices much lower. The United States took the lead in bolstering the IMF and seeking additional sources of income to bail out countries such as Argentina, Brazil, and Mexico that had fallen in arrears and could not pay their debts. With new funds from the IMF, the World Bank, and a variety of private and public sources, along with rescheduling of the debts and imposition of national austerity measures in the affected countries, defaults on loans were avoided.

However, the situation in many much smaller and less wealthy countries was equally bad and grew worse during the 1970s and 1980s. Much of the development aid invested in developing countries was badly mismanaged or squandered by national bureaucracies. In the 1970s, the "basic needs" philosophy emerged to promote agricultural development in order to encourage more effective use of Bank resources. In many cases, however, new loans to countries couldn't even pay the debt service with the old loans, putting countries on a treadmill in which they lost further ground. In the mid-1970s these circumstances led to calls for a New International Economic Order (NIEO) by developing countries and demands for generous debt rescheduling and debt cancellation and for huge increases in concessional aid. The IMF came under heavy fire from developing countries during this time owing to the austerity measures it required countries to undertake to qualify for loans.

A further strategy of developing countries during these years of economic instability was to proliferate the number of UN development agencies. Some made sense, such as the establishment of the UN Development Program, whereas others evoked the nonsupport of the wealthier countries. An example of the latter was the creation of the UN Capital Development Fund to assist in promotion of community development programs in the least-developed countries. Because this Fund relied on voluntary contributions and most developed states opposed its creation, the Fund has been seriously undersubscribed. For most of their support, developing countries would need to turn to the World Bank affiliates and the IMF or to private investment and bilateral aid.

During the 1980s, international efforts to get hold of the development assistance process led to the regular holding of in-country development strategy discussions by development agencies to hammer out with the local government a long-term development strategy. These, coupled with roundtable discussions held by governments seeking loans, with donor governments and with World Bank officials, helped to give a country's overall development plan a degree of cohesion. Absent such a process, duplication and mismanagement would multiply, given the large number and wide range of development agencies and private sources for investment.

In 1988, in a further effort to leverage funds for investment in the Third World, the Bank established the Multilateral Investment Guarantee Agency (MIGA), which attempts to promote private investment in the least-developed countries by insuring investors against risks often associated with investing in Third World countries, such as expropriation, civil war, and host country efforts to block repatriation of corporate assets.

During the 1990s, the major challenge for the international monetary system came in the form of otherwise good news: the collapse of communism. The rapid degeneration of the economies of the former Soviet Union and other Communist countries, followed by the death of communism, led the newly formed governments to seek membership in world monetary organizations. This put a great deal of pressure on existing resources in the early 1990s, placing other developing countries in the position of competing for foreign aid with countries that had once been a source of foreign aid. The sustained growth experienced by wealthier members of the IMF and World Bank has permitted these agencies, coupled with the even vaster private markets that have seen huge accumulations in the 1990s, to continue to be a source of potential income to meet the additional strain put on the international monetary system by integration of the former Communist world.

OUTCOME OF THE DEBATE

The debate concerning international financial and monetary policy is an interminable one. Throughout recent history, the movements of finance and capital among nations have been governed not only by the wealthier countries but by private banking institutions, along with the UN specialized agencies in this field. The World Bank and IMF have routinely borne criticism and resentment. They have responded to such criticisms in many instances with shifts in policy. Attacked for trickle-down economic aid approaches in the 1960s, they adopted "basic needs" approaches in the 1970s. Attacked in the 1970s and 1980s for insensitivity to environmental concerns, they adopted policies in the 1980s and 1990s to ensure greater attention to the environment. Attacked for conditioning loans on the enactment of painful austerity policies and national economic reforms, they bent but did not break. In the long run, painful reforms of national policy were essential in putting many developing countries that had previously imposed wasteful and inefficient subsidies and state-run enterprises on a more stable footing, by unleashing private enterprise, boosting the productive capacity of their agricultural sector, and promoting greater foreign investment.

After the painful period of the 1980s, many, though certainly not all, countries turned the corner in the 1990s. Even in Asia, where a severe economic crisis hit in the late 1990s, recovery was well under way by the close of the decade. The economies of many former Communist countries, particularly that of the Russian Federation, remain a major problem, as do the economies of many developing countries that continue to face a debt crisis, leading to continuing calls for debt rescheduling and debt cancellation. One of the more poignant voices in this regard was that of Pope John Paul II, who called upon wealthy nations and international lending agencies in 1999 to forgive the debts of the poorest nations entirely as an act of grace at the onset of the third millennium. As yet, there has been no rush to take the pope up on his offer, and indeed, the problems facing many developing countries remain quite daunting.

However, the international monetary system was established precisely to deal with long-term economic and development problems. Thus, there continues to be a need for such institutions. The nearly universal participation by states in them at the end of the 1990s attests to the belief of governments that this is so, even when they grumble over the terms of a loan agreement.

See also Global Environment (Debate 27); New International Economic Order (Debate 30); Third World Development Programming (Debate 25); Trade and Development (Debate 24).

FOR FURTHER READING

Bennett, A. LeRoy. *International Organizations: Principles and Issues.* Englewood Cliffs, NJ: Prentice-Hall, 1995.

Culpeper, Roy, et al. *Global Development Fifty Years after Bretton Woods.* New York: St. Martin's, 1997.

Danaher, Kevin. *50 Years Is Enough: The Case against the World Bank and the International Monetary Fund.* Cambridge, MA: South End, 1994.

Kapur, Devesh, et al. *The World Bank: Its First Half Century.* Washington, DC: Brookings Institution, 1997.

Khan, Shahrukh. *Do World Bank and IMF Policies Work?* New York: St. Martin's, 1999.

Ul Haq, Mahbub, et al., eds. *The UN and the Bretton Woods Institutions: New Challenges for the Twenty-first Century.* New York: St. Martin's, 1995.

UN Yearbooks, 1990, 1995.

---------------------- *Debate 6* ----------------------

Arab-Israeli Dispute (1947)

SIGNIFICANCE OF THE ISSUE

No single political conflict has proved more tenacious and persistent during nearly the entire life of the United Nations as has the Arab-Israeli dispute. The UN Trusteeship Council, the General Assembly, the Security Council, the Economic and Social Council (ECOSOC), and the United Nations Relief and Works Agency for Palestine (UNRWA) have all been engaged in what first was called the Palestine Question, introduced onto the agendas of the General Assembly in its second session and of the Trusteeship Council in 1947. Wars in 1948, 1956, 1967, and 1973 punctuated a tense regional environment that called upon the full diplomatic resources of the United Nations and the entire international community. Peaceful resolution of the dispute gained momentum in the 1970s and again in the 1990s, but full implementation of peace agreements eludes the region.

BACKGROUND TO THE DEBATE

Palestine is home to the ancient Holy Lands of Judaism and Christianity. Jerusalem, site of the Jewish Temple until destroyed by the Roman legions in A.D. 70, is also revered by Christians as the site of the Passion, death, and Resurrection of Jesus and considered a holy site by Islam. With the dispersion of the Jewish people in A.D. 70, Palestine eventually became a predominantly Christian region by the fourth century A.D. until conquered by Muslim armies in the seventh century A.D. The Crusades marked a further point of conflict between Christian Europe and Muslim occupiers of Palestine in the eleventh to twelfth centuries, after which Palestine was invaded by Mongolian armies in the fourteenth and fifteenth centuries. In 1516 it fell under the control of the Ottoman Turks until the end of World War I, when the United Kingdom undertook administration of the area under a League of Nations mandate in 1920. Palestine suffered considerable neglect under

Ottoman rule, and this enabled Jews to return. Under the British mandate, Jewish immigration increased in the wake of Nazi persecution of Jews after 1933. In 1917, Britain acknowledged the legitimacy of Zionist claims to establish a homeland for the Jewish people. However, Arabs objected strenuously to the idea of a Jewish state, to Jewish immigration, and to the sale of lands to Jewish immigrants. Riots broke out in 1920, 1921, 1929, and 1933 and sporadically from 1936 to 1939. Britain halted Jewish immigration in 1939. After World War II, unable to resolve the conflicting demands of the now-sizable Jewish population with those of the Arab Palestinian majority, Britain handed the issue over to the United Nations in 1947. The United Nations in turn decided in favor of partition into a Jewish state and a Palestinian state. In 1948, Israel declared its independence and immediately was attacked by her Arab neighbors, who refused to accept or recognize Israel's existence as a state. Overwhelmingly superior armed forces from Egypt, Jordan, Syria, Lebanon, Iraq, and Saudi Arabia attacked Israel, hoping to destroy the fledgling state and restore Palestinian rights. But Israel successfully fended off the attacks and actually increased its territory at the expense of the Palestinians.

Thus, the first of four major Arab-Israeli wars began, much to the disadvantage of the Palestinians, some 700,000 of whom fled into neighboring Arab states, even as Egypt seized the Gaza Strip and Jordan the West Bank of the Jordan River and Old Jerusalem. Neither Egypt nor Jordan granted Palestinians autonomy in these areas, and the remaining parts of the intended Palestinian state were absorbed by Israel. This displacement and disfranchisement of the Palestinians served to heighten animosities in the region in subsequent years as four generations of Palestinians were born in exile and prone to radical, violent, and terrorist methods against their prime enemy, the Jewish state of Israel. Conversely, Israel lived in a state of continuous insecurity owing to a lack of Arab recognition and to the fact that it was surrounded by hostile and increasingly well-armed Arab nations.

HISTORY OF THE DEBATE

The debate about Palestine began in the UN General Assembly in its Second Session in 1947. On 29 November, the General Assembly voted to partition Palestine into a Jewish and a Palestinian state, once the UK mandate had formally ended. This transpired on 14 May 1948 and was followed immediately by the Arab attacks. The United Nations made numerous attempts to mediate the conflict. Count Folke Bernadotte, the United Nations mediator, was assassinated on 17 September 1948 in Jerusalem, and his successor, Dr. Ralph Bunche, worked for months to obtain a series of cease-fire agreements. During the fighting, Israel continued to gain territory, especially in the southern Negev desert region. After intensive negotiations,

Egypt and Israel agreed to an armistice on 7 January 1949. This was followed by an agreement with Lebanon on 22 March, with Jordan on 3 April, and with Syria on 20 July. While the armistices brought an end to the fighting, they did not guarantee the peace. Arab countries deeply resented the presence of Israel and the humiliation of defeat. They supported Palestinian terrorist attacks against Israel and blockaded the Gulf of Aqaba, which was Israel's only access to the Red Sea.

In October 1956, Israel invaded the Sinai region of Egypt and the Gaza Strip to halt Palestinian terrorist attacks and to break the Egyptian blockade of the Gulf of Aqaba, Israel's only access to the Red Sea. Britain and France intervened as well, to prevent Egyptian president Gamal Abdel Nasser from successfully nationalizing the Suez Canal. The United States and the Soviet Union both opposed this intervention. On 6 November, a cease-fire was arranged. Israeli, British, and French forces were withdrawn and a United Nations Emergency Force (UNEF) was introduced to patrol the Egyptian/Israeli border with the agreement of both countries. In late October 1956, the UN General Assembly, acting under the Uniting for Peace Resolution, in its First Special Emergency Session called upon Secretary-General Dag Hammarskjöld to submit plans for the UNEF. The Assembly action was necessary given that the UN Security Council was stymied by potential British and French vetoes and because the Soviet Union threatened to intervene directly on Egypt's behalf. Tensions were high. In a vote of 64 to 5 (Britain, France, Israel, Australia, and New Zealand), the Assembly called for an immediate cease-fire, withdrawal of Israeli forces behind preexisting armistice lines, an embargo on military aid, and steps to reopen the Suez Canal. The United States, which had not been consulted by Britain or France, publicly criticized its allies and put pressure on them and Israel to comply with the UN demands. Under this pressure the invading powers eventually buckled, and UNEF was deployed under the direct supervision of Hammarsjköld, who was answerable to the Assembly and Security Council. The permission of Egypt (Israel refused to allow UNEF forces to operate on its territory) was secured for UNEF deployment. UNEF operated as a peacekeeping force intended merely to serve as an international buffer between the conflicting parties. It was strictly enjoined not to use force.

The UNEF remained until 19 May 1967, when Nasser ordered them to leave. Secretary-General U Thant complied with Nasser's demand, although the original understanding of the deployment of UNEF was that Egypt would not seek its withdrawal until its mandate had been fulfilled, a mandate that included prevention of the resumption of hostilities. U Thant did not press this point, believing that Egypt had the right to demand withdrawal. Nasser then seized the Gaza Strip and reintroduced the blockade of the Gulf of Aqaba. On 5 June, Israel, sensing an imminent threat to its security, unleashed a powerful attack on all fronts, rapidly occupying all of

Egypt's Sinai Peninsula, seizing the Golan Heights from Syria, and Old Jerusalem and the West Bank from Jordan, all within six days. On 10 June, the fighting ceased under UN arranged agreements. The Six Day War shocked the Arab world, and this time Israel refused to budge from the newly occupied territories without recognition and guarantees of peace from its Arab neighbors. The Arabs refused to recognize Israel. In the meantime, the Soviet Union began to provide heavy military assistance to Arab governments, while Israel relied heavily on military aid from the United States.

In November 1967, at the request of the United Arab Republic (Egypt), the Security Council was called into session to deliberate the persisting problems of Israeli occupation of Arab lands. Despite the acrimonious exchanges that took place, with the Soviet Union siding with the Arab states in condemning Israeli aggression and calling for Israel's immediate withdrawal to prewar boundaries and Western powers insisting that guarantees of Israeli security were essential to any lasting peace, a compromise draft resolution sponsored by the United Kingdom won unanimous endorsement on 22 November as Security Council Resolution 242 in which the Council declared that lasting peace could only be achieved in the Arab-Israeli dispute through the return of occupied territories to the rightful sovereigns and through Arab recognition of Israel's right to existence (see Appendix 8 for a text of this landmark resolution). This land for peace strategy remained a keystone of all subsequent international efforts to resolve the Arab-Israeli dispute. However, the wider Cold War between the superpowers continued to provoke tension in the Middle East, which intensified during the 1960s and 1970s, as the region was further destabilized by a massive arms race.

Rankling under yet another defeat at Israeli hands, Egypt under President Anwar Sadat and Syria under Hafez Assad attacked Israel during the high holy days of Yom Kippur on 6 October 1973. The Soviet Union supplied Egypt and Syria by a massive airlift during the fighting, and the United States responded in kind with support to Israel, during one of the most tense Cold War confrontations ever. Although Israel suffered early and heavy losses, it swiftly recovered and managed to resist Syrian advances and to cross over the Suez Canal in order to trap invading Egyptian forces. On 24 October after more than two weeks of intense fighting, the United Nations brokered a cease-fire, leaving Egypt in a position to claim at least a partial victory and a vindication of past defeats. After negotiations in 1974, brokered by U.S. Secretary of State Henry Kissinger, Israel withdrew from the West Bank of the Suez Canal.

Momentum toward peace between Israel and Egypt gathered in subsequent years and culminated in the Camp David Peace Accords, brokered by President Jimmy Carter and agreed to by Anwar Sadat and Israel's Menachem Begin, on 26 March 1979. Thirty years of war between the two countries came to an end and diplomatic relations were established. In

Security Council members vote on the historic Resolution 242 establishing the land for peace principle as a basis for resolution of the Arab-Israeli dispute on 22 November 1967. UN/DPI Photo Yutaka Nagata

1982, Israel formally returned the Sinai to Egypt. Although this agreement was crucial in momentum toward peace in the Middle East, insofar as no major war between Israel and the Arab states has occurred since then, Israel's relations with Lebanon, Jordan, and Syria, continued to be problematical, as did the plight of the militant Palestinians, who were expelled from one Arab country after another. Palestinian forces eventually concentrated their efforts in southern Lebanon during the early 1970s, and Israel did not hesitate to retaliate against Palestinian attacks on Israeli towns and citizens with reprisals against Palestinian settlements in Lebanon. Lebanon's civil war between Muslims and Christians in 1975–1976 complicated matters further, allowing the Palestine Liberation Organization (PLO) to make use of southern Lebanon for its raids into Israel. In March 1978, Israel invaded southern Lebanon in retaliation for a PLO terrorist attack, but it later withdrew to permit the insertion of a United Nations Interim Force in Lebanon (UNIFIL). Matters came to a head in 1982, as PLO forces continued to use

Lebanon as a base for terrorist attacks against Israel. Israel again invaded Lebanon, forcing the PLO to evacuate, and Israeli and Syrian forces briefly clashed before agreeing to a truce. Syria, backed by Soviet military assistance, nevertheless avoided major direct conflict with Israel, which could now concentrate its military forces in the north without fear of Egyptian attack in the south. This strategic advantage prevented all-out conflicts but guaranteed nothing more than a very uneasy peace. With the PLO deprived of bases in Lebanon, Israel still had enemies to the east, but Syria and Jordan refrained from overt hostilities in subsequent years. Restive Palestinian populations, especially in the West Bank, provided the main source of instability during the 1980s. The *intifada*, or uprising, gathered momentum as Palestinians expressed their anger at continued Israeli occupation and at the creation of new Jewish settlements in the occupied territories of the West Bank. These settlements were considered violations of international law by the United Nations because occupying belligerent powers are forbidden to treat occupied territory as their own. UN bodies voiced condemnation of their construction, and they served as an ongoing point of conflict between Israeli occupying forces and the Palestinians. The movement of Israel's capital from Tel Aviv to Jerusalem also sparked great controversy, given Arab Palestinan claims to Old Jerusalem.

While tensions existed throughout the 1980s, the collapse of the Communist world, especially the Soviet Union, in the late 1980s and early 1990s deprived Israel's enemies of military support. Further momentum toward the fashioning of peace in the Arab-Israeli dispute followed the 1991 Persian Gulf War. In that conflict, Israel refrained from retaliating against Iraqi Scud missile attacks, whereas the United States, France, United Kingdom, and other Western powers, in collaboration with the Soviet Union and a coalition of Arab states, including Saudi Arabia, Kuwait, the Gulf States, Egypt, and Syria, agreed to retaliate against Iraq for its invasion of Kuwait. Following Iraq's crushing defeat in the Persian Gulf War, the PLO realized that its only hope for a return to Palestine rested in recognizing Israel's right to exist. In 1993, a peace agreement between the PLO and Israel was achieved. With the blessings of Jordan, the peace process now moved to another level, as various Israeli governments and Yasir Arafat of the PLO spent subsequent years haggling over how to grant Palestinian autonomy in the Gaza Strip and portions of the West Bank.

OUTCOME OF THE DEBATE

Over the course of the Arab-Israeli dispute, the United Nations has played the part of mediator and conciliator, the fashioner of cease-fires, and the peacekeeper. Starting with the cease-fire negotiations of UN mediators and the deployment of the United Nations Truce Supervision Organization (UNTSO) after the 1948 war, the United Nations has repeatedly responded

United Nations Disengagement Observer Force (UNDOF) forces, established after
the 1973 Yom Kippur war, monitor activities in the Golan Heights between Israel
and Syria in December of 1990. UN/DPI Photo John Isaac

to the conflicts in this region. In 1956, UNEF I was deployed to separate hostile forces in the Sinai. In 1973, UNEF II was deployed for similar reasons
until the Egypt/Israel peace agreement of 1979. A United Nations Disengagement Observer Force (UNDOF) was also deployed along the Golan
Heights between Israel and Syria in 1974, and in 1978 the UNIFIL was deployed to monitor hostilities in southern Lebanon. UN peacekeeping strategies were honed and developed in the crucible of the Arab-Israeli conflict.
They could not prevent wars from occurring, but they did contribute to
more stable interim periods of genuine, if uneasy, stability. As long as the
superpowers continued to line up in support of the opposing parties in the
region, the establishment of lasting peace was quite difficult, but when hostilities threatened to provoke direct superpower confrontation, the United
States and the Soviet Union had the good sense to pull back from the brink
and call upon UN bodies, such as the General Assembly or more frequently
the Security Council, to deploy peacekeeping forces.

The end of the Cold War opened new opportunities for peace in the
1990s, and these continue to bode well for a lasting peace in the region. Jordan has formally recognized Israel's right to exist, and the Israeli-PLO
peace agreement continues to make progress in fits and starts. Israel still remains concerned about its security in the face of ongoing terrorist attempts
by radical Palestinian factions to disrupt the peace process, but the creation

of a real Palestinian state is now within sight after more than five decades of strife, and the lone major threat to Israeli security, Syria, has moderated its approach to Israel in view of the fact that other Arab states have come to terms with the existence of Israel. As the region slowly gains greater stability, and moves toward a genuine and lasting peace, the United Nations will be remembered for having substantially contributed to the peace process.

The real source of a lasting peace must ultimately come from agreements between Israel and her neighbors. This is largely accomplished with Egypt and Jordan. Full accommodation with Syria has yet to be achieved. Great strides have been made in direct talks between Israeli and Palestinian leaders. In November 1999, final-status discussions began between newly elected Israeli Prime Minister Ehud Barak and Palestinian leader Yasir Arafat. Sticking points included the status of large Jewish settlements on the West Bank, final determinations of territorial borders for a Palestinian state, the right of Palestinian refugees to return to territory now under Israel's control, the future status of Jerusalem, and the timing of the declaration of a new Palestinian state. These difficult issues must be resolved before the Palestinian Question is retired from the UN agenda, a point underscored by renewed violence in the region in the fall of 2000.

See also Persian Gulf War (Debate 44); Zionism as Racism (Debate 34).

FOR FURTHER READING

Finklestein, Norman. *Image and Reality of the Israel-Palestine Conflict*. New York: Verso Books, 1995.

Guyatt, Nicolas. *The Absence of Peace: Understanding the Israeli-Palestinian Conflict*. London: Zed Books, 1998.

Herzog, Chaim. *The Arab-Israeli Wars: War and Peace in the Middle East*. New York: Random House, 1984.

Lesch, Ann, and Dan Tschingi. *Origins and Development of the Arab-Israeli Conflict*. Westport, CT: Greenwood Press, 1998.

Robinson, Glenn E. *Building a Palestinian State: The Incomplete Revolution*. Bloomington: Indiana University Press, 1997.

Rosner, Gabriella. *The United Nations Emergency Force*. New York: Columbia University Press, 1963.

Stjernfelt, Bertil. *The Sinai Peace Front: UN Peacekeeping Operations in the Middle East, 1973–1980*. New York: St. Martin's, 1992.

UN Yearbooks, 1948–1949, 1956–1957, 1967.

India-Pakistan Dispute (1948)

SIGNIFICANCE OF THE ISSUE

One of the first major issues involving the granting of independence to former colonies and the resulting conflicts concerned the partition of India
and Pakistan in 1947, the massive flows of Hindu and Muslim refugees that
followed partition and the conflict, and a dispute over the princely state of
Kashmir-Jammu, which was free to become independent or accede to either India or Pakistan. This was but the first of many conflicts between India and Pakistan in subsequent years, making it one of the most prolonged,
difficult, and still unsettled disputes in UN history. The United Nations
Military Observer Group in India and Pakistan (UNMOGIP), established
by the UN Security Council to monitor the Kashmir dispute in January
1949, still exists. Only the UN Truce Supervision Organization in the Middle East, established only eight months prior to UNMOGIP, has a lengthier
pedigree.

BACKGROUND TO THE DEBATE

The history of the Indian subcontinent is marked by the existence of hundreds of princely states, never completely unified under a single ruler, although several imperial dynasties did succeed in uniting parts of northern
India at various times. Predominantly Hindu in religious orientation, Bud-
dhism also originated in India. Apart from the Gupta empire of the fourth
and fifth centuries A.D., the only successful efforts at unifying northern India
came with the Mogul empires of the sixteenth and seventeenth centuries,
when Islamic rulers began to dominate the region. Under the great emperor
Akbar, Islamic rule was extended substantially, but Hindus also gained
equal subject status. The British entered the subcontinent through Calcutta
to establish a factory. They took control of Calcutta, then the predominantly
Islamic region of Bengal, and eventually all of India in 1757. Indians of both

Indian soldiers land in Srinigar as tensions rise with Pakistan over the status of Kashmir. © Bettmann/CORBIS

the Islamic and Hindu religions chaffed under British rule, and the last major effort to dislodge them in the mid-1800s, failed, and the British government assumed direct authority over rule of the colony from the British East India Company in 1858.

Indian nationalism continued to grow, however, especially with the advent of the educational system established by the British. In the 1880s the Indian National Congress was formed and led the struggle for independence; it produced great spokesmen for the cause, including in the 1920s and 1930s Mahatma Gandhi, who returned to India after many years in South Africa after World War I during which the British had promised to grant greater political autonomy to India. Facing British foot-dragging, he organized the famous nonviolent campaigns of civil disobedience and passive resistance during the 1930s. While some constitutional concessions were granted in 1935, full independence was not granted. In 1942, during World War II, Britain granted India autonomy, but the nationalists wanted complete independence, and the Indian National Congress passed the "Quit India" resolution. In the turmoil that followed, Gandhi, and Jawaharlal Nehru, the eventual political heir of India, spent much time in jail. Agitation for independence continued during the war and intensified afterward, but a complicating factor was a major split in the Indian National Congress, between the Muslim League, led by Mohammed Ali Jinnah, and the Hindus. The Muslim League demanded a separate state of Pakistan. Although Gandhi and Nehru were opposed to partition, they eventually conceded to the reality so that independence itself might be achieved. In 1947, the partition and the full independence of India and Pakistan were effected, although technically each of the 584 princely states gained independence separately. With the exception of three princely states, the majority of the states, many quite small, chose to join either India or Pakistan even before independence. The exceptions were Hyderabad, Junagadh, and Kashmir. Hyderabad and Junagadh were Hindu areas governed by Muslim rulers. Hyderabad's Muslim ruler sought independence, and Junagadh's sought union with Pakistan. India invaded and incorporated both areas, in the case of Junagadh, after a plebiscite. Kashmir, by contrast, was a predominantly Muslim area ruled by an unpopular and autocratic Hindu. He stalled making a decision on independence or union, leaving the question to be resolved after partition and full independence.

By arrangement of the great powers, India was granted original membership in the United Nations in 1945, and after partition, Pakistan joined the United Nations in 1947. The partition of India in 1947 disrupted the lives of millions. Sectarian violence broke out in both Pakistan and India, with the repression of Muslim minorities in India and Hindu minorities in Pakistan. Refugees fled in huge numbers—over 12 million—both ways across the newly established borders. The violence continued into 1948 and left a bitter legacy between the two countries, which has yet to be overcome.

HISTORY OF THE DEBATE

The humanitarian nightmare created by the partition of India did not directly involve the United Nations. However, in the state of Kashmir/Jammu, problems continued to simmer into 1948. According to the independence agreement, Kashmir/Jammu was free to remain independent, or to join either Pakistan or India. The majority of the population was Muslim, but the ruling prince, Maharajah Sir Hari Singh, was a Hindu, and when fighting broke out after the partition, he requested accession with India. India accepted the offer, noting that a final determination would have to be made in light of the wishes of the people. On 1 January 1948, India reported to the Security Council that the state of Kashmir and Jammu had been invaded by tribesmen with the assistance of Pakistan. Pakistan countered that Jammu and Kashmir had been illegally occupied by India and that an extermination campaign of Muslims was underway. Both countries agreed to the fielding of a United Nations Commission for India and Pakistan (UNCIP) to investigate and mediate the dispute. UNCIP, consisting of representatives from five countries (Argentia, Belgium, Colombia, Czechoslovakia, and the United States), visited the region in the summer of 1948. It recommended, among other things, a mutual cease-fire and a

UN-sponsored plebiscite in the region. To monitor the cease-fire in the region the Security Council established UNMOGIP in January 1949. UNCIP continued to function in an effort to mediate the dispute; however, little progress toward a plebiscite was made in subsequent years, and when a constituent assembly met in Srinigar, Kashmir's capital, to consider integration with India, Pakistan objected to the Security Council in November 1956. Council recommendations failed to result in any agreement, as did subsequent Security Council sessions in 1962 and 1964. The dispute defied resolution. Throughout 1965, as in previous years, dozens of violations by both parties of the cease-fire were reported. Matters heated up in September as India invaded portions of Pakistan. Secretary-General U Thant traveled to the troubled region, negotiating in both India and Pakistan. A new cease-fire agreement was reached on 22 September, and a new United Nations India-Pakistan Observation Mission (UNIPOM) was dispatched by the Security Council to patrol and observe the border areas where the Indian intervention into Pakistan occurred. In 1966, talks held under the auspices of the Soviet Union led to a mutual agreement for withdrawal of forces, which was completed by 25 February, after which UNIPOM was disbanded. However, the Security Council continued to renew the mandate of UNMOGIP.

The next outbreak of conflict occurred in 1971 with the secession of East Pakistan and its declaration of independence as Bangladesh, following a civil war there that had precipitated an Indian intervention. The crisis in the east Bengal State produced about 10 million refugees who fled into India. War flared briefly between India and Pakistan, but the collapse of Pakistani forces in East Pakistan quickly settled the matter, and a cease-fire was reached along the western border with India. Fighting occurred along the border with Kashmir, but the status quo continued to prevail. Not until 1976 did India and Pakistan resume normal diplomatic relations. In the meantime, India moved quickly to establish friendly ties with Bangladesh, which took UN membership in 1974.

During the 1980s and 1990s no progress was made in resolving the Kashmir dispute, although no outbreaks of conflict occurred. In the meantime, both India and Pakistan made significant strides in developing nuclear weapons capabilities, adding a new and ominous tone to the dispute. An underground test explosion by India in 1998 was followed by a similar test in Pakistan as tensions between the two countries mounted.

OUTCOME OF THE DEBATE

Although the General Assembly issued a resolution on the occasion of the fighting in Bangladesh in 1971, the India-Pakistan dispute over Kashmir has remained largely within the purview of the Security Council, which has explored all measures available to settle the dispute. These efforts have been largely fruitless. However, if the dispute has resisted full resolution, for much of the time a fair degree of calm has prevailed since the war of 1971. India has sought over the decades to treat the Kashmir question as though it were simply an internal matter of domestic affairs. However, the United Nations is on record favoring a plebiscite to finally determine Kashmir's destiny, and the ongoing UN presence in the region may be seen as a stubborn commitment by the United Nations to this principle, even though its attainment any time soon is unlikely.

Episodic violations of the border between Pakistan and India along the Kashmir frontier have occurred, and most recently, in the fall of 1999, violence increased with cross-border artillery duels, reminding the United Nations that one of its longest and most intransigent disputes remains very much alive and kicking.

See also Decolonization (Debate 18).

FOR FURTHER READING

Bennett, A. LeRoy. *International Organizations: Principles and Issues.* Englewood Cliffs, NJ: Prentice-Hall, 1995.

Birgisson, Karl Th. "United Nations Military Observer Group in India and Pakistan." In William J. Durch, ed., *The Evolution of UN Peacekeeping.* New York: St. Martin's, 1993. 273–284.

Harrison, Selig, Paul H. Kreisburg, and Dennis Kux, eds. *India and Pakistan: The First Fifty Years.* Cambridge, UK: Cambridge University Press, 1998.

United Nations Office of Public Information. *Everyone's United Nations.* New York: United Nations, 1968.

UN Yearbooks.

Wirsing, Robert G. *India, Pakistan, and the Kashmir Dispute: On Regional Conflict and Its Resolution.* New York: St. Martin's, 1997.

Health (1948)

SIGNIFICANCE OF THE ISSUE

Although health programs are the primary responsibility of governments, infectious diseases recognize no boundaries, and so international cooperation is necessary to cope with epidemics. In addition, one of the great obstacles to human productivity is illness, especially in the developing world where poverty exacerbates health issues. Thus, the United Nations has been seen by governments from a very early stage as a means of cooperating in the area of health policy, as well as in the control and eradication of diseases. In an age of globalization in travel and trade, the opportunity for the rapid spread of exotic diseases has increased, placing even more pressure on international cooperation to prevent and control epidemics.

BACKGROUND TO THE DEBATE

The fear of plagues is one of the ancient dreads of humanity and is represented in the biblical tradition as one of the Four Horsemen of the Apocalypse. Lacking modern knowledge of microbiology, until the nineteenth century, little could be done by governments in facing infectious diseases other than quarantines, and so typically people and governments resigned themselves to their fate and little international cooperation was pursued. Efforts by European countries during the mid- to late 1800s explored the possibility of establishing quarantines and disinfection of incoming ships at ports. But this was a shot in the dark, as knowledge of which ships were infectious and of the incubation periods of various diseases was limited. The effort shifted in the latter part of the nineteenth century to quarantines at the ports and countries of origin. But these systems were imposed by European states only in areas that could not prevent such an infringement on sovereignty, and they caused resentment. Systems involving imposition of quarantines were ineffective and politically unpalatable. Still a series of health conferences and attempted conventions allowed governments to share knowledge and ideas. The ad hoc conference approach led in 1907 to the formation of a regular multilateral mechanism for the sharing of health information through the establishment of the International Office of Public Health (OIHP), which was headquartered in Paris. It served as a clearing-house for information on the occurrence and spread of diseases. By the mid-1920s, nearly forty countries had accepted the idea of submitting compulsory reports to OIHP. In 1923, the League of Nations, acting on a request of the International Committee of the Red Cross (ICRC), developed a Health Organization but incorporated it into the League Technical Committee process rather than giving it autonomous status. Like the OIHP, which continued to function outside the League, the Health Organization served as an instrument of passive information sharing, but it quickly evolved into a service-supplying agency as well, by providing resources to governments to help combat the spread of epidemics. Although this more activist approach was opposed by some countries as an infringement on sovereignty, it continued to characterize much of the work of the League Health Organization and set a precedent for later international health agencies.

With the outbreak of World War II, Allied governments began to cooperate on a range of relief and assistance activities through the United Nations Relief and Rehabilitation Agency (UNRRA), which included special attention to health matters in recently liberated war zones. After World War II, the United Nations International Children's Emergency Fund (UNICEF) was established to provide special assistance, including health assistance to children. But there was a general feeling that a specialized agency was needed to comprehend and coordinate wider cooperation in health matters, and so at the Economic and Social Council (ECOSOC) intergovernmental conference in July 1946, sixty-one countries adopted the World Health Organization (WHO) Constitution. The Constitution came into force in 1948, and WHO became an operational agency under the supervision of an intergovernmental body known as the World Health Assembly. WHO assumed the functions of OIHP and the League of Nations Health Organization, as well as the operational functions of UNRRA at that time. The Pan-American Health Organization (PAHO), which was established in 1902, continued to exist as an independent agency but also as a regional office of the WHO.

HISTORY OF THE DEBATE

From the start, the WHO was charged with three related goals in connection with response to disease: prevention of disease, controlling the spread of disease after its outbreak, and curing disease. The prevention strategy included efforts to eradicate specific diseases through immunization.

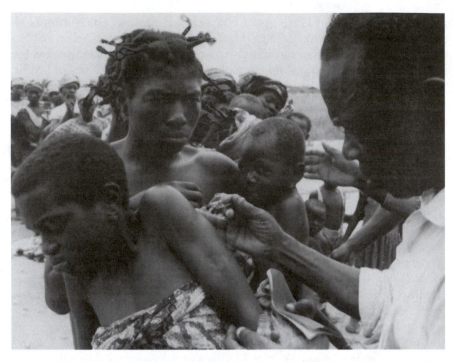

Preventions of epidemics is a major concern of the international health policy. Here young girls and mothers in Leopoldville, Congo, are vaccinated against smallpox, which broke out in January 1962. UN/DPI Photo B. Zarov

Small-pox, one of the ancient scourges of humanity, is one of the diseases that WHO has largely eliminated through international cooperation. In connection with other diseases, such as malaria, which is spread by mosquitoes, development of programs to eliminate or reduce the vector population has been another strategy of the WHO in cooperation with governments. The three-pronged strategy for coping with disease also involved seeing health as related to sanitation, hygiene, mental health, and health education as well, and WHO's programmatic activity increased enormously over the decades in order to promote the development of effective national health agencies. In short, WHO became a major player in the development agency network. It provided training programs, conferences, and seminars for national health professionals; it financed pilot projects in health programs to give national health care personnel hands-on experience. It gradually, in cooperation with the Food and Agriculture Organization (FAO), developed environmental projects as well. The WHO continued the work of its predecessors in terms of conducting research and studies on health and in disseminating reports to the international community, all considered by then as largely uncontroversial and routine. Another area in which WHO conducts research relates to the problem of narcotics and the use of illegal drugs. Its Expert Committee on Drug Dependence monitors illegal drug usage throughout the world and publishes annual reports concerning narcotics usage. In this area, WHO has warned governments and the United Nations about the need for preventing new forms of drug dependency and has offered recommendations on treatment for narcotics users and addicted persons.

Controversy and political differences have not been absent either within WHO or in ECOSOC and the General Assembly to which WHO reports and where further health programs are often initiated. Budget problems began to affect WHO as its policies and programs expanded. Rarely did contribution levels of member states keep pace with the scope of the work WHO might have done. Setting priorities in a climate of budgetary scarcity always creates frictions within UN bureaucracies and among member states, some of which seek substantial assistance, while others foot the bill. The establishment of regional commissions, a step taken to enhance performance when the WHO Constitution was first adopted, became difficult to coordinate and led to wasteful duplication of efforts. While many founders of WHO conceived of the agency as a functional organization that would lead to an integrated global system of health cooperation, in fact much of the organization's budget is spent on programs meant to enhance and strengthen the independent capacity of each member state's health sector to provide contained health services within their own territories.

Political problems have also come into play in WHO debates. Until 1965, Latin American and Islamic nations prevented WHO from undertaking population-related programs at the request of certain Asian countries such as India, Sri Lanka, and Sweden, especially in the family planning area, a hot-potato issue for many governments. Refusals to seat delegations from South Africa and Portugal during the mid-1960s, along with the animosities surrounding the Middle East dispute that prevented health cooperation between Israel and various Arab nations, were among the political issues that marred the debates on health.

In 1976, the UN General Assembly declared the year 1981 the International Year of Disabled Persons. In 1981, the World Health Assembly adopted a Global Strategy for Health for All by the Year 2000, which was aimed at attaining a level of health throughout the world that would allow all people to "lead a socially and economically productive life." This ambitious project had clear implications in the field of economic development, especially in the Third World. The General Assembly approved the Strategy by consensus.

In the early 1980s, as the acquired immunodeficiency syndrome (AIDS) epidemic first emerged, WHO cooperated with various national organizations in sponsoring conferences to discuss the dangers posed by this new affliction. Its work in this area continued into the 1990s in efforts to strengthen national capacities of response to the AIDS problem, in promoting biomedical research, in halting the spread of the human immunodeficiency virus (HIV), and in providing care to AIDS victims. In 1987, WHO established a Global Program on AIDS. Programs on a host of sexually transmitted and communicable diseases continued during the 1980s and 1990s as well.

During the 1980s, as civil wars and natural disasters such as drought and famine struck throughout the world, but especially in Africa, WHO developed its capacities to respond to disaster situations in consultation and co-operation with governments. But its long-term programs dominated its work. A combined WHO/UNICEF initiative known as the Expanded Program on Immunization, which had been established in 1974, gained substantial momentum during the 1980s, and by 1990 over 80 percent of all infants had been vaccinated against poliomyelitis, measles, tuberculosis, diphtheria, whooping cough, and tetanus, a major accomplishment. Still, tuberculosis continued to spread out of control in many parts of the world, and AIDS was decimating certain countries in Africa.

OUTCOME OF THE DEBATE

Thousands of scientists have been employed by the WHO over the years to conduct research on health-related issues. Nearly 100,000 people have been trained under WHO auspices in heath-related fields and now work throughout the world in government ministries and localities. WHO has sponsored the development of new drugs in an attempt to stop the epidemic spread of tropical diseases. The vast majority of WHO personnel live and work in the field rather than at headquarters in Geneva. Through WHO efforts, smallpox has been virtually eradicated. Polio and leprosy are also within range of eradication. World cooperation in the health arena has made these advances possible.

However, AIDS, along with many other sexually transmitted diseases, continues to spread in epidemic proportions, and many people in the tropics continue to be afflicted by tropical diseases. The recognition that health issues are related to development has linked WHO to a range of development agencies and to a range of other issues, including human settlements, the environment, food, and social services.

Although controversial issues do arise in the international health field, this is one area in which governments by and large have pursued policies of moderation and common sense. The debates have generally focused on how countries can, within their own economic development policies and national health care systems, better promote health for their peoples and coordinate their policies at the international level to the same end.

See also Global Environment (Debate 27); Human Settlements (Debate 36); Narcotics Control (Debate 19); Status and Condition of Children (Debate 2); Third World Development Programming (Debate 25).

FOR FURTHER READING

Beibeder, Yves, et al. *The World Health Organization.* The Hague: Kluwer Law International, 1999.

Jacob, Philip E., Alexine L. Atherton, and Arthur M. Wallenstein. *The Dynamics of International Organization.* Homewood, IL: Dorsey Press, 1972.

Lee, Kelley. *Historical Dictionary of the World Health Organization.* Lanham, MD: Scarecrow, 1998.

Siddiqi, Javed. *World Health and World Politics: The World Health Organization and the UN System.* Columbia: University of South Carolina Press, 1995.

World Health Organization. *Coping with Natural Disasters.* Geneva: WHO, 1990.

Genocide (1948)

SIGNIFICANCE OF THE ISSUE

During World War II, the Nazi government of Germany committed many humanitarian outrages, including a determined effort to exterminate the Jewish people. About 6 million Jewish civilians were slaughtered, along with a similar number of East European Slavs and gypsies, all of whom were considered subhumans by the racist-minded Nazi regime. These horrors shocked the conscience of humanity, provoking UN condemnation of genocide in 1948 in the aftermath of World War II after the true enormity of the Holocaust had been fully discovered.

BACKGROUND TO THE DEBATE

Throughout history, various forms of genocide have been practiced by warring armies and peoples. Widespread slaughters of innocent civilian populations, forced expulsions of peoples, and extermination of cultural and religious practices were not uncommon. However, as governments entered the twentieth century, under the influence of enlightenment, a general sentiment prevailed that human beings had grown more civilized. Customary laws of war emerged to protect civilian populations from barbaric practices, and governments acknowledged an obligation to observe principles of international humanitarian law. Thus when, at the close of World War II, invading Allied forces discovered the death camps and survivors began to tell their stories to the world, the international community expressed shock at the enormity of Nazi policies of exterminating Jews, working Jews and other people to death in concentration camps, and torturing opponents of the Nazi regime, among many other atrocities.

The term *genocide* was first used by Raphaël Lempkin in his book *Axis Rule in Occupied Europe* (1944), in which he chronicled Nazi atrocities. *Genocide* is defined as the act of destroying completely or partially a national,

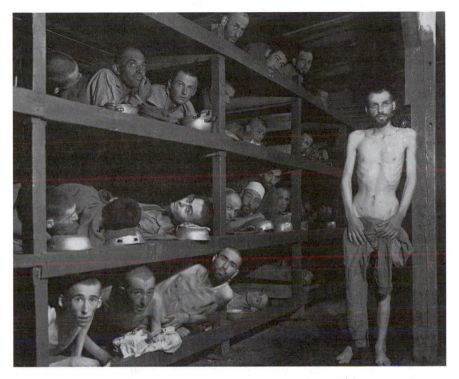

Starved survivors of Buchenwald camp in 1945 give evidence of the policy of genocide adopted by the Nazis during World War II, which provoked the world's outrage and gave rise to the passage of the Genocide Convention. © CORBIS

ethnic, racial, or religious group. Although genocide was nowhere listed as
an explicit crime in the international law prevailing during World War II, it
clearly both violated existing laws of war aimed at protecting civilian populations and fundamentally violated the foremost obligation of governments to protect and secure the lives of innocent civilians, whether their
own nationals or foreign nationals under a state's occupation. The international community, during the creation and operation of the Nuremberg
Tribunal, identified the Holocaust and other genocidal practices by the Nazis as crimes against humanity. But punishment for the past criminal acts of
Nazi officials was only one necessary step. Many governments believed
that an international convention should be promulgated to condemn genocide and provide for its punishment. On 11 December 1946, the UN General
Assembly requested that the Economic and Social Council (ECOSOC) undertake studies for drawing up a draft convention on genocide, and
ECOSOC in turn directed the secretary-general to consult with appropriate
experts, the Commission on Human Rights, and governments in preparing
a draft convention. This draft was then later further revised by an Ad Hoc

Committee on Genocide appointed by ECOSOC to draft the convention. The committee was composed of representatives from China, France, Lebanon, Poland, the United States, the Soviet Union, and Venezuela. They met at Lake Placid in the spring of 1948 and produced a draft convention that was submitted to the General Assembly and further debated by the Sixth Committee.

HISTORY OF THE DEBATE

Although virtually all UN member states supported the idea of promulgating a Convention on the Prevention and Punishment of Genocide, there was disagreement concerning the exact acts that should constitute genocide, on the extent of the definition of genocide, and on the question of jurisdiction for the punishment of genocide. Poland and the Soviet Union supported the idea that actions preparatory to the commission of genocide such as study and research, propaganda, or incitement to genocide should be punishable, but representatives from the United States and the majority of other countries opposed this on grounds that defining preparatory acts to genocide was a definitional quagmire. Language was later included in the convention that held "direct and public incitement to genocide" as a punishable act.

The governments of Byelorussia, Poland, Venezuela, and Brazil supported the idea of including provisions regarding cultural genocide, but representatives from the United States, United Kingdom, France, and Canada opposed this, preferring that the convention focus on the acts of physical genocide and that cultural genocide be dealt with by a separate agreement. Thus, formal references to cultural genocide were not included in the convention. A similar battle took place over whether to include political groups, along with ethnic, national, racial, or religious groups, as groups protected from genocide. The United States and France supported the inclusion of political groups, but the Soviet Union, Venezuela, Poland, and Brazil opposed the idea, and political groups were eventually not incorporated as protected classes under the convention.

Several delegations outright opposed the establishment of an international tribunal to adjudicate allegations of genocide, and most other delegations, though not opposed in principle, agreed that the idea required further study. Indeed, the General Assembly decided to postpone the establishment of a criminal tribunal and directed the International Law Commission to study the matter. It was not until five decades later that a Permanent International Criminal Court was established to address the prosecution of genocide and other violations of humanitarian law.

The UN General Assembly adopted the text of the Genocide Convention by a unanimous vote of fifty-six countries on 9 December 1948. The convention defined genocide as a crime under international law and as applying to acts committed whether during war or peace with the intent to destroy, in whole or in part, a national, ethnical, racial, or religious group. Acts falling within this definition included "killing members of the group; causing serious bodily or mental harm to members of the group; deliberately inflicting on the group conditions of life calculated to bring about its physical destruction in whole or in part; imposing measures intended to prevent births within the group; and forcibly transferring children of the group to another group." In addition, the convention prohibited not only acts of genocide but conspiracy to commit genocide, direct and public incitement to commit genocide, attempts to commit genocide, and complicity in genocide as punishable acts. The convention entered into force in January of 1951 and has been subsequently ratified by well over a hundred countries.

OUTCOME OF THE DEBATE

Not all countries that signed the Genocide Convention ratified it in a timely fashion. The United States, for instance, deferred ratification with reservations until 23 February 1989 as legal questions arose concerning whether provisions of the convention might be inconsistent with U.S. government policies toward Native American populations. Nor has the existence of the convention prevented numerous genocidal acts by governments, including murderous genocides in Cambodia by the Khmer Rouge in the 1970s, as well as similar activities by Idi Amin in Uganda, by various Sudanese regimes against the Christian and animistic populations living in Southern Sudan, by various parties in the Balkan wars of the 1990s, and by Rwandan Hutus against Tutsis in 1994. The use of "ethnic cleansing" techniques in the former Yugoslavia during the Bosnian conflict and by Hutus against Tutsis in Rwanda at last excited the UN Security Council to establish on the recommendation of the secretary-general two International Tribunals to enforce the Genocide Convention for crimes committed within the Former Yugoslavia and in Rwanda. Events in those countries stimulated renewed interest in the establishment of a Permanent International Criminal Court, which was opened for ratification in 1998. The United States refrained from ratifying the International Criminal Court on grounds that its provisions might be used to advance spurious claims against U.S. forces participating in international peacemaking capacities. Most European countries strongly supported and subsequently signed it.

Still, the Genocide Convention has increased international awareness of and repugnance to the crime of genocide, and there is a gradual building of institutions aimed at providing more effective legal prosecution and punishment of genocide whether at the international level or through the domestic courts of various countries.

See also Balkan Civil Wars (Debate 45); Cambodia Situation (Debate 38); Human Rights (Debate 10); Rwandan Civil War (Debate 49).

FOR FURTHER READING

Andreapolous, George J. *Genocide: Conceptual and Historical Dimensions*. Philadelphia: University of Pennsylvania Press, 1997.

Minow, Martha. *Between Vengeance and Forgiveness: Facing History after Genocide and Mass Violence*. New York: Beacon Press, 1999.

Prunier, Gerard. *The Rwanda Crisis: History of Genocide*. New York: Columbia University Press, 1997.

Ratner, Stephen, and Jason S. Adams. *Accountability for Human Rights Atrocities in International Law: Beyond the Nuremburg Legacy*. Oxford: Clarendon, 1997.

Totten, Samuel, William S. Parsons, and Israel Charny. *Century of Genocide: Eyewitness Accounts and Critical Views*. New York: Garland Publishers, 1997.

UN Yearbooks, 1948–1949.

Human Rights (1948)

SIGNIFICANCE OF THE ISSUE

Although governments retained their sovereignty, they acknowledged their responsibility to promote and protect human rights and fundamental freedoms in the UN Charter and have continued to do so in dozens of subsequent human rights declarations and treaties that call upon governments to implement domestic measures to ensure the promotion and protection of these rights. Governmental adherence to human rights norms is highly variable, illustrating an often very wide gap between principle and practice; however, a growing human rights advocacy community and international political awareness among nations ensure that few major human rights abuses go undetected, though many go unpunished.

BACKGROUND TO THE DEBATE

The concept of human rights is rooted in very old notions about the dignity and equality of the human person that may be traced to the Judeo-Christian traditions. However, it was the birth of the idea of natural rights in the seventeeth-century thought of social contract thinkers such as Thomas Hobbes and later John Locke and others that gave rise to the modern idea that each individual possesses certain inalienable rights. These ideas inspired the U.S. Declaration of Independence, the U.S. Constitution and Bill of Rights, and the French Declaration of the Rights of Man. As parliamentary democracies emerged in Europe, political and civil rights were increasingly extended to the common people, practices such as slavery came under attack, and the political rights of women were advanced. The emergence of the International Committee of the Red Cross and of national Red Cross societies represented the first formal emergence of human rights and humanitarian organizations dedicated to the care of the sick and wounded during times of war or emergency.

Although the League of Nations Covenant did not explicitly mention human rights, Article 23 called for the maintenance of humane conditions for labor, the just treatment of native inhabitants of non-self-governing territories, and the control of international traffic in women and children. During the life of the League, several bodies created for the protection of refugees and for the provision of humanitarian aid were established, including the League of Nations High Commissioner for Refugees Coming from Russia.

The outbreak of World War II and the immense human misery wrought during that war stimulated a great deal of concern about human rights. Nazi treatment of the German Jewish population had given rise to the creation of a High Commissioner for Refugees Coming from Germany in the late 1930s and to the establishment of the Intergovernmental Committee for Refugees (IGCR) in 1938. The IGCR continued to operate on a reduced level during the war and expanded its activities to include non-Jewish refugees and displaced persons as well as small numbers of Jewish refugees who managed to escape the Holocaust. In the Declaration of the United Nations of 1 January 1942 that was pronounced by the Allied governments of twenty-six nations, the preservation of human rights and justice was explicitly mentioned and served as a harbinger of the importance to be attached to human rights in the UN Charter. Thus, by the time governments sat down to hammer out the terms of the Charter, they were already inclined to include human rights matters as a major activity of the new global postwar organization. Indeed, the preamble of the UN Charter asserts that member states are "determined . . . to reaffirm faith in fundamental human rights, in the dignity and worth of the human person, in the equal rights of men and women." The achievement of international cooperation in "promoting and encouraging respect for human rights and for fundamental freedoms for all without distinction as to race, sex, language, or religion" is listed in Article 1 of the Charter as one of the main purposes of the United Nations. In Chapters IX and X of the Charter, institutional mechanisms are provided for the "Universal respect for, and observance of, human rights and fundamental freedoms," and the UN Economic and Social Council (ECOSOC) is given authority to make recommendations "for the purpose of promoting respect for and observance of human rights" and to create commissions for the promotion of human rights.

While the UN Charter makes numerous references to human rights, the underlying norm emphasized is the sovereignty of its member states. Thus the UN Charter and the governments that drafted and later ratified it intended for human rights to be promoted and protected by the governments themselves within their domestic jurisdictions. Interference in the domestic affairs of states by the United Nations directly was not anticipated. However, violations of human rights take place within and under the jurisdiction of particular countries. Thus, all debates about the effective enforcement of human rights encounter squarely the norm of state sovereignty and they have been conditioned by this fundamental reality. Moreover, in actual practice, human rights typically flourish under democratic governments, but many, even the vast majority of, governments of member states of the United Nations over the years were nondemocratic. Such governments often signed human rights treaties and applauded human rights norms in the abstract but failed to observe them in practice. Thus the true advancement of human rights has always been grounded on the effective incorporation and enforcement of these norms in the domestic law of member states. Commitment to this process among UN member states has been highly variable.

HISTORY OF THE DEBATE

In February 1946, ECOSOC established the UN Commission on Human Rights and called for it to submit proposals for the establishment of an International Bill of Human Rights. In December 1948, the first fruit of the Commission's work, the Universal Declaration of Human Rights, was debated and approved by the UN General Assembly by a vote of forty-eight in favor with no opposition and eight abstentions. The abstentions in-

Mrs. Eleanor Roosevelt holds a copy of the Universal Declaration of Human Rights at Lake Success, New York, in November 1949. UN/DPI Photo

cluded the Communist countries of Byelorussia, Czechoslovakia, Poland, Ukraine, the Soviet Union, and Yugoslavia, as well as Saudi Arabia and South Africa. The Declaration was not a legally binding treaty but rather a statement of aspirations and goals. The Declaration included a broad list of rights including civil and political rights, on one hand, and economic, social, and cultural rights, on the other. As a general rule, Communist and socialist governments applauded the inclusion of economic, social, and cultural rights but resisted imposition of civil and political rights inconsistent with their centrist and nondemocratic regimes. Western democratic states tended to see the civil and political rights as more essential rights and tended to look upon the economic, social, and cultural, rights as flowing from free political systems and free enterprise economies. Third World countries that joined the United Nations and this debate in large numbers during the early 1960s tended to emphasize the importance of the economic, social, and cultural rights as well, although many were in a poor financial position to guarantee work and primary education for all of their citizens.

This fundamentally different approach to understanding human rights would continue to mark UN debates and cause the UN Commission on Human Rights, of which Eleanor Roosevelt was a prominent member, to draft a separate legally binding covenant to treat civil and political rights, with an accompanying protocol, and an additional covenant on economic, social, and cultural rights. The work of drafting these covenants took place from 1956 to 1966, when the UN General Assembly adopted them and urged member states to ratify them. It became clear that most governments would not ratify a covenant on civil and political rights that contained provisions giving individuals a capacity to lodge human rights claims against their own governments. Thus the idea was put forward to develop an optional protocol to the covenant on civil and political rights that would give states an opportunity to submit to this potentially more invasive form of enforcement if they chose to do so. The Covenant restricted its enforcement mechanism to the creation of a Human Rights Committee to which member states were obliged to submit reports concerning their compliance to Covenant provisions. States could also submit questions and complaints about another state's party, but this aspect of the Covenant has not been widely adverted to since raising complaints against other states is a sure way for a government to invite retaliatory complaints. In short, most governments did not seek in the Covenant to invite international interference in their domestic affairs.

State compliance with the civil and political rights of citizens is a fairly simple matter of governmental will. Compliance with economic, social, and political rights requires resources as well as will. Thus, governments did not in this latter Covenant oblige themselves to immediate adherence to the enumerated rights. Rather, they agreed as far as possible and where feasible to progressively achieve their full realization. Civil rights may be directly achieved by a simple decision to ensure their enforcement, but ensuring that all citizens get an education, adequate welfare services, and heath care depends on the economic capacity of the particular society. Since the Covenant on Economic, Social and Cultural rights acknowledged this reality, countries could ratify it without incurring burdensome obligations.

Although the Covenants did not enter into force until 1976, and still do not enjoy universal ratification, many additional human rights declarations and treaties have been promulgated by UN bodies in subsequent years. Over the years several nonbinding declarations have been asserted by the United Nations, including a declaration on the rights of the child (1959), on the elimination of all forms of racial discrimination (1963), on the elimination of all forms of discrimination against women (1967), on the eradication of hunger and malnutrition (1974), on the prohibition of torture and other cruel, inhuman or degrading treatment or punishment (1975), on the rights of disabled persons (1975), and on the right to development (1986). Legally binding treaties on many subjects were also negotiated including conventions on the political rights of women (1952), on the stateless persons (1954), on the nationality of married women (1958), on the elimination of all forms of racial discrimination (1965), on the suppression and punishment of the crime of apartheid (1973), on the elimination of all forms of discrimination against women (1979), on torture (1984), and on the rights of the child (1989).

The proliferation in the number of declarations and conventions should not be confused with actual progress in state compliance with human rights norms. The declarations implied no legal obligations, and the conventions contained only minimal means of enforcement. Moreover, human rights became a kind of ideological battleground. During the Cold War, Western democratic states regularly pointed out the failure of Communist governments to comply with basic civil and political rights such as fair trials, freedom of movement, and freedom of speech and religion. An increasing number of Third World countries accused Western powers of imperialism and neocolonialism and of responsibility for depriving them of economic development. Communist countries joined this chorus. Western countries were quick to point out that Third World countries, like the Communist nations, were deficient in providing civil and political rights. With growing majorities, Southern states focused the glare of human rights advancement on the apartheid policies of South Africa and on issues of racial discrimination. Such declarations and treaties won widespread support from Southern nations and lukewarm reactions or reservations from some developed states.

A number of the human rights conventions established committees to receive reports from member states or complaints from governments regarding human abuses committed by other states. Among these are the Human Rights Committee, the Committee against Torture, the Committee on Economic, Social and Cultural Rights, the Committee on the Elimination of Discrimination against Women, the Committee on the Elimination of Racial Discrimination, and the Committee on the Rights of the Child. These bodies, in turn, submit reports to the UN General Assembly through ECOSOC. The UN General Assembly receives such reports and routinely makes recommendations concerning them. These recommendations are not binding, and they often excite considerable opposition or reservations among member states, depending upon which country or what human rights issue is the subject of debate, although many recommendations that are less controversial are adopted by consensus.

During the 1990s, the global collapse of communism and the increasing recognition among Southern nations about the need for democratic political development have reduced the ideological contention that has marked the UN debate on human rights. Nevertheless, controversy still surrounds the elevation of development to the status of a right. In 1998, the UN General Assembly reaffirmed in a nonbinding recommendation that the right to development was an integral part of human rights. The debate on this question broke down along North-South lines, with the developing countries advancing the notion that development was an integral human right, and many Western or developed states expressing reservations on the matter. The United States was the only country to vote against the resolution, although more than forty countries abstained on the measure. The United States rejected the idea of convention on the right to development and characterized as misleading the idea of linking international macroeconomic policy, debt burdens and relief, and global trade policy directly to causes of poverty and underdevelopment.

In 1993, the World Human Rights Conference was held in Vienna, which emphasized the connection of both democracy and development to human rights. The Conference proposed, and at its recommendation the UN General Assembly established, the United Nations High Commissioner for Human Rights (UNHCHR) as a means of consolidating and elevating UN attention to the coordination of human rights activities. Among the issues that the UNHCHR supervises is the recent activity in the realm of human rights education.

OUTCOME OF THE DEBATE

After fifty-five years of debate, there can be little doubt that the United Nations has made significant institutional strides in dealing with human rights issues. Since 1993, this area of UN activity is now supervised by the highly visible UNHCHR office, which coordinates the work of various UN human rights bodies. The UN Commission on Human Rights has evolved from a body devoted to the drafting of human rights treaties to one that has become much more involved in investigating and reporting on human rights situations throughout the world. It dispatches fact-finding missions to monitor state compliance with human rights law. During the 1990s an additional and increasingly important focus of the Commission has been to actually provide UN member states with the technical support and legal advice to improve their human rights performance.

In addition to the expanded UN machinery for human rights observation, the growth of private advocacy organizations and nongovernmental organizations (NGOs) in this area has been phenomenal, especially in the 1990s. Thousands of grass-roots human rights organizations exist throughout the world. Thus, very few significant violations of international human rights law will go unreported. The growth of telecommunications, computer, and Internet technology ensures that violations of human rights in a remote corner of the globe will become news everywhere. Governments, under these conditions, have an increased incentive to more progressively respect and promote human rights. Nonetheless, political disputes, domestic instabilities, and ethnic division and sectarian conflicts continue to mark the domestic political life of many nations. As long as this remains true, human rights abuses will continue to occur. As compared to the global situation at the inception of the UN Charter, however, governments that choose to abuse human rights will be subjected to ever greater international scrutiny and pressure to respect and protect human rights. The state remains the main enforcer of human rights, but prying eyes and concerned words from many quarters now urge governments to take this job of enforcement more seriously.

See also Genocide (Debate 9); Refugees and Stateless Persons (Debate 4); Terrorism (Debate 28); Third World Development Programming (Debate 25).

FOR FURTHER READING

Baehr, Peter. *The Role of Human Rights in Foreign Policy.* New York: St. Martin's, 1994.

Donnelly, Jack. *Universal Human Rights in Theory and Practice.* Ithaca, NY: Cornell University Press, 1989.

Forsythe, David P., ed. *Human Rights and Development: International Views.* New York: St. Martin's, 1989.

Gorman, Robert F. *Historical Dictionary of Human Rights and Humanitarian Organizations.* Lanham, MD: Scarecrow Press, 1995.

Langley, Winston E. *Encyclopedia of Human Rights Issues since 1945.* Westport, CT: Greenwood Press, 1999.

Lawson, Edward. *Encyclopedia of Human Rights.* New York: Taylor and Francis, 1991.

Vincent, R. J. *Human Rights and International Relations.* Cambridge: Cambridge University Press, 1986.

Membership and Representation Questions (1950)

SIGNIFICANCE OF THE ISSUE

During the first ten years of the United Nations, Cold War bickering between the Communist countries and the Western bloc led to a stalemate within the UN Security Council concerning approval of new members. The Soviet Union vetoed membership of countries allied with the Western nations and the dominance of the Security Council by pro-Western powers led to a "collective veto" of pro-Communist states. This stalemate was broken in 1955 when a "package deal" was agreed to, and a host of states were admitted. This largely ended the use of the veto by permanent members of the Security Council on membership questions. However, other disputes over membership and representation continued with regard to divided states, and annual battles over representation of China continued until 1971.

BACKGROUND TO THE DEBATE

Under Chapter II, Article 4, paragraph 2 of the UN Charter, countries seeking membership in the United Nations must be approved by a vote of the General Assembly upon the recommendation of the Security Council. Because admission of new members is considered an important question, the General Assembly must approve membership by a two-thirds vote only after the Security Council has voted to recommend membership. As a substantive question, membership applications are subject to a permanent member's veto in the Security Council. Although in principle the United Nations is open to all peace-loving states with the goal of achieving universal membership, in practice disputes have arisen over what constitutes a "peace-loving" state, and the legitimate government of a state when more than one government claims sovereign rights to jurisdiction of a state. Owing to such disputes the United Nations has yet to achieve truly universal representation, although it has come increasingly close to that ideal.

Presumably, states granted admission to the United Nations should have independent governments capable of carrying out international acts and obligations. Moreover, the government seeking admission should have effective control over the territory and population it claims to represent. Such issues are sometimes difficult to sort out. Membership issues arose even during the negotiation of the UN Charter. Joseph Stalin, for instance, fearing that the United Nations would be dominated by Western interests, demanded that each of the Soviet Union's sixteen Soviet Socialist Republics be admitted. In a compromise, the United Kingdom and the United States agreed to allow separate admission of Byelorussia and the Ukraine even though they were integral parts of the Soviet Union and exercised very little real autonomy. Such compromises have long been a part of UN practice when political difficulties arise.

Complicating the membership question during the first decade of the United Nations' existence was the emergence of the Cold War and the outbreak of the Korean War. During this early phase of UN practice, membership applications received rough treatment. In the afterglow of Allied cooperation during World War II, Afghanistan, Iceland, Sweden, and Thailand, all of which had remained neutral during the war, were admitted in 1946. In 1947 Yemen and Pakistan were admitted. Burma and Israel were admitted in 1949 and Indonesia in 1950. But while nine members were accepted during the first five years of the United Nations' existence, twice that many were denied, and the crisis worsened during the period from 1951 to 1955, during which no new members were accepted despite the frequent annual applications for membership. The International Court of Justice ruled in an Advisory Opinion of 3 March 1950 that a Security Council recommendation in favor of membership was required by the UN Charter, placing all countries applying for membership at the mercy of the veto. The growing animosities of the Cold War, to which was added the hot war of Korea from 1950 to 1953, produced a membership stalemate rooted in ideological and political contention.

HISTORY OF THE DEBATE

Throughout the first decade of the United Nations' existence, the West and the Soviet Union prevented admission into the United Nations of countries closely allied to either ideological bloc. Because Western governments occupied a majority of seats on the Security Council, applications for membership by such Communist states as Albania, Bulgaria, Hungary, Romania, and Mongolia failed to achieve the seven-vote majority then needed (today the necessary margin for admission is nine votes) for recommendation of membership to the General Assembly. Governments opposing membership of Communist governments often invoked their failure to live up to treaties or UN resolutions regarding protection of and respect for human rights. The Soviet Union, standing alone, vetoed membership of pro-Western states, observing that many of these governments did not maintain diplomatic relations with it and insisting that their admission be linked to the admission of pro-Soviet states.

This situation, as noted, came to a head in 1950, producing a five-year stalemate during which no country gained admission to the United Nations. Several efforts were undertaken to break the logjam and to allow the settlement of the membership question. Australia, which had been a foe of the veto provisions for permanent members even at the San Francisco Conference of 1945, resurrected efforts to curtail Security Council involvement in the membership process, insisting that this function should be the primary responsibility of the non-veto-bound General Assembly. Argentina made a similar suggestion, arguing that regardless of Security Council action the General Assembly ought o vote on admission of members. As early as 1949, the UN General Assembly itself had recommended that the Security Council actions on membership ought to go forward with a vote of any seven members, regardless of the concurrence of permanent members. When asked for an Advisory Opinion on such matters, the International Court of Justice held in 1950 that the Charter forbade General Assembly action on membership applications that failed to win Security Council approval. Although the General Assembly had on two occasions noted that candidates for admission vetoed by the Soviet Union met all requirements for acceptance to the United Nations, such protestations had little effect. The stalemate continued, and nothing short of an amendment of the UN Charter, which was even less likely in the rancor of the Cold War dispute, could change the situation legally.

Governments, then, turned to more quiet forms of negotiation. In 1953, the General Assembly established a good offices committee to explore ways to resolve the membership issue, as the list of potential applicants continued to grow. By 1955 mounting support for resolution of the membership question led to a proposal to admit all applicants except the controversial applications of the divided states of Korea and Vietnam. When China vetoed the application of Mongolia, the Soviet Union backed out of the package deal but then countered with a proposal to set aside the applications of Mongolia (a pro-Soviet state) and Japan (a pro-Western state). This formulation won the support of both the Security Council and the General Assembly, and with the impasse broken, sixteen new members, including Albania, Austria, Bulgaria, Cambodia, Ceylon (Sri Lanka), Finland, Hungary, Ireland, Italy, Jordan, Laos, Libya, Nepal, Portugal, Romania, and Spain, were formally admitted on 14 December 1955. Japan was admitted a year later, and Mongolia's admission was approved in 1961.

Membership questions, though greatly eased, owing to the 1955 package deal, did continue to be occasions of controversy. Divided states such as Germany, Vietnam, and Korea were not admitted until political circumstances permitted it. An agreement for simultaneous admission of the Federal Republic of Germany (West Germany) and the German Democratic Republic (East Germany) was not achieved until 1973, and the unification of Germany later mooted the issue of separate German states. Vietnam was not admitted until 1977, after the victory of the North and the absorption of the South by Communist forces. The Koreas were admitted separately in 1991.

The question of Chinese representation, which had been complicated by the events surrounding the Korean War, remained an ongoing source of controversy. Efforts by the Communist government on the mainland to be recognized as the legitimate government of China for purposes of representation in the United Nations were routinely rebuffed until 1971, in part because the Communist government's peace-loving status could be questioned owing to its aggressive attack on UN forces in Korea. By 1971, many governments had reversed position and regarded the government on Taiwan as the problem. The United States tried to get the United Nations to adopt at that point a two-China policy that would allow membership for both competing governments and thus preserve the ideal of universality of UN membership. But even Taiwan rejected the idea of two Chinas, insisting that China was one and could have but one government. Many countries then bowed to the reality that the Communist government had the superior claim to sovereignty governing the vast majority of the territory and population of China. In 1971, the General Assembly, by a vote of 75 to 35 with 17 abstentions, expelled the Republic of Taiwan and awarded the UN seat to the People's Republic of China.

OUTCOME OF THE DEBATE

Generally speaking, applications for UN membership are now almost routinely accepted. In 1960 seventeen countries, all but one being former African colonies, were admitted into the United Nations, and the march of new members has continued in breathtaking fashion. Today the United Nations has 185 members. Very small states, such as the island countries of the Maldive Islands, Nauru, Palau, and Tuvalu and such European ministates as Andorra, Liechtenstein, and San Marino have been admitted even where their independence and capacity to carry out international acts have been in question.

The United Nations has drawn ever closer to the principle of universality of membership, although some areas of the globe, such as Taiwan, continue to lack formal representation at the United Nations. Switzerland has chosen to remain outside of the United Nations owing to concern about

Representatives of the People's Republic of China (PRC) take their seat for the first time in the UN General Assembly after years of credentials battles with representatives of the Republic of China on Taiwan over which government should represent China at the United Nations. UN/DPI Photo Yutaka Nagata

how the collective security provisions of the Charter might compromise its neutrality. However, Switzerland is an active member of many UN specialized agencies, a large number of which make their headquarters on Swiss soil. For the vast majority of independent nations, UN membership has become a necessary attribute of sovereign statehood, and today 98 percent of the world's population is officially represented in the United Nations.

See also Korean War (Debate 12).

FOR FURTHER READING

Bennett, A. LeRoy. *International Organizations: Principles and Issues*. Englewood Cliffs, NJ: Prentice-Hall, 1995.

Goodrich, Leland, Edvard Hambro, and Anne P. Simons. *Charter of the United Nations: Commentary and Documents*. 3rd rev. ed. New York: Columbia University Press, 1969.

Luard, Evan. *A History of the United Nations*. New York: St. Martin's, 1982.

UN Yearbooks, 1946–1955.

Korean War (1950)

SIGNIFICANCE OF THE ISSUE

The Korean War marked the first time that the UN Security Council invoked Chapter VII of the UN Charter to authorize the deployment of armed forces to fight against an unlawful invasion and punish aggression. It led to the passage of the Uniting for Peace Resolution, which, in turn, provided the UN General Assembly with greater authority to make recommendations on matters of peace and security in the absence of Security Council action. The Korean War demonstrated that the Cold War could quickly become a hot one. After the negotiation of an armistice, Korea remained divided, as it had been before the war, into a Communist state in the North and a pro-Western state in the South—a symbol of Cold War tensions that remains unresolved even with the passage of the Cold War era.

BACKGROUND TO THE DEBATE

Korea's strategic location at the crossroads of East Asia has historically made it a battleground where Chinese, Japanese, and Russian forces have struggled for control of its territory. Japan occupied Korea during the Russo-Japanese war of 1904–1905 and annexed Korea in 1910. Its occupation of Korea ended only with its defeat at the end of World War II. The United States occupied South Korea, and the Soviet Union took control of North Korea, with the 38th parallel designated as the border between the two zones of occupation. Shortly thereafter, at the Moscow Conference, Korea was designated as a trusteeship under the administration of four powers, the United States, the Soviet Union, Great Britain, and China. In 1947, the UN General Assembly established a Temporary Commission to pave the way for free elections, which were held in South Korea during 1948. However, since the Soviet Union refused to allow the United Nations access in the North, elections there were not possible. The Soviet Union established a Communist government in the North without the benefit of elections, and it declared the UN Temporary Commission and the elections it supervised in the South invalid. At its Third Session in December 1948, the UN General Assembly (Resolution 195 [III]), declared the government of South Korea the sole legitimate representative of Korea and called upon governments to recognize it. In the meantime, occupying forces were withdrawn from both South and North Korea in 1949, and the United Nations set up a Commission on Korea to work toward unification of the country by peaceful means, a measure opposed by the Soviet Union and other Communist governments.

Matters in Korea were complicated by the civil war in China, which culminated in 1949 with the victory of the Communist forces, which took control of mainland China, while the government of the Republic of China fled to the island of Formosa. Although the Soviet Union and other Communist governments of Eastern Europe recognized the Communist People's Republic of China (PRC) as the legitimate government of the country, other governments continued to recognize the Republic of China (ROC), now situated on Taiwan, as the only legal representative of China. This led to a dispute within the United Nations over representation, which was resolved in favor of the ROC government on Taiwan. In a pique of anger and protest, the Soviet Union boycotted meetings of the United Nations including the Security Council during 1950. On 25 June 1950, North Korean troops invaded South Korea, bent on reunifying the country by force under a Communist government, and the United Nations faced the first major test of its collective security provisions.

HISTORY OF THE DEBATE

With the Soviet Union boycotting the United Nations from January into the summer of 1950, the Security Council was in a position to meet and take action on the North Korean aggression without the interposition of a Soviet veto. On the very day of the invasion of the South, the Security Council met and passed a resolution that determined, under Article 39 of the UN Charter, that North Korea had committed a breach of the peace. It called for an immediate cessation of hostilities and withdrawal of North Korean forces and for all UN member states to assist the United Nations and refrain from supporting the North Korean aggression. The resolution passed with nine affirmative votes and only one abstention by Yugoslavia, which expressed concern that assignment of blame for aggression was premature until the situation was clarified. Two days later, the Security Council passed another U.S.-sponsored resolution by a vote of seven votes to one (Yugoslavia), while two members, Egypt and India, did not participate in the vote. The continued absence of the Soviet Union prevented it from vetoing the resolution, which recommended that all UN member states furnish support to the Republic of Korea to repel the invading forces and restore peace and security. On 7 July, the Security Council called upon the United States to establish a unified command to coordinate and direct the deployment of UN forces. General Douglas MacArthur was named by U.S. President Harry S Truman as the Commander of the UN forces in Korea. The United States acted quickly in deploying air, sea, and limited ground forces to assist South Korea, and by the end of 1950, forty-two of the fifty-nine member states of the United Nations had provided military, economic, or humanitarian support to Korea. Ten countries supplied ground forces, eight supplied naval forces and five supplied air forces in defense of South Korea.

The swift reaction of the United States and its allies under UN authorization surprised the Soviet Union, which returned to its Security Council seat on 27 July to prevent any further UN actions on Korea at odds with its interests. The Soviet Union maintained that the Security Council votes were illegal since the illegitimate government of the ROC rather than the PRC had cast the votes, and it accused the United States of planning and provoking the aggression and illegally intervening before the Security Council had met. These accusations found little support among the majority of UN members, and efforts by the Soviet Union during its tenure as president of the Security Council to condemn U.S. actions and to link the Korean conflict to the Chinese representation issue were defeated.

Realizing that the veto-bound Security Council could present future problems for the UN organization in dealing with threats to peace and acts of aggression, the UN General Assembly on 3 November 1950 adopted a "Uniting for Peace" resolution in which it asserted that the General Assembly could meet within twenty-four hours at the request of any seven Security Council members or a majority of the members of the General Assembly to consider measures that might be taken to address any threat to the peace, breach of the peace, or act of aggression in cases where the Security Council, owing to a lack of consensus among its permanent members, failed to exercise its primary authority over collective security. (For a text of this landmark resolution, see Appendix 8.) The General Assembly under this resolution could recommend to member states that they deploy armed forces if necessary. Unlike the Security Council, however, which could legally bind member states in collective security situations, any action by the General Assembly would be only recommendatory.

In the fall of 1950, UN forces expelled North Korean armies from the South, passed beyond the 38th parallel, and rapidly advanced toward the Yalu river boundary with China in the North. Chinese Communist Red Army forces intervened in October, ominously complicating both the war and diplomatic efforts to resolve it, as UN forces retreated well into South Korea in the face of the powerful Chinese counterattack. The Security Council was unable to condemn the Chinese invasion owing to the veto of the Soviet Union. However, other UN bodies, including the General As-

A UN press officer interviews Korean refugees with the help of an interpreter in September 1950. UN/DPI Photo

sembly's First Committee and the General Assembly, undertook actions to explore the possibility of obtaining a cease-fire, the restoration of peace, economic rehabilitation, and negotiations for the unification of Korea. The General Assembly established a UN Commission for the Unification and Rehabilitation of Korea, and on the recommendation of the Economic and Social Council (ECOSOC) it also established the United Nations Korean Reconstruction Agency (UNKRA), on 25 November, in an effort to address the humanitarian needs of the beleaguered and suffering people of Korea. For two years the conflict raged on, as neither the Communist Chinese forces nor those of the United Nations could attain a decisive victory. A propaganda war accompanied the stalemate on the ground, as the Communist and Western blocs jockeyed for international favor and traded charges and countercharges. Despite disingenuous efforts by the Communist powers to lay all blame on the United States and Western powers, the United Nations consistently called upon China to end its aggressive intervention in Korea (GA Res. 498 V), continued to urge international support for the UN military action against the ongoing aggression (GA Res. 498 V), and called for an arms and strategic materials embargo on China and North Korea (GA Res. 500 V).

Truce talks continued during 1951 as UN forces pushed Chinese units north of the 38th parallel, and by the end of 1952, the negotiations had produced agreement on all of the major issues in dispute, except the issue of repatriation of prisoners of war, which was largely resolved by May 1953, and an armistice was signed on 27 July 1953. Attention turned even more vigorously to the daunting humanitarian problems and the quest for rehabilitation and reconstruction. Peace talks in subsequent months proved contentious. The original boundary between the North and South, the 38th parallel, continued to serve as a reminder of Cold War tensions in subsequent decades.

OUTCOME OF THE DEBATE

The United Nations proved itself capable during the Korean War of undertaking deployment of forces against aggression, but its capacity to do so was the result of the coincidence that the Soviet Union was boycotting Security Council sessions. The UN action preserved South Korea from aggressive subjugation by the North and punished the North Korean action. However, the entry of Communist China into the war complicated the UN action and prolonged the war much to the disadvantage of millions of suffering Koreans. The Chinese aggression was also contained after initial difficulty, and months of truce negotiations produced an armistice that led to the end of open hostilities.

Massive amounts of humanitarian relief, rehabilitation, and reconstruction assistance was subsequently provided through UNKRA and gradually Korea recovered from the effects of the war. Still, political instabilities wracked South Korea in the 1960s, and disputes along the demilitarized zone of the 38th parallel prolonged the Cold War tensions in the country. South Korea's astonishing economic growth during the 1970s and 1980s was accompanied by episodic political unrest, while North Korea made substantially less progress in economic development, so much so that a prolonged famine in the late 1990s took hundreds of thousands of lives. The end of the Cold War in the early 1990s did not produce a political resolution to the Korea problem, although tentative steps in that direction were taken when the two countries' leaders met in June 2000 for direct bilateral talks. The Communist government in the North continued to serve as a military threat to the South, and the development of nuclear weapons and missile launch capabilities continued to serve as a source of instability in East Asia. After five decades of attempts to negotiate a reconciliation between the two Koreas, Korea remains divided with no immediate prospect of reunification, thus serving as a lingering reminder of the Cold War and the bitter legacy of East-West rivalry.

See also Membership and Representation Questions (Debate 11).

FOR FURTHER READING

Kaufman, Burton I. *The Korean Conflict*. Westport, CT: Greenwood Press, 1999.

Kim, Joungwon. *Divided Korea: The Politics of Development 1945–72*. New York: Hollym International Corporation, 1999.

Pores, Susan, and James E. Hoare. *Conflict in Korea: An Encyclopedia*. New York: ABC-Clio, 1999.

Stueck, William. *The Korean War: An International History*. Princeton, NJ: Princeton University Press, 1997.

UN Yearbooks, 1950–1953.

Defining Aggression (1950)

SIGNIFICANCE OF THE ISSUE

The very operation of a successful collective security organization such as the United Nations requires that member states know what constitutes aggression so that measures can be taken to punish the offender and protect states victimized by aggression. Generally, *aggression* is defined as an attack by one or more states against another, but circumstances of the attack, the level and type of force used, and the nature of any prior provocation are all matters that qualify the general definition. Efforts by governments to define and prohibit aggression speak to the general desire of the international community to avoid war. Although it might seem to be an easy matter to do this and to avoid and punish aggression, the effort to define aggression itself took nearly twenty-five years of debate in various UN bodies.

BACKGROUND TO THE DEBATE

Work to define and prohibit aggression began under the aegis of the League of Nations. The League Covenant, itself, called upon member states to refrain from war, to resort first to peaceful settlement of disputes, and to avoid aggressive war. However, governments retained a right to self-defense and to take action necessary "for the maintenance of right and justice." In 1928, France and the United States promoted an initiative to prevent recourse to war. Known as the Kellogg-Briand Pact, which was initially signed by fifteen states and ultimately ratified or adhered to by sixty-five nations, this treaty condemned and renounced war as a means of national policy. Disputes were to be resolved only by peaceful means. The treaty did not outlaw defensive war or collective actions by such bodies as the League of Nations. More important, it stipulated no means of actual enforcement, and the outbreak of World War II eleven years later illustrated that the treaty ignored the underlying realities of international relations.

The League collective security system also proved to be flawed, and nation-alistic sentiments prevailed over international efforts to prevent and control aggression.

With the creation of the United Nations and its renewed emphasis on collective security, governments reiterated their desire to resolve disputes by peaceful means and collectively to prevent, control, and punish aggression through the Security Council. The Nuremberg Tribunal also identified the "planning, preparing and initiating" of wars of aggression as a crime against peace. Thus, after the horrors of World War II, the international community once again committed itself to a process of promoting international peace and security. As before, however, international and civil wars continued to bedevil the foreign and domestic affairs of nations.

HISTORY OF THE DEBATE

In 1950, the Soviet Union introduced a proposal to define aggression, and the UN General Assembly passed the matter on to its Committee on In-

The effects of wartime aggression are seen in the devastation of Warsaw, Poland, which was reduced to rubble during a three-week siege by German military forces at the outbreak of World War II in September 1939. UN/DPI Photo

ternational Law for further study. In 1952, the Assembly set up a special commission for the definition of aggression, which after being reconstituted in 1954 with twenty-one member states began to hold periodic sessions in 1956. Further sessions were held in 1959, 1962, 1965, and 1967. The General Assembly established a new and larger Special Committee of thirty-four experts in 1967, which eventually produced a consensus draft on the definition of aggression in 1973, for final General Assembly consideration.

The Special Committee reported annually to the General Assembly regarding its deliberations, where further debate took place in the United Nations' Sixth Committee for Legal Affairs and in plenary sessions of the Assembly itself. The process of drafting a treaty, declaration, or legal definition involves consideration of draft proposals made by member states, which are then subject to negotiation. Such was the case in the Special Committee's efforts to draft a definition of aggression. In 1969, three proposals were submitted to the Special Committee, one from the Soviet Union, a second proposal sponsored by thirteen countries (Colombia, Cyprus, Ecuador, Ghana, Guyana, Haiti, Iran, Madagascar, Mexico, Spain, Uganda, Uruguay, and Yugoslavia), and a third great power proposal sponsored by Australia, Canada, Italy, Japan, the United Kingdom, and the United States. The committee considered each of the proposals paragraph by paragraph in an effort to find common principles. In the process several different issues were considered. The issue of how the definition of aggression would be applied especially in relation to the functions of the Security Council was considered. Would the definition apply only to states or also to belligerent communities or insurgent groups? What might constitute direct, as opposed to indirect, aggression? Consideration was given to the kinds of acts that constituted aggression such as declarations of war, use of weapons of mass destruction, invasion, attack, military occupation, annexation, bombardment, attack by land, sea, or air forces, blockades, armed insurgencies, terrorist activity, and subversive tactics. Then there was the question of priority. Should the state that first used force be considered the aggressor, or was there such a thing as provocation or threat that might mitigate the first use of force? This in turn raised the question of aggressive intent, the legitimate use of force for self-defense, and collective security. Even if used in self-defense, the principle of proportionality was held to be an important limiting factor in the types of justified retaliation a government might legitimately use in its self-defense. Finally, there was the issue of defining the consequences of aggression, assigning responsibility for it, denying recognition of territorial gains made by conquest, and possibly even the issue of reparations.

While debate proceeded, it became apparent that states differed among themselves concerning whether the whole process of defining aggression was useful. In plenary debates of the General Assembly in 1970, Ceylon (Sri

Lanka), Cyprus and Poland argued that securing a definition on aggression would greatly assist the United Nations in maintaining international peace. China, Israel, and Sweden expressed doubts on this point. Some countries believed that even discussion of the matter was premature, whereas other delegations emphasized that any definition must attract overwhelming support of UN members and especially among the permanent members of the Security Council where, ultimately, decisions about punishing acts of aggression must be taken. Hungary, Japan, Kuwait, Mongolia, and the United States were among those asserting this view. Wide-ranging discussions and views on the content of a definition of aggression were expressed. The United Kingdom and the United States insisted that indirect forms of aggression were even more destabilizing than direct acts of aggression and that covert forms of aggression must be included in the definition. Many small countries supported this view, while the Soviet Union suggested that direct forms of aggression should be addressed first. Members differed over whether a declaration of war was by itself an act of aggression, with Bolivia and Greece holding that it was, and Canada and Ceylon holding that it was not necessarily so. No country directly objected to the first use of force as at least a key part of a definition of aggression, but most acknowledged that other factors had to be considered as well. Italy and the United States insisted that aggressive intent was an essential ingredient of an act of aggression, since unauthorized or accidental attacks should not be treated as intentional acts of aggression, but other delegations, such as Colombia, Cyprus, France, and Iraq, thought real aggressors could dodge responsibility by making spurious claims of accidental or unauthorized attacks. States differed on whether the principle of proportionality should be included in the definition, over whether revolutionary wars of self-determination should be exempted from or included in a definition of aggression, and over whether or not the issue of state responsibility and legal consequences for aggression should be included.

To deal with this range of disagreement, the Special Committee set up a Working Group to draft acceptable compromise language for presentation to the General Assembly. Over the course of the next three years, the Working Group and Special Committee were able to achieve a consensus agreement that balanced the interests and views of various governments. In the end the draft limited itself to the issue of armed aggression by states or groups of states against one another. First use of force was seen as "prima facie" evidence of aggression, but this depended on the actual circumstances and the gravity of the use of force, which had to be determined on a case-by-case basis by the Security Council. A range of acts, whether or not war had been actually declared, constituted acts of aggression, including invasion, military occupation and annexation of territory, bombardment, blockades, attacks on the air and sea fleets of another country, allowing one's territory to be used by another state to perpetrate an act of aggression on a third state, and the sending of armed bands, groups, irregulars, or mercenaries by one state into the territory of another to commit serious acts of aggression. The list of acts was not seen as exhaustive, and the Security Council could determine on a case-by-case basis that other acts could constitute aggression. The draft indicated that aggression could not give rise to valid claims of territorial acquisition and that aggression gives rise to international responsibility. Another provision of the draft provided that people under colonial domination had a right to struggle for self-determination in accordance with the UN Charter and other legal instruments. Some countries, such as Algeria, China, Egypt, Ghana, Kenya, Senegal, the Soviet Union, and Yugoslavia, interpreted this to mean that people under colonial domination had a right to armed struggle, but this was expressly denied by Canada, Italy, the Netherlands, and the United States who pointed out that the struggle of oppressed peoples envisioned in the draft must always be a peaceful struggle in accordance with the purposes and principles of the UN Charter, not armed struggle. Various provisions of the draft drew comment and reservations by member states, including China, which continued to believe that the language of the definition would be manipulated by the superpowers to their own ends. However, the General Assembly adopted the definition without a vote, indicating that any differences nations had over the language were insufficient to block passage of the statement as a whole.

OUTCOME OF THE DEBATE

As with all previous international efforts to define and prevent aggression, the decision by the UN General Assembly in 1974 to adopt a definition on aggression did not itself change the behavior of states. Many highly destructive international and civil wars involving external intervention have occurred since the adoption of the definition of aggression. During the 1970s and 1980s, the Security Council remained largely unable to serve as a means of collective security owing to the ongoing divisions among permanent members of the Security Council and a worldwide struggle between the forces of the Western and Communist worlds. Iran and Iraq fought the bloodiest war since Korea in the 1980s, largely without an international response. Genocide in Cambodia was perpetrated without international sanction in the mid-1970s. Wars in the Horn of Africa, Central America, and Southeast Asia continued. The Soviet Union invaded Afghanistan. The United States intervened in Central America wars. Cold War competition, in short, largely mooted the admirable effort to define aggression, demonstrating that a legal definition is one thing and the actual practice of nations often quite another.

Still, with the end of the Cold War, the incidence of international armed conflict has declined substantially. Now the problem lies in the civil wars that are often as bloody and destructive as international wars. For these, the definition of aggression arrived at in 1974 has only marginal application. Thus, the international community continues to be faced with a major challenge, not only of definition but of collective will in dealing with such conflicts. In the case of the Kosovo war, the North Atlantic Treaty Organization (NATO) forces bombed Serbia for what they considered illegitimate acts by the Serbian government against its Albanian population in its province of Kosovo. Serbia had committed no formal act of aggression against another state, NATO bombed first, and it failed to secure authorization for that bombing from the Security Council. NATO countries, though apparently in violation of the definition of aggression, held that the anticipatory commission of genocide by Serbian forces justified its action and that the brutal attacks unleashed by Serbian forces in the wake of the bombing proved that fears of genocide were real, thus justifying further the first use of force. It would appear that as far as the issue of applying any standard of aggression is concerned governments will continue to do as they have always done, namely, use force whenever they believe they are justified, regardless of whether a consensus exists on its legality or validity.

See also Decolonization (Debate 18); Kosovo Situation (Debate 50); Terrorism (Debate 28).

FOR FURTHER READING

Nyiri, Nicolas. *The United Nations' Search for a Definition of Aggression*. New York: Peter Lang, 1989.

Stone, Julius. *Aggression and World Order*. Westport, CT: Greenwood Press, 1976.

UN Yearbooks, 1970–1974.

Von Glahn, Gerhard. *Law among Nations: An Introduction to Public International Law*. New York: Allyn and Bacon, 1996.

Apartheid in South Africa (1952)

SIGNIFICANCE OF THE ISSUE

First inscribed on the UN General Assembly agenda in 1952, the problem of apartheid, the policy in South Africa of the separation of the races, remained a contentious issue in UN debates until the early 1990s when reforms were initiated by the white minority regime of South Africa, which culminated in the election of a black majority government in 1994. The most extreme form of racial discrimination practiced by any country in the world, the policy of apartheid was condemned by most nations, although pressures for actual reform and proposals for sanctions did not arise until the independence of many black African states, who engineered international declarations classifying apartheid as an international crime.

BACKGROUND TO THE DEBATE

The Union of South Africa (established in 1910), which became known as South Africa in 1961 when it seceded from the British Commonwealth, was an original member of the League of Nations and of the United Nations. In 1948, the National Party, supported by the white Dutch population known as Afrikaaners, took power under the leadership of Dr. D. F. Malan, who ran for office on a program for apartheid. South Africa had long practiced a policy of racial separation in housing and education. The policy of separation was rooted in the complicated history of the region. In the late seventeenth century, Dutch settlers landed at the Cape of Good Hope and began a gradual settlement in southern Africa. At first they encountered little resistance from the local Hottentots and Bushmen who sparsely populated the area. However, as the Dutch began migrating north and east after the British took control of South Africa in 1795, they encountered the much more numerous and warlike Zulu peoples who were migrating from the north. The British and Dutch vied for the region in the early 1800s, but the

British formerly took control in 1814. The Dutch, or Boer, settlers, who practiced slavery in connection with exploitation of the indigenous inhabitants, continued to clash with the British administration. Two years after the British abolished slavery in the colony, the Boers began their famous Great Trek into the uninhabited areas of the interior of South Africa. Separate Boer states emerged in the Transvaal, the Orange Free State, and Natal. The British annexed the latter in 1842 and parts of the Orange Free State in 1871 after diamonds were discovered in the Kimberley area. Disputes between the British and Dutch eventually culminated in the Boer Wars of 1899–1903. The Union of South Africa was established in 1910 when the Transvaal and Orange Free State joined the British cape colony and Natal as a unified dominion of Great Britain.

Throughout South Africa, whether in Dutch- or British-controlled areas, policies of racial segregation were practiced. The vast majority of the population in South Africa was black (about 75 percent), whereas a substantial number of Indian people and people of mixed race also populated the area. The majority of whites, about 60 percent, were Dutch, and together with

Segregation of the races is starkly displayed in Bloemfontein, South Africa, at a sports arena, just one manifestation of the policy of apartheid. UN/DPI Photo H. Vassal

those of British descent, they outnumbered the Asians and colored peoples but were a mere 15 percent of the total population. Still, they dominated the government of the area, as neither blacks, people of mixed race, nor Asians could vote or participate in the political process. After World War II, the racial policies of South Africa came under closer international scrutiny and more severe criticism.

HISTORY OF THE DEBATE

UN action on the question of South Africa and its racial policies began with a complaint by India in 1946 concerning South African discrimination against Asians, a battle that was joined by Pakistan in 1947. South Africa's National Party, which took control in 1948, however, had even more ambitious plans, and its agenda included a much wider extension of separation of the races. In 1950, the National Party introduced the Group Areas and Population Registration Acts. In the meantime, efforts by the United Nations to extend its good offices to mediate the complaints by India and Pakistan with South Africa failed to materialize. In this setting, the UN General Assembly in December 1952 established a three-man commission to study the racial situation in South Africa and noted that all countries should bring their domestic policies and legislation in line with their Charter obligations to promote and protect human rights, which in the case of South Africa were egregiously flouted by the apartheid policies. South Africa's response to the UN actions was to invoke its rights under Article 2 (7), claiming that its apartheid policy was a matter of domestic jurisdiction and of no concern to the international community. Thus, it refused to acknowledge the legitimacy of the UN Commission, which nevertheless met and made reports to the General Assembly in subsequent years. The General Assembly routinely passed resolutions in the 1950s calling upon South Africa to reform its apartheid policies and expressing regret and concern over South Africa's intransigence in failing to undertake revision of the policy.

However, a full-scale UN treatment of apartheid did not commence until the 1960s. In 1960, sixteen newly independent African states joined the United Nations, and sixteen more joined during the 1960s. These countries vociferously opposed the racist policies of the government of South Africa, and they increasingly and loudly proclaimed their objections in UN forums. Adding to this chorus of criticism of apartheid was the deteriorating situation inside South Africa itself. In 1959, the white minority regime promulgated the Bantu Self-Government Act, by which 13 percent of the least productive lands in South Africa were to be given independence as black homeland areas. The rest of South Africa would be under the direct control of whites. This deepening of apartheid was widely condemned, as was the Sharpeville incident of 21 March 1960, in which sixty-nine unarmed South African protestors were killed by government forces. The UN Security

Council began meeting to discuss the effects of apartheid on international peace and security. On 1 April the Council called upon South Africa to renounce its policy of apartheid. In 1962, for the first time, the UN General Assembly declared apartheid a danger to international peace and security and called for UN members to break diplomatic relations with South Africa and to establish export embargoes against South Africa and boycotts of South African goods. The vote on this resolution was 67 to 16 with 27 abstentions. Most of the countries opposing the proposed sanctions were Western trade partners of South Africa, including major powers such as Great Britain, France, Japan, and the United States. South Africa rejected the validity of all these UN recommendations, and the nonparticipation of such major trade powers guaranteed the ineffectiveness of the sanctions imposed by other countries. But over the long run a broadening and deepening of sanctions by UN member states did occur.

In the years and decades that followed, various UN bodies were engaged in the debate on South African policies, particularly the special UN body for monitoring apartheid established in 1962, which, commencing in 1974, was known as the Special Committee against Apartheid. In 1963, the UN Security Council determined that the situation in South Africa comprised a threat to international peace and security, and it called upon states to impose a voluntary embargo against the sale of arms to South Africa, an embargo that was made mandatory by the Council in 1977. The Council remained actively involved with the situation in South Africa from 1960 to 1988, a period during which it adopted twenty-five resolutions dealing with apartheid or its consequences, one of the more significant decisions being a call for suspension of all new investment in South Africa in 1985. In 1966, the International Court of Justice (ICJ) heard a complaint filed by Ethiopia and Liberia concerning the legitimacy of South Africa's administration of the Southwest Africa Trust Territory. The Court eventually ruled that Liberia and Ethiopia did not have standing to bring suit against South Africa, but the UN General Assembly voted in the aftermath of the decision to revoke South Africa's mandate over Southwest Africa, which was renamed and thenceforth referred to in UN debates as Namibia.

With the establishment of the Organization of African Unity (OAU) in 1963, which was dedicated in large part to the rapid decolonization of Africa, to the elimination of racial discrimination, and to opposition of apartheid in South Africa, yet another venue for concentration of international debate concerning South African racial policies came into being. The OAU served as a constant official opponent of South African policies, although individual member states, such as Malawi, Lesotho, and Botswana, maintained relations with South Africa, owing to its overwhelming influence on their national economies. Other African countries tolerated black market trading with South Africa, although most African countries continued officially to condemn South Africa's racial policies. The UN General Assembly adopted the UN Declaration on Elimination of All Forms of Racial Discrimination in 1963, a statement motivated to a large extent by opponents of South Africa's racial policies. In 1965 the General Assembly adopted an International Convention on the Elimination of all Forms of Racial Discrimination that established a Committee to receive reports and hear complaints about racial discrimination. This Convention entered into force in 1969. Similarly, on 30 November 1973, the Assembly adopted the International Convention on the Suppression and Punishment of the Crime of Apartheid, which entered into force in July 1976. This treaty condemned the policy of apartheid as a crime against humanity and in certain respects as a form of genocide. It called upon states party to take legislative, executive, and judicial measures to ensure the apprehension and punishment of those guilty of participating in acts of apartheid. In 1974, the Assembly recommended that South Africa be refused participation in all international organizations and bodies, but a proposal in the Security Council to expel South Africa from the United Nations was defeated. In December 1979 the Assembly called upon member states to impose an oil embargo on South Africa.

The General Assembly subsequently held special or emergency sessions in 1978, 1981, and 1986 to consider South African policies in Namibia and to call for Namibia's full and complete independence. The Assembly proclaimed the year 1982 to be the International Year of Mobilization of Sanctions against South Africa, and during the 1980s, imposition of economic sanctions on South Africa by additional countries, including major powers such as the United States, increased external pressures on South Africa for reform. South African electoral reforms in 1984 that extended voting rights to Coloreds and Asians only infuriated the black African population, leading to increased domestic instability. The General Assembly held an additional special session in 1989 to consider the question of apartheid. In a resolution adopted by consensus, the special session issued a Declaration on Apartheid and its Destructive Consequences in Southern Africa that urged South Africans to end the apartheid system by peaceful and democratic means.

Indeed, matters were moving rapidly toward reform inside South Africa itself, even as the regional situation in southern Africa experienced success on the diplomatic front. In 1984 Mozambique decided to negotiate directly with South Africa to help end its civil war. After lengthy negotiations brokered by the United States, South Africa agreed to withdraw from Namibia in 1988, as Cuban forces withdrew from neighboring Angola. Namibians repatriated in large numbers during 1989 prior to elections, which led to the nation's independence. In 1990, Namibia became a member of the United Nations. With normalized relations coming into play with its major neighboring countries in the late 1980s, South Africa witnessed a number of major internal reforms in subsequent years leading up to the transition to black majority rule.

OUTCOME OF THE DEBATE

These external and internal developments coalesced after the election of F. W. de Klerk in 1989 as president of South Africa. President de Klerk released Nelson Mandela of the African National Congress from prison and began to negotiate with him and other black African leaders. Gradually, the South African Parliament began to dismantle the legislative basis for apartheid. The Separate Amenities Acts was repealed in June 1990. In June 1991, at the urging of de Klerk, the South African Parliament voted to repeal the Lands Act, the Group Areas Act, and the Population Registration Act, but negotiation of terms by which black Africans could participate in elections still awaited action. On 17 March 1992, over two-thirds of white South Africans voted to give de Klerk a mandate to end the apartheid system totally by negotiating a new national constitution that would extend voting rights to the black population. The United Nations fielded the first members of its Observer Mission in South Africa in September 1993 to monitor constitutional talks in South Africa, and in October the UN General Assembly ended, by a consensus vote of its 184 members, its thirty-one-year ban on trade after South African parties agreed to an interim Constitution. After months of difficult negotiations and preparations, elections were held in April 1994 that led to the election of Nelson Mandela as president. On 23 June 1994, the new government of South Africa took its seat in the General Assembly, a body that had refused for twenty previous years to accept the credentials of the South African white minority regime. The Assembly also terminated the mandates of the UN Trust Fund for South Africa and of the Special Committee against Apartheid.

The end of the long and bitter global debate over apartheid saw other international bodies also accept the credentials of the new government. Relations with the white minority population continued to be marked by ongoing difficulties and differences, but the peaceful transition in power was a major accomplishment after so many decades of rancor and protest. The United Nations served for nearly five decades as the focal point of international opposition to the racial policies of the South African government, and although tactics about how an end to apartheid might best be achieved was a subject of ongoing controversy, few nations disputed the moral bankruptcy of the policy itself. International rejection of apartheid as a legitimate means of public policy ultimately triumphed in the largely peaceful reforms undertaken by South African leaders after so many years years of bitter debate. The wider debate in the United Nations about racial discrimination, which was fueled in large part by the existence of white minority regimes in Southern Africa, reduced the visibility of debates on racial discrimination during the 1990s, except in its more egregious forms of ethnic cleansing and genocide where international attentions and energies continued owing to the especially heinous nature of such acts.

See also Angola Situation (Debate 42); Decolonization (Debate 18); Genocide (Debate 9); Human Rights (Debate 10); Mozambique Situation (Debate 47); Rhodesian Question (Debate 21); Southwest Africa (Namibia) Dispute (Debate 3); Zionism as Racism (Debate 34).

FOR FURTHER READING

Christopher, A. J. *Atlas of Apartheid*. London: Routledge, 1994.

Eades, Lindsay Michie. *The End of Apartheid in South Africa*. Westport, CT: Greenwood Press, 1999.

Klotz, Audie. *Norms in International Relations: The Struggle against Apartheid*. 2nd ed. Ithaca, NY: Cornell University Press, 1999.

Price, Robert M. *The Apartheid State in Crisis: Political Transformation of South Africa, 1975–1990*. New York: Oxford University Press, 1991.

The United Nations and Apartheid, 1948–1994. New York: UN Publications, 1994.

UN Chronicle (Sept. 1994): 4–14.

UN Yearbooks, various 1948–1994.

Waldmier, Patti. *Anatomy of a Miracle: The End of Apartheid and the Birth of the New South Africa*. New Brunswick, NJ: Rutgers University Press, 1998.

Population (1954)

SIGNIFICANCE OF THE ISSUE

Apart from collection of statistical and demographic data by the United Nations, which is widely accepted as a routine matter, debates about population policy in UN settings have proved to be highly controversial. The degree to which the United Nations should participate actively in population control policies is a matter of ongoing controversy, even with a growing number of governments adopting population control measures of their own. Disagreement about what constitutes *over*population, about whether population growth is a detriment or a spur to economic development, and about who should be in the business of controlling populations continues both in international and academic debates.

BACKGROUND TO THE DEBATE

Population has been a matter of concern for the United Nations from its very inception. In 1947, the Economic and Social Council (ECOSOC) replaced its Demographic Commission with a Population Commission that was to conduct studies on population, encourage the collection of accurate population data, and advise ECOSOC on population trends and the relationship of such trends to economic and social conditions and migration. Thus the United Nations encouraged the conduct of national and regional censuses, provided technical and demographic assistance to countries to enhance their capacity for collection of population data, published the *UN Demographic Yearbook*, and promoted the study of population growth and its effects on the economy.

The issue of population was seen in the first two decades of UN debate primarily from its scientific and statistical aspects. But as time passed and the global population continued to increase, many governments began to view population growth as a potential problem. Because questions of fam-

Rapid urbanization and crowded cities are one by-product of population growth. Here in the crowded Ginza area of Tokyo, Japan, streets are closed to automobiles to allow full use by urban pedestrians. UN/DPI Photo Guthrie

ily size have always been matters of the most personal and intimate nature within families, and tied to the deepest religious convictions about the sacredness of life, many governments were reluctant to interfere in what had been traditionally regarded as a matter beyond their proper sphere of authority. Whether families used any methods of family planning at all, or some form of natural family planning or artificial means of contraception, was highly variable in different cultural and religious settings. Although family planning programs and the use of artificial contraception gradually became more prevalent during the 1960s and subsequent decades, in part because of national and international programs to promote them, the underlying moral and ethical questions concerning the methods of population control policies, including the related and highly controversial issues of abortion and sterilization, remain explosively divisive matters of both national policy and international debate.

Generally, the growth of national populations is highly connected to their state of economic development. As countries develop economically, the natural tendency is for population growth rates to decline as both death rates and birthrates decline. It is an irony that the wealthier, more secularized governments whose countries once passed through stages of high population growth now view the high population growth rates of developing countries as a threat to international development and stability, and thus they generally support the introduction of population control measures. Many developing countries have noticed this apparent contradiction and have insisted in successive world population conferences that they will not be viewed as objects of the population control policies of developed states. They have asserted their right to establish national policies relating to population. They have argued that their population is their main resource. Many Third World governments have insisted that the developed country obsession with population growth in the developing world is misplaced and that the best way to tackle a perceived problem of *over*population is through generous policies of economic development. Thus, UN debates tended until recently to be dominated by a population control focus of developed states and a suspicious counteraction by developing countries that insisted on national autonomy and emphasized the primacy of economic development.

HISTORY OF THE DEBATE

The very first international census was conducted in 1950, and it was followed in 1954 by the First World Population Conference, which was held in Rome and attended by sixty-eight governments as well as hundreds of demographers who presented scientific papers. At this time, the primary focus of international debate centered on the introduction of standardized statistical measures and census instruments. Prior to the Second World Population Conference in Belgrade in 1965, the UN General Assembly held a heated debate in 1962 concerning a proposal to authorize UN technical assistance in birth control. The issue of artificial contraception as a means of controlling population was highly controversial, and the proposed resolution failed by a vote of 34 to 34 with 32 abstentions.

The issue was revisited at Belgrade where concerns about a demographic explosion worried many national delegations. The controversial question of family planning was taken up at Belgrade by eighty-eight countries. In 1966, the UN General Assembly addressed the population explosion question by asserting (Res. 2111/XXI) that "the number of children in the family should depend on the free will of each family." In 1967, the UN Declaration on Social Progress and Development asserted that each family had a right, subject to the limits of national population policies, to "know the measures that will enable it to decide on the number of its children." In a gingerly fashion, governments and the United Nations wished to uphold the rights of couples to determine family size, while making available to families information that would enable them to regulate the number and spacing of births. In December 1966 the UN General Assembly also established a Population Trust Fund, which became operational in 1969 and later became known as the United Nations Fund for Population Activities

(UNFPA). This body, which is supported by voluntary contributions, was established to assist developing countries to study demographic problems and their effects on social and economic development. Increasingly, however, UNFPA became the focal point for lobbying by governments and family planning nongovernmental organizations (NGOs) for the wider dissemination of family planning services in the developing world.

The Third World Population Conference was held in Bucharest in 1974. Here, in an effort to fashion a consensus among developed states preoccupied with finding means for limiting population growth and developing states who were preoccupied with economic development, 140 governments agreed to a plan of action that underscored the sovereign right of each country to develop its own population policies and their duty to do so in the wider context of global economic and social development. The plan of action reiterated the right of couples and individuals having "the basic human right to decide freely and responsibly the number and spacing of their children and to have the information, education and means to do so."

The Fourth World Population Conference was held in Mexico City in 1984. Many of the same themes raised at Bucharest were reiterated at Mexico City, but the conference was under heavy lobbying by family planning NGOs and many Western governments to broaden the agenda on population control, to consider the question of abortion as a means of population control, and to promote more expansive UN participation in family planning activities. The United States, under the conservative Reagan administration, lobbied heavily against the initiative to define abortion as a legally enforceable universal human right and pointed to the use by China of coercive abortion as a means of strict population control as an example of where such a right tended. At Mexico City, governments approved wider international efforts to promote family planning initiatives but stipulated that abortion was not a legitimate means of family planning.

A decade later, a more liberal Clinton administration governed the United States. As preparatory documents were developed for the International Conference on Population and Development in Cairo in 1994, the Clinton administration, coupled with UNFPA officials, and many family planning NGOs, such as the International Planned Parenthood Federation, heavily influenced the drafting process for the principles and plan of action to be presented at Cairo. The draft opened the door to consideration of abortion as an international human reproductive right, to state-oriented as opposed to family-oriented sex education, to the right of teenagers to sexual activity free of parental oversight, and to unions other than traditional marriage as legitimate forms of family life. The subtle interjection of such principles into the draft plan of action for the Cairo Conference raised much concern internationally in the year prior to the Conference. The Holy See spent months pointing out to delegations the serious moral and social implications of the innovations, much to the displeasure of the Clinton administration. Although the Holy See played a pivotal role in organizing opposition to the U.S. innovations, by the time the Cairo Conference met, numerous countries in the developing world also expressed serious reservations with the draft document. Catholic nations of Latin America and Muslim nations of the Middle East, Africa, and Asia came to the Conference with serious objections. In one of the most hotly contested international conferences on record, virtually no portion of the draft program of action escaped amendment, and some of the more controversial chapters were entirely revised. The heavily amended document remained controversial at the end of the day, and over 20 countries of the nearly 180 present asserted oral or written reservations to language that might be construed to legitimize abortion, premarital sexual relations, or nontraditional sexual unions. Countries expressing reservations of this sort included: Afghanistan, Argentina, Brunei Darussalam, Djibouti, the Dominican Republic, Ecuador, Egypt, El Salvador, Guatemala, Honduras, Iran, Jordan, Kuwait, Libya, Malta, Nicaragua, Paraguay, Peru, Syria, United Arab Emirates, and Yemen.

Nevertheless, the Cairo Conference broke new ground in changing the focus of population debates from population control to free and informed choice. The document rejected all forms of coercion in population policies. Although it mentioned, unlike the Bucharest or Mexico City documents, that abortion was a dimension of population policy and of primary health care, it reaffirmed that abortion should not be promoted as a measure of family planning. It reaffirmed the family, founded on marriage, as the basic unit of society. It also underscored the critical need for economic development in the developing world and the need for the education and advancement of women on the basis of full equality.

OUTCOME OF THE DEBATE

The Cairo Conference illustrated that issues concerning population control are matters of ongoing controversy. Future population conferences will no doubt provoke ongoing disputes about how to deal most effectively and appropriately with population growth. For now, however, the Cairo Conference clearly stipulated the connection between population and development, the need for the education and advancement of women on the basis of equality, the right of countries to develop national strategies for the regulation of population growth, and the right of families freely and responsibly to choose how to regulate the size of their families.

In the meantime, there has been a steady decline in recent decades in the global population growth rate. This is attributed variously to negative growth rates in some developed countries, to economic development in many Third World countries, and to the wider availability of family planning services. The population explosion scare of the 1960s and 1970s has been replaced by more sober and realistic projections about population growth, which see global population growth rates continuing to slow until stabilizing around the middle part of the twenty-first century.

Future UN debates on the subject of population will no doubt continue to address the interrelationships between and among population trends, the environment, economic and social development, renewable and nonrenewable resources, technological developments, urbanization, migration, and human rights. The interdependency of these issues is now widely accepted by the international community.

See also Global Environment (Debate 27); Health (Debate 8); Human Settlements (Debate 36); Status and Condition of Children (Debate 2); Status of Women (Debate 33); Third World Development Programming (Debate 25).

FOR FURTHER READING

Brown, Lester. *Beyond Malthus: Nineteen Dimensions of the Population Challenge.* New York: W. W. Norton, 1999.

Cromartie, Michael. *The Nine Lives of Population Control.* Grand Rapids, MI: Eerdmans, 1995.

Erlich, Paul. *The Population Bomb.* Reprint. Cutchogue, NY: Buccaneer Books, 1991.

Hollingsworth, William G. *Ending the Explosion: Population Policies and Ethics for a Humane Future.* Santa Ana, CA: Seven Locks Press, 1996.

Kasun, Jacqueline, and Julian Simon. *The War against Population: The Economics and Ideology of Population Control.* San Francisco: Ignatius Press, 1988.

Livi-Baci, Massimo. *A Concise History of World Population.* Trans. Carl Ipsen. London: Blackwell, 1997.

Report of the International Conference on Population and Development. UN Document A/CONF.171/13 (18 Oct. 1994).

Simon, Julian L. *The Ultimate Resource 2.* Princeton, NJ: Princeton University Press, 1997.

UN Yearbooks, 1947, 1954, 1974, 1984, 1994.

Hungarian Question (1956)

SIGNIFICANCE OF THE ISSUE

The invasion of Hungary by the military forces of the Soviet Union in October 1956 deepened Cold War hostilities between the East and the West. The United Nations could take no formal collective security action owing to the veto power of the Soviet Union in the Security Council. However, it did call an emergency session of the General Assembly that called for withdrawal of Soviet forces. The installation of a new Hungarian government by the Soviet Union complicated international efforts to rectify the situation, and the eruption of the Suez Crisis eventually deflected attention from the Soviet use of force. However, the effective response to Hungarian refugee flows by the United Nations High Commissioner for Refugees (UNHCR) and other humanitarian agencies solidified the work of these agencies and established their credentials as essential mechanisms of humanitarian response to international conflicts.

BACKGROUND TO THE DEBATE

After World War II, military forces of the Soviet Union occupied much of Eastern Europe, including Hungary. Hungary, which had supported Germany during World War II, sued for peace as Russian forces advanced through Eastern Europe. Germany seized the state and ordered continued resistance to Russian advances. Hungarians then suffered through months of fighting between German and Russian forces on Hungarian soil. After World War II, Hungary established a republican form of government and elected a National Assembly. However, as elsewhere in Eastern Europe, the Soviet Union put pressure on the anti-Communist elements of the government and eventually forced Hungarians to hold new elections in which the Communist Party emerged victorious. Communist opponents were subsequently purged. Events such as this, repeated in other East European countries, led to the descent of what Winston Churchill called the "Iron Curtain," as Communist governments were installed in Soviet-occupied states. Confrontations in Berlin and Korea added to the Cold War climate in subsequent years.

Hungary's entry into the United Nations was stalled for several years as the Western powers and the Soviet Union squabbled over a range of issues, and each side prevented allies of the other side from becoming UN members. With the resolution of the membership crisis in 1955, Hungary became a UN member. Hungarians generally chaffed under the boot of Soviet repression, and in the fall of 1956, a popular nationalist revolt broke out that supported a nationalist-oriented Communist government under Imre Nagy, who threatened to break Hungary's military ties with the Soviet Union and the Warsaw Pact states.

The Soviet Union was in no mood to brook this kind of expression of independence and disobedience, and on 22 October Soviet military forces intervened with troops and tanks and began a brutal crackdown on civilians and dissidents. Nagy announced on 28 October his desire to negotiate with the Soviet Union in an effort to secure the withdrawal of Soviet forces on mutually agreeable terms. However, on 1 November, even more Soviet forces entered Hungary. The Nagy government protested this action, repudiated its membership in the Warsaw Treaty, declared its neutrality, called upon the four great powers to defend its neutrality, and requested that Hungary's situation be placed on the agenda of the UN General Assembly. Within days, Nagy and members of his government were arrested and many were eventually executed. With a new puppet government installed by the Soviet Union, Hungary argued that any UN action would represent a violation of its territorial integrity, interference in its domestic affairs, and an affront to its political independence.

HISTORY OF THE DEBATE

Several days after the initial Soviet intervention, representatives of the United Kingdom, France, and the United States requested a meeting of the UN Security Council to consider the Hungarian situation under Article 34 of the UN Charter and to investigate the dispute as a potential threat to international peace and security. The Hungarian representative to the United Nations and the Soviet Union both argued that the situation in Hungary constituted a domestic matter under Article 2 (7) of the Charter and that discussion by the Council of the question would constitute unjustifiable interference into Hungary's domestic affairs. Western governments countered that the fact that foreign troops were fighting on Hungarian soil clearly indicated that the question was of international concern, and they successfully passed a resolution to place the matter on the Council agenda, despite Soviet objections and an abstention by Yugoslavia.

In the debates that followed, Cold War rhetoric and ideological pronouncements thickened the air. Western governments noted that a massive
invasion and much bloodshed were already evident in Hungary and that
fair and free expressions of the people's will would constitute the only legitimate way to restore peace. The Soviet Union charged that the United
States was actively assisting reactionary and Fascist elements in Hungary
and that Soviet troops already stationed in Hungary had simply gone to the
aid of the Hungarian government, at its request, to restore order. Claims by
Western governments that the rights of Hungarians were being violated
was merely a smokescreen by which Western governments hoped to interfere in the sovereign affairs of the free people of Hungary.

Messages to the world by Imre Nagy indicated that the Soviet version of
events in Hungary was at odds with the reality of repression and violence
against Hungarians by Soviet forces, and the intervention of even more Soviet forces on 1 November reaffirmed the validity of this view. At further
meetings of the Security Council, Western governments condemned the
use of force by the Soviet Union, which responded that it was ready to withdraw all its forces at the request of the legitimate government of Hungary.
This contradicted squarely the 1 November appeal of the Nagy regime. The
Soviet Union persisted in denying any further intervention by its forces,
pointing out that this was merely a ruse concocted by Western powers to divert attention from the British and French aggression in the Middle East
that had commenced on 29 October. A U.S.-sponsored resolution was submitted on 3 November that called upon the Soviet Union to desist from further military intervention and to withdraw its forces. The resolution also
reaffirmed Hungary's right to independence and called upon the mobilization of humanitarian assistance. The resolution was vetoed by the Soviet
Union on 3 November, and the Council then called upon the General Assembly to hold a special emergency session to consider the Hungarian situation.

The General Assembly met the following day to take up consideration of
the Hungarian crisis. Despite Soviet opposition, the matter was placed on
the agenda, and after brief debate, a revised and amended version of the vetoed Security Council resolution was adopted by a roll-call vote of 50 to 8
with 15 abstentions. In subsequent days the General Assembly passed resolutions calling for the Soviet Union and Hungary to cease interfering with
the provision of humanitarian aid to the people of Hungary, calling upon
the UNHCR to coordinate emergency assistance for fleeing Hungarian refugees, and calling upon UN member states to assist countries bordering
Hungary who were affected by the influx of refugees.

The failure of the United Nations to resist the Soviet intervention into
Hungary and the increasingly brutal crackdown that occurred in Hungary
against all dissident activities resulted in subsequent weeks and months in
a steady stream of Hungarian refugees. In the week of 20–26 November

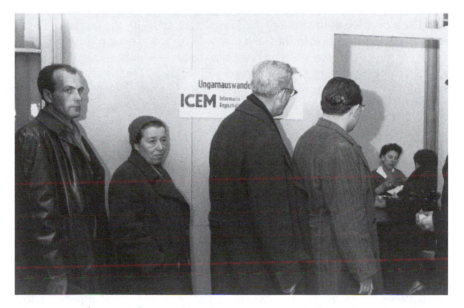

Hungarian refugees seeking asylum in Vienna, Austria, in December 1956 line up to register for resettlement and assistance. The Inter-governmental Committee for European Migration (ICEM) together with the UN High Commissioner for Refugees worked diligently to meet the needs of Hungarian refugees. UN/DPI Photo

alone, about 46,000 Hungarian refugees fled into Austria. Austria and Yugoslavia together received about 200,000 Hungarians during the crisis. In addition to the UNHCR, which coordinated relief aid to refugees, the International Committee of the Red Cross worked with the Hungarian Red Cross to deliver assistance inside Hungary. The Food and Agriculture Organization monitored food needs inside Hungary, and the United Nations Children's Fund provided additional relief aid. Working with the UNHCR in Austria and Yugoslavia to cope with refugee needs was the Intergovernmental Committee for European Migration, which helped to pay transportation assistance for the nearly 120,000 Hungarian refugees who resettled in countries after first seeking asylum in Austria or Yugoslavia. The UNHCR also assisted in the repatriation of more than 5,000 refugees who voluntarily decided to return to Hungary.

OUTCOME OF THE DEBATE

The lack of will on the part of the Western powers to directly and militarily confront the Soviet Union in Hungary put an end to the idea championed in earlier years of the Cold War by U.S. Secretary of State John Foster Dulles, to roll back the forces of communism in Eastern Europe. The West was itself divided at the time of the Hungarian crisis by the fact of the British-French intervention in the Suez that was opposed by the United States. Under these circumstances, the West was in no position to threaten or use counterforce against the Soviet Union in Hungary. Tacitly, the Cold War settled down into a war of words as the West resigned itself to the reality of the Iron Curtain and to a policy of containing communism within its current borders rather than seeking the liberation of Soviet client states. The UN General Assembly passed numerous resolutions concerning the situation in Hungary in subsequent years. In November 1959, however, the Hungarian government announced that Russian troops would be permitted to remain as long as the Hungarian government deemed necessary.

The one area in which Western cooperation had shown great resolve was in the handling of the refugee situation from Hungary. International agencies, such as the UNHCR, which had been established as temporary stop-gap means of resettling post–World War II refugees and displaced persons, now became major players as providers of emergency assistance and protection to refugees. The efficient response by the humanitarian agencies, especially the UNHCR, assured its survival as an increasingly important and active UN humanitarian agency.

Not until the collapse of communism in Eastern Europe in 1989 did Hungarians enjoy full and complete independence from Soviet hegemony. In subsequent years they rejected communism in favor of democratic government, and in 1999, Hungary was admitted to membership in the North Atlantic Treaty Organization, an ironically symbolic act of defiance against their former Russian mentors.

See also Membership and Representation Questions (Debate 11); Refugees and Stateless Persons (Debate 4).

FOR FURTHER READING

Brzezinski, Zbigniew. *The Soviet Bloc: Unity and Conflict*. New York: Praeger, 1961.
Litvan, Gyorgy. *The Hungarian Revolution of 1956: Reform, Revolt and Repression 1953–1963*. New York: Addison-Wesley, 1996.
Marrus, Michael. *The Unwanted: European Refugees in the Twentieth Century*. New York: Oxford University Press, 1985.
Stokes, Gale, ed. *From Stalinism to Pluralism: A Documentary History of Eastern Europe since 1945*. New York: Oxford University Press, 1981.
Sugar, Peter, et al. *A History of Hungary*. Bloomington: Indiana University Press, 1994.
UN Yearbook, 1956.

Congo Crisis (1960)

SIGNIFICANCE OF THE ISSUE

For the first time since Korea, UN peacekeeping activities in the Congo crisis extended into peacemaking and the use of force in a complicated postcolonial struggle among political forces in this newly independent country. Until 1990 the Congo Operation was the largest and most expensive as well as most controversial deployment of forces. Although the United Nations Operation in the Congo (ONUC) was authorized by the Security Council, secretary-general Dag Hammarskjöld exercised considerable authority in its deployment, angering the Soviet Union, which attacked the office of secretary-general. Hammarskjöld died in a plane crash in the Congo in 1961. The General Assembly held an emergency session on the crisis in the Congo and played a part with the Security Council in shaping the ONUC mission. The expanded role ONUC took, in large part opposed by the Soviet Union, led to the latter's refusal to participate or to pay for its portion of ONUC expenses, leading to a major UN financial crisis in 1963–1964. Still, the four-year ONUC operation did succeed in holding the Congo together.

BACKGROUND TO THE DEBATE

The Belgian Congo was a colony little prepared for the independence it was suddenly granted on 30 June 1960. Held by Belgium since 1885, first as a personal property of King Leopold, then placed under the authority of the Belgian government after reports of the scandalous treatment of Congolese laborers in the mining industry in 1908, the Congo faced independence as a large, unintegrated, ethnically diverse population spread out over a large area and led by divided elites. In the two years preceding independence a total of ten political parties, many based explicitly on ethnic or regional claims, emerged. No consensus existed among these competing parties regarding what the appropriate form of government should be or how the new country should orient its affairs toward Belgium. Ideology also divided the various leaders of the country, with some being pro-Western and others professing socialist and Marxist leanings. Moreover, the mineral-rich country was experiencing economic recession. Riots in Leopoldville in 1959 proved an ominous harbinger of things to come.

From the outset of independence, political differences among leaders contributed to the Congo's instability. Joseph Kasavubu served as president and Patrice Lumumba as prime minister. The armed forces mutinied on 5 July, just days after independence and tribal violence flared up against Belgian officials, causing a mass exodus of Belgian administrators, leaving the country at an economic and administrative standstill. Belgium intervened to protect its nationals and other foreigners and to restore order in mineral-rich Katanga province, where Moise Tshombe declared a separate independence on 11 July. Kasavubu and Lumumba called for a withdrawal of Belgian forces. Tshombe welcomed the Belgian presence, but his declaration of Katangan independence was opposed by both Lumumba and Kasavubu. In the midst of this confusion, Lumumba and Kasavubu sent a telegram to Secretary-General Dag Hammarskjöld asking for UN intervention to restore order to the fledgling country. Hammarskjöld notified the UN Security Council, which adpted a resolution on 14 July calling for a withdrawal of Belgian forces and authorizing the secretary-general to provide such military and technical assistance as necessary to help the government of the Congo restore order. The resolution, though commanding the support of the Council, survived amendments by the Soviet Union, which would have condemned Belgium and offered military assistance to African member states. These minor differences between the majority of the Council and the Soviet Union signified a difference in policy and ideology that would later grow into major points of controversy. Using the authority vested in him under the resolution, Hammarskjöld established the ONUC to secure the withdrawal of Belgian forces, to maintain law and order, to assist the government of the Congo in overcoming its constitutional crisis, to deal with the Katanga secession, and to provide technical assistance. Both military and civilian operations were planned to cope with the growing crisis. The first UN contingents from Tunisia and Ghana entered the Congo on 15 July, and within a month, the number of UN forces had grown to over 14,000. The ONUC presence would prove to be a long and arduous one, given the complicated and fluid internal and international situation.

HISTORY OF THE DEBATE

The ONUC forces achieved one of their major goals within two months, as Belgian troops cooperated with the arriving UN forces and gradually withdrew. However, entry of UN forces into Katanga proved to be controversial. Lumumba demanded that they assist him in crushing the secessionist efforts of Tshombe forces, but this, Hammarskjöld held, would violate ONUC's mandate, a position later affirmed on 9 August by the Security Council, which wished to avoid using force in internal conflicts. Belgium cooperated with the peaceful intervention of ONUC forces into Katanga, but an angry Lumumba refused to cooperate with Hammarskjöld. This was followed on 5 September by a constitutional crisis in which Kasavubu and Lumumba issued pronouncements of mutual dismissal. Amid the confusion, Army Chief of Staff Colonel Joseph Mobutu seized power and arrested Lumumba. For nearly a year, no officially recognized government existed for the United Nations to deal with, and rival governments began to emerge. The UN Security Council failed, owing to ideological differences, to decide on a course of action, and the UN General Assembly convened an emergency special session from 17 September to 20 September. It called upon a peaceful resolution of the dispute, established a Conciliation Commission to that end, and called upon foreign powers to refrain from providing military assistance to any parties to the Congolese conflict.

Complicating the Congolese drama in late November 1960 through January 1961 was the flight of Lumumba from his house arrest where he at least enjoyed protection by UN forces, his capture by Congolese troops on 1 December, and his transfer to Katanga in January 1961, where he was murdered. These events, which the Security Council was helpless to prevent, caused the Soviet Union in February to demand the dismissal of Hammarskjöld and to assert their refusal to acknowledge him as secretary-general. They even proposed a complete reorganization of the Secretariat in the form of a three-member (troika) executive position, in which the veto could be exercised within the Secretariat. This troika proposal found no support among the majority of member states, which affirmed their support for Hammarskjöld and for the Congo operation.

In the meantime, Mobutu and Kasavubu asserted control in Leopoldville (now Kinshasa), the capital of the Congo, and constituted the main government recognized by most other states. However, Antoine Gizenga, a supporter of Lumumba and a socialist, held control of Stanleyville (now Kisangani) in the East and claimed national jurisdiction. The Soviet Union and several African countries recognized Gizenga's as the legitimate government of the country and on this central issue turned the dispute between the Soviet Union and the Western powers on the Security Council. The Soviet Union and some African countries with forces in ONUC withdrew their forces in protest over the United Nations' recognition of the Kasavuvu-Mobutu regime and its failure to recognize the Lumumba-Gizenga faction. Then there was Katanga itself, where Tshombe continued to claim sovereignty, without making claims to authority over the nation as a whole. To enforce his secessionist claims, Tshombe retained

Belgian mercenaries, which clashed with ONUC forces in August and September of 1961. Albert Kalonji in Kasai province also sought to achieve autonomy from the Congo. ONUC worked diligently in this complicated situation to get contending parties to negotiate their differences. Eventually a national unity government was proclaimed on 2 August 1961 with Cyrille Adoula as premier. Gizenga and Tshombe continued to offer resistance to this government. Gizenga, however, was censured and later apprehended by the government. Tshombe proved to be a more formidable adversary to the United Nations. Hammarskjöld arranged to meet with him personally after ONUC units clashed with Tshombe's mercenary forces in August and September, but Hammarskjöld and seven members of his staff were killed when their plane crashed on 17 September en route to the meeting. Negotiations proceeded nonetheless, and a cease-fire was reached between ONUC and Tshombe just three days later. This agreement was frequently violated by Tshombe's forces, driving the Security Council on 24 November 1961 to authorize the new secretary-general, U Thant, to use force to ensure the cessation of mercenary activity. Fighting resumed in Katanga in December, with ONUC forces making substantial gains. Further peace negotiations were held, but instability continued throughout 1962 as efforts to arrange a national unity plan were redoubled. Tshombe eventually agreed to end the Katanga secession in January 1963, after reneging on many similar previous promises, and in the weeks that followed, ONUC forces entered the remaining secessionist strongholds. The secession came to an end offcially on 4 February 1963, but ONUC forces remained in the Congo until 30 June 1964 at the request of the Congolese government, which sought ongoing UN help in maintaining law and order in the country.

OUTCOME OF THE DEBATE

Repercussions of the Congo crisis were numerous and significant. Although the ONUC forces had secured the withdrawal of Belgian forces and the eventual unity of the Congo, while civilian operations had provided much needed humanitarian relief to refugees and persons displaced by the civil conflict, instabilities continued in the Congo in subsequent years. Indeed, in the month after the withdrawal of UN forces, rebellion prevailed in much of the eastern part of the Congo, including Stanleyville. There rebel groups held a thousand foreign nationals hostage in November 1964, precipitating a joint U.S.-Belgian intervention to secure their release. A number of African member states and East bloc countries demanded that the Security Council meet to discuss this U.S.-Belgian action, which they viewed as an unwarranted intervention in African affairs, despite the fact that the Congolese government had authorized the action. The government of the Congo countered with a demand that the Council consider the problem of

Lieutenant General Sean Mckeown, commander of the United Nations Operation in the Congo (ONUC), bids farewell to an Ethiopian contingent at Stanleyville, Congo, on 5 March 1962. UN/DPI Photo

foreign assistance to the rebel groups. The Council called for an end to all foreign interference in the Congo, to a withdrawal of mercenaries, and to support of the Organization of African Unity as a means of promoting stability in the Congo. This hope was not immediately realized, as governmental instability continued. Kasavubu, who had appointed Tshombe prime minister in 1964, removed him in 1965 shortly before he, himself, was overthrown by Joseph Mobutu. Mobutu, who renamed the Congo as Zaire in 1971, began a more than thirty-year reign as the nation's head of state. His authoritarian style brought some stability to Zaire, punctuated by civil disturbances in the Shaba region (formerly Katanga). Eventually, however, civil war resumed in the late 1990s, and Mobutu was ousted in 1997 by rebel forces from Eastern Zaire. But civil war continued into the late 1990s as Zaire, now renamed the Democratic Republic of the Congo, became immersed in a civil war of continent-wide involvement.

Apart from the ongoing political woes of the Congo, which were not permanently settled by the UN intervention, a financial crisis over funding of the ONUC operation emerged in 1963, as the Soviet Union refused to pay its share of the peacekeeping expenses. The Soviet Union believed that the entire operation had been illegally hijacked by the Western powers in the General Assembly and by the secretary-general. Its socialist allies in the Congo had been murdered or defeated, and it was in no mood to pay for operations to which it did not fully consent. This crisis was eventually re-solved by the General Assembly, which placed UN peacekeeping operations on an ad hoc voluntary basis in subsequent years. The United Nations would be much more careful in subsequent peacekeeping opera-tions not to become mired down in domestic disputes and civil wars. Peacekeeping operations were once again largely recaptured by the Secu-rity Council, which during the next two and a half decades only authorized seven peacekeeping or peace observation operations before the explosion of renewed UN peacekeeping activities associated with the end of the Cold War.

See also Rwandan Civil War (Debate 49); UN Financing Crisis (Debate 20).

FOR FURTHER READING

Bennett, A. LeRoy. *International Organizations: Principles and Issues*. Englewood Cliffs, NJ: Prentice-Hall, 1995.
Bobb, F. Scott. *Historical Dictionary of the Democratic Republic of the Congo (Zaire)*. 2nd ed. Lanham, MD: Scarecrow Press, 1999.
Everyman's United Nations. New York: UN Office of Public Information, 1968.
Hochschild, Adam. *King Leopold's Ghost: A Story of Greed, Terror and Heroism in Co-lonial Africa*. New York: Houghton Mifflin, 1998.
LeFever, Ernest W. *Crisis in the Congo: A United Nations Force in Action*. Washing-ton, DC: Brookings Institution, 1965.
Lemarchand, Rene. *Political Awakening in the Belgian Congo*. New York: Green-wood Press, 1982.
Meditz, Sandra W., et al. *Zaire: A Country Study*. Washington, DC: American Uni-versity Area Handbook Series, 1995.
Schatzberg, Michael G. *Mobutu of Chaos: The United States and Zaire, 1960–1990*. Lanham, MD: University Press of America, 1991.

Decolonization (1960)

SIGNIFICANCE OF THE ISSUE

The idea of self-determination of peoples and states is enshrined as one of the basic purposes and principles of the UN Charter and in the formation of the Trusteeship Council and in the Declaration on Non-Self-Governing Territories. The pace of decolonization, however, was a matter of much contentious debate both in the relations of colonizing countries and colonized peoples and, increasingly, in the late 1950s and early 1960s at the United Nations as well, where it was often entangled with claims and counterclaims of imperialism between Communist bloc and Western countries. Regardless of the contentiousness of the debate, the inexorable trend throughout the life of the United Nations was for the progressive achievement of independence of non-self-governing territories and their eventual membership in the international community.

BACKGROUND TO THE DEBATE

In one sense, the roots of the decolonization process go back to the formation of the international state system as reflected in the Peace of Westphalia among European states in 1648, which ended the bloody Thirty Years War and reorganized the international sovereign state system. Implicit in the emergence of the idea of sovereignty, including the independence and equality of states, was the notion that the European states extending mutual recognition to one another constituted the original states and that any other peoples seeking admission into the state system would require the recognition of existing states. In a sense, then, the rest of the world was regarded as subject to discovery and occupation by European governments. The fact that Europe rapidly expanded its exploration of the world and that its economy rapidly industrialized gave European governments an advantage in dealing with the less powerful governing systems found in the New World, Asia, and Africa, areas that in due course were al-most completely colonized by European countries.

To gain independence from European colonial occupation, colonized peoples had either to fight wars of independence or to seek through more peaceful means recognition as an independent state from the mother coun-try and other European governments. Many countries of the New World, including the United States, and later several Latin American states fought successful revolutionary wars of independence and became full-fledged members of the international community after being recognized by exist-ing European states. Some areas in Southern Africa and in Asia labored un-der colonial control for centuries, while most of Africa was not colonized until the end of the nineteenth century.

Colonization, though not equally brutal or repressive in its many expres-sions, was almost always resented by the colonized peoples, and as the in-ternational community entered the twentieth century, calls for independence grew more common in many colonial areas. This process was hastened by the effects of World War I, after which the League of Na-tions established a mandate system to supervise the administration of colo-nies stripped from the Axis powers and given to various victorious Allied powers to administer as sacred trusts for the benefit of native populations. Although the emphasis of the mandate system related to opening colonial administration to external scrutiny and to ensuring the imposition of en-lightened policies of colonial administration, it did not create an actual right to independence.

After World War II and the establishment of the UN Trusteeship Council in 1945, the mandate idea was extended. Any territory placed under the su-pervision of the Trusteeship Council would, ipso facto, be eligible for even-tual self-government and independence. This idea was strongly favored by the United States. European colonial powers agreed to the idea as long as it only applied to those territories grandfathered in from the League mandate system or other enemy territories seized by the Allies during World War II and placed under the trusteeship arrangement. Other colonies held by the victorious Allied states of Europe still fell under the control of the coloniz-ing country. However, Chapter XI of the UN Charter, the Declaration Re-garding Non-Self-Governing Territories, while leaving the ultimate question of independence to the discretion of the colonizing state, did call upon the administering powers to respect the local culture, to work toward self-government at a pace consistent with the particular circumstances of each territory, to promote economic development, and to transmit reports to the secretary-general concerning the economic, social, and educational situation in territories under their administration. The UN system repre-sented an advance over the League mandate system, and the idea of pro-moting "respect for the principle of equal rights and self-determination of peoples" was included as a purpose of the UN Charter. Still, all efforts by various governments in the early years of the United Nations to convert this principle of self-determination into a right were resisted by the major powers.

HISTORY OF THE DEBATE

However, the heyday of colonialism was largely spent by the end of World War II, and momentum began to grow toward the granting of independence toward former colonies typically, but not always, after a significant period of preparation. By the late 1950s most of the European countries had come to view the colonial systems as a burden, and the claim of colonial peoples to liberty and self-determination could not much longer be denied by parliamentary democracies in Europe that subscribed to such principles in their own political life. Thus, during the first fifteen years of the United Nations, most of the activity centered on the operations of the Trusteeship Council, where the movement toward independence was required, and on the collection of information concerning colonial territories where granting of independence was not required. In 1947 the General Assembly set up an Ad Hoc Committee on Information to examine reports required by the Declaration on Non-Self-Governing Territories. Although the committee was routinely renewed for periods of three years after 1949, efforts by noncolonial powers to establish it as a permanent body were rebuffed by the colonial powers, and it did not have the authority to comment on political or constitutional developments.

This situation changed dramatically in the early 1960s after the adoption by the UN General Assembly of the Declaration on the Granting of Independence to Colonial Countries and Peoples, which represented a watershed development of UN involvement in the decolonization process. The success of the Declaration was in part a reflection of the fatigue of the colonial powers, who had already moved aggressively to grant independence to dozens of former territorial dependencies and who no longer sought to stall efforts by these newly independent states to accelerate the process of decolonization. With former colonies becoming more numerous and more strident about self-determination for colonial peoples, the tone and pace of UN action in this arena changed and quickened.

The decade of the 1960s is often referred to as the decade of decolonization and independence. A total of forty-two countries gained independence and UN membership during the 1960s, more than any single decade in the history of the United Nations. In 1960 alone, seventeen countries gained independence and admission as UN members. Coincidentally, in that same year, Nikita Khrushchev, chairman of the Communist Party in the Soviet Union, submitted a draft declaration on the granting of independence to colonial peoples for consideration of the UN General Assembly. The Soviet proposal was exceptionally radical in that it called for the immediate and

Honoring the inclusion of seventeen new member states to the United Nations, a flag-raising ceremony is led by Secretary-General Dag Hammarskjöld on 30 September 1960. Most of the states admitted were former colonies in Africa. UN/DPI Photo M. Bardy

complete liberation of all colonial peoples from foreign domination. Khrushchev used the submission of the draft resolution as an opportunity to cast the Soviet Union as the true friend and ally of all colonial peoples and thus to score propaganda points against the West. The Soviet proposal met resistance. The representative of the United Kingdom expressed shock at the political nature of the Soviet proposal and at the hatred it manifested and the harm it would bring to colonial peoples. At the same time the United Kingdom accused the Soviet Union of hypocrisy, reminding the assembled delegates that the Soviet Union had forcibly annexed Latvia, Lithuania, and Estonia. It called for caution and prudence in the progress of colonial areas toward independence, especially in areas with populations less than 100,000. Western governments, including the United States, would sound this theme in subsequent years, noting that the preoccupation of newly independent members and of UN bodies with the fast-disappearing forms of Western colonial practice obscured the more ominous and threatening Communist colonial empire where democracy was systematically excluded or exterminated. The Soviet Union routinely charged that the United States was itself a colonial power, even as the United States accused the Soviet Union of colonial practices. This rhetoric continued for many years as the Soviet Union sought to cast itself as the true champion of independence for peoples of the developing world.

However, the representatives of developing and recently independent countries recognized the unfeasibility of the Soviet proposal. Thus on the same day that the Soviet proposal was introduced, Cambodia introduced a more moderate proposal on behalf of twenty-six African and Asian nations, which eventually attracted the sponsorship of forty-three developing countries (Afghanistan, Burma, Cambodia, Cameroon, Central African Republic, Ceylon, Chad, Congo [Brazzaville], Congo [Leopoldville], Cyprus, Dahomey, Ethiopia, Federation of Malaya, Gabon, Ghana, Guinea, India, Indonesia, Iran, Iraq, Ivory Coast, Jordan, Laos, Lebanon, Liberia, Libya, Madagascar, Mali, Morocco, Nepal, Niger, Nigeria, Pakistan, Philippines, Saudi Arabia, Senegal, Somalia, Sudan, Togo, Tunisia, Turkey, United Arab Republic, and Upper Volta). Many of these countries, although expressing gratitude to the Soviet Union for taking the initiative on the colonial question, pointed out that they did not want the question to become a matter of East-West dispute. Many acknowledged that much progress had already been made under the Trusteeship and Non-Self-Governing Territory provisions of the Charter, but they also expressed frustration that the process had often been too slow and cautious. They observed that economic freedom should accompany political independence. Various Latin American states expressed their concurrence in the idea that granting of independence to colonial areas should be encouraged and broadened. Representatives of the Eastern bloc states lined up predictably behind the Soviet proposal but eventually supported the forty-three–power resolution of the nonaligned countries. The representative of the United States pointed out that thirty-four countries had already achieved independence under Article 73 of the Charter, that the end of the colonial system was a certainty, but that care should be taken in the planning and granting of independence. The United States also attacked the Soviet Union as the purveyor of a "new and lethal" colonialism. Several countries, including Argentina, Israel, Portugal, France, and South Africa, countered charges made against them by the Soviet Union.

The Soviet Union, seeing that its resolution had little support, moved to amend the forty-three-power resolution to ensure that all colonial peoples would be granted independence no later than the end of 1961 and to grant the General Assembly the right to consider implementation of the declaration at its next session. The Assembly rejected the Soviet draft resolution as well as its amendments to the forty-three-power draft on 14 December 1960. The forty-three-power Resolution was adopted as resolution 1514 (XV) by a vote of 89 to 0 with 9 abstentions (Australia, Belgium, Dominican Republic, France, Portugal, Spain, Union of South Africa, United Kingdom, United States).

The Declaration stated that alien domination, subjection, or exploitation was a violation of human rights, that all peoples have the right to self-determination regardless of the inadequacy of their preparedness for independence, that armed resistance to independence movements should cease, and that immediate steps should be taken to enable territories to secure their independence. In 1961, the Assembly, noting that little progress had been achieved in the previous year regarding implementation of the Declaration, established a Special Committee to examine implementation progress. In 1962 the Committee was enlarged from seventeen to twenty-four members and became known as the Special Committee of Twenty-Four. This body, which later absorbed all other UN committees established to deal with colonial territories other than those administered by the Trusteeship Council and the Special Committee against Apartheid, was influential in making requests, appeals, and recommendations to colonial authorities regarding the granting of independence, although it had no power to enforce them under international law. Nonetheless, twenty-two countries obtained independence under the committee's auspices in the 1960s alone, and by the mid-1970s, most colonial areas had achieved their independence, with the exception of the micro-states whose size and population presented difficulties. The debates in the United Nations turned in the late 1960s and early 1970s on the circumstances of individual territories, with the most controversial areas being those in Southern Africa, including Angola, Mozambique, Namibia, and Rhodesia. As these countries gained independence in the 1970s, along with many micro-states, anticolonial rhetoric gradually focused on South Africa, which after the reforms of the late 1980s also became an object of less controversy.

OUTCOME OF THE DEBATE

By the 1980s, even the micro-states were achieving UN membership, and most other new members came into existence with the demise of Communism and the disintegration of states in the communist bloc, including the Soviet Union, Yugoslavia, and Czechoslovakia. By the end of the 1990s the United Nations was nearing its goal of universal membership. All of the Trust Territories earned independence by the early 1990s, and although territorial dependencies continue to exist, both the ideological pressure and the anticolonial rhetoric were substantially reduced in UN debates regarding such areas. In 1993, the Special Political Committee of the General Assembly, which had dealt with issues such as apartheid, racism, and decolonization issues, was collapsed into the Fourth Main Committee, which had previously dealt with trusteeship issues. The new committee became known as the Special Political and Decolonization Committee.

The decolonization debate is one that, though marked by much heat and contention, has largely spent itself, after having largely achieved the Charter's goal of promoting respect for the equality and self-determination of peoples. Major related issues now concern the treatment of indigenous peoples under the administration of independent states and the likelihood that most new claims for self-determination will come at the expense of the territorial integrity of existing states, a matter that the United Nations is not well suited in principle to address.

See also Apartheid (Debate 14); Arab-Israeli Dispute (Debate 6); Congo Crisis (Debate 17); India-Pakistan Dispute (Debate 7); Membership and Representation Questions (Debate 11); Rhodesian Question (Debate 21); Southwest Africa (Namibia) Dispute (Debate 3).

FOR FURTHER READING

Everyman's United Nations. New York: United Nations Office of Public Information, 1968.

Furedi, Frank. *Colonial Wars and the Politics of Third World Nationalism*. New York: I. B. Tauris, 1994.

Jacobs, Philip E., Alexine L. Atherton, and Arthur M. Wallenstein. *The Dynamics of International Organization*. Homewood, IL: Dorsey Press, 1972.

UN Yearbook, 1960.

Narcotics Control (1961)

SIGNIFICANCE OF THE ISSUE

The human costs of narcotics usage around the world are huge and frightening in terms of loss of health, loss of productivity, and loss of lives. Moreover, governments spend huge sums of money in combating drug trafficking and usage through their criminal justice systems. Much money can be made in drug trafficking, too, but unlike other economic activities, the result is destructive rather than productive. The United Nations has been involved in the area of narcotics control since its inception, having inherited the League of Nations efforts in this area, but unified and centralized efforts to tackle the growing problem of drug trafficking and drug usage began in 1961 with the Enactment of the Single Convention on Narcotic Drugs and the creation of the International Narcotics Control Board (INCB). Since then, UN efforts to coordinate international policy and efforts at narcotics control have been intensified.

BACKGROUND TO THE ISSUE

In the early phases of international efforts to control drugs that began in 1909 with the establishment of the International Opium Commission in Shanghai, China, where the United States and twelve other world powers met to discuss means of controlling the opium trade, the main issue facing governments was how to control the production, trade, and use of opium, a natural product, in order to ensure its use only for legitimate medicinal purposes. In 1912, when the Hague Opium Convention was signed as a result of the Shanghai conference, governments were faced with regulation of a mere handful of natural narcotic substances. In the 1990s, nearly 40 natural substances required similar control, along with almost 250 synthetic substances. Thus, during the twentieth century the problem of drug use has grown more complex, and so have efforts to control their production, trade,

Part of the global battle against narcotics trafficking begins with convincing producing countries to develop alternate crops. Here a member of the Hmong hill tribe
in northern Thailand is shown near a field that once grew poppies. Under a UNDCP
project farmers voluntarily gave up opium poppy production. UN/DPI Photo
J. Sailas

and use. In 1912, governments attacked the problem in the Hague Opium
Convention by agreeing to limit the manufacture, trade, and use of narcotics for medical purposes. They agreed to restrict use by closing opium dens,
penalizing possession of narcotics, and punishing those who sold narcotics
to unauthorized persons. This essentially three-pronged attack would
mark international efforts: (1) controlling production and availability of illegal narcotics, (2) controlling the trafficking of narcotics, and (3) controlling the use of narcotics. In the 1990s, control over money laundering, an
aspect of control of trafficking, was also strengthened.

In 1925, under the aegis of the League of Nations, the Permanent Central
Narcotics Board (PCNB) was established at Geneva, bringing narcotic substances other than opium under its jurisdiction. In 1931 a Convention for
Limiting the Manufacture and Regulating the Distribution of Narcotic
Drugs was adopted in Geneva, in an effort to impose on governments a system for estimating import needs for legitimate uses of narcotics in science
or medicine. A Drug Supervisory Body was created to administer and coordinate these international efforts. Illegal trafficking in narcotics continued

despite these efforts, and so governments attempted to strengthen control over trafficking itself by punishing those apprehended in the illegal trafficking of narcotics. This effort culminated in the ultimately abortive 1936 Convention for Suppression of the Illicit Traffic in Dangerous Drugs. As in all such attempts at national cooperation, the key is for governments to develop and enforce similar legal standards and punishments within their own national jurisdiction and to develop extradition policies that will ensure cooperation of governments in the prosecution and punishment of individuals engaged in criminal activity. In 1923 the creation in Paris of INTERPOL (International Police Organization), an intergovernmental body of cooperation among the police organizations of countries, represented a major step in advancing national efforts in sharing information on policing matters. A major function of INTERPOL is international narcotics control.

Thus, long before the establishment of the United Nations, governments were aware of and active in efforts to regulate the international narcotics trade. In 1946, at its first session, the UN General Assembly directed the Economic and Social Council (ECOSOC) to establish the United Nations Commission for Narcotic Drugs (UNCND) and a Drug Supervisory Body. In Geneva, the United Nations maintained a Narcotic Drug Laboratory for purposes of identifying confiscated drugs, and in 1948, the UN General Assembly expanded the meaning of the term "narcotics" to include a list of other natural and synthetic substances that the World Health Organization (WHO) identified as having addictive qualities. In 1953 an Opium Protocol was signed by which member states attempted to limit the legal production of narcotics, so as not to overproduce such substances, and to control the amount of stocks governments could store. At the same time, the Protocol limited production of opium for export to just seven exporting countries, Bulgaria, Greece, India, Iran, Turkey, the Soviet Union, and Yugoslavia. This agreement did not enter force until 1963, but with it, and several other control measures adopted by governments, a hodgepodge of control efforts complicated enforcement and control. Each drug treaty or protocol had different signatories. Different control bodies for enforcement existed. Some conventions contained stricter measures of control. Some substances were subject to stricter regulation than others. To address these problems, the UN General Assembly adopted the Single Convention on Narcotic Drugs in 1961.

HISTORY OF THE DEBATE

With the establishment of the Single Convention on Narcotic Drugs in 1961, governments took a giant step through the United Nations toward a more effective international regime of narcotics control. The INCB became the single administrative body for international supervision of narcotics regulation. This agreement entered into force in 1964 and became the focal point of the control of narcotics. The UNCND took the lead in preparing drafts of the Single Convention, submitting them to governments and revising the draft in light of their suggestions. In 1961 an international conference was called to finalize the draft agreement. Among its provisions was a new international restriction on states, other than those currently engaged in the legal production of opium, from entering the trade without ECOSOC permission. The treaty put all narcotics, not merely opium, under international control and supervision. Governments were required to extend licensing and recording procedures to all drugs. The supervisory efforts of the INCB extended for the first time not just to imports, as had been the case under the PNCB, but to exports of narcotics as well. The desire at the drafting stage of the Single Convention to apply export restrictions on nonsignatory states, however, was vigorously opposed by the Soviet Union and Eastern European states at the international conference. Here politics came into play because Communist China had not been invited to the final drafting conference, and Communist governments insisted no system could be imposed on governments that had not participated in or agreed to the provisions of the agreement.

Another major development in the control of narcotics was that many of the countries participating in the Single Convention on Narcotic Drugs were newly independent and lacked the experience and capacity to effectively implement treaty provisions. At the same time, for many developing countries, where poverty was pervasive, narcotics control, though theoretically desirable, was a low priority in comparison to other, more pressing issues of economic development. Thus, many countries were unlikely or even reluctant to seek special funds or technical assistance to develop their national capacity for regulating the production and trafficking of narcotics. To address this problem, the United Nations offers special technical assistance to governments wishing to take advantage of it. The system is a voluntary one and involves the sending of experts to advise governments about narcotics control issues, the provision of training programs for national administrative officials, and demonstration projects. Several UN specialized agencies such as WHO and the Food and Agriculture Organization (FAO) are involved in sponsoring such programs, along with INTERPOL. WHO is involved in treatment programs for addicts, and the FAO has developed innovative programs whereby governments develop crops to replace narcotics production so as to maintain a capacity to obtain revenues in international trade.

Further efforts by the United Nations to broaden and strengthen narcotics control took place in the early 1970s. In 1971 the Convention on Psychotropic Substances was adopted by an International Conference, thus extending international regulation to hallucinogens such as LSD as well as amphetamines and barbiturates. Also established in 1971 was a voluntary United Nations Fund for Drug Abuse Control (UNFDAC) to assist governments in their efforts at narcotics control. In 1972 a Protocol to the 1961 Single Convention stressed the need for governments to develop programs for the treatment and rehabilitation of drug addicts.

Although governmental ratification of narcotics and psychotropical drug control agreements has seen a steady increase in national participation, the growth of drug production and usage increased dramatically during the 1970s and 1980s, as cocaine and marijuana outstripped usage of opium-based drugs such as heroin. In addition, the use of sedative-type substances has also increased enormously. Opium-based drugs now constitute one of the smallest percentages of global consumption, being surpassed in the 1980s by usage of sedatives, marijuana, amphetamines, hallucinogens, and cocaine. International awareness of the changes in the production, trafficking, and consumption of various illegal drugs led to a recognition of a need to attack the problem with a new sense of urgency in the late 1980s and early 1990s. In 1988, the UN Convention against Illicit Traffic in Narcotic Drugs and Psychotropic Substances was adopted. In 1990, the United Nations held a special session devoted to the International Drug Problem, establishing a new United Nations Drug Control Program (UNDCP) to assist countries in monitoring trends in drug production, consumption, and trafficking and in promoting the implementation of drug control treaties.

During the decades of expanded drug production and usage, governments, while attempting to cooperate, tended to view the drug problem through different lenses. In countries of the developed world, where a high percentage of drug users are found and where the wealth to consume drugs exists, there was a tendency to focus on the failure of developing countries to limit the supply side of production of illegal substances, such as marijuana and cocaine. On the other hand, countries such as Colombia, Mexico, China, Laos, Myanmar, Thailand, Afghanistan, Pakistan, and other countries of Central Asia, where opium or cocaine is produced, often accused the major drug-consuming countries such as the United States and the West European nations of failing to attack the problem from the demand side. International cooperation in the 1990s has urged all countries to attend to matters of both supply and demand for illegal drugs, and with UN assistance, many countries have begun successfully to limit production and control trafficking through seizure of drugs both prior to export and during the importation and sale of drugs. Programs to encourage the cultivation of alternative crops have also born fruit, as in Laos where coffee and asparagus production programs cut opium production dramatically. By the 1990s, concerted international efforts to control the epidemic levels of drug production and usage were beginning to pay off.

OUTCOME OF THE DEBATE

Efforts by countries to attack the problem of money laundering at the national level and through regional agreements in the late 1980s and early 1990s moved international cooperation in controlling the trafficking of drugs to a new level. In 1988 at the Basel Committee on Banking Regulations and Supervisory Practices and at the UN Convention against Illicit Traffic in Narcotic Drugs and Psychotropic Substances, steps were taken to cope with the issue of money laundering. Efforts intensified at the national and regional levels in subsequent years to prosecute money launderers. In 1997, the United Nations formally launched a Global Program against Money Laundering to assist governments in this area of narcotics control.

Increasingly governments have come to realize that effective control of production of drugs is not sufficient, and many new efforts to combat the demand side in consuming countries have taken place in the 1990s. This was one of the major issues of debate in the June 1998 General Assembly Special Session on Countering the World Drug Problem held in New York, which adopted a Declaration on the Guiding Principles of Drug Demand Reduction. The special session took particular notice of the problem of drug abuse among the world's youth, and it established target dates for the reduction of drug abuse. The UNDCP will exercise an overall monitoring and coordination of national and international efforts to this end. But as always in matters of international cooperation, governments themselves will need to devote resources in the renewed efforts to reduce production, illicit trafficking, and consumption of illegal drugs. Already the 1990s saw a leveling off of opium poppy production and a decrease in coca cultivation and production. Marijuana production, however, rose during the 1990s, as did use of synthetic drugs, a new area of major concern. It is clear, then, that the international community still has a lot of work to do before it can declare victory in the war on drugs.

See also Health (Debate 8).

FOR FURTHER READING

Jacob, Philip E., Alexine L. Atherton, and Arthur M. Wallenstein. *The Dynamics of International Organization*. Homewood, IL: Dorsey Press, 1972.

Lande, Adolf. "The Single Convention on Narcotic Drugs." *International Organization* (Autumn 1962): 776–798.

McAllister, William B. *Drug Diplomacy in the Twentieth Century*. London: Routledge, 1999.

Osmañczyk, Edmund Jan. *Encyclopedia of the United Nations and International Agreements*. London: Taylor and Francis, 1985.

UN Chronicles, 1998–1999.

UN Yearbooks, 1961, 1988, 1990.

Debate 20

UN Financing Crisis (1961)

SIGNIFICANCE OF THE ISSUE

The crisis of 1961–1965 over UN financing indicated deep divisions over the deployment and mandates of UN peacekeeping forces rooted in Cold War rivalry and the ideological struggle between Communist countries of the East bloc and Western democracies. It symbolized the difficulty of implementing the collective security provisions of the UN Charter in the climate of East-West tension and caused the United Nations to change for more than two decades the system by which it financed peacekeeping operations, removing these from the mandatory assessments to voluntary contributions undertaken on an ad hoc, case-by-case basis.

BACKGROUND TO THE DEBATE

Under the terms of Article 17 of the UN Charter, the General Assembly approves the budget of the organization. The article also provides that the expenses of the United Nations "shall be borne by the members as apportioned by the General Assembly." The predominance of the UN General Assembly in the budget process reflected the practice that had developed in the League of Nations, where the League Assembly gradually assumed complete control of the budget approval process from the League Council. The United States proposed at the Dumbarton Oaks Conference of the great powers that the UN General Assembly be responsible for determining the budget and procedures for apportionment of expenses. This was widely approved at the San Francisco Conference, and the only issue that attracted debate was whether the means of apportionment ought to be specified in the Charter itself or left to the collective wisdom of the General Assembly. The founding states opted for the latter. Each member state under Article 17 is obliged to pay its share of expenses.

Under the practice of the United Nations, the secretary-general prepares an annual budget for the organization and submits it to the Advisory Committee on Administrative Budgetary Questions prior to the opening of the regular annual session of the General Assembly. The General Assembly refers the budget proposal and the Advisory Committee's report to the Fifth Committee, which deliberates on matters of budget and administration. The Fifth Committee's decisions are then reported to the General Assembly, where they are discussed and must be ultimately approved. Prior to the move in the late 1980s toward consensus adoption of budget questions, votes on budgets were made by a two-thirds majority. The General Assembly also adopts annual resolutions to meet unforeseen or extraordinary expenses. These enable the secretary-general to incur expenses not otherwise approved in the regular budget. Such expenses arise when a council, commission, or other UN body establishes a new program or responds to an emergency situation not anticipated in the regular budget. Until 1962, the secretary-general had almost unlimited authority to incur expenses for such activities. But with the large expenditures incurred from the United Nations Emergency Force (UNEF) in the Middle East and from the United Nations Operation in the Congo (ONUC), the General Assembly decided to place limits on that authority.

The issue of how to apportion UN expenses among member states was also put by Article 17 in the hands of the General Assembly. The UN Preparatory Commission proposed that an expert committee be established to devise a method for apportionment based broadly on member state capacities to pay. At its first session in 1946, the UN General Assembly adopted its Rules of Procedure, which included a provision (Rule 158) for the creation of an expert Committee on Contributions. This body initially consisted of ten members but was enlarged by subsequent decisions of the General Assembly. Members are selected to three-year terms on the basis of broad geographical representation, personal qualifications, and experience. The Committee, under Rule 160, advises the General Assembly concerning the apportionment of expenses based broadly on the capacity of each member to pay, and scales for assessment are subject to general revision every three years, unless extraordinary circumstances intervene. The Committee also advises the Assembly on assessments to be fixed for new members, and it hears appeals from member states for changes of assessments.

Factors considered by the Committee on Contributions in recommending a scale of assessments included the national income of members, per capita income, economic dislocations resulting from World War II, and the ability of members to obtain foreign currency. Initially, the United States paid about 40 percent of the UN regular budget, although based on the proposed scale, it should have paid 50 percent. This was seen as too great a dependence on one member state. In 1957, the Assembly further decided that in principle no single member should contribute more than 30 percent.

Minimum contributions were also set for member states. In the 1950s, this was 0.04 percent of the budget, but with the growth of members and the inclusion of increasingly smaller countries into membership, the Assembly has reduced the minimum contribution to 0.01 percent of the overall budget. The U.S. contribution was also reduced to 25 percent. Still, throughout the entire history of the United Nations, fewer than 10 percent of the member states have contributed anywhere from about 70 to 90 percent of the budget. This discrepancy finally caused major donors to rebel in the 1980s and to demand consensus votes on the UN budget, a practice that continued into the 1990s.

A further issue complicating the apportionment of expenses is Article 19 of the Charter, which stipulates that a member state that is in "arrears in the payment of its financial contributions . . . shall have no vote in the General Assembly if the amount of its arrears equals or exceeds the amount of the contributions due from it for the preceding two full years." The article came into play when the Soviet Union refused to pay for the peacekeeping expenses of the ONUC forces deployed in the Congo in 1960 and subsequent years. It, together with another dozen countries that were delinquent on payments largely owing to the large peacekeeping budgets for both UNEF and ONUC, ran the risk of losing its General Assembly vote.

HISTORY OF THE DEBATE

Although discussion concerning the role of UN financing for peacekeeping operations can be traced back to the formation of UNEF I in 1956, the debate came to a head in 1961, after the secretary-general was authorized by the Security Council to deploy UN forces and civilian operations in the Congo crisis. In 1961, the General Assembly was notified by the Committee on Contributions that a number of states were in substantial arrears on payment of their contributions, owing in large part to the additional peacekeeping expenses. On 20 December, the General Assembly requested an advisory opinion of the International Court of Justice (ICJ) concerning whether peacekeeping operations fell under the requirements of Article 17 of the Charter. A year later the General Assembly decided to accept the ICJ's ruling that expenses for peacekeeping operations did indeed constitute expenses of the organization under Article 17. At the same time, the Assembly established a twenty-one-member Working Group on the Examination of the Administrative and Budgetary Procedures of the United Nations to study ways in which peacekeeping operations might be handled. The matter continued to fester, as some states claimed an inability and others an unwillingness to pay for peacekeeping expenses. To focus discussion on the matter the General Assembly called its Fourth Special Session, which met from 14 May to 17 June 1963.

In the general debate of UN financing of peacekeeping operations, the United States and a majority of other members backed the secretary-general's and the ICJ's view that peacekeeping initiatives, whether authorized by the Security Council, the General Assembly, or both, were expenses of the organization that should be apportioned according to the regular assessments. The United States was joined by Iceland, Iran, Lebanon, Libya, Senegal, Thailand, the United Kingdom, and thirty-five additional member states who sponsored a resolution reiterating the collective financial responsibility of all members for payment of UN expenses. But France refused to pay for expenses associated with the UNEF operation, arguing that the United Nations was moving inappropriately in the direction of creating a world government by trying to impose costs on unwilling members. The Soviet Union balked at paying for either UNEF or, especially, ONUC expenses. Other states joined them, arguing that only the Security Council, under a strict interpretation of the UN Charter, could authorize a peacekeeping action and that General Assembly action in the face of Security Council stalemate represented an usurpation of powers granted solely to the Security Council. Because both UNEF and the ONUC operations involved General Assembly infringements on Security Council prerogatives, they considered the operations illegal. Joining the Soviet Union in a refusal to pay any expenses associated with them were Bulgaria, Byelorussia, Cuba, Czechoslovakia, Hungary, Poland, and the Ukraine. They rejected both the ICJ advisory opinion and the General Assembly resolution of 1962 arguing that neither was binding on member states. The Soviet Union and its East bloc allies argued that all peacekeeping expenses should be assessed against the aggressors. In the case of UNEF, this would include France, Israel, and the United Kingdom, and in the case of the Congo, Belgium. The East bloc countries also announced their intention to refuse to pay for elements of the UN regular budget that they considered unjustifiable or badly administered.

Countries considering themselves the victims of aggression, such as Egypt in the Suez Crisis, objected to being required to pay for the costs of UN operations. Other countries, including several Latin American states, claimed that the best method for handling peacekeeping expenses was to place a heavier burden on the permanent members of the Security Council and reduce the burden on other states, who should nevertheless make smaller payments, or even token payments, depending on the capacity to pay.

The special session passed seven resolutions concerning the financial crisis. All of them were opposed by the Soviet Union and its Eastern bloc allies including Albania, Bulgaria, Byelorussia, Cuba, Czechoslovakia, Hungary, Mongolia, Poland, Romania, and the Ukraine. France joined in opposition to several of the resolutions, as did a small number of other countries. The first resolution, adopted by a vote of 92 to 11 with 3 abstentions, reiterated the collective financial responsibility of all members, called upon richer countries and permanent members of the Security Council to bear the greatest burden for peacekeeping, and called upon all members to make voluntary contributions within their means to pay. The second and third resolutions fixed an ad hoc method for paying for UNEF and ONUC expenses and identified those countries in an economically disadvantaged position, which would pay less than half their regular assessment on the bulk of the peacekeeping expenses. Other states were called upon to add to their regular assessment with further voluntary contributions. The fourth resolution, adopted by a vote of 79 to 12 (including the East bloc and France) with 17 abstentions, called upon members in arrears to make their payments. A fifth and sixth resolution authorized the secretary-general to continue issuing UN bonds to finance operations and to discuss the establishment of a Peace Fund to be established by voluntary contributions in order to provide the United Nations greater flexibility in meeting threats to peace and security. The latter proposal was sponsored by Cyprus, Ghana, the Ivory Coast, Nigeria, and Pakistan. Both resolutions were opposed by the East bloc countries and France. The last resolution called for the Working Group to continue its work and report to the General Assembly in subsequent sessions. Thus concluded the special session.

At its Eighteenth Session the General Assembly continued to finance peacekeeping operations on an ad hoc basis, and little progress was made on the resolution of the underlying dispute. A decision on the matter was postponed until the Working Group reported in 1964. In the meantime, however, several states, including the Soviet Union by the time the Nineteenth Session met in 1964, were already delinquent under Article 19, and France would become delinquent before the completion of the session. The Soviet Union threatened to leave the United Nations if the Article 19 sanction were imposed. For the only time in its history, the General Assembly held a voteless session to avoid a direct confrontation. All business was conducted by consensus, no votes were recorded on the General Assembly floor, and votes on issues lacking consensus were avoided. The delegation from Albania attempted to force the issue, by requiring votes, but the proposal was ignored by the president of the General Assembly, and the vast majority of members tacitly accepted the device as a means of doing business for that session. The following year, at the Twentieth Session, the United States reluctantly withdrew its insistence that states in arrears be denied their vote, allowing voting to resume in its normal fashion despite the ongoing refusal of member states to pay arrears. At the same session a Committee of Thirty-three was established to carry on the tasks of the Working Group. But its work and that of other succeeding committees failed to reach any resolution of the dispute.

OUTCOME OF THE DEBATE

Even while the debate on financing raged, the United Nations was called upon to address threats to international peace and security, and in doing so it gradually developed a policy of ad hoc responses to financing such operations. In 1962, the Netherlands and Indonesia agreed to share on an equal basis the costs of the United Nations Temporary Executive Authority (UNTEA) and Security Force dispatched by the General Assembly to monitor the situation in West Irian. In June 1963, Saudi Arabia and the United Arab Republic (Egypt) agreed to pay for the cost associated with the deployment of the United Nations Yemen Observation Mission (UNYOM). The Soviet Union acquiesced, despite its general view that costs should be borne by aggressors, and the Security Council was thus able to authorize UNYOM deployment. In March 1964, the Security Council approved the deployment of the United Nations Forces in Cyprus (UNFICYP), on condition that all costs would be met by the governments of Cyprus, Greece, Turkey, and the United Kingdom or other governments providing troop contingents or voluntary contributions.

This ad hoc approach to funding continued with the Security Council authorizing a 7,000-man UN force in 1973 following the Yom Kippur War, and another smaller force in Lebanon in 1978. In both cases the operations were funded by a modified assessment scale agreed to by France and the Soviet Union since the Security Council, not the General Assembly, was the locus of decision making.

Eventually, with the demise of communism and the end of the Cold War, the UN Security Council became heavily engaged once again in the business of peacekeeping and peacemaking, and budgets for such activities skyrocketed in the 1990s. Spurred by Secretary-General Boutros Boutros-Ghali's *Agenda for Peace* proposal in 1992, the General Assembly reiterated the principle that peacekeeping operations are the collective responsibility of all member states, and it called upon them to pay their assessments in full and in timely fashion. The financing of peacekeeping operations has thus been subjected to the more predictable provisions of Article 17. However, actual apportionment of expenses has continued to vary, with some countries incurring substantially higher proportions of the costs on a voluntary basis, as did the United States in the case of expenses associated with the Persian Gulf crisis. However, the United States and other countries continued during the 1990s to fall in arrears. When the United States is the offender, UN budgets are placed under severe strain, given the large portion of the budget covered by U.S. contributions. The United Nations has responded to the more recent budget crisis with considerable energy, cutting secretariat staff, streamlining operations, and holding its budgets to zero growth in the latter part of the 1990s.

Financing of the UN budget has proved to be a highly controversial and perennial issue in the United Nations. The capacity to pay is rarely a factor in the decision of governments not to pay their full assessments on time. Rather, political considerations are normally involved. This was the case with the Soviet Union and France in the financial crisis of the 1960s, and with the United States in that of the 1980s and 1990s. This should not be viewed, then, as unusual. Politics at both the national and international levels is at the heart of the business of making and spending budgets. Budgets are never really neutral. They are, in a larger sense, a record of which political groups are winning or losing various battles over policy. When countries are on the losing side of a budget battle at the United Nations, they are not shy about withdrawing financial support for undesirable programs. Since the United Nations is not a world government and since it lacks the real enforcement power to "collect taxes," it must learn to live within whatever means it can to grapple with its various mandates.

See also Arab-Israeli Dispute (Debate 6); Congo Crisis (Debate 17); Cyprus Question (Debate 23); Persian Gulf War (Debate 44).

FOR FURTHER READING

Bennett, A. LeRoy. *International Organizations: Principles and Issues*. Englewood Cliffs, NJ: Prentice-Hall, 1995.
Everyman's United Nations. New York: United Nations Publication Office, 1968.
Goodrich, Leland, Edvard Hambro, and Anne P. Simons. *Charter of the United Nations: Commentary and Documents*. 3rd rev. ed. New York: Columbia University Press, 1969.
McDermott, Anthony. *The New Politics of Financing the UN*. New York: St. Martin's, 1999.
Stoessinger, John G., ed. *Financing the United Nations*. Washington, DC: Brookings Institution, 1964.
UN Yearbooks, 1963, 1992.

Rhodesian Question (1962)

SIGNIFICANCE OF THE ISSUE

Next to the South African system of apartheid, one of the bitterest postcolonial disputes in which the United Nations was engaged concerned the British colony of Southern Rhodesia and the unilateral declaration of its white minority government in November 1965, which denied the black majority any part in the political life of the country. In 1966, the Security Council imposed economic sanctions on Rhodesia under Chapter VII of the UN Charter, marking the first time such a step had been taken by it. During the 1970s, a bloody civil war in the country defied internal or external reso-lution until 1979 when a democratically elected black majority government took power and proclaimed the independence of the new state of Zimba-bwe. Tied to issues of decolonization and racism, two of the most highly charged issues debated in UN settings, the Rhodesian question remained a controversial agenda item until the birth of Zimbabwe.

BACKGROUND TO THE DEBATE

The history of Rhodesia hearkens back to the twelfth century and the ad-vanced Zimbabwe civilization. In the centuries that followed, numerous African peoples settled in the interior of southern Africa, including the Mashona (who constituted the majority) along with smaller numbers of Ndebele and Zulus. Portuguese explorers entered the area in the 1500s but left no lasting mark on the area. A modern European presence was not es-tablished until Cecil Rhodes and his British South Africa Company moved into the region in the 1890s. From that time until 1923, the region was ad-ministered by the local British settlers associated with the British South Af-rica Company. This circumstance gave the local British authorities a good deal more autonomy in their administration of the area than was true of other British colonies, and this would be a major factor in controversial political developments of the 1960s and 1970s.

Great Britain formally annexed Rhodesia, then known as Southern Rhodesia, but allowed it to govern itself in a semiautonomous fashion. White settlers, though a very small minority, enjoyed complete control of colonial administration and of the economy. In 1953, a Federation of Rhodesia, composed of Southern Rhodesia, Northern Rhodesia (later Zambia), and Nyasaland (later Malawi), was formed, in which white settlers continued to enjoy control, but the arrangement continued to provoke resentment from the black majority populations. Zambia and Malawi gained independence in 1964 from the Federation of Rhodesia with black majority governments, a condition that the United Kingdom insisted upon as a condition of granting independence. This left Southern Rhodesia as the lone exception, where whites continued to enjoy political control and where they also agitated for full independence from Britain. In 1961, whites in Southern Rhodesia approved a constitution that denied black majority participation and began to agitate for independence based on this constitution. The United Kingdom resisted its efforts to proclaim independence, precisely because such a move by the white minority would not be broadly democratic and would ignore the wishes of the black majority. The formation of indigenous political organizations, such as Joshua Nkomo's Zimbabwe African People's Union (ZAPU) and Paul Mushonga's Zimbabwe National Party, gave voice to the black majority's aspirations for political participation. During the years 1964 and 1965, controversy swirled both in Rhodesia and Britain over the contemplated unilateral declaration of independence being considered by the white minority government of Rhodesia. The matter also was of concern to the United Nations and its Special Committee charged with implementing the General Assembly's Declaration on the Granting of Independence to Colonial Countries and Peoples, which heard testimony from Nkomo and Mashonga as early as the spring of 1962. Rhodesia gradually became a subject of international concern.

HISTORY OF THE DEBATE

Although the United Kingdom was the chief international actor in the early stages of the battle over Rhodesian independence, the United Nations did become involved through its Special Committee on matters of colonial peoples. In 1962, this body established a subcommittee to remain in close contact with the United Kingdom concerning future steps toward the independence of Southern Rhodesia. After consultations with the British government the subcommittee reported that a drift toward independence under the flawed 1961 white minority constitution should be halted, that genuine self-government could not possibly be achieved when a white minority of only 10 percent ignored the legitimate rights of the black majority of 90 percent, and that a resolution of the problem was likely to ensure great upheaval and conflict. Its observations were tellingly prescient.

The General Assembly took up the Question of Southern Rhodesia for the first time in its sixteenth regular session of 1962. Fifty members took part in the general debate, the majority throwing their full support behind ZAPU in its opposition to the white minority constitution of 1961, pointing out that it violated universally accepted norms of democratic participation. The majority supported a resolution that would call upon the United Kingdom to immediately call a constitutional conference of all peoples in Southern Rhodesia, to restore all rights of the non-European peoples, and to release all political prisoners. East bloc states such as the Soviet Union, Albania, Bulgaria, Hungary, Romania, and the Ukraine supported the resolution but urged that a black majority government be granted independence immediately. Western governments, such as the United States, Australia, Canada, France, Italy, and New Zealand, sympathized with the overall desire to promote democracy in Rhodesia but were reluctant to ask the United Kingdom to undertake initiatives inconsistent with its own constitutional capacities. The resolution was adopted by a vote of 73 to 1 (South Africa) with 27 abstentions, while the United Kingdom and Portugal did not participate in the vote. Stronger language calling for the immediate suspension of the 1961 constitution was adopted at the Seventeenth Session of the General Assembly in the fall of 1962. The United Kingdom held, during these discussions, that Southern Rhodesia fell beyond the competence of UN bodies since it was not a non-self-governing territory but a self-governing territory with a responsible government and that, since 1923, the United Kingdom had no direct authority to legislate the internal affairs of Southern Rhodesia. Thus, when the matter was brought to the attention of the Security Council in the fall of 1963, the United Kingdom vetoed a resolution that called upon it to implement prior General Assembly resolutions. The United States and France abstained on the same resolution. A resolution similar to that which failed in the Security Council was adopted by the General Assembly a month later at its Eighteenth Session.

The real drama, however, began as the white minority government considered a formal unilateral declaration of independence during 1964. When this declaration was formally announced on 11 November 1965, both the Security Council and the General Assembly called upon the United Kingdom to take immediate steps to bring the minority regime to an end. They also called on all member states to refrain from recognizing the illegal white regime. At its November meeting, the Security Council invited seventeen nonaligned states, the majority African states, to participate in its debate on the unilateral declaration of independence. The United Kingdom indicated at the debate that it considered the unilateral declaration of independence invalid, as only the British Parliament could grant independence, and that it would never do so until the wishes of the entire population of Southern

Rhodesia were affirmed. It further observed that since an illegal step had been taken by the white minority regime, that the United Kingdom was now the sole legitimate government and sovereign authority in Rhodesia. The United Kingdom asked all nations to refuse recognition of the illegal regime, it imposed an embargo on the export of all arms, and welcomed a like UN initiative and various economic sanctions. The Council passed a resolution (10 to 0 with 1 abstention [France]) in which it condemned the unilateral declaration of independence and called upon states to refrain from recognizing or rendering assistance to the illegal government. In a second resolution, in an identical vote it adopted language calling upon states to impose an arms embargo and to do their "utmost" to break all economic relations with Southern Rhodesia.

In the years that followed, both the Security Council and the General Assembly passed resolutions condemning the illegal regime and calling upon states to impose economic sanctions. In a key and unprecedented resolution of 15 December 1966, the Security Council invoked Chapter VII of the Charter by imposing compulsory economic sanctions against Southern Rhodesia, marking the first time it had taken such a step. In 1968 the Council expanded the list of items subject to economic sanctions and established a committee to monitor implementation of the resolution and to report on which member states failed to abide by it. Throughout the late 1960s and into the 1970s, the Security Council broadened and strengthened the sanctions against Southern Rhodesia. Portugal and South Africa persisted in ignoring such resolutions, which caused them to be the subject of indirect or direct rebuke in the Security Council and in the General Assembly. The latter also repeatedly called for Security Council action against Southern Rhodesia and made statements of concern over the failure of economic sanctions alone to force changes in the area.

During the 1970s, the rebellion against the white regime by black nationalist organizations intensified. Joshua Nkomo's ZAPU received military support from the Soviet Union and generally took refuge in neighboring Zambia. In Mozambique, Robert Mugabe's Zimbabwe African Nationalist Union (ZANU) formed an even more impressive opposition army, with aid from the People's Republic of China. Under pressure from the military activities of these groups, the civil war in Rhodesia intensified and spilled over into the neighboring countries that harbored opposition forces. Hundreds of thousands of black Rhodesian refugees fled into neighboring countries where they were assisted by the United Nations High Commissioner for Refugees (UNHCR). Internally, the white minority regime of Ian Smith, began in the mid- to late 1970s to negotiate with black leaders, such as Bishop Abel Muzorewa, over establishing a new constitution that would provide for limited political participation by the black majority. In 1977, elections were held under this new constitution, and the country of Zimbabwe-Rhodesia was proclaimed, with Muzorewa participating in government with Smith. The international community broadly rejected these reforms and called for full, free, fair, and internationally monitored elections in Rhodesia following a return of opposition groups. The civil war continued in brutal intensity after 1977, indicating that the experimental reforms were unsatisfactory and that only a comprehensive settlement involving ZANU and ZAPU would ever restore order.

OUTCOME OF THE DEBATE

By 1979, the general fatigue with conflict on all sides, and a diplomatic offensive launched by the United Kingdom, finally brought all sides to the negotiation table, where in the Lancaster House agreement they eventually committed themselves to a cease-fire, a repatriation of all refugees, a demobilization of forces, free and fair, internationally monitored elections, and a transfer of authority to a new black majority government. The Lancaster House agreement was successfully implemented. In 1979, Robert Mugabe won a substantial majority of votes and became Zimbabwe's first prime minister. In 1980, Zimbabwe joined the United Nations, and the long-term task of rebuilding the country after fifteen years of civil war began. Mugabe continued as ruler, in subsequent decades, exercising a firm hand in the country's political life. Although many whites fled Rhodesia, a good many stayed to cast their lot with the new country and to work toward a prosperous and peaceful future. With the independence of Zimbabwe, the question of Rhodesia was resolved, and it no longer appeared on the agenda of UN bodies. Sanctions imposed in earlier years were revoked, and the new government enjoyed widespread recognition and attracted considerable international assistance.

See also Angola Situation (Debate 42); Apartheid (Debate 14); Decolonization (Debate 18); Mozambique Situation (Debate 47); Southwest Africa (Namibia) Dispute (Debate 3).

FOR FURTHER READING

Chamberlain, Waldo, Thomas Hovet, Jr., and Erika Hovet. *A Chronology and Fact Book of the United Nations, 1941–1976*. Dobbs Ferry, NY: Oceana Publications, 1976.

Keppel-Jones, Arthur. *Rhodes and Rhodesia: The White Conquest of Zimbabwe 1884–1902*. Montreal: McGill Queens University Press, 1983.

Morris-Jones, W. H. *From Rhodesia to Zimbabwe: Behind and Beyond Lancaster House*. London: Frank Cass, 1980.

Strack, Harry. *Sanctions: The Case of Rhodesia*. Syracuse, NY: Syracuse University Press, 1978.

UN Yearbooks, 1962, 1963, 1964, 1965, 1966.

Vietnam Question (1963)

SIGNIFICANCE OF THE ISSUE

The civil war in Vietnam was a multifaceted situation involving the disposition of French colonial rule, the independence of Vietnam, the interplay of Communist and Western democratic ideologies, foreign intervention, superpower relations, and Cold War ideology. Because of the direct involvement of various great powers, including France, the United States, the Soviet Union, and Communist China, the matter could be dealt with only tangentially by the UN Security Council, and other bodies, such as the General Assembly, could only issue nonbinding recommendations. Most of the major decisions taken during the course of the conflict were made outside of the United Nations by the respective governments most directly involved. Still, the UN debate reflected broader world opinion, and quiet diplomacy by the secretary-general's office was in evidence.

BACKGROUND TO THE DEBATE

In the latter half of the nineteenth century, France undertook control of Vietnam and maintained colonial authority there until the Japanese occupation during World War II. In 1862 Annam ceded control of its eastern provinces of Cochin-China to France as a colony. In 1864 Siam granted France control of Cambodia as a protectorate. French colonial administration further expanded in Indochina with the Saigon agreement with Annam, in which France obtained Tongking as a protectorate. In 1882, France extended its control over all of Annam and Tongking after occupying Hanoi—acquisitions acknowledged by the Treaty of Hue in 1883. In 1885, a reluctant China recognized French claims to Annam following French occupation of Taiwan. France later incorporated Laos as a protectorate in 1887, thus consolidating its holdings in Indochina. Nevertheless, the local populations remained highly restive, and French occupation of the region was marked by periodic conflicts until its final withdrawal from the region in 1954. The Japanese occupation of much of Indochina during World War II was a watershed period. Vietnamese nationalists gained considerable strength during the occupation, and at the war's end, a coalition of Communist parties declared independence. In 1949 France recognized the independence of Vietnam but refused to deal with Communists, instead recognizing an anti-Communist government. French military forces remained in Vietnam to stave off the Communist forces. However, in the decisive battle of Dien Bien Phu of 1954, French forces were defeated, following a U.S. refusal to intervene militarily or to supply nuclear weapons, and in the Geneva Accords that were subsequently negotiated, Vietnam was divided into two zones, one dominated by Communists in the North and the other dominated by anti-Communists in the South. The Geneva Conference was attended by representatives of Cambodia, Laos, the Democratic People's Republic of Vietnam, South Vietnam, China, France, the Soviet Union, the United Kingdom, and the United States. The Geneva Accords provided that a free general election should be held in 1955.

In 1955, South Vietnam held elections that resulted in the proclamation of a republican form of government under president Ngo Dinh Diem. Ho Chi Minh, president of the North, however, insisted on general elections that would effect the reunification of the country. Diem, fearing that a general election might lead to a Communist victory, declined to participate in general elections leading to reunification. Communist Vietcong emerged in the South in opposition to Diem, and eventually they received both military supplies and troop support from the North and indirectly from the Soviet Union and Communist China. As Vietcong and North Vietnamese attacks grew in intensity, the government of South Vietnam sought external support. The United States under President John F. Kennedy sent military advisers in 1962, American bombing of North Vietnam began in 1964, and ground troops were committed in 1965. At about this same time, the war was gaining larger attention from the international community, and UN bodies began to consider the question of Vietnam.

HISTORY OF THE DEBATE

Problems relating to the Vietnam Question first reached the United Nations in September 1963 in the form of a complaint lodged or sponsored by sixteen countries, including Afghanistan, Algeria, Cambodia, Ceylon, Guinea, India, Indonesia, Mali, Mongolia, Nepal, Nigeria, Pakistan, Rwanda, Sierra Leone, Somalia, and Trinidad and Tobago. They charged that the government of South Vietnam had interfered with Buddhist religious practices and that this constituted a violation of human rights. President Ngo Dinh Diem denied the charges in a letter to the secretary-general, and the General Assembly agreed to send a fact-finding mission to Vietnam to ascertain the truth of the matter. The assassination of Diem and the over-throw of his government while the fact-finding team was in Vietnam largely mooted its report, and the General Assembly shelved the matter.

However, during the following spring, Cambodia, a neutral country, lodged the first of several complaints regarding incursions into its territory by Vietnamese and American military forces. Vietnam and the United States expressed regrets over the incidents, noting that the frontiers be-tween Cambodia and Vietnam were ill-marked. Apart from establishing a three-member committee consisting of the representatives of Brazil, the Ivory Coast, and Morocco to visit sites where border incidents had oc-curred, the Council took no further action. Later in the same year, the Gulf of Tonkin incident occurred, in which American naval vessels were alleg-edly attacked by North Vietnamese vessels. Although the Security Council met to discuss the incident, representatives of North Vietnam refused to ap-pear, and the Council took no action.

In 1964, the United States bombed North Vietnam for the first time, and in March 1965 it introduced the first regular combat troops into Vietnam, in-stead of just military advisers. The war rapidly escalated at this time, as large numbers of American forces, along with smaller numbers from Aus-tralia, New Zealand, the Philippines, South Korea, and Thailand, entered the fray.

In 1966, the United States brought the matter of Vietnam to the attention of the Security Council. The ensuing debate had a surreal quality, as no in-formed observer could expect any substantive action by the Council, given the ongoing Cold War, the superpower confrontations occurring on a global scale, and the veto power held by several interested parties, includ-ing the United States and the Soviet Union. Moreover, the argument in-volved a divided country with two governments, neither of which held membership in the United Nations, a point made by Bulgaria in the Secu-rity Council debate that ensued.

The United States proposed in a draft resolution that immediate and un-conditional discussions among the contesting parties should begin with a view to implementing the Geneva Accords of 1954 and 1962 and that there be an immediate cessation of hostilities under appropriate international su-pervision. The United States charged that neither North Vietnam nor Com-munist China (not yet a government recognized by the United Nations) had shown interest in diplomatic solutions, nor had the Soviet Union shown support. The United States claimed that its suspension of bombing in December of the previous year had been made as a goodwill gesture and to ascertain whether the bombing itself had been an obstacle to the com-mencement of peace talks; but the United States also claimed that Hanoi continued the infiltration of troops and military supplies during the bomb-ing cessation and only belatedly replied to the offer for resumption of peace talks with an ultimatum that showed virtually no flexibility. Under those

U.S. soldiers enter a Vietnamese village during the U.S. involvement in the Vietnamese War. © Bettmann/CORBIS

conditions, the United States could not continue a suspension of the bombing, although it continued to desire a means of seeking a peaceful solution, including bringing the matter to the Security Council.

The Soviet Union argued that the Security Council was an inappropriate venue for discussions on Vietnam, as these should be done in the context of the Geneva Accords. It chastised the United States for duplicity in seeking Security Council action while simultaneously resuming the bombing campaign in the North. It accused the United States of attempting to stage a crude propaganda campaign while it continued its aggression in Vietnam against the legal and peace-loving North Vietnamese government.

Although Bulgaria viewed the Security Council as an inappropriate venue for debating the issue since neither North nor South Vietnam was a member state, most members of the Council, including Argentina, China (Republic of), Japan, the Netherlands, New Zealand, the United Kingdom, and Uruguay, did not object to the U.S. effort to consult with it. The Netherlands observed that the Charter permitted the Council to deal with threats to peace and security regardless of whether the states involved were UN members.

But other members voiced reservations. France noted that the idea that the Security Council could serve as an effective venue for resolving the dispute was flawed, since the United States was the only principal in the conflict present. Mali and Nigeria, while acknowledging any member state's right to request a meeting of the Council, did not believe that the timing or circumstances were auspicious for any hope of a reasonable settlement. Uganda expressed similar doubts. Although the matter was placed on the agenda for discussion, the president of the Council proposed that private consultations be held to determine how best to continue the debate. After these consultations, no further formal debate was held, and the president of the Council reported that Council members expressed a fairly common sense of anxiety over the continued hostilities in Vietnam and a desire to see them swiftly brought to a peaceful resolution through some appropriate forum in which the Geneva Accords could be implemented.

OUTCOME OF THE DEBATE

Resolution of the Vietnamese conflict took place largely beyond the framework of UN organs. The Paris Peace Accords provided a legal context in which the United States could gracefully extricate itself from Vietnam. But no elections were held to determine the fate of the South, which was absorbed through no democratic process but rather through military means. The Communist government of Vietnam took its seat as a member of the United Nations in 1977.

The political repression experienced in the South after the Communist takeover eventually stimulated a huge flow of refugees in the form of boat people, from the mid-1970s into the early 1990s. Over a million and a half Vietnamese fled their homeland during the subsequent decade and a half. The United Nations was deeply involved through the UN High Commissioner for Refugees in responding to the needs of these refugees, which received a generally hostile reception from neighboring Southeast Asian countries. Under the terms of the 1979 Indochinese Refugee Conference, countries in the region agreed to open their borders to Vietnamese refugees on a temporary basis, with the understanding that other nations would resettle them and pay for the costs associated with their temporary settlement. The United States, France, Australia, and Canada resettled the largest numbers of Vietnamese boat people, although many other countries participated in this humanitarian program.

The invasion and occupation of Cambodia by Vietnam in 1978 led to even more refugee flows from Cambodia and to condemnation by the United Nations, despite the ironic fact that the Vietnamese invasion had rid Cambodia of the genocidal Khmer Rouge regime of Pol Pot. The People's Republic of China invaded Vietnam in 1979 partly in retaliation for its invasion in Cambodia. Chinese forces were easily repulsed by the well-armed and battle-hardened Vietnamese army. These acts of war among Communist nations suggested that the deeper factor in much of the conflict in the region for years was rooted in nationalistic rather than fraternal Communist sentiments.

The refugee situation in Southeast Asia was largely resolved in the late 1980s with the convening of a second conference on Indochinese refugees, at which Vietnam agreed to the principle of voluntary repatriation. Under severe economic distress, and facing the collapse of communism throughout the world, Vietnam decided to normalize its relations with non-Communist nations. It agreed to withdraw from Cambodia in 1991, paving the way for resolution of the Cambodian crisis and as a prelude to better ties with Western democracies. It began a process of economic liberalization designed to seek international financial and monetary support and to establish commercial ties in the international trade system. Under these circumstances, the economy and quality of life in Vietnam began to improve even as its political system liberalized and ties with the United States and other Western countries grew friendlier.

See also Cambodia Situation (Debate 38); Decolonization (Debate 18); Genocide (Debate 9); Refugees and Stateless Persons (Debate 4).

FOR FURTHER READING

Chapius, Oscar M. *A History of Vietnam.* Westport, CT: Greenwood Press, 1995.

Davidson, Phillip B. *Vietnam at War: The History 1946–1975.* Oxford: Oxford University Press, 1991.

Everyman's United Nations. New York: United Nations Office of Public Information, 1968.

Kolko, Gabriel. *Vietnam: Anatomy of Peace.* London: Routledge, 1997.

Murray, Geoffrey. *Vietnam: Dawn of a New Market.* New York: St. Martin's, 1997.

UN Yearbook, 1966.

Wain, Barry. *The Refused: The Agony of the Indochina Refugees.* New York: Simon and Schuster, 1981.

Cyprus Question (1963)

SIGNIFICANCE OF THE ISSUE

The Cyprus dispute raised at an early time in UN history a difficult question that that body has faced with increasing frequency since the end of the Cold War, namely, how to ensure stable independence for colonies or independent countries having serious ethnic conflicts without involving UN forces in interminable policelike operations. One of the longest-lasting UN operations, the Cyprus situation has remained on the Security Council's active agenda since 1964.

BACKGROUND TO THE DEBATE

Cyprus, the third largest island in the Mediterranean Sea, is located south of Turkey and east of Syria. For many centuries the majority of the population of the island has been Greek. In the late sixteenth century, Ottoman Turks took control of the island, and a sizable minority population of Turks came to live on the northern side of the island. In 1878, the British assumed control of Cyprus, and with the outbreak of World War I, they annexed it as British territory. The Greek population proved restive during the British dominion. They increasingly demanded union with Greece. This, of course, was unacceptable to the Turkish population and to the British as well. But the Greeks continued to press demands for union with Greece and took arms in 1955 to impress their wishes on the British government.

After long and difficult negotiations, the United Kingdom agreed in 1959 to terms for the independence of Cyprus with Greece and Turkey as well as with the Greek and Turkish Cypriot populations. Cyprus achieved independence on 16 August 1960 as a republic in which both Greek and Turkish Cypriots would enjoy guarantees of their rights and interests in a political system calling for ethnic balance and a pursuit of common goals.

For example, the constitution called for a Greek Cypriot president and a Turkish Cypriot vice president. Furthermore, to guarantee the security of both populations as they tentatively agreed to cooperate in furtherance of the goal of independence and national stability, Cyprus, Greece, Turkey, and the United Kingdom signed a Treaty of Guarantee, which provided for joint consultations among any three parties should any one fail to live up to its obligations under the agreement, and failing the success of joint consultation, each party was free to take steps to preserve the terms of the treaty.

Renewed violence between Greek and Turkish Cypriots erupted in 1963, and efforts by the four parties to the Treaty of Guarantee seemed at first to work as a combined force of British, Greek, and Turkish units under British command entered Cyprus in late December with the government's permission to help restore order. The Greek-dominated government of Cyprus, however, complained almost immediately about the depredations of Turkish units and expressed a fear that Turkey was preparing to invade the island. It appealed to the United Nations for help.

HISTORY OF THE DEBATE

The crisis of late 1963 and early 1964 did not represent the first time that the question of Cyprus had found its way onto the agenda of the United Nations. Greece brought the question of Cyprus to the attention of the UN General Assembly in 1954, seeking a pronouncement calling for recognition of the rights of the inhabitants of Cyprus to self-determination. This initiative was not acted upon by the General Assembly. However, when both Greece and the United Kingdom called for UN discussion of Cyprus in 1956, the issue received more attention. Greece sought to have the United Nations affirm the Greek Cypriot's right to self-determination, while the United Kingdom asked the Assembly to address the problem of Greek support for terrorist activities on the island. In 1957, the General Assembly adopted a compromise course, calling upon the parties to the dispute to resolve their differences peacefully through negotiation. A Greek-sponsored measure calling for an immediate plebiscite in Cyprus failed to win a majority in the Assembly. With slow progress being made in negotiations, the General Assembly reiterated in 1958 its desire to see a just and democratic solution negotiated by the parties. These came to fruition in February 1959, when an agreement was signed in London providing for the independence of Cyprus, under special constitutional and treaty guarantees.

About a month after its independence, Cyprus became a member of the United Nations and enjoyed a brief respite of calm for its first three years of existence. After Greek Cypriot president Archbishop Makarios proposed numerous amendments to the constitution, fighting broke out between Greek and Turkish Cypriots. In this context Cyprus appealed for a meeting of the UN Security Council to address what it called Turkish violations of the Treaty of Guarantee and of Cypriot sovereignty and territorial integrity. At a 27 December 1963 meeting of the Security Council, representatives of Cyprus, Turkey, and Greece were invited to participate in Council debate without vote. Cyprus indicated that although a cease-fire had been negotiated prior to the meeting, thus reducing its urgency, nevertheless Turkish forces continued to play "gunboat diplomacy," including violations of airspace and territorial waters in Cyprus. The root cause of the problem in Cyprus, he asserted, were flaws in the nation's constitution that had divided towns never previously divided into separate ethnic communities. This had been done in haste and without due consideration in negotiations prior to independence and needed to be rectified, along with a divided, inconsistent, and unsatisfactory judicial system, poor fiscal provisions, and impossible provisions for amendment.

These were legitimate concerns raised by Makarios with Turkish Cypriots that were rejected by the Turkish vice president, the Turkish government, and the Turkish Cypriot community. Countering these charges and explanations, the Turkish representative to the Security Council asserted that the Greek Cypriots had unleashed a campaign of extermination against Turkish Cypriots and that Turkey merely sought to protect both its rights and Turkish lives. He denied that any invasion of the island by his government was planned or under way. The Greek representative welcomed the Turkish assurance that no attack was planned but noted that the recent buildup of military forces in southern Turkey could certainly be mistaken as a potentially ominous act. He noted also that the violence precipitated in prior days was the work of armed Turkish Cypriots and called upon the Council to support the cease-fire now in effect. The Council took no formal action at the meeting.

Pursuant to the cease-fire agreement, the interested parties met in London on 15 January 1964, where the Greeks insisted on the establishment of a unitary state with appropriate protections for Turkish Cypriots, whereas the latter demanded geographical separation from the Greek community. Efforts to determine the composition of a new peacekeeping force failed. UN Secretary-General U Thant appointed a Personal Representative to observe the progress of peacekeeping operations in Cyprus. From 18 February to 4 March, the Security Council remained seized of the Cyprus situation, taking up issues regarding the Cypriot constitution and the call by Cyprus for a UN peacekeeping force. On 4 March, it adopted a resolution calling for peaceful resolution of the dispute on the part of all disputants and parties, and for the establishment by the secretary-general in consultation with the involved parties of a temporary UN force to preserve peace and security. The resolution, sponsored by Bolivia, Brazil, the Ivory Coast, Morocco, and Norway, was unanimously adopted. This force became operational on 17 March as the United Nations Peacekeeping Force in Cyprus (UNFICYP) and reached a level of 6,000 troops by June. Countries

supplying either troops or civilian police to the operation included Australia, Austria, Canada, Denmark, Finland, Ireland, Sweden, and the United
Kingdom. The island was divided into zones in which military contingents
of particular countries exercised primary oversight. Although random acts
of violence were committed by both Cypriot communities, UNFICYP had a
positive impact on security, and its mandate was extended for a further
three months, in June, September, and December 1964 and March 1965. In
subsequent years, the Security Council has routinely extended the
UNFICYP mandate usually in six-month intervals. Although fighting
broke out in August 1964, prompting further steps by the Security Council
and a call for both sides to observe the terms of previous Security Council
resolutions, by December the secretary-general reported some improvement attributable to the stabilizing UN presence.

The General Assembly took up the question of Cyprus in 1965, passing a
controversial resolution recognizing the "full sovereignty and complete independence" of Cyprus, which the government of Cyprus considered a
victory for all small states facing imperialist threats. But many states observed that such a declaration seemed to dispute the legitimacy of the special treaties and constitutional measures included in the Cypriot
constitution as protections for the Turkish minority. Although the resolution passed, the majority of the delegations either abstained or voted no.
The vote, 47 to 5 with 54 abstentions, was hardly a ringing endorsement,
and interestingly the United States joined Albania, Pakistan, Iran, and Turkey in voting against it.

In subsequent years, an uneasy truce prevailed on Cyprus, until
intercommunal violence recurred in the mid-1970s, provoking an actual invasion of Turkish forces in the summer of 1974. UNFICYP was helpless to
prevent the invasion but did serve as a stabilizing influence in its aftermath
and was called upon formally to monitor and observe the cease-fire lines
for the protection and assistance of both communities. During this phase of
the UNFICYP operation, Danish, British, Canadian, and Austrian forces
were concentrated in four separate sectors along the cease-fire lines between Turkish-occupied northern Cyprus and the Greek-occupied south,
rather than being dispersed throughout the country. Calls by the General
Assembly in November 1974 for all foreign troops to withdraw from Cyprus were ignored. Mutual recriminations by the Greek and Turkish governments and Greek and Turkish Cypriot communities continued at
Security Council meetings held in 1975. The Council officially notified Turkey of its regret at the step taken by Turkey to recognize a Federated Turkish
State in the Turkish-occupied portions of Cyprus, and it called for the direct
involvement of the secretary-general's office in the negotiation process. In
the meantime, renewed conflict on the island created a larger refugee problem. As early as August 1974, the secretary-general nominated Sadruddin
Aga Khan, United Nations High Commissioner for Refugees (UNCHR), as

UN involvement in Cyprus began in 1963 and continues, making it one of the longest-lasting UN efforts at peacekeeping. Here a Swedish UN peackeeping unit is shown outside the city of Famagusta at an observation post located near the Greek Cypriot village of Dherinia after fighting broke out between Greek and Turkish Cypriots in 1974. UN/DPI Photo Yutaka Nagata

the coordinator for humanitarian assistance to Cyprus. The World Food Program provided substantial amounts of food aid to displaced persons in cooperation with UNFICYP.

In 1994, the Security Council reaffirmed that any settlement in Cyprus must be based upon a single state, with single sovereignty and a single citizenship composed of two politically equal communities in federation, and avoid any form of partition, secession, or union with any other country. These principles, earlier articulated by the United Nations in 1993, were agreed to in principle by the two parties in January 1994. But efforts to create a "bi-zonal and bi-communal" agreement made little progress throughout the late 1990s in a context of generally reduced tension as one of the longest UN peacekeeping operations continues to drag on well into its fourth decade.

OUTCOME OF THE DEBATE

Although the situation in Cyprus continues to remain on the UN agenda, the security situation has normalized to a substantial degree. The humanitarian situation on the island no longer requires major international attention or presence. Nonetheless, absent a final resolution of the ongoing geographical separation and communal segregation on the island, the possibility of renewed hostilities remains. Thus, the UN Security Council continues routinely to renew the UNFICYP mandate every six months, although the size of the UNFICYP contingent is much reduced compared to its earlier levels.

See also UN Financing Crisis (Debate 20); UN Reforms (Debate 43).

FOR FURTHER READING

Everyman's United Nations. New York: United Nations Office of Public Information, 1968.

Goodspeed, Stephen. *The Nature and Function of International Organization.* New York: Oxford University Press, 1967.

Jospeh, Joseph S. *Cyprus Ethnic Conflict and International Politics: From Independence to the Threshold of the European Union.* New York: St. Martin's, 1999.

Kaloudis, George S. *The Role of the UN in Cyprus from 1964 to 1979.* New York: Peter Lang, 1991.

Mirbagheri, Farid. *Cyprus and International Peacemaking 1964–1986.* London: Routledge, 1998.

O'Malley, Brendan, and Ian Craig. *The Cyprus Conspiracy: America, Espionage and the Turkish Invasion.* New York: St. Martin's, 2000.

Richmond, Oliver. *Mediating in Cyprus: The Cypriot Communities and the United Nations.* London: Frank Cass, 1998.

Stefanidis, Ioannis D., and Yiannis Stefanidis. *Isle of Discord: Nationalism, Imperialism and the Making of the Cyprus Problem.* New York: New York University Press, 1999.

UN Monthly Chronicle, 1994–1999.

UN Yearbooks, 1963, 1964, 1965, 1975, 1992.

Debate 24

Trade and Development (1964)

SIGNIFICANCE OF THE ISSUE

Trade issues have long occupied the attention of the United Nations. In 1947 the General Agreement on Tariffs and Trade (GATT) was founded, resulting in periodic trade negotiations or "Rounds." Developing countries, however, considered the GATT rules discriminatory in relation to their economic circumstances. Through the establishment of they United Nations Conference on Trade and Development (UNCTAD), they sought to highlight how trade issues affected their economic development situation. After its inception in 1964, principles asserted by UNCTAD were gradually recognized as justified, particularly in connection with relaxation of the GATT principle of reciprocity in tariff reductions and in the establishment of a preferential trade policy less harmful to the economic situation of developing countries.

BACKGROUND TO THE DEBATE

International acceptance of free trade principles after World War II was rooted in the belief that the Great Depression of the 1930s was at least partially a result of the restrictive trade policies that governments imposed in order to protect their domestic industries from foreign competition in the 1920s and early 1930s. Thus when governments of the Western world met in the first round of discussions leading to the creation of the GATT, they adopted policies that would favor the widest possible extension of free trade. In doing this they stipulated that countries in negotiating bilateral trade agreements with one another should observe the principle of reciprocity, that is, a mutual and proportional reduction of tariffs on one another's imports. This was seen to be the fairest way to ensure a reduction in tariffs, an increase in international trade, and both greater efficiency in production and competitiveness in pricing. Consumers of all nations should benefit from the process. The most-favored nation (MFN) principle, which countries were encouraged to include in the commercial agreements, also called for states to extend the lowest possible tariffs to all other countries whenever it gave a lower or preferred tariff to any one of its other trade partners. In this way tariffs for all trade partners could be automatically reduced without the necessity for formal renegotiation of tariff rates for other parties. Any advantage given to a commodity of one trade partner would be automatically conferred on others. MFN coupled with the reciprocity principle stimulated a tremendous growth in world trade after World War II, leading to higher levels of prosperity for many nations.

A problem arose, however, when former colonies gained their independence in large numbers during the 1950s and 1960s. Many of these countries, unlike the wealthier, more established, and highly industrialized countries of the North, depended solely on agricultural or mineral commodities, as opposed to manufacturing and industrial goods, for export. The problem with this was that most commodities fluctuated in price and rarely increased in value or price at a rate comparable to that of manufactured goods. Thus, developing countries of the Third World found themselves paying increasingly higher prices for the manufactured goods they needed, while receiving less for their commodity-based exports. If they stayed on such a treadmill for very long, they would never be able to save the resources necessary to establish a manufacturing capability of their own and would become permanently dependent on wealthier states for industrial products and permanently consigned to an agricultural class economy as long, at least, as their terms of trade remained unfavorable.

There was a way out of the problem. If wealthier countries would ignore the reciprocity principle of GATT in favor of a preferential trade system with developing countries, then the latter might hope to graduate into industrial status. The idea went something like this: If a poorer country relying largely on commodities for export was given low tariff access to the economies of wealthier states, and also given the right to erect higher tariffs on manufactured goods imported from wealthy states, then manufacturing enterprises within the poorer country would have an ability to develop at least a domestic market; and perhaps, after once getting on their feet and developing a more competitive edge, they might also begin to export manufactured goods at more competitive prices. If this kind of preference were not allowed, infant industries in poorer countries would have a very hard time competing with the bigger and more sophisticated industrial operations of wealthy countries and would be driven out of business by them. In short, developing countries pointed out that a strictly reciprocal trade policy discriminated against them and hampered their economic development.

During the 1950s, the Economic and Social Council (ECOSOC) dealt with commodity problems by authorizing the secretary-general to convene special international conferences to deal with problems in the trade of commodities. Conferences were held to deal with problems in the trade of tin, sugar, wheat, and olive oil, as well as exploratory meetings on copper, lead, and zinc. In 1954, ECOSOC established a subsidiary organ known as the Commission on International Commodity Trade to make recommendations on how to reduce the wide fluctuations characteristic of trade in many commodities. This commission pointed out in 1962 that a long-term trend in the decline of commodity markets was emerging.

It was out of consideration of problems such as this that the idea emerged among developing countries that they needed an organizational mechanism to articulate such concerns at the global level. So it was that the idea for the UN Conference on Trade and Development came into being as a kind of parallel trade negotiating body that would allow developing countries to advance their concerns about the effects of trade on their overall prospects for economic development.

HISTORY OF THE DEBATE

In 1962, the Economic and Social Council recommended to the General Assembly that a conference on trade and development be called to deal with commodity markets. The General Assembly agreed with the ECOSOC proposal and scheduled preparatory meetings for such a conference in 1963. UNCTAD met for the first time from 23 March to 16 June 1964 in Geneva, where, after being incorporated by the UN General Assembly later the same year as one of its specialized agencies, it continues to maintain its headquarters and a full-time secretariat. At the Conference 120 states were represented. The final act of the Conference was adopted by consensus, but 34 countries registered reservations and observations on the resolution. Many indicated that they had signed the final act merely as an accurate record of the Conference proceedings with the understanding that their comments and reservations of many of the principles asserted in the discussion and debate would be acknowledged, and several governments expressed specific reservations to particular clauses or recommendations of the Conference. For example, a number of developed countries disagreed with the principle that developing countries should be extended preferential trade rights. The Conference proposed, among other things, that the UNCTAD be established as an organ of the General Assembly, with a permanent executive body, a fifty-five-member Trade and Development Board. The Conference proposed the need to study and improve the wide discrepancies of economic growth among countries at different levels of development, along with measures to assist or relieve countries with accumulating debts and to promote private and public capital flows to developing countries. While many developed nations expressed their reservations with the final Conference act, 77 developing countries, who came to be

The United Nations Conference on Trade and Development (UNCTAD) meets in Geneva in 1964 as delegations from developing countries discuss the effects of global trade policy on their development prospects. The Geneva 77 was later influential in seeking a reform agenda through UNCTAD and other UN bodies. UN/DPI Photo

known as the Geneva 77, issued a joint declaration hailing the beginning of a new era of trade negotiations in which the voices of developing states would be heard along with their interests in promoting balanced trade and development. But they insisted that years of neglect and of intolerable international class distinctions among the very rich and the intolerably poor could no longer prevail and that the Conference was but a first step toward rectification of long-standing international economic injustices. They promised to press the issue of the "trade gap" between basic commodities and manufactured goods in the years ahead.

In giving life to UNCTAD, the General Assembly noted that trade was an important aspect of a country's economic development and that many developing countries had expressed a strong desire to see a comprehensive and global body established in which they could advance principles and policies conducive to their economic growth and to harmonious trade relations at the multilateral level. It approved the creation of UNCTAD as a permanent organ with a fifty-five-member Trade and Development Board, reporting directly to it rather than through the coordinating authority of ECOSOC. In the long run, this arrangement proved to be problematical as it complicated the ability of UNCTAD to cooperate with other UN economic and development agencies, but from the developing country perspective, it allowed UNCTAD to remain a freestanding voice for articulation of Third World demands on trade issues and their impact on development. Because of the UN financial crisis and the decision taken to avoid contentious votes during the 1964 regular session of the General Assembly so as to avoid a confrontation over the potential loss of the Soviet vote in the Assembly because of its delinquency in paying peacekeeping-related assessments, no official vote was taken on the resolution providing for the establishment of UNCTAD. Governments having reservations were content to allow the body to be created and to fight over any differences on commodity policy and other issues at a later date.

Like GATT, UNCTAD has periodic rounds of negotiation, at three- or four-year intervals. It has met at various locations including New Delhi in 1968, Santiago in 1972, Nairobi in 1976, Manila in 1979, Belgrade in 1983, Geneva in 1987, Cartagena in 1992, and Midsrand, South Africa, in 1996. At the outset UNCTAD articulated its central concerns, and these have been reiterated time and again at its periodic conferences. It is concerned with developing fair trade policies for primary commodities, manufactures, and semimanufactures; encouraging transfer of technology from developed to developing states; developing compensatory financing; developing standards for shipping and regulation of invisible commerce (transfers of wealth through banking transaction, tourism, insurance, investment transfers or services); improving trade between socialist and nonsocialist countries; encouraging trade expansion and economic integration among developing countries; and promoting other special measures in favor of developing and least-developed countries. UNCTAD is set up in seven committees to deal with these issues.

One of the eventual successes after constant pressure by UNCTAD was the establishment of a system of trade preferences by various developed countries, beginning with the member states of the European Economic Community (EEC). Although UNCTAD criticized the early preferences system adopted by the EEC in 1970 as ineffective, in 1972 the EEC extended preferences to all UNCTAD states and in 1977 brought the system into compliance with UNCTAD recommendations. The United States also recognized a General System of Preferences approach in its dealings with many UNCTAD states.

With less success UNCTAD has also emphasized the development of an Integrated Programme for Commodities (Nairobi, 1976), but this initiative got mired down in the shrill and unproductive New International Economic Order (NIEO) debates. Similar efforts to guarantee transfers of technology and a restructuring of the international monetary and financial system favorable to deeply indebted developing states have also proved to be difficult areas in which only marginal progress has been made. UNCTAD sessions, facing frustration with achievement of many central goals, thus often became strident affairs where a drumbeat of relentless criticism of Western capitalist countries could be heard. However, in its 1992 Recommendations, the UNCTAD VIII session called for a more reconciliatory strategy aimed at creating a "new partnership for development." The failure of the confrontational tactics of the NIEO debates led developing states in UNCTAD and other UN development bodies to seek a more realistic way to seek development aims, even as a large number of developing countries began to take more responsibility for their own economic problems rather than shifting blame to developed states.

OUTCOME OF THE DEBATE

UNCTAD's role in international trade and development issues came under reevaluation during the mid-1990s, as UN member states negotiated a new World Trade Organization (WTO) to replace the GATT. Although UNCTAD was not superseded entirely by the WTO, many of its functions and concerns are incorporated into WTO provisions. In 1996, the UN General Assembly called upon UNCTAD to review its role in the new system of global trade, especially in light of the establishment of the World Trade Organization as a successor to GATT in 1995. In subsequent years, it has emphasized the need to focus special attention on the least developed countries, to fully integrate the former countries of the socialist bloc into the global economic system, and to protect the transit rights of land-locked developing countries. In 1997 UNCTAD issued a report on the situation of heavily indebted poor countries (HIPCs), which included about twenty-nine of the forty-eight countries classified as least-developed countries. Steps were taken by the World Bank and the International Monetary Fund with the approval of the international community in 1994 to address the debt situation of HIPCs. Under this initiative, the debt situation of the HIPCs is monitored closely to determine the level of debt rescheduling, debt reduction, or debt cancellation justified, given the performance of each HIPC's economy.

During the 1990s, UNCTAD's role in the formation of international trade and development policy diminished. However, it is likely to remain an ongoing voice for developing country needs, especially those of the least-developed countries, as the effects of the globalization of trade on the economies of those countries clarify themselves in future years.

See also Decolonization (Debate 18); New International Economic Order (Debate 30); Third World Development Programming (Debate 25); World Monetary System (Debate 5).

FOR FURTHER READING

Bennett, A. LeRoy. *International Organizations: Principles and Issues.* Englewood
     Cliffs, NJ: Prentice-Hall, 1995.
Everyman's United Nations. New York: United Nations Office of Public Informa-
     tion, 1968.
Hoekman, Bernard, and Michael Kostecki. *The Political Economy of the World
     Trading System: From GATT to WTO.* Oxford: Oxford University Press,
     1995.
Krueger, Anne O. *The WTO as an International Organization.* Chicago: Chicago Uni-
     versity Press, 1998.
Osmañczyk, Edmund Jan. *Encyclopedia of the United Nations and International Agree-
     ments.* London: Taylor and Francis, 1985 and 1990.
UN Chronicles, 1991–1999.
UN Yearbooks.
Weiss, Thomas G. *Multilateral Development Diplomacy in UNCTAD: The Lessons of
     Group Negotiations, 1964–84.* London: Macmillan, 1986.
Williams, Marc. *Third World Cooperation: The Group of 77 in UNCTAD.* New York:
     St. Martin's, 1991.

Third World Development Programming (1964)

SIGNIFICANCE OF THE ISSUE

Apart from the disarmament question that dominated East-West debates in the United Nations for several decades, the issue of development in the Third World has been—and remains—the dominant issue in North-South debates at the United Nations. The degree of attention to the problem of economic development in United Nations setting grew dramatically in the 1960s, especially after the creation of the United Nations Development Program (UNDP) in 1965, and today the vast majority of the UN budget, and the activities of its specialized agencies, deals broadly with development-related issues. Often debates over development have been heated and rancorous, although in recent decades the rhetorical animosities of previous years have been replaced by a sober realism, as poverty persists despite four decades of UN attention to the matter. No issue has received more attention in terms of time or resources in the UN system.

BACKGROUND TO THE DEBATE

Traditionally, countries were largely on their own in terms of developing their economies and promoting agricultural self-sufficiency and industrial development. The first intergovernmental efforts to promote economic growth and prosperity as such did not come into existence until after World War I. Of course, a country could rely on trade relations and the goodwill of friendly nations and investors from other countries to help it develop its resources, but these were matters lying largely within the bilateral diplomacy of nations. Indeed, to a very large extent, the modern state as a director of its own economic growth and development really didn't develop until the late 1800s. International efforts to promote commerce began somewhat earlier with the Rhine and Danube River Commissions. European and international conferences were held to promote free navigation of the Elbe in 1861, to promote postal cooperation in 1863, to regulate marine signaling in 1864, to promote railways and railway regulation in 1878 and 1882, to deal with the emplacement of submarine cables in 1882, to regulate copyrights in 1884–1885, to deal with the status of the Suez Canal in 1885, to promote maritime law and radiotelegraphy in numerous conferences from 1889 to 1910, and to develop aerial law in 1910. This increasing intergovernmental contact was also felt in the area of monetary and trade policy in the late 1880s and early 1900s and was broadly related to exploration of ways that international cooperation among governments could promote the mutual economic welfare of states.

A positive impact of World War I was the emergence of deepening multilateral economic cooperation and its gradual institutionalization. In 1919 alone the International Institute of Commerce, the International Labor Organization (ILO), and the League of Nations were established. The League, in turn, established technical organizations to deal with economic and financial issues, communication and transit issues, and health issues. In 1939, a special report by Australia's Stanley Bruce recommended that many of the economic and social bodies of the League should be brought into greater coordination and collaboration. As negotiations for the United Nations took shape during World War II, this message was remembered, and the UN Economic and Social Council (ECOSOC) emerged as a major organ, not merely an ancillary committee.

Even before the inauguration of the United Nations, governments established the Food and Agriculture Organization (FAO) to enhance agricultural cooperation and development, and the International Bank for Reconstruction and Development (IBRD), or World Bank, and the International Monetary Fund (IMF) to help with the economic reconstruction of a war-torn world. The United Nations Educational, Scientific, and Cultural Organization (UNESCO), established in 1945, devoted substantial sums of its technical activities to developing countries. These organizations were followed in 1948 by the entering into force of the General Agreement on Tariffs and Trade (GATT), which was established to promote free trade in international commercial markets and thereby stimulate general economic growth and production, and the World Health Organization (WHO), which though established in 1946 did not commence operations until 1948. UN activities in the relief area were undertaken by the United Nations Relief and Rehabilitation Administration (UNRRA) from 1943 to 1947, the United Nations Children's Fund (UNICEF) in 1946, the International Refugee Organization (IRO) from 1947 to 1951, the United Nations Relief and Works Agency for Palestine (UNRWA) in 1949, the United Nations High Commissioner for Refugees (UNHCR) in 1951.

In the 1950s, UN institution building for international development continued with establishment of the Expanded Program of Technical Assistance (EPTA) in 1950 to supplement and expand the efforts of the many specialized agencies and ECOSOC's efforts on behalf of economic development activities. The EPTA was an initiative of U.S. President Harry S Truman. During its first decade of operations the EPTA eventually attracted an increasing number of voluntary contributions from governments, and contributions rose from about $20 to $50 million from 1950 to the early 1960s. The United States underwrote up to 60 percent of the funds in the early years but cut back to 40 percent as more countries joined the voluntary initiative. At about the same time as the EPTA was initiated, a Technical Assistance Administration was added to the UN Secretariat to enable it to administer and coordinate the growing number of agencies involved in technical and development assistance activities. An intergovernmental body known as the Technical Assistance Board was also created in order to provide governmental oversight of these activities. In the later 1950s, the International Finance Corporation (IFC) of the World Bank and the Special UN Fund for Development of (1957) were established to augment development assistance resources. In 1960, the World Bank added the International Development Association (IDA) to provide funds for the special needs of developing countries, and in 1963, the World Food Program (WFP) was created to supplement FAO activities in the food assistance arena, with the special purpose of meeting emergency food aid needs, most of which existed in the developing world.

The whole idea of the EPTA was to provide technical assistance advisers to countries lacking adequate administrative and technical support personnel. But with the alphabet soup of UN assistance agencies piling up, and the scope of needs and demands made by growing numbers of newly independent and relatively poor countries, the EPTA process was necessarily highly fragmented. The Special Fund established in 1957 attempted to concentrate UN development assistance activities. Poorer UN member countries had hoped to establish an even larger and more heavily endowed Special United Nations Fund for Economic Development (SUNFED), but the richer states who would have to foot the bill were not enthusiastic, and the Special Fund, a scaled-down version of SUNFED, was the compromise. Eventually, voluntary contributions by member states to the Special Fund exceeded those to the EPTA, by nearly double in 1965, the year that the two programs were finally collapsed into the United Nations Development Program (UNDP). Between 1960 and 1965, over thirty new members, all of them developing countries, joined the United Nations, and the number of voices calling for more active UN involvement in the eradication of poverty and in the promotion of economic prosperity for poor countries increased dramatically. The first of four consecutive UN Development Decades was declared in 1961, as developing countries appealed for attention to their economic woes. The tone of UN debates thus began to shift, and often the language of cooperation was replaced by that of confrontation.

HISTORY OF THE DEBATE

The creation of the UNDP was first proposed in 1962 and was debated by an ECOSOC committee and studied by the UN Secretariat from 1963 to 1964. ECOSOC voted in 1964 to recommend to the General Assembly the consolidation of the UN Special Fund and the EPTA with a view to consolidating and expanding their activities in a new UNDP. Given the financial crisis over peacekeeping and the consensus vote rule that prevailed during the 1964 session, the General Assembly postponed action on the creation of UNDP to the following year in its Second Committee. The ECOSOC proposal was amended in the Second Committee, which recommended a thirty-seven-member governing body for the UNDP composed of nineteen developing countries and seventeen developed countries. The United States, Belgium, Canada, France, and the Netherlands favored a smaller body with equally divided membership, but the developing country proposal was adopted in Committee and in the General Assembly by a vote of 89 to 0, with 11 abstentions. Under UNDP, the Special Program and the EPTA continued to operate, though in a more coordinated fashion.

Starting with an initial budget of just over $145 million in 1965, the UNDP saw its revenues rise substantially in subsequent years, reaching the $1 billion mark in 1989 and $1.5 billion just two years later. The rise in funds, must, however, be viewed in light of both the significant inflation that occurred over those years and the growth in numbers of poor countries requiring assistance. In the 1990s this included dozens of new countries of the former Soviet Union and Soviet bloc. Thus, while revenues have expanded, so have needs.

The role of UNDP was and remains largely coordinative in nature. Despite its growth in revenue, large operational development programs are not funded directly by UNDP but rather by the World Bank, IMF, and a host of other UN specialized agencies, bringing the total resources spent on development into the $15 to $20 billion range annually. UNDP helps to give these programs focus within the country of assistance, through the activities of its resident representative who has responsibility for coordinating development planning by host country agencies and the range of UN agencies operating within the country. Such coordination at the host country level is highly desirable to ensure a rational and efficient expenditure of resources in a planned fashion. However, interagency tensions and turf wars, both within host country and donor governments and within the UN system itself, routinely complicate the efforts by UNDP to impose a degree of order on development planning and programming.

The first UN Development Decade passed with little progress having been made in the objective condition of many developing countries. However, the developing countries had succeeded in establishing new UN agencies that were susceptible to their perspectives on the best means of achieving development. The creation of UNDP was a positive step forward. At Geneva, in 1964, the creation of the United Nations Conference on Trade and Development (UNCTAD) provided developing countries direct entrée into the UN General Assembly, where its often strident membership began to articulate the need for an increasingly radical restructuring of the international economy to ensure economic progress in the developing world. In 1965, acting on the demands of developing countries, the UN General Assembly unanimously endorsed the establishment of yet another international bureaucracy, the United Nations Industrial Development Organization (UNIDO), which became functional in 1967.

Throughout the 1960s, the creation of new layers of UN development bureaucracy added to the complexity of an already complicated and overlapping set of agency jurisdictions and mandates. As new issues or problems arose, the General Assembly, now dominated by developing countries, often just created new agencies to cope with them, rather than considering how such issues might best be addressed within existing UN machinery. Developed countries that paid virtually the entire bill for such agencies and their programs grew increasingly skeptical in the 1970s and 1980s about simply writing checks for the activities of such agencies. Resentful that multilateral funds were being mismanaged and wasted, they began to oppose expanded authorities and programs at the multilateral level.

Opposed to the developed states were the so-called Geneva 77, whose numbers rapidly escalated to over a hundred in the 1970s and 1980s. In the view of many representatives of these countries of Africa, Asia, and Latin America, the international economic system was stacked in favor of the rich states of the industrialized North. This basic standoff in views was already emerging in the 1960s, but in the 1970s, the attitudes hardened and the level of ideological rhetoric intensified. This was at least in part a function of the trends toward socialist governance in much of the Third World and the tendency of the Soviet Union and its Eastern European allies and, after 1973, the Communist government of the People's Republic of China to side with the developing countries against the industrialized states of the Western world in development-related debates.

The demands of the developing world were straightforward. They wanted more development assistance on more favorable terms, and they wanted a preferential system of tariffs to counteract what they viewed as unjust trade policy calling for reciprocal reduction of tariffs. Much of this debate was advanced by UNCTAD and in the General Assembly where the developing states enjoyed numerical superiority. But when the General Assembly set as a goal for its Second Development Decade in 1970 that developed states transfer 0.7 percent of their gross national product (GNP) in public sector aid to developing countries, the gap between General Assembly voting majorities and the performance of wealthy nations in adhering to the foreign assistance goal became obvious. Rich countries as a general

The Prek Thnot River basin of Cambodia was one of the first tributaries of the Mekong River studied by the UN Development Program as a potential multipurpose development project. Here heavy equipment is in operation in March 1970 at the site of the Prek Thnot Dam, which was constructed to enhance rice cultivation in the region. UN/DPI Photo

rule simply were not in a generous mood, and the vast majority of them fell far short of the goal. The Netherlands and the Scandinavian countries of Norway, Sweden, and Denmark were the only ones to come close, and their share of the overall foreign assistance budget was quite small.

Coupled with the frustration of rich country unresponsiveness to their demands, many developing countries faced real economic hardship in the 1970s, with energy-driven inflation, high oil prices, high food prices, and poor performance of basic commodities other than oil on international markets. Developed countries were hit hard by inflation and stagnating economies, too, and were in a much less generous mood to succor the needs of other nations when their own economies were experiencing significant price shocks.

It was at this very time that the Third World made its big push for a radical restructuring of the international economy, following a UN Special Session on Raw Materials in 1974, calling for the creation of a New International Economic Order (NIEO). This debate, which is chronicled more extensively in Debate 30, led to an even deeper rift between the chief aid-giving countries, such as the United Kingdom, France, Germany, and the United States, and the countries of the developing world. By the end of the 1970s, many Third World countries had actually lost ground in their struggle for economic development.

Despite the failures, in 1980 the UN General Assembly was able in a consensus vote to establish new targets for increases in foreign aid to developing countries, for increases in developing country exports, for increases in developing country domestic savings, and for increases in agricultural and industrial production. But expectations fell far short of these illusory targets. Conservative governments won election in the 1980s in the United States and in many European countries. They emphasized programs of budget cutting, not figuring out how to spend more money on foreign economic aid. Civil wars in many parts of the Third World sapped already bare-bones development budgets of resources as national security interests took precedence. Population growth in many developing countries often washed out absolute economic gains when calculated on a per capita basis. Inefficient and sometimes utterly corrupt governments in Third World countries mismanaged national resources. Debt among Third World countries skyrocketed. A development crisis of major proportions was brewing, and shrill charges and countercharges were hurled back and forth between the developed countries whose governments were no longer in a mood to be blamed for what they viewed as the utter irresponsibility of many developing country regimes. The latter, frustrated with years of mediocre economic performance and often negative growth, looked with anger and bitterness at a distribution of wealth that was growing even more skewed to the advantage of already wealthy states. Part of the problem facing the poorest countries concerned their heavy dependence on imported oil, which increased dramatically in price during the 1970s, producing a large flow of precious reserve currencies from the poorer countries to the Organization of Petroleum Exporting Countries (OPEC). One group of developing states, mainly but not exclusively Arab and Middle East countries, thus benefited economically, whereas the poor countries, called at the time the most seriously affected countries (MSAs), suffered. This shift in income to oil-rich states could not be blamed on the developed countries. Sensing their vulnerability to criticism, many Arab oil-exporting countries substantially increased their own foreign assistance budgets, but the vast majority of this aid found its way through bilateral programs to other less fortunate Arab nations. Non-Arab MSAs continued to experience difficulty owing to the oil shocks of the 1970s.

The worst area of crisis during the 1980s was, without doubt, Africa, where poverty was the most intense and widespread and accompanied by a host of nasty and brutal civil wars. A special session was convened by the General Assembly in 1986 to consider the terrible plight of many African countries, whose economies, already set back by the factors mentioned above, also were facing one of the worst continent-wide droughts in history. A five-year UN Program of Action for African Economic Recovery and

Development was adopted by unanimous consent. In the meantime, many African countries began to realize that not all of the blame could be placed on a colonial past or on developed country foreign aid policy. Slowly, but surely, many began a process of gradual reform of their economic policies, discarding centrally planned and socialist parastatal operations for a more free enterprise economy. They took often painful steps to reduce domestic subsidies, to invest more heavily in the agriculture sector and in rural areas, facing the reality that conservative governments in the West would not provide aid absent such reforms. Moreover, many countries, which had relied on economic ties with the Soviet Union, realized that their socialist benefactor was having serious economic problems of its own. By the late 1980s, the global political situation was rapidly moving against socialism and in favor of the revitalized free enterprise economies of the West. These underlying realities eventually had their effect on the rhetoric of debates at the United Nations, which grew increasingly more sober as the old days of East-West rivalry gave way to a world where there was only one development game in town: that dominated by the capitalist nations of the Western world.

OUTCOME OF THE DEBATE

No one doubts that the development of the Third World will eventually be of benefit to all concerned, even the wealthy states. The question is how this ought to be done. The effort by developing countries to use multilateral mechanisms during the NIEO debate largely failed. But clearly there was much truth to their underlying argument about the structural barriers developing countries face in attempting to develop their economies. Fairer trade, debt rescheduling, and new, larger, and more intelligently designed aid packages were much in need and continued to occupy the concern of developing countries throughout the 1990s.

A major obstacle to the achievement of greater development in the 1990s concerned the fact that dozens of newly created states, resulting from the collapse of communism and of the Soviet Union, now joined the ranks of aid-receiving countries, where many had been aid-givers in previous years. Just then, as many countries in the Third World, but especially in Africa, were undertaking serious domestic reforms and establishing a context in which larger amounts of Western aid could do some real good in jump-starting and consolidating their economic reforms, Western donor nations were becoming increasingly preoccupied with the political instabilities and economic problems of former Communist countries of the East bloc. This problem continued into the late 1990s and poses an ongoing challenge to the United Nations and all countries seriously interested in promoting the progressive development of the developing world.

Success stories in democratic reform and in economic growth do exist in many parts of the developing world. But for about forty of the least-developed countries, the prospects remain bleak. Thus, the development debate will doubtless continue well into the first decade of the Third Millennium, with at least some hope that the sustained growth experienced among the developed countries will finally be felt more broadly and deeply in much of the developing world where malnutrition, hunger, illiteracy, and disease still threaten well over half of humanity.

See also New International Economic Order (Debate 30); Trade and Development (Debate 24).

FOR FURTHER READING

Bennett, A. LeRoy. *International Organizations: Principles and Issues*. Englewood Cliffs, NJ: Prentice-Hall, 1995.

Boutros-Ghali, Boutros. *An Agenda for Development 1995*. New York: UN Publications, 1995.

Lewis, John P., and Valerina Kallab, eds. *Development Strategies Reconsidered*. New Brunswick, NJ: Transaction Books, 1986.

Murphy, Craig N. *International Organization and Industrial Change: Global Governance since 1850*. Oxford: Oxford University Press, 1994.

UN Development Yearbooks.

UN Yearbooks, various, 1959–1990.

Weiss, Thomas G. *Multilateral Development Diplomacy in UNCTAD: The Lessons of Group Negotiations, 1964–84*. London: Macmillan, 1986.

Nonproliferation of Nuclear Weapons (1965)

SIGNIFICANCE OF THE ISSUE

Of all the issues involving disarmament and arms control, one of the most difficult surrounds the principle of nonproliferation, which attempts to prevent the spread of nuclear weapons. This is not a principle that can be forced on nation-states because of the principle of sovereignty. However, given the tremendous destructiveness and destabilizing effects weapons of mass destruction entail, many countries have proved willing to promise to refrain from developing such systems. A few countries have refused to participate in nonproliferation regimes, and in some cases their refusal has increased instabilities in their regions. At the request of governments UN agencies have undertaken the monitoring of proliferation of weapons, giving the United Nations a pivotal role in the implementation of this important area of arms control policy. During the 1990s, the United Nations sponsored a convention banning chemical weapons, thus extending the concern about proliferation from nuclear weapons to biological and chemical weapons as well.

BACKGROUND TO THE DEBATE

During the early 1950s, only the United States and the Soviet Union possessed nuclear weapons. Indeed, after World War II the United States alone had the atomic bomb. Unfortunately, its proposal in 1946 to establish an international system for the development of nuclear power for peaceful means alone, with provisions for investigation and regulation of nuclear materials and prohibitions against the development of nuclear weaponry, the so-called Baruch Plan, was rejected by the Soviet Union, which countered with a proposal unacceptable to the West.

The opportunity thus passed for the pacification of nuclear technology, and the nuclear arms race had begun. Thus, the Soviet Union rapidly developed nuclear weapons technology. However, as time passed, other countries also joined the nuclear club, including the United Kingdom, which tested its first weapon in 1952, and France, which commenced testing in 1960. The People's Republic of China undertook its first nuclear test in 1964. India and Pakistan have also tested nuclear weapons, and several other countries are known to have advanced nuclear weapons capacities, including Israel, South Africa (with the change in governments in 1994 South Africa agreed to denuclearize), Brazil, Iraq, and North Korea. Concern about the proliferation of nuclear weapons increased during the 1950s and 1960s as more nations achieved nuclear power status. Almost any country with a sufficient amount of fissionable materials and enough money for research could begin building and testing such weapons. Given the political instability existing in many countries and regions, the spread of nuclear weapons was indeed a frightening prospect. But to do anything about it would require many acts of will on the part of many governments to refrain from acquiring this destructive technology.

HISTORY OF THE DEBATE

The issue of nonproliferation first came to the UN agenda in 1965 at the request of eight countries—Brazil, Burma, Ethiopia, India, Mexico, Nigeria, Sweden, and the United Kingdom. These governments proposed that the United Nations consider the promulgation of an agreement on nonproliferation. The General Assembly referred the question to its Disarmament Commission, deferring discussion in the Assembly on the item until the following year. In the meantime, both the United States and the Soviet Union submitted nonproliferation proposals for consideration by the commission that could not agree on compromise language, and the General Assembly could only exhort them to come to agreement. In 1968, the United States and Soviet Union submitted a joint draft of an agreement on nonproliferation to the commission that was reviewed by the General Assembly and approved by it in June by a vote of 95 to 4 (Albania, Cuba, Tanzania, and Zambia), with 21 abstentions. Most of the countries abstaining were developing countries with the exception of France, Spain, and Portugal. Days later, the UN Security Council adopted a three-power declaration (United Kingdom, United States, and Soviet Union) on the nonproliferation agreement. In the Non-proliferation Treaty (NPT), nuclear powers agreed to refrain from transferring nuclear weapons or technology to nonnuclear powers. Nonnuclear powers agreed not to receive or develop such weapons, and they agreed to accept safeguards monitored by the International Atomic Energy Agency (IAEA) in order to verify their compliance with the obligations entered into under the treaty. These safeguards allow the use and development of nuclear materials for peaceful purposes. The treaty entered into force on 5 March 1970. Most of the nonnuclear powers of East and West Europe ratified the agreement with the notable exception of France. Every five years since the entry into force of the NPT in 1970, states party have held a review conference.

The problem with the NPT lies in the ability of nonsignatory states to ignore its provisions, a simple fact of life in international relations. Although 170 member states had ratified the NPT by 1995, important nonsignatories included major regional powers, such as India, Pakistan, Iraq, and North Korea. The situation in Iraq, which was required under the cease-fire agreement with the UN Security Council in 1991 to subject itself to IAEA inspections to ensure the destruction of all nuclear, as well as chemical and biological, weapons-making capacities, illustrated the ways in which a determined government can frustrate the capacity of the United Nations to undertake verification processes. Iraq, though not a party to the NPT, was obliged under the Security Council resolutions to allow such inspections to be undertaken by the IAEA through the United Nations Special Commission (UNSCOM). Iraq managed to drag its feet and complain about the unfair composition of the inspection teams, attacking them as intrusions by the United States and the United Kingdom. In 1998, Iraq refused to permit

After the Iraqi invasion of Kuwait, the UN Security Council called for the destruction of all Iraqi nuclear, chemical, and bacteriological weapons and weapons-making facilities. The United Nations Special Commission (UNSCOM) was tasked with monitoring Iraqi compliance. Here an inspection team oversees the destruction of ballistic missiles at Dawrah, Iraq. UN/DPI Photo H. Arvidsson

any further inspections and was attacked in retaliation by U.S. and UK air forces. These bombings did nothing to ease Iraqi recalcitrance, and not until March 2000 did the United Nations make headway in restoring inspections of Iraq's capabilities for the production of weapons of mass destruction. With the creation of the United Nations Monitoring, Verification, and Inspection Commission (UNMOVIC), which replaced UNSCOM, Iraq renewed cooperation in the context of relaxed sanctions.

Apart from the NPT, governments have been encouraged to declare regional nuclear free zones. Such zones were established in Latin America and the Caribbean and in the South Pacific and South Atlantic, but efforts to promote the idea in the Middle East and South Asia have not born fruit to date.

Concern about nonproliferation of weapons of mass destruction also turned to biological and chemical weapons, which are even more easily and cheaply produced than nuclear weapons, leading some to refer to them as the "poor man's" bomb. In 1972, the UN General Assembly adopted the Convention on the Prohibition of the Development, Production and Stockpiling of Bacteriological and Toxin Weapons and on Their Destruction. It entered into force in 1975. In 1992, the Chemical Weapons Convention was adopted, extending the idea of eliminating such weapons from signatory state arsenals.

OUTCOME OF THE DEBATE

The United Nations was unable to play a direct role in many of the arms control agreements reached among contesting powers during the years of the Cold War. However, the one area in which the two superpowers did share an interest was in preventing an uncontrolled and thus destabilizing spread of nuclear weapons to other countries. They agreed to use the United Nations as the vehicle for the adoption of the NPT, which has gradually attracted very wide ratification by states. There remain a few holdouts, but the larger norm that now prevails in international law for well over 180 states is the duty of nonproliferation rather than the right to develop nuclear weapons.

With the collapse of the Soviet Union, there still exists a concern that nuclear materials could be sold on the black market to terrorist organizations or rogue governments who could use the materials and possibly even the technological knowledge of disaffected members of the scientific community of the former Soviet Union to develop nuclear weapons. Thus, while NPT has made vast strides through UN action, there are still some major hurdles to clear before the United Nations can say that the problem of nuclear proliferation has been solved and that the nuclear genie, let loose in the post–World War II years, has been finally contained.

See also Disarmament (Debate 1); Terrorism (Debate 28).

FOR FURTHER READING

Forsberg, Randall. *Arms Control in the New Era*. Cambridge, MA: MIT Press, 2000.
Forsberg, Randall, et al. *Nonproliferation Primer: Preventing the Spread of Nuclear, Chemical and Biological Weapons*. Cambridge, MA: MIT Press, 1995.
Osmañczyk, Edmund Jan. *Encyclopedia of the United Nations and International Agreements*. London: Taylor and Francis, 1985.
UN Yearbooks, 1965–1995.

Debate 27

Global Environment (1972)

SIGNIFICANCE OF THE ISSUE

One of the areas of global policy in which the United Nations has played a leading role is the environment. Its first Conference on the Human Environment in Stockholm in June 1972 represented a milestone in multilateral conference diplomacy by increasing international awareness to the problem of environmental degradation, its international scope, its international implications, and its relations to other issues such as economic development and population. Resulting from the Conference was the first UN body to serve as a focal point for international environmental policy, the United Nations Environment Program (UNEP). A controversial follow-up Earth Summit in Rio de Janeiro in 1992 again focused world attention on the problems of air and water pollution, acid rain, global warming, ozone depletion, deforestation, desertification, and loss of biodiversity, matters that call for explicit national action but also international cooperation.

BACKGROUND TO THE DEBATE

Prior to the 1960s, little international attention was paid to questions relating to the environment. Indeed, little attention was paid to such matters even in the national legislation of countries. But decades of scientific research and the visible results of pollution of the air and the rivers, lakes, and oceans on the environment began to get the attention of both national and international policymakers during the 1960s. As early as 1898, scientists had warned that carbon dioxide emissions could lead to global warming. Others, however, believed that the opposite effect was also possible and that a new ice age could be precipitated by such emissions. But the adverse health effects of industrial pollution and the inadequate treatment of human waste were becoming more obvious. Medical research indicated a higher incidence of lung cancer in cities with high levels of smog and air pollution and of other forms of cancer in areas with polluted water supplies. Armed with such information, legislators in the United States passed clean air and water acts in the 1960s, providing for regulation of industries engaged in pollution. Public awareness of the hazards of pollution for the environment and human health increased dramatically during this time. Countries in Western Europe and in other parts of the world also began to take steps to cope with the problem of environmental degradation.

In the late 1960s, a series of private meetings of businessmen and specialists from a variety of fields began studying the future effects of industrial and population growth on the availability of natural resources, the pollution of the environment, and the capacity to produce food and other renewable resources. Known as the Club of Rome, this private initiative led to controversial research results predicting disastrous consequences for the world if population and industrial growth were not immediately checked.

Less apocalyptic but still sober studies funded by the United Nations and undertaken by the secretary-general, pursuant to UN General Assembly Resolution 2398/XXII in 1968, suggested that the world had a decade in which to begin seriously addressing issues related to population, rampant and unplanned urban growth, resource depletion, pollution, the extinction of species, and food production. Known as the "U Thant Report" or "Man and His Environment," this study was published in 1969. The sense of urgency created by both the private studies and the UN research led to a General Assembly request in 1969 for the United Nations Educational, Scientific, and Cultural Organization (UNESCO) to undertake a series of regional symposia around the world in preparation for a World Conference on the Protection of Man's Environment to be held in Stockholm in 1972. The regional symposia were conducted in 1971 by the UN Economic Commissions for Africa, Asia and the Far East, Latin America, and Europe and a UNESCO session in Beirut. From 5 June to 14 June 1972, the first historic international meeting ever held to discuss the condition of the global environment was held at Stockholm.

HISTORY OF THE DEBATE

A total of 113 member states of the United Nations gathered in Stockholm to consider the state of the global environment. Even so, the conference was marred from the outset by Cold War controversy, centering on German representation at the conference. Neither of the Germanys, the Federal Republic or the German Democratic Republic, was then yet a member of the United Nations. Both became members in the following year. The East bloc sought first to delay the meeting until 1973 (the year in which both Germanics were admitted to the United Nations), and when this proposal failed, it sought to include language that would invite "other interested states" to the meeting in addition to UN members or members of other spe-

Representatives of more than 100 nations gather in Stockholm, Sweden, for a two-week UN Conference on the Global Environment (5–16 June 1972). The Second Committee of the Conference here deliberates issues concerning environment and development. UN/DPI Photo Yutaka Nagata

cialized agencies, including the International Atomic Energy Agency. Under the criteria established by the General Assembly, the Federal Republic of Germany was invited to the conference, but the German Democratic Republic was not. For this reason, the Soviet Union and most of the East European countries boycotted the meeting.

Three main committees were established to examine the six substantive issues on the conference agenda. The First Committee discussed human settlements and the noneconomic aspects of environmental issues. The Second Committee discussed natural resources management and its relation to development. The Third Committee studied issues pertaining to pollution and to an appropriate institutional response to environmental questions. A Working Group on the Declaration on the Human Environment was also established by the conference. Setting the tone for the gathering, the opening speech by the secretary-general of the conference noted that governments were launching a new approach in coping with man-made environmental problems and that while a no-growth policy was unrealistic, governments would need to reexamine the basic purposes and processes of such growth. On 16 June, the conference adopted a Declaration on the Human Environment, which acknowledged the fact that environmental problems in the developing world were often a consequence of underdevelopment and in the developed world a function of industrial activity.

In the twenty-six principles that followed, it was declared that governments should strive to protect the environment through conservation and antipollution measures, to provide assistance to developing countries to guard against natural disaster, to promote stable prices for commodities, to promote the rational and planned development of human settlements and housing, to encourage the rational management of resources, to pursue environmental education and scientific research, to encourage just compensation to victims of pollution or environmental damage, and to seek the elimination of nuclear weapons. The text of the Declaration was adopted by acclamation, although a number of countries expressed reservations and other observations concerning various provisions.

The conference also made a total of 109 recommendations in its Action Plan for international environmental action, including in the areas of human settlements, natural resource management, pollution measurement and control, the relationship of environment to development and trade policy, and the pursuit of environmental education. Although adopted by the conference, several states indicated their opposition to particular provisions. The United States and several other states did not accept the principle that when environmental regulations restricted trade with developing countries, that compensation should be paid. The United States, Canada, Japan, and a number of West European states opposed the creation of a separate financial mechanism for human settlements, and Japan voiced its opposition to a recommendation calling for a ten-year moratorium on whaling.

In other action, China, France, and Gabon opposed a conference condemnation of nuclear tests, especially above-ground testing, which otherwise was adopted by a vote of 56 to 3, with 29 abstentions. Finally, the conference proposed the creation of a governing council for environmental programs, the establishment of a small secretariat to carry out the recommendation of the governing council, and a voluntary fund to support environmental projects. It also called upon the General Assembly to establish 5 June of each year as World Environment Day.

On 15 December, the UN General Assembly passed by overwhelming majorities resolutions that established World Environment Day and created the UNEP with a secretariat, a governing council, a voluntary environmental fund, and Earthwatch, an international environmental information network. Recommendations concerning various aspects of the conference plan of action were also approved, some overwhelmingly (action to prevent pollution) and others with smaller majorities or greater opposition. Separate financing for human settlements, for instance, continued to arouse Western opposition.

The issue of the environment and its relation to development illustrated divisions between how developed and developing states viewed the environmental debate. The wealthy states, which were already industrialized and able financially to consider imposition of stricter environmental regulations through national action, emphasized the need for national legislation to prevent pollution. By contrast, the developing states, not yet industrialized but hoping to achieve that status, noted that such national action on their part would be very expensive and thus an obstacle to development. They insisted that wealthier states should assist them in this process, to ensure both their increased development and the preservation of a safe environment. The industrialized states, though unwilling to recognize an international duty to provide such assistance, did over time realize that some compensatory financing scheme would be necessary if substantial progress were to be made in improving the global environment.

The creation of UNEP was an important step for the UN system, although other UN bodies such as UNESCO and the International Labor Organization (ILO) also took action on environmental issues in subsequent years. UNESCO developed its Man and the Biosphere project in 1976—a program that sets aside biosphere reserves to protect endangered species—and it also held a conference in Tblisi in 1977 regarding environmental education. The ILO drafted a convention in 1977 on environmental hazards in the workplace. UNEP established its Global Environmental Monitoring System (GEMS) in 1975, initiated an International Register of Potentially Toxic Chemicals in 1976, launched a World Conservation Strategy in 1980, and produced its first report on the state of the world's environment in 1983.

In the meantime, governments began to negotiate a variety of new treaties establishing various protections of the environment as international awareness of environmental problems grew. In 1975 several global environmental conventions entered into force, including the Convention on Wetlands of International Importance, the Convention on the Prevention of Marine Pollution by Dumping of Wastes and Other Matter, the Convention Concerning the Protection of the World Cultural and Natural Heritage, and the Convention on International Trade in Endangered Species of Wild Fauna and Flora. In 1976, under UNEP auspices, the Convention for the Protection of the Mediterranean Sea against Pollution was negotiated. After nearly a decade of intense negotiation, the UN Convention on the Law of the Sea, which included provisions for the protection of the marine environment, was signed in 1982. In the following year, the first ever international agreement regulating air pollution, the Convention on Long-Range Transboundary Air Pollution (Acid Rain), entered into force, as did a Convention on the Conservation of Migratory Species of Wild Animals and a Convention on the Prevention of Pollution from Ships. Further treaties on conserving tropical timber (1985), on early notification of nuclear accidents (1986), and emergency assistance in case of nuclear accidents (1987) entered into force in subsequent years.

In 1985, governments began negotiations on a treaty to protect the ozone layer. Scientific studies had demonstrated that the use of chlorofluoro-carbons (CFCs) in refrigerants, solvents, propellants, and other products was leading to a substantial depletion in the ozone layer, which protects the earth from excessive ultraviolet radiation from the sun. While developed states could afford to eliminate the production and use of CFCs, and begin using other more expensive refrigerants and coolants for air conditioning and cooling, developing countries were in no position to do so. Eventually developed states recognized their need and provided for the inclusion of a Fund from which developing states could draw resources to ensure the eventual ban of CFCs on a global scale. The Vienna Convention for the Protection of the Ozone Layer entered into force in 1988, and a year later, the Montreal Protocol on Substances that Deplete the Ozone Layer also entered into force.

After years of haggling over the need for a second International Conference on the Environment, and after nearly two decades of progress in developing international environmental law, many parts of the developing world continued to experience a degradation of the environment, and in this context, the UN General Assembly voted in 1989 to convene a United Nations Conference on Environment and Development (UNCED) in 1992 at Rio de Janeiro, Brazil. In 1990, for the first time, the World Bank, whose programs had been widely criticized for their antienvironmental impacts, joined with UNEP and the UN Development Program to establish the Global Environment Facility to fund environmental projects in developing countries. Momentum was growing to place international environmental issues in a development-related context.

The ambitious agenda of the UNCED, otherwise known as the Rio Earth Summit, recognized that while much progress in international environmental awareness and law had been made, much of the world's population, especially in the developing world, lived in a context of increasing environmental degradation. With the biodiversity of the planet under attack, with increased deforestation and desertification, with ongoing air and water pollution, especially in Eastern Europe and in much of the developing world continuing largely unabated, consensus had developed that a more global and sustained program for environmental protection and development was necessary. Representatives of 182 nations gathered at Rio together with 650 nongovernmental organizations (NGOs) and representatives of other concerned citizens for the earth summit. An estimated 17,000 people participated in events leading up to or including the conference, including 7,000 representatives of NGOs from 165 countries. In the first week of the conference itself, more than 200 speeches by governments, NGOs, and various intergovernmental organizations (IGOs) were heard. This was followed by a two-day summit of 118 world leaders, which included a roundtable session among government leaders, the largest such gathering ever held. Resulting from UNCED were the Rio Declaration, a Program of Action, known as Agenda 21, an 800-page document including hundreds of programmatic proposals for action, and a Statement of Forest Principles, aimed at promoting more sustainable management of the world's forests. As always, the major issues of controversy concerned financing and implementation of the proposed agenda. Conference president Maurice Strong estimated that the $125 billion required to implement the program of action was $70 million more than the then-existing level of the global Official Development Assistance provided by governments. Only about $7 billion was officially committed by governments at the conference, far short of its ambitious agenda. The conference acknowledged the long-standing right of nations to exploit their own natural resources, but it called upon governments to recognize their duty to ensure that such activities did not damage the environment of neighboring states. The traditional split between developed and developing countries was again reflected in the desire of the former to emphasize the need to protect the environment and by the latter to see that the Declaration reflected a concrete and detailed recognition of the relationship of development to the environment. The United States specifically objected to Principle 3 in the Declaration, which established a right to development. The twenty-seven principles included in the Rio Declaration represented a clarion call to the protection of the environment and the promotion of sustained development. However, the principles, as in all declarations, required national action for full implementation. The conference did establish a Commission on Sustainable Development, which meets annually to monitor progress on implementation of the Rio Declaration and to which member governments submit annual reports.

The conference also unveiled two new environmental treaties for signature, including the Convention on Biological Diversity, which the United States refused to sign owing to its provisions on the transfer of ideas and technology and its presumably unworkable financing scheme, and the UN Framework Convention on Climate Change aimed at the voluntary reduction of greenhouse gas emissions by the end of the 1990s. The latter treaty entered into force in 1994 and won widespread adherence among states. The Conference of Parties consisting of the representatives of ratifying governments has met annually since 1995 to review progress on implementation of the treaty. The countries of the European Union (EU) and Small Island States have been among the strongest supporters of the Convention of Climate Change. The industrialized countries of the former Eastern bloc are large potential producers of greenhouse gases and so may find it difficult to meet the treaty goals. The Organization of Petroleum Exporting Countries' (OPEC's) main concern turns on the effect of lower oil consumption on their national economies. Although developing countries, including China, are not subject to the same restrictions under the treaty as are industrialized states, their highly variable economic circumstances and resource bases make many potentially subject to greater regulation. Finally, countries such as the United States, Japan, Canada, Australia, New Zealand, and Norway seek to achieve flexible approaches to limiting greenhouse gas emissions. The essential obligation such countries and the EU states make is to reduce their greenhouse gas emissions to 1990 levels by the year 2000, a goal that proved to be far too optimistic. The developed industrial states produce about three-quarters of greenhouse gas emissions, but are best situated to protect themselves from their effects. Developing countries, however, seek relief from imposing strict emissions so that they might proceed with economic development. At the same time they are more vulnerable to climate change than are the developed states.

OUTCOME OF THE DEBATE

The condition of the global environment continues to be of considerable concern to UN environmental bodies and to governments. Responding to the Agenda 21 program of the Rio Earth Summit, the UN Secretariat established an Inter-agency Committee on Sustainable Development to coordinate the work of the various UN specialized agencies responsible for following up on various provisions of Agenda 21. The secretary-general also established a High-Level Advisory Board on Sustainable Development, consisting of experts and eminent persons to advise him directly on emerging environmental issues and their impact on development. A follow-up review of the Rio Conference took place on its five-year anniversary in 1997. National reports, with the exception of Eastern European countries, where economic recession had limited industrial activity, showed an increase in greenhouse gas production. Expectations on the speed with which reductions could be achieved were downsized. Instead of reaching 1990 levels by the year 2000 by voluntary efforts, governments began to explore ways of achieving legally binding targets by 2005, 2010, or 2015. At Kyoto, in 1997, a Protocol Amending the Climate Change Convention was negotiated under which the industrialized countries are obliged to cut greenhouse gas emissions by 5.2 percent, but entry into force of the agreement awaits the ratification of at least six countries with the largest emissions in 1990. The Kyoto protocol meets stiff opposition in the U.S. Senate. UN experts at UNEP and the World Meteorological Organization reported record-high temperatures in 1998 and worry that the greenhouse gas effect is a major contributor. There is no scientific consensus that this is in fact the case, but many continue to worry that delay on the part of major greenhouse gas–producing countries in trimming their emissions will only contribute to further global warming. If the latter does in fact occur, it will lead to the melting of polar ice caps and to a rise in the sea level, threatening inundation of coastal areas. Debate continues as to whether this is a realistic worry, but in the meantime various UN bodies are now gathering and disseminating more reliable data on global temperature fluctuations, on climate change and the chemical composition of the atmosphere, on the transfer and deposit of harmful substances through the atmosphere, and on the relationship between atmospheric changes in composition and changes in regional and global climate. The fact that such data for previous decades is at best spotty raises an ongoing debate about comparability of data and the meaning of short-term shifts or trends.

As for efforts to increase development assistance, this too has not lived up to the expectations of Rio. In 1991 the average percentage of donor country gross national product dedicated to foreign aid was 0.34. Far from increasing, under the influence of Rio, this had dropped to 0.27 by 1995, illustrating the inability of international declarations to elicit binding responses in national legislation. Connecting environment to development did little to change the ongoing reality of the struggle for development in the Third World, leading to considerable frustration among leaders of developing countries.

Not all of the news is pessimistic, however. There is substantial evidence of improvements in the quality of the air and water in many developed states and some developing countries. Several developing countries have realized substantial improvement in their economies. Many of the Asian states that experienced economic setbacks and crises in the period 1995–1997, after many years of spectacular previous growth, have begun to recover. Many countries have begun programs of reforestation, water development, and conservation, often with UN help.

The battle for a clean environment is a matter of ongoing concern for the United Nations and will doubtless remain a main preoccupation in future decades. It will most certainly continue to be linked to the problems of development in the South as well, promising to make for continued spirited debate between countries on different sides of the North-South division.

See also Health (Debate 8); Human Settlements (Debate 36); Law of the Sea (Debate 29); Population (Debate 15); Status of Women (Debate 33); Third World Development Programming (Debate 25); World Monetary System (Debate 5).

FOR FURTHER READING

Brown, Lester R., et al. *The State of the World 1984* [and subsequent years]. New York: Norton, 1984 (and subsequent years).

Finlay, David J., and Thomas Hovet, Jr. *7304: International Relations on the Planet Earth*. New York: Harper and Row, 1975.

Gosovic, Branislav. *The Quest for World Environmental Cooperation: The Case of the UN Global Monitoring System*. London: Routledge, 1992.

Meadows, Donella, Dennis Meadows, Jorgen Randers, and William W. Behrens III. *The Limits of Growth*. New York: Universe Books, 1972.

Moore, Thomas Gale. *Climate of Fear: Why We Shouldn't Worry about Global Warming*. Washington, DC: CATO Institute, 1998.

Rayner, Steve, and Elizabeth Malone. *Human Choice and Climate Change*. 4 vols. Columbus, OH: Batelle Press, 1998.

Spector, Bertram, et al. *Negotiating International Regimes: Lessons Learned from the UN Conference on Environment and Development (UNCED)*. Norwell, MA: Graham and Troutman, 1994.

Tolba, Mustafa, et al. *Global Environmental Diplomacy*. Cambridge, MA: MIT Press, 1998.

UN Chronicles, 1990–1999.

UN Economic and Social Council. *Problems of the Human Environment: Report of the Secretary-General*. New York: UN Document E/4667, 1969.

UN Yearbooks, 1971–1972.

Young, Oran, ed. *The Effectiveness of International Environmental Regimes*. Cambridge, MA: MIT Press, 1999.

Terrorism (1972)

SIGNIFICANCE OF THE ISSUE

Terrorism is a form of violence directed explicitly against innocent civilian populations for the purpose of spreading terror. Although international law tolerates acts of war undertaken by states for legitimate reasons, such as self-defense and as a collective punishment for aggression, especially when they are undertaken by the armed forces of countries and protect innocent civilians, terrorism explicitly targets innocent civilians. Acts of terrorism have been very common in the post–World War II era, often in connection with struggles for national liberation and self-determination, which complicates any effort to outlaw or punish terrorist activities, especially when they are financed or supported by the policies of governments. The issue was also significant in the UN setting, because the secretary-general himself sought to have the matter included on the General Assembly agenda.

BACKGROUND TO THE DEBATE

Terrorist activities are not new, although modern communications have both made awareness of acts of terrorism more widely known and probably also stimulated a higher incidence of such acts insofar as one goal of terrorism is to gain public attention. Assassinations of heads of state and diplomatic figures trace back to ancient history. In more modern times, pirates have continued to use terrorist tactics on the high seas, and during the 1960s, a huge increase in air hijackings occurred, sometimes accompanied by threats against passengers who were held as hostages.

The earliest international effort to respond to and counter terrorism took place under the League of Nations in 1937, which adopted a Convention for the Prevention and Punishment of Terrorism, but that instrument failed to attract ratification by states and never entered into force. Major efforts to

Terrorists employ attacks on both government buildings and innocent civilian populations to air their grievances. Here bomb devastation caused by and Irish Republican Army attack on Whitehall is depicted. Hulton-Deutsch Collection/CORBIS

counter terrorism were undertaken by governments in the 1960s and 1970s with the passage of treaties aimed at curbing crimes aboard aircraft, air piracy, and acts of violence against civil aviation. The International Civil Aviation Organization (ICAO) was the principal agency through which such agreements were undertaken by governments. The first ICAO Convention on Offenses and Certain Other Acts Committed on Board Aircraft was signed in Tokyo in 1963. It was followed by an ICAO Convention for the Suppression or Unlawful Seizure of Aircraft done at The Hague in 1970 and the ICAO Convention to Discourage Acts of Violence against Civil Aviation done at Montreal in 1971. These treaties were considered necessary by governments, given the increasing incidence of air hijacking and other acts against the safety of aviation that occurred during the 1960s.

Coupled with air piracy was the growing number of terrorist organizations associated with various national liberation movements throughout the world, including the Middle East where Palestinian groups used terrorism as a routine instrument of violence against the citizens and state of Israel and against Western nations supporting Israel. But many other areas of the world where political grievances of non-self-governing peoples remained unresolved also produced terrorist activities, including such groups as the South Molluccans, the Basques, the Irish Republican Army, Armenian nationalists, and Puerto Rican nationalists. The political turmoil of the 1960s also produced domestic terrorist organizations in Japan, the United States, and various European countries.

HISTORY OF THE DEBATE

Against the backdrop of increasing terrorist incidents, including acts of violence against national leaders, diplomats, international passengers, and civilians in the late 1960s and early 1970s, UN Secretary-General Kurt Waldheim asked the General Assembly to place the issue of terrorism on its agenda in 1972. He acknowledged that the problem was complex and not easy to solve but pointed out that far from being an isolated domestic activity, terrorism was taking on an increasingly international character, both in terms of its violent expression and its root causes, that it was becoming increasingly sophisticated owing to modern technology, and for these reasons, that it needed to be discussed in an international setting. The General Assembly, in referring the agenda item to its Sixth Committee on legal affairs, foreshadowed the basic outlines of the debate on terrorism that followed by giving the agenda item the rather explicit title of: "Measures to prevent international terrorism which endangers or takes innocent human lives or jeopardizes fundamental freedoms, and study of the underlying causes of those forms of terrorism and acts of violence which lie in misery, frustration, grievance and despair and which cause some people to sacrifice human lives, including their own, in an attempt to effect radical changes." Debate over this verbose title evoked considerable controversy, and the decision to include it on the agenda was effected by a vote of 66 to 27, with 33 abstentions, indicating that many states even had reservations about discussing this thorny issue.

In committee, the United States introduced a draft convention for the prevention and punishment of certain acts of international terrorism, which provided that ratifying states would impose severe penalties in punishment of terrorist acts. Weighing heavily on the minds of many speakers were the recent attacks on Israeli athletes at the Olympic Games in Munich. Many delegations held that all such acts undermined international order and required priority attention. The United States supported the convening of an international conference to establish a convention. The Soviet Union preferred that a convention result after consideration by the International Law Commission. Both countries disavowed the use of terrorism for any purpose, including that of national liberation. However, a number of Third World countries expressed the view that Western governments had long tolerated brutal, inhumane, and terrorist treatment of oppressed and colonized peoples and only now reacted when this mistreatment manifested itself in international terrorism. Thus, they emphasized, it was critical to consider the underlying causes of terrorism, not just its symptoms. Israel pointed out that Arab countries had opposed the adoption of the agenda item owing to the fact that they were responsible directly or indirectly for the terrorist activities in the Middle East. Arab states stressed that Palestinian patriots were not terrorists but fighters for national liberation and self-determination. China supported this position, striking out at Israel, Portugal, and South Africa as major sources of imperialism, colonialism, racism, and Zionism.

Three draft resolutions on the subject of terrorism were submitted, one by the United States, one by several Western powers, and one by sixteen members of the Geneva 77. Owing to the majority of developing countries, the only resolution voted on and adopted by the Sixth Committee was the sixteen-power resolution favored by the developing countries, which gave special attention to the underlying causes of terrorism while condemning terrorist acts. The committee vote was 76 to 34, with 16 abstentions. Its resolution was adopted by the General Assembly by a vote of 76 to 35, with 17 abstentions, and provided for the creation of a thirty-five-member Ad Hoc Committee on International Terrorism, three subcommittees of which subsequently considered the questions of drafting a definition of international terrorism, dealing with the underlying causes of terrorism, and studying measures for the prevention of international terrorism. Debate was deferred in the following two years until taken up again in 1976 and 1977. Divisions between developed states and the developing countries persisted over whether or not to treat the activities of liberation groups as falling under the rubric of terrorist acts. Commanding majorities, developing countries persisted in distinguishing between individual acts of terrorism and acts committed by groups in pursuit of national liberation.

In 1973, the UN General Assembly did pass by consensus the UN Convention for the Protection and Punishment of Crimes against Internationally Protected Persons, Including Diplomatic Agents. In 1979 it also approved the Convention against the Taking of Hostages. During these and subsequent years the General Assembly repeatedly passed resolutions in which all acts of terror were condemned in strong terms. However, specific efforts to define terrorism eluded consensus.

OUTCOME OF THE DEBATE

The international community has not been able to gain full consensus on how to treat terrorist acts, on how to deal with terrorists, nor on how to define terrorism. Most steps against terrorist activities have been undertaken by international or regional agreements. In 1988 the United Nations turned its attention to the connection between terrorism and narcotics trafficking at a conference in Vienna that produced a Convention against Illicit Traffic in Narcotic Drugs and Psychotropic Substances.

Real progress in preventing terrorist acts depends on state agreement and practice in prohibiting the use of their territories for terrorist training and activity and in either punishing terrorists through domestic action or extraditing them to other states for trial and punishment. Some progress has been made in these areas by recent actions of the UN General Assembly and other UN bodies. In 1994, the General Assembly adopted a Declaration on Measures to Eliminate International Terrorism, which addressed issues relating to extradition and on sharing information about terrorists. In the same year, the UN International Law Commission, acting under a General Assembly request to act as a matter of priority, adopted a draft statute of the International Criminal Court, which would have jurisdiction over genocide, serious war crimes, torture, hostage taking, hijacking, and illicit trafficking in narcotic drugs. This convention was opened for signature in 1998 after the UN Diplomatic Conference in Rome decided to establish a permanent International Criminal Court and adopted its Statute by a vote of 120 to 7, with 21 abstentions.

In 1997, the General Assembly adopted the International Convention for the Suppression of Terrorist Bombings, which for the first time made no distinction between terrorist acts and the activities of national liberation groups. Some countries believed that the actions of the military forces of states should have been included in this convention, but they are exempted from the treaties provisions. This convention calls for states to take steps for the suppression and punishment of terrorist bombings within their own jurisdictions, lists extraditable offenses, and provides that states may exercise jurisdiction over acts committed against their own nationals abroad. In the same year the Assembly adopted one of its strongest resolutions against terrorist acts, declaring them to be "criminal acts intended or calculated to provoke a state of terror in the general public, a group of persons or particular persons for political purposes." Such acts were condemned as unjustifiable under all circumstances "whatever the considerations of a political, philosophical, ideological, racial, ethnic, religious or any other nature that may be invoked to justify them." This represented an advance over the debates of the 1970s and 1980s.

While terrorist acts, such as the bombing of the U.S. embassies in Kenya and Tanzania, continue to attract widespread attention, the frequency of terrorist acts declined in the 1990s, even as the United Nations and related bodies reached a consensus that such acts needed to be more aggressively investigated, tried, and punished. Terrorist acts are unlikely to be totally eradicated, but through international cooperation, they can be suppressed and reduced.

See also Arab-Israeli Dispute (Debate 6); Decolonization (Debate 18); Defining Aggression (Debate 13); Zionism as Racism (Debate 34).

FOR FURTHER READING

Alexander, Yonah. *International Terrorism: National, Regional and Global Perspectives*. New York: Praeger, 1981.

Guelke, Adrian. *The Age of Terrorism and the International System*. New York: St. Martin's, 1998.

Laqueur, Walter. *The New Terrorism: Fanaticism and the Arms of Mass Destruction*. Oxford: Oxford University Press, 1999.

Lesser, Ian O., et al. *The New Terrorism*. Santa Monica, CA: Rand Corporation, 1999.

Reich, Walter, ed. *Origins of Terrorism: Psychologies, Ideologies, States of Mind*. Washington, DC: Woodrow Wilson Center Press, 1998.

UN Chronicles, 1990–1999.

UN Yearbooks, 1972–1995.

Von Glahn, Gerhard. *Law among Nations: An Introduction to Public International Law*. New York: Allyn and Bacon, 1996.

Law of the Sea (1973)

SIGNIFICANCE OF THE ISSUE

Seventy percent of the earth's surface is covered by seas and oceans, and these waterways serve as highways of international commerce and contain vast reserves of living and mineral resources. Rights of navigation and access to marine commerce and fisheries have been sources of concern and conflict among nations throughout history. With the discovery during the International Geophysical Year in 1957 that trillions of dollars' worth of metallic nodules existed on the floor of the deep seabeds, a new potential dimension of either conflict or cooperation among nations was realized. Efforts to manage national exploitation of deep seabed resources became one of the most high-stakes games of international negotiation during the 1970s as the nearly decade-long Third United Nations Conference on the Law of the Sea haggled over how to ensure the fair and peaceful means by which exploitation of ocean resources should be governed. The controversy continued after a Convention on the Law of the Sea was established, but in the 1990s, after revisions to the treaty, an international authority to govern the high seas was slowly implemented on the principle that resources found beyond the limit of national jurisdiction should be treated as the common heritage of mankind.

BACKGROUND TO THE DEBATE

For centuries, countries attempted to cordon off various parts of the seas and oceans as private national domains. Enforcing such policies, however, was always difficult. During the seventeenth century, governments hotly contested for control of the seas; some countries, such as Portugal, which was a dominant seagoing power, advanced the idea of closed seas, but famous Dutch legal scholar Hugo von Groot (known as Grotius) argued persuasively for the freedom of the seas doctrine. In the practice of states,

especially during the eighteenth and nineteenth centuries, the latter principle prevailed. According to this principle, all governments had a right to
establish navies and commercial fleets and to make use of the oceans for
navigation, trade, and fishing. At about the same time, states in northern
Europe asserted that coastal states could exert jurisdiction over a territorial
sea of 3 miles in width, roughly the distance a cannon could fire, thus giving rise to the "cannon-shot rule." A coastal state could claim exclusive
rights to fishing, to exploitation of other resources, and to imposition of
customs regulations in this zone. Gradually most coastal states accepted
this rule, although some states, such as those in Latin America, asserted territorial sea claim as wide as 200 miles. Thus, while freedom of the seas prevailed on the high seas, the notion that coastal states could make claims to a
territorial sea, and even a contiguous zone beyond it, in time became acknowledged in the practice and law of nations.

Issues relating to the law of the sea, such as the laying of submarine cables and their protection, rules for navigation and adjustment of claims resulting from collisions at sea, and rules for registry of vessels and
suppression of piracy, also emerged in the late 1800s and early 1900s. The
League of Nations addressed such issues as the limits of the territorial sea,
the use of living resources of the sea, and the protection of whales in the
1920s and 1930s.

During the latter half of the twentieth century, however, the discovery of
valuable resources, including oil, on continental shelves, which in many
cases extend well beyond the territorial sea claims of states, on the average
about 30 miles but sometimes as far as 600 miles before descending into the
deep seabed, led countries to assert exclusive jurisdiction over them. Argentina was the first to do so in 1944, and the United States followed suit in
1945, with the Truman proclamation. Initially, other governments protested these actions, but within a relatively short period of time, many
coastal states exerted similar claims to their continental shelf and the resources found on the seabed or in the subsoil of the shelf. Because the width
of the continental shelf varies considerably, sometimes less than a mile, as
on the Pacific coast of South America, to hundreds of miles in areas of the
South Pacific, the International Law Commission of the United Nations
suggested that claims should be limited to "a depth of 200 meters, or beyond that limit, to where the depth of the superjacent waters admit of the
exploitation of the natural resources." This definition was also adopted in
the language of the 1958 Convention on the Continental Shelf, which was
negotiated at the First UN Conference on the Law of the Sea at Geneva.
Other conventions resulting from this Conference attended by eighty-six
states governed rules for demarking the territorial sea, reiterating the principle of the freedom of the seas on the high sea, and conservation of fisheries and other living resources. A Second UN Conference on the Law of the
Sea in 1960 failed to produce further progress on issues regarding the terri-

torial sea and fishing rights. However, in other UN settings, rules for protecting the rights of landlocked states were discussed at a conference of landlocked states including Afghanistan, Austria, Byelorussia, Bolivia, Czechoslovakia, Hungary, Luxembourg, Nepal, San Marino, Switzerland, and the Vatican. Such states were concerned about rights of access to the high seas. The UN International Law Commission studied measures for the codification of the law of the sea during the 1950s that served as useful groundwork for subsequent UN conferences.

During the late 1960s, the UN General Assembly took steps to reevaluate the entire law of the sea in light of scientific knowledge and technical developments, especially as they applied on the high seas beyond the limits of national jurisdiction. It set up an ad hoc committee in 1967 to study the matter, after an impassioned and eloquent speech by Ambassador Arvid Pardo of Malta captured the imagination of the Assembly. He called for the United Nations to adapt the law of the sea to a new and rapidly changing international landscape. In 1968 the ad hoc committee was enlarged and renamed the Committee on the Peaceful Uses of the Sea-Bed and the Ocean Floor beyond the Limits of National Jurisdiction, As a result of this committee's work, in 1970, the General Assembly adopted a Declaration on the deep seabed and ocean floor beyond the limits of national jurisdiction, asserting that the resources found therein are the "common heritage of mankind." It also decided to call a Third Law of the Sea Conference to convene in 1973.

Already the basic outlines of the political debate and the bloc politics of the law of the sea were becoming manifest, and they were rooted in basic considerations of geographical location, ocean topography, development status, national resource availability, historical fishing rights, military security, and ideological status. To understand the history of the Third Law of the Sea Conference, by far the largest and most important of the sea law conferences, it is necessary to explore the various interest groups that formed. First, developing states in general, but with some notable exceptions, favored the idea of placing deep seabed resources under the management of an international regime that could ensure that the wealth garnered from deep seabed mining activities could be equitably distributed among all nations but most particularly to the developing nations who lacked the technological capacity to exploit ocean resources. Thus they emphasized the "common heritage of mankind" doctrine. This desire was felt perhaps most acutely by landlocked developing countries who could make no territorial sea or continental shelf claims and by geographically disadvantaged states, who could exert only limited claims owing to their limited coastal access or because they were hemmed in by neighboring or nearby states. Support for the idea of an international regulatory regime extended even to the wealthier landlocked states who supported this general approach.

Exceptions to this general pattern included Third World countries whose economies were based substantially on the production and trade of basic minerals such as manganese, cobalt, copper, zinc, and other metals contained in the deep seabed nodules. A sudden or massive dumping of seabed-related metals such as these on international markets could ruin the economies of land-based producers of such metals. Thus, countries such as Zambia, Zaire, Zimbabwe, Bolivia, and others, though generally supportive of the idea of an international seabed authority and regime, wanted guarantees that their economies would not be adversely affected. Moreover, some developing countries had substantial coast lines and could protect resources found within their continental shelves. For them, the right to exert these claims was a priority, even when they supported the general notion of an international seabed authority.

For wealthier states who possessed the technology to undertake deep-seabed mining, the idea of a common heritage was fine, so long as it did not prevent businesses from obtaining licenses to do the mining. But developing country demands for a transfer of such technology to them or to an internationally controlled enterprise that would exploit resources on their behalf were stoutly opposed by several wealthy states, including the United States, United Kingdom, France, and Germany.

The two superpowers, though at odds over a host of ideological matters, shared a common national security concern and similar military interests in keeping sea lanes, international straits, and other maritime passages open for transit of their naval vessels and submarines. For them, any deal to establish an international zone of exploitation for deep seabed resources was of secondary importance to this larger geostrategic consideration. Because pressures to expand territorial sea claims beyond three to twelve miles was growing, over 200 international straits through which transit of all vessels, including naval vessels, was guaranteed could suddenly be closed off by the assertion of wider territorial seas. The superpowers sought, then, to emphasize the right of transit through straits, even where broader territorial sea claims were asserted.

The issue of fisheries was also a matter of concern, especially to countries such as the Soviet Union, Portugal, Iceland, the United Kingdom, Poland, and Spain, among others, who maintained long-distance fishing fleets. To the extent that coastal states extended fishery claims further than their territorial seas, the fishing vessels of these countries might suddenly be excluded from waters in which they had historically fished. They emphasized the historical rights principle to protect their fishing industries. At the same time coastal states of both the developed and developing world insisted on their priority rights to protect, conserve, and exploit fishing resources in their coastal waters, and they pressed for the idea of extending an exclusive economic zone to a limit of 200 miles from their shores. Such claims would have to be adjusted to take into account the historic fishing rights of those countries whose fishermen had fished in what before had been international waters.

These were the broad outlines of the various interests that came into play as 116 countries met at the First Session of the Third UN Conference on the Law of the Sea convened in New York in 1973. In the eleven subsequent sessions that took place over the following decade at such sites as New York, Caracas, Geneva, and Kingston, Jamaica, the various competing interests haggled over the elaboration of the UN Convention on the Law of the Sea, a massive document of 320 articles, which resulted from what some observers called the "greatest international gambling match" ever held.

HISTORY OF THE DEBATE

The bloc politics of the debate over the law of the sea was evident from the action taken during the First Session of the conference, where in New York thirty-one vice presidents were elected based on regional distribution among the African Group, the Asian Group, the Eastern European Group, the Latin American Group, and the Western European and Other Group (e.g., the United States). Although the First Session was largely procedural, the bloc politics dimension of the negotiations was acknowledged from the start by the election of officers. In the debates that followed, it would become clear that the various blocs were not at all unified in their views on the range of issues to be dealt with by the conference. Matters would be much more complicated than merely accommodating bloc interests. The work of the conference was to be done in three main committees and by a drafting committee that would consolidate committee reports.

At the Second Session held in Caracas in 1974, 138 countries participated in a general debate in which they also began to grapple with alternative texts prepared for consideration by the preparatory seabed committee or submitted by member states. These included the Kampala statement resulting from a conference of landlocked and geographically disadvantaged states, a statement by the Intergovernmental Maritime Consultative Organization (IMCO) regarding shipping, and a report of the secretary-general and the Organization of African Unity (OAU) on sea law issues. While the conference held plenary discussions on the peaceful uses of the oceans, zones of peace and security, and enhancing global participation, the three main committees began to consider various draft texts. The First Committee was assigned issues relating to the establishment of an international regime for the seabed and ocean floor beyond national jurisdiction and institutional mechanisms for its realization. Controversy existed in this committee from the start. Colombia submitted a draft text on behalf of the Geneva 77 providing that the international authority should exercise direct control over exploration and exploitation of seabed resources. Colombia's proposal had the support of more than a hundred states, including China,

most developing countries, and a few European states such as Spain and
Romania. Approaches proposed by several governments of Western Europe and the United States would grant the seabed authority general regulatory oversight and the capacity to contract with member states. Similar
proposals made by other countries sought to allow the actual exploration
and exploitation of resources to be undertaken by countries or their private
corporations, under the general supervision of the seabed authority. The
United States expressed a concern that investments by countries or corporations be protected. France and Japan sought explicit definitions of the respective rights and duties of all parties in the exploration and exploitation
process, whereas the German Democratic Republic insisted that governments should have a sovereign right to conduct exploration and mining,
rather than a supranational agency. The First Committee also grappled
with the economic implications of mining and land-based producers. Zaire
supported a scheme for compensation of lost revenue to land-based producers, but representatives of the United States and the United Kingdom
doubted the necessity or wisdom of such a proposal.

The Second Committee discussed the establishment of legal rules governing territorial seas, contiguous zones, exclusive economic zones, straits,
archipelagoes, and the continental shelf, as well as the high seas in connection with fishing rights, mineral exploitation, and the like. Regarding the
territorial sea, the United Kingdom proposed extending the traditional
limit of 3 miles to 12. Ecuador, which like other Latin American states already claimed a 200-mile territorial sea limit, proposed that 200 miles be
adopted, not the 12-mile proposal of the United Kingdom. Ecuador was
formally supported by Cuba, Guinea, and Peru, among others. Guyana
proposed that no further extension of the territorial sea be considered.

The extension of the territorial sea raised the issue of innocent passage
rights through straits from one part of the high seas to another. The Soviet
Union and various East European countries insisted on innocent passage
for all vessels, as did the United Kingdom and Denmark. But Algeria, Peru,
and Tanzania, among others, sought a distinction between merchant vessels, which should retain rights of free passage, and warships, which would
be subject only to innocent passage. China opposed free passage of warships through straits, proposing that advance notice and authorization for
innocent passage of warships should be adopted.

Discussion on the continental shelf revealed concerns of landlocked
states such as Nepal, which proposed that the continental shelf claims be
eliminated or placed under common management. Many states such as
Australia and El Salvador rejected this idea while emphasizing coastal state
rights. Other states, such as Austria, Egypt, Singapore, and Uganda, believed that no shelf claims should extend beyond 200 miles, in light of the
growing consensus in favor of a 200-mile exclusive economic zone. Regarding the latter idea, countries evinced a high degree of support and consen-

sus. Coastal states, it was felt, should exercise rights of management and control over resources beyond the territorial sea to a limit of 200 miles. Coastal states would not exercise territorial jurisdiction as such, however, and thus freedom of navigation, overflight, and laying of cables and pipelines by other countries would be permitted.

Belgium, Denmark, France, the Federal Republic of Germany, Ireland, Italy, Luxembourg, and the Netherlands provided for preferential rights for coastal state fishing, while acknowledging historical rights of foreign fishermen. The Soviet Union and several East European states supported the idea of preferential rights, but China opposed it. Debate also ensued on the rights of landlocked states to access to exploitation of the living resources of the sea and on how to measure archipelagoes in light of new rules for territorial sea extension and implementation of economic zones.

The Third Committee considered the questions of preservation of the marine environment, scientific research, and the development and transfer of technology. Substantial progress was made in this committee concerning measures to protect the marine environment from pollution, which included provisions for notification of accidents, preferential assistance for developing countries in coping with accidents causing pollution, and preferential rights of coastal states to exercise protection over its coastal waters. On marine scientific research a major split was revealed between states who wanted coastal states to have rights to advance notification and consent to authorize research in all areas under its jurisdiction and states who sought a right of freedom of research beyond the territorial sea. In the former camp were such countries as Canada, China, India, Mexico, Tanzania, and Yugoslavia; in the latter were Israel, the United States, and the Soviet Union, among others. The committee did not fully address the issue of transfer of technology, which would eventually prove to be its most controversial subject. A number of developing countries, however, insisted that this was a critical necessity, a view much out of favor among wealthier developed states.

At the 1975 session, where 141 countries convened at Geneva, a single negotiating text was formulated. The First Committee proposed establishment of a three-part international governance process for seabed mining: an International Seabed Authority (ISA) consisting of all members, a smaller Council, and a business-related arm of the ISA, the Enterprise, to serve under the aegis of the ISA or in contractual partnership with third parties for purposes of exploring and exploiting deep seabed resources. The proposal also called for a system of international dispute resolution to adjudicate conflicting seabed claims. This arrangement was supported by the Geneva 77 group of developing countries, but the United States and numerous West and East European states expressed reservations. In the Second Committee, informal groups debated the fine points of implementation of the exclusive economic zone and protection and conservation of fisheries, among other issues. In the Third Committee, disputes arose over the rights of flag states versus coastal states in taking action concerning marine pollution. Countries such as Canada, whose arctic areas are environmentally sensitive, sought maximum rights for coastal states, whereas countries such as the United Kingdom sought to limit concessions to coastal states. Similar differences continued to exist over scientific research, and controversy over transfer of technology continued to evoke disagreement.

In 1976, a revised single negotiating text was developed at the Fourth Session and further debated at the Fifth Session of the conference, both sessions being held in New York. The major impasse concerned the regulation and institutional framework for deep seabed mining. In 1977, at the Sixth Session, an informal composite negotiating text was produced evidencing gradual progress in several areas among the 146 participating states on such issues as the territorial sea and economic zone claims, rules applying to archipelagoes, and rules on extending rights of coastal states to exploitation of their continental shelves beyond 200 miles, coupled with a sharing of resources in such areas with the ISA for ultimate disbursement to states party, especially developing states. Progress was also noted in settlement of disputes and in the principles that would guide deep seabed mining. The ISA would have the authority to mine, in conjunction with the Enterprise, but states parties would have the right to contract with the ISA to conduct individual operations. This represented a compromise between the position of the developing and developed countries.

In 1978, seven working groups were established to tackle the areas of major disagreement left after five years of discussion, and in subsequent sessions governments focused on remaining areas of difference. An informal text of the Draft convention was readied in 1980, and at its Tenth Session in 1981, the official text of the convention was produced, although the United States continued to express reservations about the deep seabed mining provisions. Jamaica was approved as the seat of the ISA and the Federal Republic of Germany as the site for the International Tribunal of the Law of the Sea, the convention's chief judicial body. In 1982, despite continued disagreement on seabed provisions, the conference voted on final amendments and produced a final text. The vote on the convention was 130 to 4, with 17 abstentions, indicating that full consensus had not been achieved despite nine years of arduous negotiation. In December 1982, 119 countries signed the convention, and in the following year a preparatory committee met to lay the groundwork for implementing the provisions of the agreement once sufficient numbers of countries had formally ratified it.

OUTCOME OF THE DEBATE

Although the Third Conference on the Law of the Sea produced a convention for signature and ratification, it did so without actual consensus on the part of important and powerful member states, including the United States, the Federal Republic of Germany, Israel, Ecuador, Peru, Brazil and Venezuela, most of which had reservations. Most of these states eventually signed the agreement, in the case of the United States, not until amendments to the seabed provisions of Chapter XI of the Treaty were renegotiated in 1994.

In September 1982, the United States, the United Kingdom, the Federal Republic of Germany, and France established a separate "Agreement Concerning Interim Arrangements Relating to Polymetallic Nodules of the Deep Sea Bed" that provided for means to prevent overlapping mining claims and disputes among these states that moved forward with national legislation to authorize deep seabed mining. Two years later, Belgium, Italy, Japan, and the Netherlands joined these countries in developing a separate system for resolution of mining claim disputes, even though many of them had signed the Law of the Sea Convention. This evoked the almost immediate denunciation of the Geneva 77 group, which declared the eight-power agreement illegal. But the United States proved stubborn on this issue, and bowing to the realities, other states agreed to renegotiate those portions of Chapter XI of the Law of the Sea Treaty that the United States and other parties found most objectionable, including the provisions calling for produc-

The UN Law of the Sea Treaty was signed in December 1982 at Montego Bay, Jamaica, after nearly a decade of arduous negotiations. Edward Seaga, prime minister of Jamaica is greeted upon his arrival at the Rose Hall Beach Hotel where the conference was held. UN/DPI Photo

tion limits to be imposed on deep seabed mining and for mandatory technology transfers, a question that had proved to be highly contentious in all international forums concerned with promoting development in the South. The United States was not prepared to grant a duty to export technology under the guise of the Law of the Sea treaty, a notion it had opposed in all other venues. Moreover, the United States was endowed essentially with a veto over decisions of the Enterprise.

The UN Convention on the Law of the Sea achieved its sixtieth ratification on 16 November 1993, and it entered into force on 16 November 1994. Although not all of the ratifying states had been able by that time to consider the amendments negotiated with the United States and other Western countries, many did so in subsequent years, assuring its full entry into force. The First Session of the International Seabed Authority met in Kingston, Jamaica, in 1995.

The UN convention didn't prevent ongoing controversy over conservation of straddling fish stocks, that is, fisheries that exist both within national economic zones and on the high seas. Canada engaged in a long-running dispute with European Union countries, particularly Spain, in attempting to prevent the latter from fishing halibut in areas lying beyond its economic zone where highly sensitive stocks of fish were located. The halibut fishery, Canada claimed, was under stress, and it had forbidden fishing even by its own fleet inside its economic zone. Spanish fishing just outside the zone was seen as provocative. In 1992 the General Assembly authorized a conference on the problem of conservation of straddling stocks, which produced a draft treaty in 1995 that won the swift signature of thirty-one states, though entry into force awaited actual ratification by thirty states.

The UN General Assembly named 1998 the International Year of the Ocean, as calls began to emerge from several countries concerning the need for a new UN conference on ocean affairs to deal with a range of issues including environmental impacts on the oceans; the degradation of coral reefs; land-based sources of marine pollution, which was at least partially addressed in a 1995 intergovernmental plan of action; and the establishment of an ocean affairs observatory to monitor ocean policy issues—indicating that the international community will continue to be occupied with matters of ocean management in future decades.

See also Global Environment (Debate 27); New International Economic Order (Debate 30); Third World Development Programming (Debate 25); Trade and Development (Debate 24).

FOR FURTHER READING

Galdoris, George V., and Kevin R. Vienna. *Beyond the Law of the Sea.* Westport, CT:
         Praeger, 1997.
Ocean Development and International Law (journal).

Oxman, Bernard. "The 1994 Agreement and the Convention." *American Journal of International Law* 88 (1994): 687.

Sebenius, James K. *Negotiating the Law of the Sea*. Cambridge, MA: Harvard University Press, 1984.

UN Yearbooks, 1967–1995.

UN Chronicles, 1994–1999.

Vasciannie, Stephen C. *Landlocked and Geographically Disadvantaged States and the International Law of the Sea*. Oxford: Clarendon Press, 1990.

Von Glahn, Gerhard. *Law among Nations: An Introduction to Public International Law*. New York: Allyn and Bacon, 1996.

New International Economic Order (1974)

SIGNIFICANCE OF THE ISSUE

Debates about economic development occupy the largest amounts of time and attention of UN bodies. The New International Economic Order (NIEO) debates, begun in the mid-1970s, initiated a lengthy and sometimes heated struggle between developed and developing states over the distribution of wealth among and within nations, the degree to which the wealthy were responsible to the poor for their development, and the specific actions that ought to be undertaken to decrease the gap between the rich and the poor nations. While the NIEO debate largely failed to gain the overall objectives of the developing world to restructure the international trade, aid, investment, and monetary systems in any comprehensive way, the echoes of the earlier argument continue to appear in international deliberations.

BACKGROUND TO THE DEBATE

International development has been a concern of the United Nations since its inception, although the intensity and frequency of discussion surrounding it increased dramatically in the 1960s with the addition of dozens of new developing nations as UN member states. Commanding increasingly larger majorities of the UN General Assembly and in an enlarged Economic and Social Council (ECOSOC), the developing nations persisted in elevating economic development to the very top of the UN agenda and in dominating the discussions and decisions of UN bodies and conferences called to deal with a range of subjects concerning development.

As they had demonstrated in 1964 with the establishment of the United Nations Conference on Trade and Development (UNCTAD), the Geneva 77 group of developing nations, which later grew to include well over a hundred nations, was able largely to dictate the terms of international declarations and documents concerning development, to force discussion of issues and policies favorable to developing country interests, and to heighten awareness to the problems of poverty and underdevelopment that they faced.

In these discussions, a predominant theme of developing countries was that the international economic system was structurally skewed in favor of the already wealthy developing states, which led to an ongoing and increasing inequality in distribution of wealth, which many developing countries saw as a major contributing cause—if not *the* major cause—of their poverty. The tendency to look elsewhere than the domestic policies of nations for causes of poverty tended to divert attention away from the often glaring disparities of wealth that existed within developing countries, from domestic policies that contributed to the persistence of poverty among their people, and from the inefficient and too often corrupt bureaucracies that mismanaged the nations' resources. Developed countries, not willing to shoulder the blame for the poverty of developing nations, were not shy about raising these points in arguments over where responsibility for poverty rested.

Although the blame game was almost always lurking beneath the surface of UN debates on the subject of the underdevelopment of Third World countries, many of the early efforts by the United Nations to address the issue of promoting a fairer international economic system were actually quite civil. Indeed, as the history of the debate shows, most of the special sessions of the UN General Assembly devoted to questions of the NIEO achieved a fair degree of consensus, at least on the surface. But deep divisions actually existed between the developed and developing countries regarding how far reform of international aid, trade, investment, and monetary policy should go. Thus, while general standards and goals were asserted, rarely were they achieved in the full and actual practice of nations.

HISTORY OF THE DEBATE

In 1974, Algeria requested a special session of the UN General Assembly to study the problems of raw materials and development. This request was made as a result of a conference of nonaligned countries in 1973, which determined that the goals of the Second UN Development Decade had failed, owing to the intransigence, lack of cooperation, and lack of political will of the developed states, some of whom, together with their multinational corporations, continued in the "plundering of developing countries." To rectify the situation, developing countries needed to mobilize and exploit their own natural resources, as had the oil-producing states who were now in a position to leverage international markets on behalf of their development. The tone of the request was clearly condemnatory, but its timing was ironic, as it was related to the oil embargo imposed on Western governments by the Arab petroleum exporting countries, following the Yom Kippur War in 1973, and the consequent rise in oil, gas, and energy prices. Although a global inflation resulting from this was evident in the industrialized world, hardest hit were the developing countries, who had to pay not only higher oil prices in precious but scarce hard currency but also higher prices for other imports.

The upshot of the Algerian request was that Secretary-General Kurt Waldheim called for a Sixth Special Session of the General Assembly in April 1974, which debated, for three weeks, the question of raw materials and development. The result of this debate was the formulation of a Declaration and a Program of Action on the Establishment of a New International Economic Order, which had been proposed and advocated by the Geneva 77 group of developing nations. These called for governments to recognize the sovereignty, independence, and territorial integrity of all nations; the right of every country to develop its own economic system; the full sovereignty of every state over its natural resources, including the right to nationalization or transfer of ownership to its nationals; the need for regulation of transnational corporations by host countries; the need for just and equitable prices of raw materials and goods exported and imported by developing countries; the provision of economic assistance to developing countries without political conditions; the reform of the international monetary system; the provision of preferential trade rights to developing countries; the transfer of technology to developing countries; and the cooperation of commodity-producing nations in forming producer associations. Coupled with references to apartheid, racial domination, and calls for full compensation for exploitation and depletion of national resources during colonialism, this list of developing country demands was nothing less than a call for revolutionary reform of the international economic system. Wisely, conference participants decided not to press the matter to a vote, and the documents were adopted without vote, even as thirty-nine countries made observations or reservations on the contents.

In the debate regarding the price of commodities, some countries proposed commodity indexation schemes, whereby prices of basic commodities would fluctuate on a par with prices of manufactured goods. Bahrain, Bolivia, India, Kenya, Morocco, Thailand, and Venezuela urged such an approach. But developed countries, such as Finland, Japan, the Netherlands, Sweden, and the United States, voiced opposition to indexation schemes as artificial distortions of markets, preferring instead more flexible commodity market schemes. Developing countries urged a broader expansion of preferential trade on behalf of their imports and exports, for greater access to technology, for debt rescheduling and cancellation, and for the right to regulate transnational corporations and nationalize foreign investments.

Developed states took exception to many of the Declaration principles. Australia, Belgium, Canada, France, Japan, the Netherlands, New Zealand,

Norway, Sweden, and the United Kingdom, though joining in the consensus, expressed reservations, as did the Federal Republic of Germany speaking on behalf of European Economic Community (EEC) nations. Many observed that the "right to nationalization" failed to mention the attendant duty under international law for just compensation to investors. Indexation schemes were cited as unworkable. The establishment of producers organizations like that of the Organization of Petroleum Exporting Countries (OPEC) could hamper trade relations and ignore consuming country needs. The notion that colonial peoples had a right of compensation and restitution for exploitation and depletion of their natural resources was rejected. The United States argued in view of its and several other nations' serious reservations that one could not argue that any real consensus existed and that the inclusion of provocative and controversial positions of just one faction, even if a large faction of nations, was not conducive to real consensus or indicative of any real creation of new legal rights. Algeria and Iraq criticized the statements of states with reservations as damaging the effort on the part of developing countries to establish consensus. Round One of the NIEO debate ended with the agreement to disagree.

Round Two of the NIEO debate resumed the following year in the Seventh Special Session of the General Assembly devoted to Development and International Economic Cooperation, where many of the same issues raised in the Sixth Special Session were revisited. Nearly all countries agreed that the trade system provided one of the most direct ways of garnering national income for development. While developing countries pressed for indexation schemes, many developed countries continued to have reservations. However, the EEC countries, the United States, and others noted their willingness to participate in case-by-case negotiations between producer and consumer countries. They also announced various preferential trade policies that would be implemented within their own national legislation. Differences continued to exist over the effects of producer organizations such as OPEC on the economies of consumer countries. Developing countries called for developed countries to transfer to them a minimum of 1 percent of the gross national product (GNP) in financial resources, of which 0.7 percent of GNP should take the form of official development assistance. While France, Norway, Sweden, and Italy, speaking on behalf of the EEC countries, affirmed the need to fulfill such a commitment, other developed states questioned the usefulness of the targets themselves. Developing countries called for various schemes providing for automatic transfers of wealth to developing countries and for various immediate forms of relief on payment of debt. Several developed countries expressed concerns about the workability of such arrangements. Despite the disagreements that continued to prevail on key issues, the tone of the Seventh Special Session remained civil, and the final Declaration of the Assembly was adopted unanimously.

The Seventh Special Session of the UN General Assembly is convened on 1 September 1975 to discuss the problems of development and international economic cooperation. Assembly President Abdelaziz Bouteflika of Algeria is flanked by Secretary-General Kurt Waldheim on the left and Bradford Morse, under-secretary-general for Political and General Assembly Affairs, on the right. UN/DPI Photo Yutaka Nagata

In the four years that followed, some progress was made in the establishment of preferential trade rights for developing countries, as both the EEC nations and the United States, among others, introduced concessions on behalf of developing country imports. In addition, at the 1977 Paris Conference on International Economic Cooperation, the establishment of a Common Fund to finance stabilization of commodity prices had been endorsed but not implemented. Provisions for transfer of technology had not affected the actual practices of nations, and only a few developed countries achieved the 0.7 percent of GNP for official development assistance. Thus, when the Eleventh Special Session of the General Assembly was held in June and July of 1980, which we might call Round Three of the NIEO debate, while some progress had been achieved, developing countries noted that it fell far short of the structural changes called for by the NIEO. Moreover, the economic dislocations, inflation and recession, and other economic shocks that had marked the global economy continued to hamper efforts at economic development. Many Geneva 77 countries continued to demand that developed countries fulfill earlier commitments to transfer real wealth. Many expressed ongoing frustration at their perceived unwillingness to do so. They called for the establishment of a Common Fund for stabilization of commodity prices of at least $6 billion. The final recommendation of the session on financing of the Common Fund was eight times less this amount, a modest $750 million, and the effort to establish an Integrated Program Commodities was only partially implemented in subsequent years.

Developed countries generally argued that the ongoing problem of poverty was something for which developing countries themselves must take responsibility. Poor investment climates resulting from inefficient policies and programs in developing countries that were unattractive to corporations were a problem that only the developing country governments themselves could address. Indeed, the radical NIEO program and threats to foreign investment led in the 1980s to a flight of capital resources from unstable countries of the Third World, as corporations sought to invest in more secure areas. So while developing countries might deserve special attention and assistance in meeting the consequences of international recession, much could be done by them to alleviate poverty and attract resources by national action and domestic economic reform. Moreover, the developed countries were less hesitant to point out certain hypocrisies among the oil-producing states who had garnered much wealth at the expense of other developing countries without participating in foreign aid giving and among the Communist countries who readily joined in criticism of market-oriented nations but failed to give any noticeable aid to the developing world. That developing countries tended to ignore the nonparticipation in foreign aid of these nations and continued to blame Western nations for development assistance shortfalls was unfair. Communist countries agreed that developing countries had to take responsibility for their own development but denied the charge that their development aid was less than that of the West, and they urged developing countries not to open their economies to private foreign investment since this would only ensure further alien control over their resources. The Soviet Union accused the capitalist states of being the main culprits for the continued lack of progress in achieving a new international economic order. While countries clearly continued to share major differences on a whole range of issues on the NIEO agenda, they did adopt session resolutions by consensus. Round Three of the NIEO debate finished much as the previous rounds did, with a superficial consensus and an underlying reality of profound ongoing differences among the developed and developing states.

OUTCOME OF THE DEBATE

During the 1980s, frequent denunciation of developed countries' failure to meet foreign assistance targets and other calls for reform of the international economic system indicated ongoing frustrations among developing countries. But several other factors were at work as well. In the United States and Europe, conservative governments took office that refused to take blame for what they saw as the ongoing mismanagement of national economies by the governments of the developing world. Less money than ever was available for development assistance, as these governments trimmed their budgets and began to invest in defense spending to prevent the victory of leftist opposition groups in Central America, Africa, and Asia. The Soviet Union and the Eastern bloc began a slow process of economic meltdown, having themselves overextended their economic capacities in support of revolutionary movements around the world. The United States began to insist that if other countries wanted American foreign aid, they must reform their domestic economies, shed themselves of socialist governments and inefficient, centrally planned economies, and embrace free enterprise. In Africa, a terrible drought and economic crisis led many governments to heed this advice. In the meantime, by the end of the 1980s, communism had utterly collapsed, and developing countries around the world realized that their economic future would rest on their own capacities to reform and develop with whatever assistance they might be able to garner from developed countries who were now preoccupied with providing aid to a host of former Communist nations whose economies were in desperate straits. Moreover, developing countries began to undertake economic reforms that would create a more stable investment climate to attract private foreign investment. Instead of viewing such investment with hostility or imposing regulation on it, many developing countries realized that they needed to take realistic steps to compete with other nations to attract foreign capital, and this included dropping the radical antibusiness rhetoric of the NIEO.

Thus, by the 1990s, the shrill and largely unproductive debates of the NIEO had passed into history, and nations throughout the globe sought new and more productive ways and means of achieving economic process. This new realism promoted a great deal of national economic and political reform, as democracy made a comeback in many areas where authoritarian governments had held sway. While economic development continues to elude many governments and poverty continues to plague many parts of the developing world, especially in Africa, which was the locus of many unfortunate and destructive civil wars during the 1990s, there nonetheless existed a broader spirit of cooperation in international deliberations on economic development at the close of the 1990s. Occasional echoes of old NIEO principles—such as calls for transfer of technology, the assertion of the principle that developed countries should pay 0.7 percent of GNP in official development assistance—continue to crop up in international conference documents. Such issues remain the subject of disagreement among nations, but most countries realize that real progress is made in the day-to-day decisions of governments, not merely in the assertion of targets or goals or in the assertion of rights that have little relation to the practice or the capacity of nations.

See also Codes of Conduct for Transnational Corporations (Debate 31); Law of the Sea (Debate 29); New International Information Order (Debate 40); Third World Development Programming (Debate 25); Trade and Development (Debate 24); World Monetary System (Debate 5).

FOR FURTHER READING

Hudson, Michael. *Global Fracture: The New International Economic Order*. New York: Harper and Row, 1977.

Keohane, Robert. *After Hegemony: Cooperation and Discord in the World Political Economy*. Princeton, NJ: Princeton University Press, 1984.

Jacobson, Harold K., and Dusam Aidjanski, eds. *The Emerging International Economic Order: Dynamic Processes, Constraints and Opportunities*. Beverly Hills, CA: Sage, 1982.

Lazlo, Ervin, et al. *The New International Economic Order (NIEO)*. New York: Pergamon Press, 1983.

Murphy, Craig N. *The Emergence of the NIEO Ideology*. Boulder, CO: Westview Press, 1984.

Onwuka, Ralph I. *The Future of Africa and the New International Economic Order (NIEO)*. New York: St. Martin's, 1986.

South Commission. *The Challenge to the South: The Report of the South Commission*. Oxford: Oxford University Press, 1990.

UN Yearbooks, 1974, 1975, 1980.

Codes of Conduct for Transnational Corporations (1974)

SIGNIFICANCE OF THE ISSUE

The rise of transnational corporations (TNCs), the term used by the United Nations in referring to multinational corporations, in the post–World War II era is a significant development in the evolution of international economic relations. Because corporations command huge sums of money, with their annual sales capacities often outstripping the entire gross national products of many individual nations, they can exert considerable influence on the economic health of a host country's economy as well as the global economy generally. As this reality dawned on many developing countries in the 1970s, they saw the United Nations as an appropriate venue for gathering and sharing information on the activities of TNCs and as a forum to press for a code of conduct to regulate their activities. At that point the issue proved to be controversial in the relations of developing and developed states, and it was embroiled in the often-heated debates about creating a New International Economic Order (NIEO). However, with the globalization of the world economy in the 1990s, the attitude toward corporate investment has grown more acceptable.

BACKGROUND TO THE DEBATE

After World War II, in view of the tremendous need for capital in reconstructing a war-ravaged world, private firms discovered a welcome climate for foreign investment. Initially, American companies dominated the international arena, but in time private corporations from Europe and Japan, and eventually from other countries, began to explore investment opportunities in other countries. As both the number of corporations involved in transnational investment increased and the volume of foreign investment rose, scholars and national leaders alike began to pay more attention to their role in the international political economy. While governments recognized the need for capital flows in the form of investments by private corporations, as one means of garnering resources for development, transfer of technology, and diversification of their national economies, they also worried that control over their natural resources and over the health and long-term welfare of their economies might be compromised.

Eastern bloc Communist states explicitly condemned corporate investment as a means of capitalist exploitation. Socialist governments in the developing world expressed increasing concern about corporate repatriation of profits, and several moved to nationalize all foreign investment. Under traditional international law, any nationalization of foreign property required adequate compensation, but several developing countries declared such principles invalid. Although they sought foreign investments, and generally viewed them as beneficial, even capitalist-oriented countries of the developing world worried about the loss of national economic autonomy. During the early 1970s, a consensus emerged among the Geneva 77 group of developing countries that the issue of TNCs needed closer scrutiny and perhaps some form of international regulation.

HISTORY OF THE DEBATE

It is important to note at the outset that during the three decades in which the United Nations has deliberated the role of TNCs, and the establishment of a code of conduct regulating their activities, political and economic trends dictated the tenor and substance of the UN discussions. During the 1970s, the climate of suspicion and hostility that existed among developing countries and the Communist world concerning corporate activity colored both the rhetoric and the substance of UN work. Matters concerning Southern Africa and apartheid were thrust into the discussions on TNCs by developing countries, which expressed frequent and loud frustration over the tangled and lengthy effort to develop even a draft code of conduct. But during the 1980s, as the crisis in the developing world peaked, especially in Africa, governments of developing countries warmed to the need for additional foreign investment. Ironically, even indigenous TNCs began to emerge in many developing countries at this time. The collapse of communism in the late 1980s led to a new climate in which even former Communist countries sought foreign investment. The globalization of the international economy in the 1990s created an even more favorable and competitive environment for foreign investment. With these developments, the Communist rhetoric of condemnation of corporate investments was replaced by a global concern about how best to take advantage of the globalization process.

As a result of the UN General Assembly's Sixth Special Session of April–May 1974 on Raw Materials and Development, which led to the Declaration on the Establishment of a New International Economic Order

The chambers of the UN Economic and Social Council (ECOSOC) in New York depicted here serve as the primary venue of UN discussions about economic development, including issues concerning the effects of transnational corporations. UN/DPI Photo Milton Grant

(NIEO), several principles concerning the activities of TNCs were enunciated. In affirming the full sovereignty of a country over its natural resources and economic activities, the Declaration asserted a country's right to nationalization or transfer of ownership of foreign assets to its nationals and its right to regulate and supervise the activities of TNCs. The Economic and Social Council (ECOSOC), which met in the summer of 1974, received a report commissioned by it two years earlier from its twenty-member Group of Eminent Persons on the Impact of Multinational Corporations on Development and on International Relations. Based on this report, ECOSOC decided to establish an Information and Research Center on Transnational Corporations, and in December 1974, it also established a Commission on Transnational Corporations, which held its first session in March 1975.

The UN General Assembly, in passing the Charter of Economic Rights and Duties of States, also took action related to TNCs. Article 2 of the Charter asserted the right of states to regulate and supervise foreign investment and noted that no states could be compelled to grant preferential treatment to such investment. TNCs were forbidden to interfere in the domestic affairs of states, and any state could nationalize investments or transfer property to its citizens. If a dispute over just compensation arose, this was to be dealt with by the domestic legal system of the nationalizing state. The Charter was adopted by a vote of 115 to 6, with 10 abstentions. Belgium, Denmark, the Federal Republic of Germany, Luxembourg, the United Kingdom, and the United States voted against it, although not always or explicitly because of its provisions concerning TNCs.

At its first session in March 1975, the Commission on Transnational Corporations spent much of its time deliberating the question of drafting a code of conduct concerning TNCs. The notion evoked a major difference of opinion between those who believed that no such code should be compulsory and those who wanted an obligatory code complete with punishments for nonobservance. The commission also called for the establishment of a comprehensive information system, for ongoing research of the activities of TNCs, and for the establishment of a definition of TNCs. During its regular session of 1975, the UN General Assembly passed a resolution condemning corrupt practices and bribery by TNCs.

Work on the drafting of a code of conduct and for the establishment of a comprehensive information system continued throughout the 1970s. Studies on corporate activities in a variety of economic sectors, such as pharmaceutics, advertising, and mining in Southern Africa, were conducted, as were studies on corporate influences on economic integration and transfer of technology. The comprehensive information center was further consolidated during this time as well. However, discussions on the drafting of a legal code proved difficult, and Communist countries accused Western powers of dragging their feet, whereas many developing countries expressed frustration at the delay in completion of the code. The United States, viewing foreign investment as a positive inducement to development, saw no reason to proceed as though the matter were of a crisis nature. By 1980, only about half of the provisions of a draft code had been agreed upon. ECOSOC, in the meantime, turned its attention to the issue of corporate accounting and reporting standards, owing to developing country concerns that corporations routinely underreported earnings so as to avoid taxes.

The dance among nations to develop a draft code of conduct for TNCs continued throughout the 1980s, as significant changes took place in the global economy and in the politics of international relations. Basic agreement existed that TNCs should observe local laws in countries of investment and that local governments should deal fairly in treatment of TNCs under their laws. Laws governing nationalization and expropriation were largely agreed upon. The need for consumer and environmental protection was widely acknowledged. But even as host governments were easing restrictions on private investments in the 1990s, disagreement continued on issues concerning compensation for expropriation, the right of entry, and establishment of investment. The very fact that governments were taking a liberalized rather than restrictive view of investment suggested that the drafting of a code of conduct would in many ways necessarily be an unending process, as economic trends and issues shifted and changed. Many began to doubt whether the whole process was any longer necessary, and as the vast majority of the world in a post-Communist age now desperately sought and often competed for foreign direct investment, the issue shifted from one of suspicious regulation to one of facilitating foreign direct investment in such a way that developing countries could enhance their overall development prospects.

OUTCOME OF THE DEBATE

One of the consequences of the hostile climate toward TNCs and foreign investment during the 1970s and 1980s was that of capital flight. TNCs removed investments from unstable countries of the developing world, preferring to invest in safer countries where expropriation, nationalization, and general hostility to foreign capital represented less of a risk to investments. This drain of actual investment and reduced prospects for potential investment left many developing states desperately short of capital, a situation they bore partial blame for creating with their hostile attitude and pointed rhetoric toward TNCs and TNC investments. Realizing this error, many countries began to change their tune, and by the 1990s, a host of developing countries began to compete once again for TNC investments.

As governments began to move toward the creation of a World Trade Organization (WTO) in the 1990s, the old UN machinery for dealing with TNCs needed a revamping and a reorientation of purpose and function. In 1994, ECOSOC recommended—and the General Assembly approved—the integration of the commission on TNCs into the institutional machinery of the United Nations Conference on Trade and Development (UNCTAD). It was given a new title, "Commission on International Investment and Transnational Corporations," under the Trade and Development Board of UNCTAD—the new title suggesting that its functions would be expanded and reoriented. Now instead of regulating corporations, its function would be to assist in governmental, intergovernmental, and nongovernmental efforts to promote a climate favorable for private sector and enterprise development. Whereas free enterprise had been previously an object of condemnation and ridicule, it was now acknowledged as a necessary tool in achieving development.

The globalization process in the latter half of the 1990s gained even more momentum, as economic interdependence deepened in the trade and investment sectors of the world economy. While a sea change has occurred in the attitude among nations toward TNCs, and the climate is more favorable now than ever for foreign investment, the globalization process does have its potential downside. The old questions about loss of control of the national economy are even more pertinent today than three decades ago. The problem of determining environmental regulation at the local, provincial, or even national level is now often dictated by international trade agreements among states that guarantee access to companies and goods that may not meet local environmental standards. The latter have often taken a back seat to the international trade obligations, raising storms of controversy over how globalization may trump and tyrannize over local decision-making bodies.

As the impacts of globalization are increasingly felt in every corner of the globe, there will doubtless be further consideration of the role of TNCs on the development of the economies of nations. That discussion will of necessity continue to be conducted at UN bodies and gatherings as governments cope with the effects of globalization.

See also New International Economic Order (Debate 30); New International Information Order (Debate 40); Third World Development Programming (Debate 25); Trade and Development (Debate 24); World Monetary System (Debate 5).

FOR FURTHER READING

Barnet, Richard J., and John Cavanagh. *Global Dreams: Imperial Corporations and the New World Order*. Reprint. New York: Simon and Schuster, 1995.

Dugger, William M. *Corporate Hegemony*. Westport, CT: Greenwood Press, 1989.

Gilpin, Robert. *U.S. Power and the Multinational Corporation: The Political Economy of Foreign Direct Investment*. New York: Basic Books, 1975.

Korten, David. *When Corporations Rule the World*. West Hartford, CT: Kumarian Press, 1995.

Leach, William. *Land of Desire: Merchants, Power, and the Rise of a New American Culture*. New York: Pantheon Books, 1993.

Office of Technology Assessment. U.S. Congress. *Multinationals and the National Interest: Playing by Different Rules*. Washington, DC: U.S. Government Printing Office, 1993.

UN Yearbooks, 1974–1995.

Food Issues (1974)

SIGNIFICANCE OF THE ISSUE

Hundreds of millions of people in developing countries teeter on the brink of starvation. In the poorest areas of the world, a civil war or a drought can place millions of people at risk of starvation in a short period of time. Debates over both emergency humanitarian aid and development at the United Nations ultimately center on how to promote the capacity of peoples throughout the world to achieve self-reliance in food production. The issue is tied to controversial matters of national economic policy, economic development debates, environmental issues, and population. The world currently produces enough food to feed everyone on the planet, but the actual availability of food resources, distribution of arable land, and population distribution are highly variable, and thus many people in developing countries suffer from chronic malnutrition and, during famine emergencies, from starvation.

BACKGROUND TO THE DEBATE

Even before the United Nations was established, governments saw a need for global cooperation concerning matters of food production. In 1943, the Food and Agriculture Organization (FAO) was initiated by a conference of allied nations at Hot Springs, Virginia, although it did not become operational until October 1945. Its work included the collection and dissemination of data on food and agriculture; the promotion of programs for the improvement of agricultural production, distribution, and marketing; and the promotion, protection, and conservation of fishery and forest resources. With the creation of the United Nations, the FAO was brought into cooperation with the Economic and Social Council (ECOSOC), which was charged with coordination of UN economic activities. The principal focus of FAO work, in cooperation with ECOSOC and other UN agencies, has been in the area of development programming.

Owing, however, to the growing frequency of emergency food aid situations—often coupled with drought—that faced many parts of the developing world, the UN General Assembly and the FAO established a World Food Program (WFP) in 1961. This body commenced operations in 1963 on a trial basis and achieved permanent status in 1966. As distinct from FAO, WFP has the mandate to provide food on an emergency basis to areas experiencing disaster or famine. The WFP's work in disaster and famine relief has been exceptional and wide reaching. Nor has it been confined to emergency aid, as its food-for-work programs in developing countries attests. These programs offer food assistance for public works and infrastructure programs of a developmental nature. WFP has also attempted to help governments improve their food production, storage, and distribution systems.

The UN system was equipped in the form of the FAO and WFP to promote international cooperation in both the developmental and emergency facets of global food production and distribution. However, as a growing number of developing countries experienced problems in food

Girls pose for a moment with sickles in hand during the grain harvest near Lunauada, Gujarat State in India in 1977. UN assistance helped India increase food production through modernization of irrigation and planting of high-yield varieties of grain. UN/DPI Photo P. Laffont

self-sufficiency during the late 1960s and early 1970s, concerns about their continuing inability to adequately feed their growing populations arose. In December 1973, the UN General Assembly decided to convene a World Food Conference at Rome to study the world food situation. A preparatory committee was established by ECOSOC to undertake planning for the conference. In establishing a substantive focus for discussions at the conference, the preparatory committee relied heavily on a report of the secretary-general of the conference entitled "Assessment of the World Food Sitution, Present and Future." This studied asserted that the long-term imbalance between supply of and demand for food in developing countries was increasingly serious, especially in view of the fact that a fifth of the population in developing countries suffered from inadequate nutrition. This chronic malnutrition was related to short-term food supplies that were highly vulnerable to variations in weather and drought, which could rapidly throw the poorly fed into a condition of famine. Thus the chronic inability of developing countries to produce adequate amounts of basic cereal grains put many countries at risk of famine and disaster. The report also concluded that the problem was not simply one of too little production of food in developing countries but also of poor distribution. Some countries had significant food surpluses, whereas others ran chronic deficits. To cope with the problems, it was clear that not only increased food production in developing countries was necessary but also better food data-gathering systems and early warning systems of acute shortages, better systems for emergency distribution of food aid, more comprehensive food reserve policies, better long-term development focuses on nutrition programs, especially for highly vulnerable populations, and better systems for international trade of food commodities. In view of these interrelated issues and problems, governments met in Rome from 5 November to 16 November 1974.

HISTORY OF THE DEBATE

Many countries came to Rome armed with proposals for improving global food management. Sri Lanka proposed the need for a world fertilizer fund. Sierra Leone, on behalf of the African Group, proposed the creation of an international fund for agricultural development. Bangladesh called for the establishment of a world food security council, a global food bank, and an international agricultural development fund. The Philippines submitted a similar plan for the latter. Yugoslavia submitted a proposal for reform of the food trade system and stabilization of food prices. Mexico sought the creation of a worldwide food information system, whereas Peru proposed a draft text for a declaration on the eradication of hunger. These and other proposals indicated that many governments were eager to review the global food situation with an eye to improving both the institutional capacity of governments and international agencies to cope with food issues and problems and the establishment of better food policies in trade, development, and emergency response. The conference was attended by 133 governments and by numerous UN and regional organizations.

The work of the conference was conducted in three main committees. The first committee dealt with issues of food production and consumption, the second with food security issues and conference follow-up mechanisms, and the third with international food trade and commodity stabilization issues. From the very outset of the general debate, a climate of urgency existed in conference proceedings. It was noted that during the year since the conference had been called, the world food situation had deteriorated owing to an energy crisis, inflation in food prices, global monetary instability, and growing unemployment. These factors affected the ability, especially of developing states, to secure adequate food stocks. Underlying this, however, was the more serious problem of the continued reliance in many parts of the developing world on traditional food production techniques that could no longer keep pace with population growth. An acute need existed for modernization of agricultural production in the developing world. Set against this view, however, was the reality that in many developing countries the traditional peasant sector of the economy was potentially the most productive sector and that the domestic food policies of states that provided subsidies to urban consumers distorted food markets in such a way as to keep food prices lower than the free market, thus discouraging the rural producers from producing more than needed for subsistence. As long as developing countries artificially distorted domestic food prices and failed to invest in the traditional food-producing sector, production would remain problematical, and countries would perversely deepen their reliance on food imports. Other policies, such as production of export crops for foreign exchange earnings, also drew land away from production of basic foods for domestic consumption. All this pointed to the fact that developing countries themselves needed as a priority to establish policies and programs supportive of enhanced food production. The conference consensus supported this principle but also called upon developed states to assist developing countries in promoting agricultural development programs. Although no specific level of assistance was stipulated, to the disappointment of some developing countries, the consensus emerged that all countries, donor nations of the developed world, and developing countries could and must contribute to an improved world food situation.

The conference approved a Universal Declaration on the Eradication of Hunger and Malnutrition, which, among other things, recognized the need for more food production and better distribution, the need for reduction of the waste of food and of postharvest loss of food to pests and poor handling and storage, and the need to reform domestic policies and obstacles to higher food production. The Declaration asserted that "every man, woman and child has the inalienable right to be free from hunger and malnutrition in order to develop fully and maintain his physical and mental faculties." In its program of action the conference called upon governments to contribute special aid to countries most seriously affected by the energy crisis as well as a proposed international fund for agricultural development proposed by the conference and to the International Fertilizer Supply Scheme for the benefit of developing countries. It called upon governments to increase their agricultural research, extension, and training programs to enhance food productivity and to promote, land, soil, and water conservation. It noted the crucial role women play in agricultural production and called for nutritional, educational, and training programs for women. It pointed out the connection of food supply to population and called upon governments to develop policies to promote nutrition and better spacing of children. It pointed out the need to protect the environment while increasing food production. It called for an increase in emergency food aid to those countries and peoples in most need. It called upon governments to expand and liberalize world trade in special regard to food products and, where possible, to extend preferential treatment to developing country agricultural commodities.

Conference recommendations drawing reservations from governments included a call for countries to reduce military expenditures so as to provide more resources for development. Albania, China, and Iran expressed reservations concerning this recommendation, and other states, including Australia, Austria, Belgium, Denmark, France, the Federal Republic of Germany, Ireland, Israel, Italy, Japan, the Netherlands, Norway, Sweden, Switzerland, the United Kingdom, and the United States, indicated that they would have abstained had the measure been pressed to a vote. Albania and China also expressed reservations concerning a provision calling for the establishment of a global information and early warning system on food and agriculture, insofar as it infringed upon national sovereignty.

In the area of institutional follow-up to its recommendations, the conference called for the establishment of a World Food Council, to function as the primary coordinating mechanism for food policy in the UN system, and for the creation of an International Fund for Agricultural Development (IFAD). Within a month the UN General Assembly took action on the conference recommendations. It endorsed the Declaration on Eradication of Hunger, established the World Food Council, and called upon states to meet for further discussions on the establishment of the IFAD, which became operational in 1977 with headquarters in Rome. In subsequent years the number of countries and the size of voluntary contributions rose substantially. By the early 1990s, voluntary contributions of members to the Fund passed the $3 billion mark. In 1977, the General Assembly adopted the Program of Action to Eliminate Hunger, which was earlier adopted by the World Food Council at its Manila meeting.

Twenty-two years after the World Food Conference, nations gathered again at Rome in November 1996 at the World Food Summit. At this gathering, nations took stock of their progress in dealing with hunger. Indeed, real progress had been made, but hundreds of millions of people remained exposed to chronic hunger in the developing world and especially in Africa. The most sobering statistic facing nations was that nearly 13 million children were dying annually owing directly or indirectly to hunger or malnutrition. Representatives of 186 countries met at the summit where they adopted, by acclamation, the Rome Declaration on World Food Security and the World Food Summit Plan of Action. The chief goal expressed in these nonbinding but sober commitments was to halve the number of hungry no later than the year 2015. Governments themselves continue to be the primary actors through national legislation and programs in combating and eradicating hunger. They pledged to take responsibility for implementing the Summit call for a Food for All campaign. Specifically, they promised to implement policies aimed at eradicating poverty and inequality and improving physical and economic access by all to nutritionally adequate and safe food, to pursue participatory strategies for agricultural and rural development to combat pests, drought, and desertification, to foster fair and equitable trade in food on international markets, and to develop national capacities for prevention and response to natural disasters, among other commitments.

Although the Declaration and Program of Action were adopted by acclamation, a number of contentious issues remained after two years of preparatory negotiations on the draft text, especially concerning language on trade, development aid, population, sanctions, and women's rights. A total of fifteen countries expressed reservations at the conference concerning such issues. The United States, while in agreement with the general thrust of the overall document, stipulated that it could not agree to the 0.7 percent of gross national product figure for official development assistance. This could not be viewed as an international obligation and indeed was a persistent holdover from the New International Economic Order debates. Still, it promised to provide quality food aid as was necessary on a case-by-case basis. Moreover, the idea that freedom from hunger was a right was a goal to be progressively realized rather than a justiciable international right, as the primary obligation to combat hunger rests with individual governments in relation to their citizens. Other delegations expressed reservations regarding economic sanctions, while the Holy See and a number of Islamic countries objected to the inclusion in the conference documents of references to the need for family planning and reproductive health care services, which are often seen as code words for promoting abortion. The UN General Assembly welcomed the Food Summit documents and later reviewed them in the 1997 special session devoted to review of the Agenda 21 of the Rio Earth Summit.

OUTCOME OF THE DEBATE

Hunger and malnutrition continue to bedevil about 800 million of the world's 6 billion people despite the best efforts and intentions of the international community. The situation, however, would most likely be much worse without these efforts; in fact, despite population increases, the number of people subject to chronic hunger has declined from about a billion in the 1970s. The World Bank estimates that with continued efforts at today's levels of technological development and assistance, the number of hungry people will decline to about 600 million in the year 2005. Indeed, global food production has continued to outpace population growth, and so the primary issue remains one of equitable distribution of food.

Food policy still lies largely within the sphere of the domestic policies of nations. However, international cooperation in promoting agricultural development and in meeting emergency food needs has been crucial in preventing and responding to famine. The World Food Council has continued to be the principal mechanism through which the United Nations makes efforts to promote a coordinated response to food issues. The FAO and WFP continue to be the primary operational programs through which food issues are addressed. Indeed, food issues have been regularly addressed in follow-up conferences on environment and population. Special sessions of the General Assembly dealing with development issues routinely address food as an area of concern. This was true of the 1980 Special Session on Economic Cooperation and the 1986 Special Session on the Critical Economic Situation in Africa. The 1974 World Food Conference, then, served as a kind of watershed event in debates over food issues, helping to draw attention to them and providing new institutional mechanisms for discussion and financial assistance, which ensure that such issues will receive due attention in the international arena. Although subsequent debates have been marked by the inclusion of controversial language concerning developed country obligations to provide foreign aid and other elements of the long-standing North-South argument over a New International Economic Order, this has not prevented governments from cooperating in food development, security, and assistance. There is every reason to expect that such cooperation will continue and that, as it does, progress will be made in reducing the number of people around the globe who face the menaces of malnutrition and starvation.

See also Global Environment (Debate 27); New International Economic Order (Debate 30); Population (Debate 15); Third World Development Progamming (Debate 25); Trade and Development (Debate 24).

FOR FURTHER READING

Conway, Gordon. *The Doubly Green Revolution: Food for All in the 21st Century*. New York: Penguin, 1997.

Cuny, Frederick C. *Famine, Conflict and Response: A Basic Guide*. West Hartford, CT: Kumarian Press, 1999.

De Wall, Alex. *Famine Crimes: Politics and the Disaster Relief Industry in Africa*. Bloomington: Indiana University Press, 1998.

UN Chronicles, 1996–1997.

UN Yearbooks, 1973–1980, 1986, 1992, 1994.

Weiss, Thomas, and Robert S. Jordan. *The World Food Conference and Global Problem Solving*. New York: Praeger, 1976.

Status of Women (1975)

SIGNIFICANCE OF THE ISSUE

The political life of most nations, until recently, has been dominated by men. In recent years, however, women have gained much wider participation in the political processes of government, and the United Nations has served as a venue in which the status, rights, health, and education of women and their role in economic development have been increasingly discussed as a matter of priority. The United Nations has held four international conferences on women, and countless other UN declarations, programs of action, and assistance measures take into account the contributions and needs of women, acknowledging that their role in agricultural production and in the rearing and education of children is paramount to the health of national economic and political life.

BACKGROUND TO THE DEBATE

Issues related to the rights and status of women have been a subject of international concern even before the establishment of the United Nations. In various countries, the women's suffrage movements produced victories in the attainment of the right to vote, in New Zealand in 1893, Australia in 1902, Finland in 1906, England in 1917, Poland in 1918, Russia in 1919, and the United States in 1920. Over the next three decades, women gained the right to vote in eleven Latin American countries. At the Montevideo Conference in 1933, a Convention on the Nationality of Women, which gave them the right to choose a nationality at the time of marriage rather than automatically following the citizenship of their husband, was adopted and later ratified by many countries of the Western Hemisphere. International conventions to prohibit the trafficking in women and children were promulgated in 1904 and 1910. The League of Nations Assembly directly supervised the enforcement of these agreements. The International Labor

Organization (ILO) took up the issues concerning the occupation and social status of women, and these have been the subject of ILO Agreements since its formation in 1919.

The UN Charter explicitly cites the protection and promotion of human rights and fundamental freedoms for all without regard to race, sex, language, or religion as one of its main purposes. In June 1946, the United Nations established a Commission on the Status of Women to explore ways in which the legal equality women had gained in many countries could be extended to equality in fact. In 1949 a Convention for the Suppression of the Traffic in Persons and the Exploitation of the Prostitution of Others was adopted by the General Assembly. The ILO adopted a Convention Concerning Equal Remuneration for Men and Women Workers for Work of Equal Value. A year later the General Assembly adopted a Convention on the Political Rights of Women, which guaranteed rights further to those enjoyed by all people under the Universal Declaration of Human Rights of 1948. In 1957 an International Convention on the Nationality of Married Women adopted the principle of the Montevideo Conference on granting women the right to choose their nationality upon marriage. The 1960s saw Conventions Concerning Discrimination in Respect to Employment and Occupation (1960) and on Consent to Marriage, Minimum Age for Marriage and Registration of Marriages (1962) and a Declaration on the Elimination of Discrimination against Women (1967) adopted by the United Nations. The UN Commission on the Status of Women saw its mandate expanded in 1962 to conduct a comprehensive study regarding how the UN system could establish a unified system for advancement of women. In 1972, based on this report and subsequent recommendations of the UN Commission as well as a variety of nongovernmental organizations (NGOs), the General Assembly decided to declare 1975 as International Women's Year and to convene a World Conference on Women in Mexico City in 1975.

HISTORY OF THE DEBATE

Prior to the convening of the World Conference on Women, regional conferences were held by the Economic Commissions for Africa, Asia, and Latin America concerning the integration of women in development with special reference to population factors. Reports from these conferences were prepared for what the UN Economic and Social Council (ECOSOC) dubbed the World Conference of the International Women's Year, to which 133 governments sent representatives. The conference produced a World Plan of Action and a Declaration of Mexico on the Equality of Women and Their Contribution to Development and Peace. The Plan of Action called for governments within a five-year period to set up national machinery to encourage and manage national efforts to advance the status of women, to improve literacy among women, to provide adequate vocational training and education to women, to increase employment opportunities for women, to promote better health education and services, sanitation, nutrition, family education family planning and welfare services for women, among many other provisions, and in particular to solve the problem of underdevelopment, which plagued women as well as developing countries generally. It called, in view of the latter issue, for the institution of a New International Economic Order.

The Conference Declaration identified thirty principles calling for measures to advance women's rights and tying these to women's advancement in the political and economic spheres. The principles included the ideas of equal pay for equal work, the right of couples freely and responsibly to decide matters concerning family size and spacing of children, a woman's free choice whether or not to marry, the need for the full integration of women into the development process, and increased opportunities for women to participate in the political process including the search for peace and justice. An additional matter of controversy was the inclusion of a condemnation of Zionism. The Declaration was adopted by a vote of 89 to 3, with 18 abstentions. The conference took up other decisions regarding the integration of women into the development process; on women's education, training, and research; on prevention of exploitation of women; and on population research and the family. In particular, it called for the establishment of an international voluntary fund for development projects concerning women and the establishment of an international training and research institute for the advancement of women.

In December 1975, the UN General Assembly approved the Plan of Action and Declaration in a series of resolutions and established a United Nations Voluntary Fund for the Decade on Women (UNIFEM) and the UN International Research and Training Institute for the Advancement of Women (INSTRAW). Four years after the Mexico Women's Conference, the UN General Assembly adopted the Convention on the Elimination of All Forms of Discrimination against Women.

A follow-up Conference on Women was held in 1980 at Copenhagen, Denmark. It reviewed progress on the Program of Action and Declaration made at Mexico City. It took further steps in emphasizing women's employment, health, and education and in noting the importance of NGOs in reaching goals in these areas of national policymaking. Controversial political issues were evident in Copenhagen, as they had been at Mexico. Developing countries dominated the elaboration of texts condemnatory of colonialism, racism, apartheid, hegemonism, and Zionism that were opposed by a dozen governments and evoked a similar number of abstentions. A program of action was adopted by a vote of 94 to 4 (Australia, Canada, Israel, United States), with 22 abstentions. The United States and Canada criticized the Plan of Action as going beyond the scope of issues of real concern to women by emphasizing political disputes and differences at odds with the real focus of the conference. Many Western European countries expressed reservations about the polemical atmosphere that had marked the conference. The Holy See regretted that the document failed to explore and honor the full range of women's roles in contributing to the society through the family, and it objected to the inclusion of language regarding family planning. The conference adopted forty-five resolutions on a range of matters concerning the role of women in development, health, education, and employment.

The third UN Conference on Women was held in Nairobi, Kenya, where Forward-looking Strategies for the Advancement of Women to the Year 2000 were adopted. By recommendation of this conference the UN General Assembly approved making UNIFEM an autonomous organization with the UN Development Program. A year after the Nairobi Conference, the first *World Survey on the Role of Women in Development* was published by the United Nations. It was followed in 1991 by the publication of *The World's Women: Trends and Statistics*, which compiled data on the condition of women throughout the world. These publications continue to be published periodically.

The 1990s saw a great deal of attention being paid to women's issues at the Rio Earth Summit on the environment in 1992, the 1993 Vienna Conference on Human Rights, and the International Conference on Population and Development in Cairo, which was the first occasion on which the international community declared the empowerment of women an integral part of the economic development process. In addition, the UN General Assembly adopted the Declaration on the Elimination of Violence against Women in 1993.

The Fourth World Conference on Women, held in Beijing in 1995, was a huge gathering that attracted 5,000 representatives of 189 governments, 4,000 representatives of NGOs, and 3,200 media representatives, along with 30,000 participants in a parallel NGO Forum on Women. It proved to be as controversial as its predecessors. Political sensitivity existed concerning the fact that it was held in Beijing, China, a country where human rights were routinely violated or ignored by the host government. In addition, during the preparatory phase of the conference, the Draft Declaration and Plan of Action were heavily influenced by individuals with little interest in the traditional notion of the family. Although the Draft contained forceful and widely accepted proposals about equality of opportunity, education, and development, it virtually ignored the idea of the family and of traditional motherhood or marriage except in references that characterized these venerable institutions as means of exploitation or as obstacles to personal advancement. Several delegations, including a number of European Union states, along with Canada, Barbados, South Africa, and Namibia, sought to reintroduce the sexual rights and abortion agenda, which had

Benazir Bhutto, prime minister of the Islamic Republic of Pakistan, addresses the opening session of the Fourth World Conference on Women, held in Beijing, China, in September 1995. UN/DPI Photo Milton Grant

been rejected at the Cairo conference on population and development. This group of governmental representatives sought to broaden the definition of marriage and to expunge the Beijing document of references to religion, ethics, and parental rights and duties in connection with the education of children. For this group, the Beijing conference represented an opportunity to rescue a radical agenda that had been rejected by governments at Cairo. But skillful diplomacy by the delegation from the Holy See brought the agenda of this minority of delegations to the attention of their governments back home, many of which were embarrassed to learn what their delegations were advocating at Beijing, after the Vatican sent a press release to European newspapers concerning what it saw as contradictions to the very idea of human rights and the dignity of the human person. The European Union (EU) delegations backed off from their more radical proposals, after governments consulted with their delegations in Beijing.

The conference generally noted progress in the advancement of women but noted many areas in which obstacles persisted. Twelve areas of concern to advancement of women included poverty; education; health issues including high maternal death rates and transmission of acquired immunodeficiency syndrome (AIDS); violence against women; armed conflicts that often most adversely affect the lives of women and children; economic structures that promote barriers to the advancement of women and sexual harassment; power sharing and decision making; adequate machinery for the advancement of women in government institutions at the highest levels; the need for gender-sensitive human rights; media portrayal of women's stereotypes; the environment; and problems associated with the girl child, including exploitation and adverse cultural practices. The final draft of the Platform for Action asserted that women have a "right to control over and decide freely and responsibly on matters related to their sexuality, including sexual and reproductive health, free of coercion, discrimination and violence." A disputed reference to elimination of discrimination due to "sexual orientation" was not included in the draft owing to a lack of support. Islamic states objected to a provision calling for the equal inheritance rights for women, so compromise language was adopted calling for such a right and for its enforcement "as appropriate." The Platform ultimately recognized the "rights and duties of parents and legal guardians" to provide guidance to young people, despite initial efforts of the EU coalition to have all such language stricken. However, the document does assert the right of young people to information, privacy, confidentiality, and informed consent on matters relating to sexuality and reproduction. On abortion the document called upon governments to review punitive laws regarding illegal abortions, but it reaffirmed the Cairo formula that "in no case should abortion be promoted as a method of family planning." With respect to the family, the conference continued to uphold it as the basic unit of society, consistent with the earliest human rights declarations such as the Universal Declaration of Human Rights. It also recognizes the social significance of motherhood and the role of parents in the rearing of children. On the issue of religion and culture, the Platform states that they contribute to fulfilling women's and men's moral, ethical, and spiritual needs and to realizing their potential in society. Rape is characterized as a war crime, and ethnic cleansing was unequivocally condemned. In its follow-up provisions, the conference also called for the establishment of a high-level adviser to the secretary-general on gender issues.

OUTCOME OF THE DEBATE

There will be further Women's Conferences in the years ahead because despite the progress that has been made in women's rights and in de facto treatment of women, the condition of women in many countries still leaves much to be desired. The ongoing recognition that the condition of women is closely connected to the overall development of the society in which they live has tied discussions of women to discussions of development issues ever since the first Women's Conference in Mexico. Women's issues also will continue to be tied to issues of population, environment, food, and human settlements.

These and other related concerns will no doubt continue to enliven debates on the advancement of women in the decades ahead. Still, as one looks back to the status and condition of women at the dawn of the twentieth century, one can see that tremendous strides have been made. Much of this progress has been the direct result of the policy and legislation of governments. However, the United Nations has proved to be a useful international venue for raising of awareness and promotion of women's issues. These settings have often been highly contentious, polemical, and hotly contested, but they have also advanced a good many sensible programs.

See also Human Rights (Debate 10); Population (Debate 15); Refugees and Stateless Persons (Debate 4); Status and Condition of Children (Debate 2).

FOR FURTHER READING

Berkovitch, Nitza. *From Motherhood to Citizenship: Women's Rights and International Organizations*. Baltimore: Johns Hopkins University Press, 1999.

Boutros-Ghali, Boutros. *The United Nations and the Advancement of Women, 1948–1996*. New York: UN Department of Public Information, 1996.

Fenster, Tori, ed. *Gender, Planning and Human Rights*. London: Routledge, 1999.

Steady, Filomina Chioma, and Remie Toure. *Women and the United Nations*. Rochester, VT: Schenkman Books, 1995.

UN Chronicle, 1995.

UN Yearbooks, 1975, 1980, 1985, 1990, 1995.

Weigel, George. *Witness to Hope: The Biography of Pope John Paul II*. New York: HarperCollins, 1999.

Young, Kate. *Planning Development with Women: Making a World of Difference*. New York: St. Martin's, 1993.

Zionism as Racism (1975)

SIGNIFICANCE OF THE ISSUE

The decision by the UN General Assembly in December 1975 to equate Zionism with racism signified the rise of Third World influence in the United Nations and the solidification of ties between anti-Israeli Arab states and antiapartheid and antiracist African states. The resolution was a symbolic unification of the issues of greatest concern to these two major blocs, and though unenforceable, it underscored the bitterness and acrimony surrounding the Arab-Israeli dispute and the relations of black Africans with the white minority regime of South Africa. Seventeen years after its enactment, the General Assembly rescinded this edict, only the second time in its history that the Assembly had reversed one of its decisions.

BACKGROUND TO THE DEBATE

Two issues of ongoing concern to the United Nations from its early years included the Arab-Israeli dispute and the racist policies of the white minority regime of South Africa, including the practice of apartheid. The Arab-Israeli dispute began with the partition of Palestine and creation of the state of Israel in 1948, events that followed from the aspirations of the Jewish people to return to Jerusalem and Palestine. In the late 1800s the Zionist movement took shape under the leadership of Theodore Herzl and others, who promoted the idea of the right of return of Jewish people to their ancestral homeland. Although Jews began to immigrate to Palestine in the nineteenth century, increased Jewish immigration into Palestine began in the early 1900s, causing Arab discontent. The British occupying authorities variously permitted and restricted Jewish immigration prior to and after World War II, provoking alternate protests from the Arab and Jewish populations. Eventually, however, international sentiment favored the establishment of both a Jewish and a Palestinian state, but Arab refusal to acknowledge Israel's existence, and their attempts to destroy the fledgling Jewish state in 1948, led to decades of intermittent war and acrimonious denunciation. Israel's survival and its devastating defeat of Arab armies in the 1967 war only deepened Arab hostility during the subsequent decade. Arab armies performed much better in 1973 when Arab states attacked Israel in what became known as the Yom Kippur War. The Arab oil embargo that followed illustrated the newfound economic power of the Arab oil-exporting states. The growth of Arab influence during this time was related in part to their diplomatic contacts with other countries of the developing world, and a sympathy of interests began to emerge among Arab states and non-Arab states of the Third World.

Through the process of decolonization, in the meantime, many new developing countries of Africa and Asia had gained UN membership. During the 1960s, these new member states began to flex their electoral muscle in UN bodies, especially in the UN General Assembly, where they now enjoyed a majority. Issues such as decolonization, racial discrimination, and apartheid propelled the African states into action, and they increasingly pressured UN bodies to pass strident denunciations of colonial powers and of the racist policies of the white minority government of South Africa. Through a process of logrolling, African and Arab states, as well as many antiimperialist powers of Asia, and many Communist countries could count on support from one another for issues relating to colonization, racism, and anti-Israeli sentiment. Indeed, both Israel and South Africa became known as international pariahs during the 1970s, having few friends and many enemies in the international arena.

HISTORY OF THE DEBATE

In 1975, the alliance of the Afro-Asian and Arab states carried their cooperation to a new level with the introduction before the General Assembly of a proposal to define Zionism as a form of "racism and racial discrimination." Debate began in the General Assembly's Third Committee, where a draft resolution equating Zionism with racism was approved by a vote of 70 to 29, with 27 abstentions. Somalia introduced the resolution in the General Assembly on behalf of other sponsors, arguing that the link between racial discrimination and Zionism was clear and unmistakable. Efforts by Belgium to have voting on the measure deferred or separated from other resolutions dealing with the UN Decade against Racism were defeated by an Assembly dominated by developing country majorities. In its preambulatory paragraphs the proposed resolution cited previous UN resolutions concerning the elimination of all forms of racial discrimination and a 1973 resolution that had condemned the "unholy" alliance between Zionism and South African racism. The debate was short-lived but acrimonious. On 10 November, the Assembly adopted resolution 3379 (XXX),

which apart from the introductory paragraphs consisted of but one opera-
tive paragraph defining Zionism as a form of racism and racial discrimination, by a vote of 72 to 35, with 32 abstentions, and three nonvoting states.
Communist bloc states were joined by twenty-seven African states, eleven
Asian states, and fifteen Arab states, along with a handful of additional
countries in voting for the proposal. Kuwait, India, Iraq, Jordan, Saudi Arabia, and the Syrian Arab Republic noted, among other points, that Zionism
was a racist and exclusive ideology and that Israel, the chief proponent of
Zionism, had close relations with South Africa, the architect of racist apartheid policies. Some supporters of the resolution, including Brazil, Iraq, Pakistan, and Yugoslavia, as well as some Arab states, qualified their votes by
noting that the resolution should not be viewed as an attack on Judaism as a
faith or religious tradition and acknowledging that even many Jews rejected Zionist ideology. Opposing the resolution were just five African
countries (Ivory Coast, Liberia, Malawi, the Central African Republic, and
Swaziland), along with many countries of Western Europe, a handful of
Latin American states, Israel, and the United States, among others. Israel
asserted that the resolution was rooted in hatred and falsehood and that it
displayed a casual arrogance and condescension toward the Jewish people
and their justifiable desire to establish a modern and independent Jewish
state. It declared the resolution totally devoid of moral or legal validity. The
United States joined in the criticism of the resolution, noting that it represented anti-Semitism, which was itself one of the most vicious forms of racism known to humankind. Thus, that the resolution was adopted in the
guise of a program to eliminate racism was "deceptive, deplorable and in-
famous." The United Kingdom, another opponent, asserted that the resolution confused nationalism with racism, hampered efforts at achieving
peace in the Middle East, and reduced UN effectiveness. Canada, Costa
Rica, the Federal Republic of Germany, Italy, the Netherlands, and New
Zealand voiced objections similar to those of the United Kingdom, some
noting that the action by the General Assembly directly contradicted the
United Nations' solemn responsibility to protect human rights. Latin
American states, such as Barbados, the Dominican Republic, and Uruguay,
who opposed the resolution, noted that it confused Zionism and racism,
which are wholly distinct terms and phenomena.

The passage of the resolution illustrated the high level of propaganda
dominating UN debates during the 1970s. It did little to move either the situation in South Africa or the Middle East dispute closer to resolution. But
as the Middle East peace process began to develop with a logic of its own,
especially after the Camp David Peace Accords between Egypt and Israel
in September 1978, it became clear that Israel would be a permanent fixture
in the region. Although the Lebanese situation continued to be marked by
conflict, after Egypt sued for peace, no coordinated or unified Arab attack

on Israel was possible. Peace in the region continued as Arab states began bowing to the reality.

At the same time, the situation in South Africa showed dramatic improvement in 1989, as a reform-minded government took power in that country, which began dismantling the apartheid system in 1990. With dramatic political improvements manifested in both the Arab-Israeli dispute and in the South African situation, sentiment began to mount for the repeal of General Assembly Resolution 3379.

OUTCOME OF THE DEBATE

Led by the United States, more than half of the UN General Assembly's membership of 166 sponsored an initiative to repeal Resolution 3379 in 1992. Arguing that the decision to equate Zionism with racism had been a relic of Cold War antagonisms and that the repeal of resolution 3379 would only help the Middle East peace process, the representative of the United States, Lawrence Eagleburger, urged member states to join in the effort begun by President George Bush, who had previously called on member states to put aside old feuds and to enhance the respectability and credibility of the United Nations. The representative of Lebanon, speaking on behalf of the Arab Group, disagreed, arguing that a repeal of the resolution would hamper the Middle East peace process by encouraging Israeli extremists and angering many Arabs.

Because the United Nations had only on one previous occasion revoked an earlier resolution (a resolution of 1946 urging member states to refrain from ties with General Francisco Franco's government in Spain because of its support for Nazi Germany), Yemen proposed that the General Assembly should treat the vote to rescind Resolution 3379 as an important question that would require a two-thirds majority. The Yemeni proposal was rejected, and Resolution 3379 was repealed by a vote of 111 to 25, with 13 abstentions. The representative of Israel noted after the vote that it was a sign of the new, sober, and more deliberative attitudes of UN member states.

See also Apartheid in South Africa (Debate 14); Arab-Israeli Dispute (Debate 6); Terrorism (Debate 28).

FOR FURTHER READING

Beker, Avi. *The United Nations and Israel: From Recognition to Reprehension.* Lexington, MA: Lexington Books, 1988.

Lacqueur, Walter. *History of Zionism.* New York: Fine Communications, 1997.

Sachar, Howard M. *A History of Israel: From the Rise of Zionism to Our Time.* New York: Knopf, 1996.

UN Chronicle, March 1992.

UN Yearbooks, 1975, 1992.

East Timor Question (1975)

SIGNIFICANCE OF THE ISSUE

For over twenty years, the problem of the self-determination of the people of East Timor, a small island in the Indonesian archipelago, north of Australia, simmered on the UN agenda unresolved until steps were taken in 1999 to ensure that the rights of the inhabitants were fulfilled in a plebiscite that won overwhelming popular approval for independence. Although Indonesian forces were called upon to withdraw, a brutal campaign of reprisals was unleashed by anti-independence activists and elements of the Indonesian military, leading to widespread killing and a large flow of refugees. International efforts to deal with the situation were tardy but nonetheless eventually helped to restore order to East Timor, one of the last areas of the South Pacific to free itself from colonial control and occupation, with direct UN assistance.

BACKGROUND TO THE DEBATE

During the sixteenth century, Portugal and Holland vied for control of the spice trade in the South Pacific, occupying much of the East Indies, including the Indonesian archipelago. The Portuguese controlled all of the island of Timor as a colony between 1586 and 1857. In 1857, they ceded the western part of the island to Holland, a deal ultimately consummated by a treaty of 1904. After a period of Japanese occupation during World War II, Portugal resumed control of East Timor in 1945, and in 1957 Portugal extended it status as an overseas province, granting Portuguese citizenship to the area's inhabitants, a majority of whom were Roman Catholics, in a region otherwise dominated by Muslims. Agitation began during the 1960s and early 1970s to wrest the colony from Portuguese control, with the formation of the Frente Revolucionária Timor Leste Independente (FRETILIN), a pro-independence party that probably reflected the opinion of a majority of the island's inhabitants. A countervailing influence also emerged with the formation of two groups with less wide appeal that called for integration with Indonesia, which in 1949 had received its independence from the Netherlands after four years of fighting. Indonesia contested the West Irian territories with the Dutch during the 1950s, as it attempted to consolidate its authority over disputed Dutch territories. In Indonesia's view, East Timor, though a Portuguese territory, rightfully belonged to it, along with the western portion of the island, which the Dutch had ceded to it on independence.

In 1974, after a change in government in Lisbon, Portugal decided to divest itself of its colonial holdings and began to set up a provisional government and a popular assembly that would then determine the manner and timing of decisions to achieve independence. Matters came to a head in 1975 as violence between FRETILIN, which acted on behalf of independence from the Portuguese, and the pro-Indonesian factions created a climate of civil war, which the Portuguese government was increasingly helpless to suppress. Portugal called upon the neighboring countries of Australia and Indonesia, along with the Red Cross, to help in providing humanitarian aid as chaotic conditions created displacement of the population. Portugal also insisted, however, that any decision on the future status of the island be decided by peaceful means of the people as a whole, not by violence. To that end Portugal attempted to get the political factions to agree to a negotiated settlement that would lead to a plebiscite, but in late November FRETILIN unilaterally declared independence, and shortly thereafter the pro-Indonesian factions did the same, calling for immediate integration with Indonesia. Portugal refused to acknowledge such claims as legitimate since no election had taken place to determine the true will of the population. But for all intents and purposes, Portugal withdrew its physical presence. In December, Indonesian forces commenced operations in East Timor. Pro-Indonesian factions later seized Dili, the capital, and formed a provisional government. They immediately requested Indonesian help in the fight against FRETILIN, which still advocated for full independence. Portugal informed the Security Council of Indonesian incursions into East Timor as early as 7 December 1975.

HISTORY OF THE DEBATE

In its meetings during December 1975 to consider the deteriorating situation in East Timor, the UN Security Council invited representatives of Indonesia, Portugal, Australia, Guinea, Guinea-Bissau, and Malaysia to participate in the discussions without vote. It also invited members of the various independence movements in Timor to be present. Portugal asked the Security Council to condemn Indonesia's interference in Portuguese

Timor, to call upon the immediate removal of its forces, and to ensure a climate suitable to the holding of elections.

Indonesia maintained that the problem in East Timor was the result of Portuguese neglect and that its own presence there had been undertaken at the request of Timorese parties. It agreed that the Timorese should decide their future for themselves and denied that any attempt was under way to annex the territory to Indonesia. FRETILIN called for a condemnation of Indonesia's aggression and asked that a fact-finding mission be sent to Timor so the United Nations could assess the situation for itself. Pro-Indonesian Timorese factions called for Timor's integration with Indonesia and for the presence of Indonesian troops to protect the people. Malaysia found Indonesia's intervention regrettably necessary after four months of bloody civil war that Portugal could not contain. China, on the other hand, condemned the Indonesian incursion as a gross violation of the UN Charter. The Soviet Union opposed outside intervention and hoped that a real process for self-determination could be achieved, while Australia stressed that the latter would only be possible through direct UN involvement. Portugal indicated that it was prepared to send troops to deal with the situation but that Indonesian forces must first withdraw. The Council then unanimously adopted a resolution calling upon Indonesia to withdraw its forces and requesting the secretary-general to send a special representative to the area to investigate the situation.

Following a report of its Fourth Committee on trusteeship matters, the UN General Assembly also adopted an earlier resolution on 12 December calling upon all states to recognize the right of the people of East Timor to self-determination, freedom, and independence. It called upon all parties to achieve a peaceful solution and deplored the military intervention by Indonesia. This resolution was adopted by a vote of 72 to 10, with 43 abstentions.

The special representative of the secretary-general visited Timor in the early months of 1976. He noted that while all parties to the dispute agreed that consultations toward a peaceful resolution of the dispute were necessary, no consensus existed regarding exactly how to proceed. The Security Council met again in April. FRETILIN accused Indonesia of occupying a fifth of the territory, accusing Indonesian forces of slaughtering tens of thousands and of using napalm and biological weapons. The special representative had been unable to visit areas under Indonesian occupation. In the meantime, Indonesia saw no need for elections, it denied the authority of Portuguese colonial administration, and it insisted that East Timor was already independent. Portugal refused to accept the legitimacy of FRETILIN but agreed that the continued presence of Indonesian forces was unacceptable. Indonesia pointed out that it was clear that none of the political groups in East Timor any longer accepted Portuguese authority. Australia noted that the withdrawal of Indonesian forces would probably lead to renewed fighting, while a number of delegations noted that there had been a normalization of life on the island, despite the lack of Indonesian withdrawal. The resulting resolution called upon Indonesia to withdraw its forces and for ongoing attempts to achieve a peaceful solution.

Given the lack of consensus among the Timorese factions, the Portuguese, as the lawful administrative authority, Indonesia, which had the advantage of proximity, and the international community about how to proceed, Indonesia moved during the summer of 1976 to respond to a call for integration of East Timor, and on 17 July, it formally annexed the area as its twenty-seventh province. This move was condemned by the UN General Assembly in December 1976 and again in November of the following year, in resolutions that rejected the claim that East Timor had been validly annexed by Indonesia. Australia, however, recognized this annexation in 1978, but the General Assembly reiterated its position in 1979 and again in 1981. It did so periodically in subsequent years as well.

For nearly twenty-five years, East Timor chaffed largely beyond the view of world attention, under the rule of Indonesia. While the UN General Assembly occasionally passed resolutions calling for the full self-determination of the people of East Timor, many countries tacitly acquiesced in the reality of Indonesian control. In 1982, at the request of the General Assembly, the secretary-general began holding consultations between Indonesia and Portugal with a view to resolving the situation to the satisfaction of all parties. In the early 1990s, the issue resurfaced as Indonesia and Australia sought to establish a treaty concerning establishment of continental shelf and economic zone claims in the Timor gap. Portugal reminded Indonesia that it had no right to engage in such negotiations on behalf of East Timor, which it illegitimately occupied. Indonesia and Australia ignored the protest and concluded the treaty. Portugal later brought the matter to the International Court of Justice, which ruled that Portugal did not have standing on the issue.

In the 1990s, FRETILIN activity increased as many Timorese grew increasingly unhappy with continued Indonesian rule. Agitation and violence and brutal Indonesian repression took place. Indonesia began to look for ways to deal with the situation. In 1997 the secretary-general appointed a personal representative for East Timor, and the governments of Indonesia and Portugal renewed efforts to achieve a solution to the problem. Indonesia favored granting East Timor autonomy but not full sovereignty, whereas Portugal would only approve of autonomy as a transition status to a full vote on independence. During 1998, these discussions continued and in May 1999 bore fruit with an agreement to hold a popular consultation on the future status of the territory. In June, by unanimous decision, the UN Security Council established the United Nations Assessment Mission in East Timor (UNAMET) to organize and conduct this consultation. The consultation would determine by secret ballot whether or not the people approved of a plan for special autonomy for East Timor within Indonesia. Rejection

Secretary-General Kofi Annan (center) meets in New York on 23 April 1999 with Foreign Minister Ali Alatas of Indonesia (left) and Foreign Minister Jaime Gama of Portugal (right) for talks on resolution of the situation in East Timor. UN/DPI Photo Milton Grant

would lead to the separation of East Timor and its independence. UNAMET consisted of nearly 300 civilian police officers to assist in providing order and 50 military liaison officers. Indonesia was held to be responsible, however, for maintaining peace and security so that the consultation could proceed on the basis of full, free, and fair participation of all. The consultation process was marred by violence carried out largely by pro-integration militias. By the end of the consultation process in August 1999, 78.5 percent of the voters rejected the autonomy arrangement with Indonesia, preferring instead the achievement of full independence.

Pro-integration militia, furious over the outcome of the vote, with assistance from elements of the Indonesian military who resented the outcome, began a brutal campaign of murder, rape, and pillage in the capital of Dili and in other major towns. A UN investigation resulted in the conclusion that the pro-Indonesian forces were engaged in a "systematic implementation of a scorched earth policy," which led to the death of thousands and the internal displacement of about 350,000 and the flight of about 270,000 refugees into West Timor. Many of the refugees and displaced simply hid in the forests to escape detection by marauding bands of militia, sometimes with the support of Indonesian regular forces. UNAMET thoroughly documented the participation of Indonesian military units in this destructive and brutal activity. In September 1999 the United Nations authorized the establishment of a multinational force, the International Force in East Timor (INTERFET), to restore peace and security, to protect UNAMET personnel, and to facilitate humanitarian operations on behalf of refugees and displaced persons. Australia agreed to provide the bulk of the initial forces deployed to these ends. In the following months, other countries contributed units as the security situation was stabilized and humanitarian aid began to flow.

OUTCOME OF THE DEBATE

A change of government in the fall of 1999 led to a more cooperative and contrite Indonesian participation in resolving the civil war in East Timor. The security situation was stabilized by the INTERFET forces, and many refugees gradually began to return to their homes. On 25 October, the UN Security Council established the United Nations Transitional Administration in East Timor (UNTAET) to oversee movement toward independence. The situation remained tenuous into the year 2000. Those pro-Indonesian refugees who fled with the militias responsible for provoking the murderous attacks on their neighbors were reluctant to return. In February 2000 UNTAET replaced UNAMET and INTERFET.

The future of East Timor, after this latest bloody episode, clearly lies in an independent status as the UNTAET operation acknowledges. Many pro-integration Indonesians are unlikely to want to live in a country in which they will be a distinct minority, especially since the pro-independence majority will harbor resentments against them. At the same time, East Timor will need to establish good relations with Indonesia so that its independence can be maintained securely, as militant pro-integration elements will no doubt attempt to advocate violence against the new nation. As long as Indonesia and its military respect the independence of East Timor, such elements can be contained.

After nearly twenty-five years of struggle, independence for East Timor lies on the immediate horizon. Whether its independence will be marked by peace, however, will depend on the wisdom of its new government and its ability to enlist its more powerful neighbors to respect its sovereignty.

See also Decolonization (Debate 18).

FOR FURTHER READING

Gunn, Geoffrey. *East Timor and the United Nations: The Case for Intervention.* Lawrenceville, NJ: Red Sea Press, 1997.
Jardine, Matthew, ed. *East Timor: Unfinished Struggle: Inside the Timorese Resistance.* Cambridge, MA: South End Press, 1996.
UN Chronicle, 1999.
UN Yearbooks, 1975–1979.

Human Settlements (1976)

SIGNIFICANCE OF THE DEBATE

The lack of adequate housing for hundreds of millions of people throughout the developing world, especially but not exclusively in increasingly
crowded and unsafe urban settings, has proved to be a difficult issue for
governments and the international community. Issues involving human
settlements are related to the problem of poverty and underdevelopment,
environmental degradation, disinvestment in rural areas, uncontrolled urbanization, high population growth rates, forced migration and refugee
flows, and civil discord—problems that have existed for some time in international relations and that remain major and ongoing concerns. Unsafe, inadequate, and substandard housing, then, is one important facet of a series
of interrelated public policy issues that have so far eluded successful national and UN responses.

BACKGROUND TO THE DEBATE

Human beings have crafted shelter since the beginning of time to protect
themselves from the elements. In tropical climates, the need for protection
from climate is less critical than in temperate or arctic climates, where winter temperatures plunge to levels that threaten human life. However, protection from monsoonal weather even in tropical climates is important for
the maintenance of health. Much of the world's population is located
within the tropics, where, all too often, especially in the twentieth century,
uncontrolled urbanization has led to the blossoming of crowded and un-
sanitary squatter settlements as huge numbers of people migrate from pov-
erty-stricken rural areas into the cities in hopes of finding employment. In
1950 only 30 percent of the world's population lived in cities, compared to
about 50 percent in the year 2000. High population growth in the poorest
countries of the developing world put immense pressure on governments

One of the most critical problems in many parts of the world is the shortage of adequate housing and the deterioration of human settlements. The crowded and dilapidated shanties of Manila, the Philippines, shown here are emblematic of the crisis in human settlements faced by many developing countries. UN/DPI Photo Oddbjorn Monsen

to keep pace in construction of housing. Many poor people crowded into unsafe areas subject to earthquakes, mud slides, and flooding, constructing makeshift housing in the highly disaster prone areas. The slums and shantytowns erected in such areas are haphazard and often hazardous to health and life. The lack of adequate physical infrastructure, electricity, running water, waste management capacities, and plumbing made many such urban zones exceptionally unhealthy places in which to live. During the 1960s and 1970s, national governments began to take more explicit notice of these problems, which began to emerge on the agendas of international bodies.

The first effort by the international community to deal with the growing problem of housing and shelter took place at the UN Conference on the Human Environment held in Stockholm in 1972. That conference called upon the UN General Assembly to convene a conference on human settlements, and it provided for a funding mechanism for projects relating to human settlements. The General Assembly approved these conference proposals and established a preparatory committee, which met in 1975–1976 to plan for the UN Conference on Human Settlements, also known as Habitat, which met in Vancouver, Canada, from 31 May to 11 June 1976.

HISTORY OF THE DEBATE

At Habitat, 132 governments, 160 nongovernmental organizations (NGOs), and a number of intergovernmental agencies met for ten days of discussion and debate on international housing and settlement issues. Unique in the history of such international conferences was the presentation of over 200 films or slide presentations by 123 governments that illustrated the state and condition of housing in their countries. The work of Habitat was conducted in three committees. The first committee worked on the draft declaration and on international programs of cooperation. The second committee considered plans of action by nations concerning their settlement policies and planning. The third committee considered plans of action by nations concerning shelter, infrastructure and services, land, and public participation. An NGO forum in which 5,000 people participated was held during the conference and established a trend for subsequent conferences.

The first committee produced a Declaration of Principles, known as the Vancouver Declaration on Human Settlements, which consisted of sixty-four recommendations for national action in the housing and settlements policy arena and was approved on 11 June by the conference as a whole by a vote of 89 to 15, with 10 abstentions. The Declaration affirmed that all human settlement policy must be aimed at recognizing human dignity and the need for provision of basic human needs and improvement in the quality of life. Rational land use policies were necessary to this end, in keeping with environmental needs. Residents of human communities had a right to participate in the process of improving communities in which they live. Two controversial provisions, one calling for the equation of Zionism with racism and the other calling for the immediate implementation of the provisions of the Declaration on the New International Economic Order (NIEO), provoked opposition. A number of the negative votes and abstentions were tied to the inclusion of such language in the Declaration, which otherwise would have met approval according to statements on the vote made by Australia, Austria, Canada, Colombia, Fiji, the Netherlands on behalf of the European Economic Community countries, New Zealand, Portugal, Spain, Switzerland, and the United States. Otherwise, there was substantial consensus on the recommendations for national action, which included a call for nations to establish formal human settlements machinery and policy, to consider the role of women in housing issues, insuring the existence and accessibility of social services, to improve urban housing, to develop disaster response capacities, to provide transportation facilities, to assist the construction industry to ensure appropriate land reform and land use, and to encourage citizen participation, among other proposals. International action called for the creation of a new international organization to serve as an advocate for international settlement cooperation among nations and to report to the Economic and Social Council (ECOSOC), creation of a secretariat to serve as an administrative body to this new organization, and creation of regional commissions on settlement issues.

After consideration by ECOSOC and its Second Committee, the UN General Assembly, in a series of resolutions at its regular session in 1976, approved the Vancouver Declaration (by a vote of 102 to 2, with 25 abstentions), which still contained language concerning Zionism and racism that delegations found objectionable. It also approved a resolution to move forward with the establishment of a new organization for human settlements, a secretariat for such a body, and establishment of regional commissions for human settlements. In 1977 ECOSOC decided to reconstitute its Committee on Housing, Building and Planning into a Commission on Human Settlements, which would promote policy objectives in the human settlement arena, propose new and cooperative solutions, and approve the use of funds for human settlements projects. It would consist of fifty-eight member governments. A secretariat to serve the commission, to be called the United Nations Centre for Human Settlements (UNCHS) or Habitat, would be established and located in Nairobi, Kenya. The General Assembly approved these decisions without vote in December 1977. UNCHS became operational in 1978, with requests for funding of human settlements projects. From a modest start of a few dozen programs in 1978, the UNCHS realized a steady growth in numbers of programs. By 1992, it was funding 262 technical projects worth about $43 million. But, as always, there were many projects for which revenue was not available—in 1992 about eighty-five projects in forty-four countries. UNCHS is funded by voluntary contributions.

In 1988, UNCHS helped to draw up and win approval of the UN General Assembly for a Global Strategy for Shelter to the Year 2000. UNCHS was also charged with follow-up responsibility for certain shelter-related provisions of the Agenda 21 established by the UN Conference on Environment and Development held in Rio de Janeiro in 1992. In that same year, the UN General Assembly decided to hold a Habitat II Conference, known as the "City Summit," to be held in Istanbul, Turkey, in 1996. Despite nearly two decades of national and international activities to deal with urban growth and provision of adequate housing and living environments, many large cities of the developing world continued to be under great stress in terms of housing availability and quality. With 500 million people in developing country urban areas living in substandard housing, with inadequate access to safe drinking water or sanitation, and often subject to unemployment or underemployment, governments and the international community still had a lot to do. Habitat II was held in order to sharpen the focus of national urban development planning and halt the worsening condition of many urban environments. It was charged with reviewing trends in human settlements programs and making recommendations regarding further steps for both local approaches to improvement of human settlements and international cooperative measures.

During the debates at Istanbul, the most difficult item concerned an initiative to declare housing a human right. Using compromise language, governments committed themselves to the "full and progressive realization of the right to adequate housing." They also agreed to explore decentralized strategies for housing decisions to allow local authorities and partnerships for urban development among governments, businesses, trade unions, and NGOs and other strategies to enhance local markets for housing. Such measures, inconceivable two decades earlier, when socialist and centralized planning was the norm in many developing countries, proved to be an innovation of Habitat II. Governments recommitted themselves in the Istanbul Declaration to address the issues of homelessness, unemployment, lack of basic infrastructure and services, urban insecurity and violence, vulnerability to disaster, gender equality, and sustainable population policies. In an echo of the old New International Economic Order debates, industrialized countries were called upon to address "unsustainable consumption and production patterns" and to strive to meet the goals of dedicating 0.7 percent of their gross national product to foreign assistance.

OUTCOME OF THE DEBATE

The outcome of Istanbul was a realization that urban housing and development issues will continue to be a major preoccupation of the UN system in the years ahead. In the year 2000 one in every two people lives in a major urban environment. By the year 2025, the expectation is that the world will have 100 megacities of populations in excess of 5 million, many with populations exceeding 20 million. By that time, more than two-thirds of humanity will live in urban settings, and 80 percent of those will be in developing countries. Under this kind of pressure, it is doubtful that housing can keep pace, barring massive and unforeseen investment in this area. Unlike previous decades, however, both governments and the international community are aware of the many problems and have organized to address them. In the area of housing, as delegates at Habitat I in Vancouver recognized in 1976, progress can only be made by acknowledging the interplay of environmental, population, rural development, migration, and domestic and international economic developments, including the increasing trend in the 1990s toward globalization of trade and investment. Effective human settlements policies must account for all of these interdependent variables.

See also Global Environment (Debate 27); Population (Debate 15); Third World Development Programming (Debate 25).

FOR FURTHER READING

UN Chronicles, 1992, 1996.

United Nations Centre for Human Settlements. *An Urbanizing World: Global Report on Human Settlements*. Oxford: Oxford University Press, 1996.

UN Yearbooks, 1972–1977, 1992, 1994, 1996.

Central American Wars (1978)

SIGNIFICANCE OF THE ISSUE

The civil wars in Central America that began in the late 1970s and raged into the 1980s were indicative of the last phase of the Cold War in which superpower competition for ascendancy within their own spheres of influence was bitterly contested in the context of Central America, a region marked by very uneven distribution of wealth and landownership and by class-based resentments. The United Nations, though powerless to prevent the conflicts, played a central role in the resolution phase of civil wars in Nicaragua, El Salvador, and Guatemala.

BACKGROUND TO THE DEBATE

One of the chief problems in several Central American countries is that from the time of the Spanish conquest the native peoples were subjected to the government and authority of the Spanish elites that settled there. Land and wealth tend to be concentrated in the hands of the descendants of the European elites, who though a minority of the population control most of the wealth. These kinds of inequalities create economic and political conditions ripe for exploitation by those who seek through revolutionary action to overturn the existing order. While Central American countries are all affected in varying degrees by the phenomena of class resentment, inequitable land distribution, and income inequalities, El Salvador, Guatemala, and Nicaragua have the longest histories of violence in connection with them, and these were the countries during the late 1970s and early 1980s that began to experience socialist revolutionary movements and crackdowns by authoritarian right-wing governments.

The events of the Cold War also led to a great fear on the part of the United States of socialist guerrilla activity in Central America, especially in view of Fidel Castro's penchant for exporting revolution from Cuba to other countries in Latin America. Moreover, during the 1970s the Soviet Union embarked on a global campaign of support to leftist opposition groups, and Central America did not escape its notice. The first country to face a real threat from revolution was Nicaragua. After decades of authoritarian rule by the Somoza dynasty and its corrupt policies, the Somoza family was enriched at the expense of the Nicaraguan people. A broad-based opposition formed including not only the leftist Sandinistas but also broad elements of the more conservative business community. This combined alliance was fatal to the regime of Anastasio Somoza, which was driven from Nicaragua in 1979. Forces sympathetic to Somoza fled into neighboring Honduras and Costa Rica, where they formed opposition groups to the new Nicaraguan government, which quickly was dominated by the hard-line Marxists under Daniel Ortega, who made it clear that they would impose a socialist order in Nicaragua, much to the chagrin of their erstwhile allies from the business community.

The emergence of a Marxist regime in Nicaragua paved the way for the Soviet Union and Cuba to provide it with assistance and to use its territory, in turn, to support a growing leftist insurgency in neighboring El Salvador. In 1979, efforts by Christian Democratic and Socialist Democratic parties to reform El Salvador's highly unequal system of landownership came to an end after a coup d'état by the right-wing military. This precipitated a civil war between the military government and the Frente Farabundo Marti para la Liberación Nacional (FMLN) and other leftist groups. The Sandinistas supported the FMLN efforts by providing arms, but the United States supported the government, creating a nasty and bloody stalemate that would produce 1.5 million refugees and displaced persons, until the reform-minded government of Alfredo Christiani took power in 1989 and began a process of reconciliation.

Guatemala also experienced domestic instability in the 1980s. Its politics had been marked by violence, external intervention, and widespread displacement of people since the 1950s. In 1982, the military nullified the results of an election it held to be fraudulent, promising to restore true democracy. But the reality was otherwise. The military instead undertook a scorched earth campaign against the native Indian peoples on the pretext that they were Communist sympathizers. This aggravated an already existing problem of internal displacement and of refugee flows into Mexico during the 1980s.

HISTORY OF THE DEBATE

The first Central American problem to reach the UN agenda was that in Nicaragua, during 1978, as the country still suffered under the rule of Anastasio Somoza and a widening civil war involving the Sandinista Liberation Front. Venezuela brought the matter to the attention of the Security

Council in September, criticizing the Somoza regime of brutally repressing its civilian population and thereby threatening the peace and security of the region. The Council's only action at the time was to warn Nicaragua not to threaten the territorial integrity of neighboring Costa Rica, where along the mutual border a number of military incidents had occurred. The General Assembly then took up the matter and in a resolution adopted by a vote of 85 to 2 (Nicaragua and Paraguay), with 45 abstentions, it voted to censure the repression of the civilian population of Nicaragua and condemn the threat to the security of Costa Rica. After the victory of the Sandinistas in 1979, the General Assembly endorsed a program of assistance to help Nicaragua rebuild itself after years of corrupt government.

The UN General Assembly first took notice of the civil war in El Salvador in 1981, with the passage of a resolution calling on Salvadoran parties to seek a negotiated solution to their differences and calling upon the government to respect the human rights of its citizens. As the civil war deepened, neither the government nor the FMLN was shy about violating the human rights of Salvadoran citizens, although the military government was by far the greater culprit. With the inauguration U.S. President Ronald Reagan in 1981, U.S. assistance for the embattled military junta in El Salvador was stepped up, as assistance to the Nicaraguan Contras harbored in Honduras and Costa Rica was initiated. Central America would become yet another battleground in a global struggle between the forces of communism and the capitalist West. The long-term effect of the Reagan policy was to deny the FMLN any hope of victory in El Salvador, and in Nicaragua, the revitalized Contras proved to be a major headache for the Sandinista regime.

As the confrontation between Washington and Managua deepened, efforts to pursue peaceful negotiations focused on the countries in the region. Apart from General Assembly denunciations of American intervention in the region, the United Nations was not well positioned to undertake forceful action. The U.S. seat on the Security Council prevented any action by that body. It vetoed, for example, a resolution framed by Panama and Guyana in April 1982, after Nicaragua called for a Security Council meeting to discuss American intervention in Central America. The Guyanan and Panamanian draft resolution would have called upon all states to refrain from either direct or indirect overt or covert use of force in the region and appealed to them to resort instead to peaceful negotiation and dialogue. In explaining its veto, the United States regretted that the resolution had not acknowledged the source of the instabilities in the region resulting from Nicaragua's intervention into the affairs of neighboring countries and that it had ignored proper means of resolving the dispute.

In 1983, Nicaragua again appealed to the Security Council to take steps to prevent attacks from Honduras by Contras financed by the United States. Honduras complained about Nicaraguan seizure of Honduran fishing vessels and a military buildup by Nicaraguan armed forces along the border. In the debate that followed, Nicaragua accused the United States of financing military infiltration into Nicaragua of counterrevolutionary forces, and it accused Honduras of collusion in this process. Honduras characterized the conflict as an internal Nicaraguan problem and denied any collusion with the United States. The United States in turn characterized the Nicaraguan Sandinista government as paranoid and as a threat to its neighbors' peace and security. The Soviet Union sided with Nicaragua. China noted cryptically that the problems in the area existed owing to the intervention of "a superpower." Libya was more direct, blaming the United States as the major culprit, as did other East European and Third World representatives. Several countries worried about the escalation of the conflict and hoped that all parties would submit to negotiation. After months of meetings during the spring of 1983, during which accusations and counteraccusations were liberally launched by or against the immediate disputants, a consensus emerged that the peace initiative of the Contadora countries (Colombia, Mexico, Panama, and Venezuela) should be commended and extended. This resolution was adopted unanimously. In 1984, Nicaragua asked the Security Council to condemn the U.S. mining of its harbors as a violation of international law. It also lodged a suit against the United States before the International Court of Justice (ICJ), which the United States refused to acknowledge as falling under the ICJ's jurisdiction. The ICJ rebuffed this claim and went forward with deliberations while the United States refused to appear. Eventually, in 1986 the Court decided in favor of the Nicaraguan claim. The United States then announced its intention to revoke its acceptance of the Court's compulsory jurisdiction. In the meantime, in Security Council action, the United States vetoed a draft resolution that would have condemned the mining and called for its immediate end. The resolution otherwise received 13 favorable votes and 1 abstention by the United Kingdom. The United States argued that the resolution was flawed insofar as it was silent about Nicaragua's persistent violations of the sovereignty of her neighbors. The General Assembly, on the other hand, unanimously adopted a much blander resolution calling for international support for the Contadora peace initiative.

In 1985, the United States imposed a trade embargo on Nicaragua. Nicaragua once again appealed to the Security Council for relief. The United States vetoed a paragraph in a resolution that was otherwise adopted unanimously; the paragraph noted that the trade embargo and other measures of economic coercion had exacerbated and aggravated the situation, and the resulting resolution, thus eviscerated, remained a repetition of earlier Council appeals for support of the Contadora process. Having failed in the Security Council, Nicaragua repaired to the General Assembly, where Nicaragua succeeded with other sponsoring states, including Algeria, Mexico, and Peru, in winning approval for a statement of the Assembly's regret at and demand for an immediate revocation of the trade embargo. In the following year, after the ICJ's judgment in favor of Nicaragua, the latter sought Security Council approval of a resolution affirming the ICJ's judgment. The resolution failed owing to a veto by the United States.

The strategy of Nicaragua in attempting to engage UN bodies during the 1980s was calculated to win it propaganda points, since even in losing every Security Council battle it maneuvered the United States into using its veto power and thus gave Nicaragua political ammunition. However, Nicaragua was increasingly pinched, both by its exorbitant military expenditures and by the economic embargo.

Thus, the struggles in Central America would be determined by conditions prevailing on the ground and by regional peace initiatives sponsored by neighboring Contadora countries who were most directly affected by the refugee flows stimulated by civil wars in El Salvador, Guatemala, and Nicaragua. The successful conclusion of the Esquipulas Peace agreements between the Contadora group and the presidents of Costa Rica, El Salvador, Guatemala, Honduras, and Nicaragua in 1987 finally paved the way towards a resolution of the Central American wars. The agreement provided for a cessation of hostilities, the establishment of amnesty and reconciliation commissions in each country, a process of democratization including free communication and political expression and organization, the cessation of military aid to irregular forces, verification and control of limits on weaponry, provision of refugee, humanitarian, and development assistance, as well as international verification and follow-up.

Despite bumpy patches, progress toward peace continued in Nicaragua in 1988 with an agreement between the Contras and the Sandinista government to cease hostilities. In this more peaceful climate, the Sandinista government was more comfortable about allowing internationally monitored elections. It announced its intention to hold such elections in 1990, but much to the Sandinistas surprise, it could not control the electoral situation in light of the international supervision; and in the free and fair elections that took place, the people of Nicaragua, dissatisfied with the economic deterioration that had taken place under the Sandinistas in large part owing to the U.S. trade embargo, voted them out of power. Prior to this, the UN Security Council had established the United Nations Observer Group in Central America (ONUCA) in November 1989 at the request of the five Central American countries most directly affected by the Esquipulas peace. ONUCA was charged with verifying the peace accords, preventing attacks against the territories of the countries in the region, and demobilizing the Nicaraguan Contras prior to the Nicaraguan elections. The electoral defeat of the Sandinistas put additional pressure on the FMLN in El Salvador, which lost a major avenue for military resupply. The El Salvadoran government was under pressure from the United States to resolve its differences with the FMLN. This led to a series of agreements and eventually the deployment by the UN Security Council of the United Nations

Observer Mission in El Salvador (ONUSAL) to monitor implementation of the agreements.

The United Nations was able to act in these situations in part because of the diplomatic rapprochement between the United States and the Soviet Union that had occurred in 1989 and continued into the early 1990s. The Soviet Union was desperately beginning to seek Western aid. It could no longer afford, nor did it wish to sustain, military and economic aid to friendly socialist regimes in opposition to pro-Western governments. The Cold War was over, and the previously veto-bound Security Council was now able to take a more active role in the settlement phases of a number of conflicts around the world, including Central America, where after a long struggle matters were finally going in a direction acceptable to the only superpower that mattered in the region, the United States.

OUTCOME OF THE DEBATE

As democratic governments took power in Nicaragua and El Salvador, hope for peace in the region justifiably grew. In 1989, the governments in the region held a conference on refugees and displaced persons, which identified ways and means for rehabilitating and reconstructing the

The United Nations played a major role in achieving implementation of peace agreements in various Central American countries. Here voters in El Salvador cast ballots in San Miguel on 20 March 1994 in elections overseen by the United Nations Observer Mission in El Salvador (ONUSAL). UN/DPI Photo Milton Grant

war-torn infrastructure of the affected countries and helping them to start back on the road to economic development. In 1992 the ONUCA forces were withdrawn, their mission having been accomplished. ONUSAL brought its work to a successful close in 1995. Even in Guatemala, which had seen human rights abuses continue into the early 1990s, governmental reforms allowed substantial repatriation of refugees. With the deployment of the UN Verification Mission in Guatemala (MINUGUA), from January 1997 to May 1997, the United Nations helped to ensure the safe return of refugees and encourage a more wholesome human rights climate.

Once again, Central American countries, after a decade of bloody warfare, could concentrate on improving their economic situation without the huge costs of ongoing wars and their accompanying destruction of lives and property. The United Nations played a useful role, in the closing phase of this drama, in providing both the peacekeeping presence to demobilize forces and secure peace and the economic interventions to help heal the wounds of war.

See also Human Rights (Debate 10); Refugees and Stateless Persons (Debate 4).

FOR FURTHER READING

Ardon, Patricia. *Post-War Reconstruction in Central America: Lessons from El Salvador, Guatemala and Nicaragua.* Herndon, VA: Stylus, 1999.

Close, David. *Nicaragua: The Chamorro Years.* Boulder, CO: Lynne Rienner, 1998.

Ferris, Elizabeth. *Central American Refugees and the Politics of Protection.* New York: Praeger, 1987.

Gallagher, Dennis, and Janelle Diller. *CIREFCA: At the Crossroads between Uprooted People and Development in Central America.* Washington, DC: Commission for the Study of International Migration and Cooperative Economic Development, 1990.

Lake, Anthony, et al. *After the Wars: Reconstruction in Afghanistan, Indochina, Central America, Southern Africa, and the Horn of Africa.* New Brunswick, NJ: Transaction Publishers with the Overseas Development Council, 1990.

MacDonald, Laura. *Supporting Civil Society: The Political Role of Non-Governmental Organizations in Central America.* New York: St. Martin's, 1997.

McCleary, Rachel M. *Dictating Democracy: Guatemala and the End of Violent Revolution.* Gainesville: University Press of Florida, 1999.

UN Yearbooks, 1977–1995.

Cambodia Situation (1979)

SIGNIFICANCE OF THE ISSUE

After many years of brutal warfare, genocide, and foreign occupation, a peace settlement brokered by the five permanent members of the United Nations (UN) Security Council in 1991 ushered in an era of peace and renewed stability in Cambodia. The United Nations Transitional Authority in Cambodia (UNTAC) forces were deployed in one of the United Nations' most ambitious peacekeeping operations. UNTAC was deployed to ensure peace, to undertake transitional administration of an entire country, and to prepare it for democratic elections. One of the largest and most expensive peacekeeping forces ever deployed by the United Nations, it completed its work successfully in September 1993.

BACKGROUND TO THE DEBATE

Cambodia became an independent state in 1953 after ninety years as a French Protectorate. Prior to the French arrival Cambodia could trace back its identity to the early Funan kingdoms of the first century A.D. In the ninth century the powerful Khmer empire emerged that encompassed much of Southeast Asia by the thirteenth century with a flourishing civilization. Encroachment by the Siamese and Vietnamese eventually reduced the size of the Khmer kingdom in subsequent centuries. Upon independence from the French, Prince Norodom Sihanouk attempted to follow a policy of neutrality. This policy was compromised in 1965 with the intervention of U.S. forces during the Vietnam War. Sihanouk also worried, however, about the Vietcong Communists arming Khmer guerrillas in the late 1960s. In 1970, Sihanouk was overthrown by General Lon Nol, and Sihanouk formed a government in exile in Paris, while the Khmer Rouge insurgents began to attack the new military regime. The United States provided military assistance to Lon Nol's regime, but the Khmer Rouge still managed to rout government forces in 1975 and to announce the end to the Khmer Republic with the formation of the new nation of Kampuchea.

The advent of the Khmer Rouge ushered in a period of great brutality and genocide. The new government forced the evacuation of the cities. Intellectuals, leaders, and persons with any connection to the former governments of Sihanouk or Lon Nol were murdered. Many city-dwellers died from hunger in the forced evacuations or in the work camps to which they were sent. Over 1 million people were killed or died owing to the new government policies, which involved a return to the "purity" of the ancient Khmer culture. Anyone with a French education or with any education was viewed as an enemy of the new state.

In 1978, fighting broke out between Khmer Rouge and Vietnamese Communist troops along their disputed border. The Vietnamese forces eventually invaded during that year, and the Vietnamese-backed Kampuchean National United Front announced the formation of a new government after the capture of Phnom Penh on 7 January 1979. The Vietnamese invasion was, for many, a blessing in disguise insofar as the bloodthirsty Khmer Rouge was no longer in a position to pursue its policies of genocide. But the invasion did result in humanitarian problems both within occupied Cambodia and along the border with Thailand, where starvation was common among the refugees and displaced persons. About 100,000 Cambodians sought refuge in Thailand or near the border with Thailand in 1978. By the early 1980s, this number had swelled to over 300,000, while large numbers of Kampucheans required assistance in their own country. The UN response to the refugee problem in Thailand was coordinated by the UN High Commissioner for Refugees, while the UN Children's Fund and the International Committee for the Red Cross were active in providing aid to displaced persons inside Cambodia. While the humanitarian situation worsened, the political situation in Southeast Asia further deteriorated in 1979, when China invaded Vietnam in retaliation for its invasion and occupation of Kampuchea, a Chinese ally. Vietnam, which had the backing of the Soviet Union, easily rebuffed the Chinese incursions across its border after a short but nasty war. No action was possible by the Security Council in responding to this situation as it involved the direct interests of two permanent members with veto powers.

HISTORY OF THE DEBATE

Presented with an awkward situation, the United Nations continued to recognize the murderous regime of the Khmer Rouge of Pol Pot rather than acknowledge the legitimacy of the new regime in Phnom Penh, which had been installed illegally by outside forces. The UN Security Council met on 11–12 January to consider the situation. A draft resolution that commanded a large majority of thirteen votes, but that excited a veto by the Soviet Union, would have accused Vietnam of an illegal aggression in Kampuchea. When the UN General Assembly met in its regular session in the fall of 1979, it refused to replace the Pol Pot delegation with the new Kampuchean regime by a vote of 91 to 21, with 29 abstentions. The same resolution called for the immediate withdrawal of Vietnamese forces.

In 1980, the General Assembly reiterated its stance in the 1979 resolution and, in addition, called for the holding of an International Conference on Kampuchea, which was held on 13–17 July 1981 in New York and attended by seventy-nine governments. A Declaration of this conference, which was boycotted by numerous governments, called for the withdrawal of all foreign forces, the restoration of Kampuchea's independence, and a commitment by all states to noninterference in its internal affairs. It asserted that a comprehensive settlement would require a cease-fire agreement by all parties, withdrawal of foreign forces under UN supervision, UN-supervised elections, and the maintenance of law and order. Many of these principles served as major features of the agreement eventually reached among the parties about a decade later. A ten-member Ad Hoc Committee was established by the conference, which continued in subsequent years to monitor the situation, explore negotiations among the parties, and report to the General Assembly. The General Assembly approved the Declaration of the Conference on Kampuchea by a vote of 110 to 25, with 19 abstentions. Opposition to the action came mainly from Communist countries, while numerous developing countries abstained.

During the 1980s, the UN General Assembly received with satisfaction several reports made by the Ad Hoc Committee on Kampuchea and praised the humanitarian support provided to refugees by Western powers while reiterating calls for a complete withdrawal of foreign troops. These resolutions evoked similar majority votes with opposition by Communist countries other than China and Kampuchea and abstentions by many developing countries. After repeated efforts to get negotiations started, success was achieved in late 1987 and early 1988 in getting the parties to agree to talk. The talks were complicated by the fact that the Khmer Rouge, though still the recognized government, was but one of three resistance parties in addition to the Vietnamese-backed Hun Sen government in Phnom Penh, which claimed a voice in the negotiations. In addition to the Khmer People's National Liberation Front (KPNLF) led by Son Sann, Norodom Sihanouk headed the National United Front for an Independent, Neutral, Peaceful, and Cooperative Cambodia (FUNCINPEC), while Khieu Samphan headed the Party of Democratic Kampuchea (PDK). Precipitating this progress was the deteriorating economic situation in Vietnam, which was only aggravated by its expensive presence in Cambodia.

Initial informal talks between the disputants were held with Vietnam, Laos, and six members of the Association of Southeast Asian Nations (Brunei Darussalam, Indonesia, Malaysia, Philippines, Singapore, and

Thailand) at Jakarta, Indonesia, in July 1988. The parties agreed that a withdrawal of Vietnamese forces coupled with assurances on nonrepetition of the policies of genocide were essential to an eventual agreement. In 1989, the parties met again in Jakarta and then again, at the invitation of France, at the International Conference on Cambodia in Paris. These meetings reiterated the need for the withdrawal of forces and the nonrecurrence of genocidal policies, but with the additional idea that these be conducted under UN supervision, in advance of internationally supervised elections. Vietnam withdrew its forces before the end of September, but fighting continued between the Hun Sen government forces and those of the resistance organizations. Against this backdrop of progress and ongoing security concerns, the parties also agreed that some sort of transitional governing authority would be necessary during the period in which elections for a new government would be held.

During 1990 the five permanent members of the Security Council weighed into the situation, holding several sessions to discuss the Cambodia situation. The demise of the Cold War made possible this unusual negotiating process, and by August the "Big Five" presented to the Cambodian parties a comprehensive framework for political settlement that provided that a Supreme National Council (SNC) would be established as a transitional authority, while refugees were repatriated, forces were demobilized and reconstituted into a national army, civil administration was rebuilt, and mine clearance could be undertaken to provide greater safety. Human rights monitoring and an elections process would also be undertaken during the transition period. The SNC, composed of a coalition of the Cambodian parties, would delegate to the United Nations Transitional Authority in Cambodia (UNTAC) all the powers necessary to ready the country for free and fair elections, at the end of which UNTAC would relinquish control to the newly elected government.

In 1991, after prolonged but productive negotiations, all parties agreed to a political settlement, to the formation of the SNC with Prince Norodom Sihanouk as its chairman, to the provisions of a new Constitution, to the deployment of UN forces, and to principles for the rehabilitation and reconstruction of Cambodia. On 16 October, the Security Council unanimously authorized the deployment of the United Nations Advance Mission in Cambodia (UNAMIC) to pave the way for the eventual establishment of the transitional authority and to provide initial security and mine-awareness programs. On 28 February 1992, the Council took the next step by establishing the UNTAC. Although numerous problems were encountered as UNTAC pursued its mandate of transitional administration, such as Khmer Rouge reluctance to disarm, human rights violations, and sporadic fighting, nevertheless, repatriation of refugees was accomplished, as was registration for and the holding of a largely free and fair election in May 1993, which led to the establishment of a new government. The elec-

After years spent in refugee camps, Cambodian refugees make their way home in 1992
under the auspices of the UN High Commissioner for Refugees repatriation program in
the early phases of the United Nations Transitional Authority in Cambodia (UNTAC)
peacemaking operation, which resulted in
elections of a new democratic government.
UN/DPI Photo J. Bleibtreu

tions were won by FUNCINPEC, led by Norodom Sihanouk's son
Norodom Ranariddh, who was named prime minister, and the elder
Sihanouk was also elected king. FUNCINPEC won fifty-eight seats in the
new Parliament, while Hun Sen's Cambodian People's Party won fifty-one
seats. Hun Sen was named second prime minister. UNTAC forces formally
withdrew after the successful conclusion to the operation on 24 September
1993.

OUTCOME OF THE DEBATE

After two and a half decades of strife, with essential help from the
United Nations, Cambodia had achieved democracy by peaceful means.

Many problems lay ahead in terms of the full reconciliation of the parties, especially Khmer Rouge units who continued to defy integration. In addition, the country continued to need reform of its public administration and help in mine clearance, in the resettlement of displaced persons, and in the repair of its physical and social infrastructure, not to mention practice in the art of democratic governance. This was underscored as the first set of elections approached in 1997–1998. Fighting broke out between the Royal government forces and those of Hun Sen. Norodom Ranariddh left the country in July 1997 as Hun Sen took control of the government—a potentially disastrous political situation that might have seen the country devolve into all-out conflict. But cooler heads prevailed, and elections again were held, leading to the return to democratic governance.

The United Nations showed that it was capable of a massive operation involving peacekeeping forces, humanitarian and development assistance, and rebuilding of civil society and administration. Although problems were experienced by the UNTAC operation, most observers agreed that the operation had been a huge success, given the breadth and complicated nature of its mission.

See also Genocide (Debate 9); Refugees and Stateless Persons (Debate 4); Vietnam Question (Debate 22).

FOR FURTHER READING

Chandler, David. *A History of Cambodia*. Boulder, CO: Westview Press, 1996.

————. *The Tragedy of Cambodian History*. New Haven, CT: Yale University Press, 1991.

Doyle, Michael W. *UN Peacekeeping in Cambodia: UNTAC's Civil Mandate*. Boulder, CO: Lynne Rienner, 1995.

Heininger, Janet. *Peacekeeping in Transition: The UN in Cambodia*. Washington, DC: Brookings Institution, 1994.

Jackson, Karl D. *Cambodia 1975–1978: Rendezvous with Death*. Princeton, NJ: Princeton University Press, 1992.

Shawcross, William. *The Quality of Mercy: Cambodia, Holocaust and the Modern Conscience*. New York: Simon and Schuster, 1984.

UN Chronicles, 1990–1998.

UN Yearbooks, 1979–1996.

Soviet Invasion of Afghanistan (1979)

SIGNIFICANCE OF THE ISSUE

The Soviet intervention into Afghanistan marked the last phase of the Cold War in which the Soviet Union embarked on an increasingly aggressive phase of attempting to exert its influence in foreign affairs. But its adventure in Afghanistan proved to be costly, not only to its economy but also to the stability of its political system, which eventually collapsed under the weight of economic crisis induced in part by its badly mismanaged and unsuccessful effort to eliminate the Afghan resistance. The Afghanistan episode marked the end of the Cold War era, the collapse of communism, and the inauguration of a world marked by vicious civil wars but also an increase in UN peacekeeping activities.

BACKGROUND TO THE DEBATE

Lying on the southern border of the Soviet Union and having common borders with the heavily Islamic Soviet Socialist Republics of Turkmen, Uzbek, and Tajik in South Central Asia, the political stability and friendliness of Afghanistan was a major consideration for the Kremlin, especially during the 1970s as Islamic fundamentalism emerged in neighboring Iran. The population of Afghanistan is almost entirely Muslim, with 80 percent being Sunnis and 20 percent Shi'ite. Although united to a large degree by religion, Afghans are divided by ethnic background. The majority, about 55 percent, are Pushtuns. The largest minority are Tajiks, who constitute about 30 percent of the population, and there are smaller numbers of Uzbeks, Hazaras, and Turkomans.

Afghanistan was ruled by a monarchical form of government from its date of independence in 1747. These governments had limited success in maintaining control of a country marked by tribal tendencies, and so establishing a central administration for the country proved difficult. Both Russia and Great Britain intervened at times as well. British influence over Afghan foreign affairs reached its peak after the Afghan War of 1878–1879, as conflict took place over where Afghanistan's borders should be fixed. British influence was ousted in the 1920s. A series of ineffectual governments ruled in subsequent decades, and in 1973 a military coup established a republican form of government under a former prince, Muhammad Daoud. The republic was short-lived, however, and in 1978 the Marxist Saur revolution took place in which Noor Mohammad Taraki, the founder of the People's Democratic Party of Afghanistan, seized power. The leftist Taraki moved to establish ties with the Soviet Union, and the two countries signed a treaty of friendship, good-neighborliness, and cooperation on 5 December 1978. Taraki, however, faced a growing rebellion within the country, which was not well disposed to Marxist rule. In September 1979, Hafizullah Amin overthrew Taraki, but though less compliant to the Kremlin, he was also not much more successful in quelling the national uprising.

In December 1979, the Kremlin moved to establish a regime more to its liking in Afghanistan. On 27 December they staged a coup d'état against Amin. Soviet troops were involved in the coup, and on the same day, Babrak Karmal, whose pro-Soviet sympathies were well known, was named Amin's successor. In subsequent days and weeks thousands of Soviet troops poured into Kabul and began fanning out over the countryside to help stem the rebellion. Karmal claimed that he had invited the Soviet intervention in order to protect Afghanistan from intervention by reactionary elements.

HISTORY OF THE DEBATE

On 31 December, China submitted a letter to the UN Security Council, notifying it of the situation in Afghanistan and condemning the Soviet action. More than fifty governments in subsequent days called for an emergency session of the Security Council to consider the question. The Council met from 5 January to 9 January 1980. The Soviet Union objected to the holding of the meeting, considering it an intrusion against Afghanistan's right to conduct its own foreign policy and its right to invite Soviet assistance to repel armed intervention from the outside. However, the debate continued since a very large number of countries insisted that the matter must be discussed, and the Council heard from thirty-two invited member states in addition to its own members. The representative of Afghanistan's newly installed government argued that his government had a right to invite Soviet military assistance and that the matter was beyond the Council's jurisdiction, a view supported by Bulgaria, Czechoslovakia, the German Democratic Republic, Hungary, the Lao People's Democratic Republic, Poland, and Vietnam. But more than two dozen countries stated that the Soviet intervention was causing instability and that it threatened the peace and security of the region. Somalia and Chile charged that the Soviet Union was pursuing an expansionist and hegemonic policy, and China went even further, accusing the Soviet Union of attempting to reach the Indian Ocean where it could seize oil fields and interrupt sea lanes. Several countries accused the Soviet Union of carrying out the coup against Amin.

A draft resolution sponsored by Bangladesh, Jamaica, Niger, the Philippines, Tunisia, and Zambia reaffirmed the right of the sovereignty, territorial integrity, and independence of member states; deplored the armed intervention in Afghanistan as being inconsistent with these principles; and called for the immediate and unconditional withdrawal of all foreign troops. The resolution was defeated by a vote of 13 in favor with 2 against (the Soviet Union and the German Democratic Republic), owing to a Soviet veto. The Council then decided, over Soviet objections, to call a special emergency session of the UN General Assembly to consider the matter. This measure, not being subject to a veto, was passed by a vote of 12 to 2, with 1 abstention.

Although East bloc states objected to the convening of the special emergency session, the session proceeded with many of these same states pointing out that Afghanistan had a right to invite military aid and the Soviet Union a right freely to respond to such a request. But Costa Rica, the Dominican Republic, and the Ivory Coast accused the Soviet Union of duplicity. Singapore pointed out that Karmal had no right to request intervention since he was only an ambassador for Afghanistan serving in Czechoslovakia at the time of the coup and the Soviet intervention. Pakistan noted that the uprising in September was motivated by devotion to Islam and its rejection of an alien ideology and that there was no evidence as the Soviet's claimed of any external intervention. The United Kingdom wondered why, if such intervention had been taking place, Afghanistan hadn't notified the Security Council, and Zaire noted that the only intervention in evidence was that by the Soviet Union. Italy, speaking for the European Community, condemned the Soviet action, as did numerous other states, including Turkey. Tiny Papua New Guinea noted that the Soviet Union's reputation as "champion of world peace" was in question, while several countries expressed fears that violence would spread or that the Cold War would resume. On 14 January, the General Assembly adopted a resolution in which it called for the immediate, unconditional, and total withdrawal of all foreign troops from Afghanistan. The resolution called for the speedy repatriation of tens of thousands of refugees who had fled in previous weeks and for humanitarian assistance to meet their needs. The resolution was adopted by a vote of 104 to 18, with 18 abstentions.

In November 1980, at its next regular session, the General Assembly again considered the matter of the Soviet intervention into Afghanistan. Pakistan was particularly concerned that the matter be addressed again, owing to the fact that 1.2 million Afghan refugees had fled into Pakistan, and the influx was continuing. In a resolution adopted by a vote of 111 to 22, with 12 abstentions, the General Assembly reaffirmed its earlier decision, renewed its call for an immediate withdrawal of foreign troops, and emphasized the need for international organizations and governments to extend humanitarian assistance to the growing numbers of refugees. In 1981, and in subsequent years, the General Assembly continued to issue similar resolutions and to call for a negotiated resolution to the ongoing conflict.

The Soviet Union, which deployed well over 100,000 troops in Afghanistan, enjoyed some initial success in pacifying areas of the country. However, Western assistance, particularly from the United States, began to flow into the mujahideen—Islamic guerrilla fighter—forces, through the refugee camps along the Pakistan border. The deployment of stinger missiles proved especially critical in reducing the effectiveness of the Soviet command of the skies in mountainous Afghanistan. The Soviet Union found itself embroiled in a war that it could not win. As the Soviet economy deteriorated, and a new leadership emerged under Mikhail Gorbachev, the Kremlin sought ways to gracefully extricate itself from its own "Vietnam." In this process, Secretary-General Javier Perez de Cuellar proved to be critical through his special representative to Afghanistan.

Following the withdrawal of Soviet forces from Afghanistan in 1988, the United Nations Office for the Coordination for Humanitarian Assistance to Afghanistan (UNOCA) was established to assist in the repatriation of refugees and reconstruction of the country. However, the pro-Soviet regime of President Najibullah continued to fight, delaying hopes of settlement of the dispute. With the defeat of his government in 1992, 1.5 million Afghan refugees repatriated, and rehabilitation efforts began.

OUTCOME OF THE DEBATE

The withdrawal of Soviet forces and the defeat of the Najibullah regime did not end Afghanistan's problems. Although refugees repatriated in large numbers, infighting emerged among the various regional, ethnic, political, and religious factions. The rise of the fundamentalist Taliban in late 1994 altered the political landscape, as their military operations succeeded in gaining ground and popular support in several provinces in the western parts of Afghanistan. Taliban forces captured Kabul in 1996 after a long siege. By this time about 4 million of Afghanistan's over 6 million refugees had returned home, and the Taliban began to restore security to many parts of the country. But the severe policies of the Taliban, its sponsorship of terrorist organizations, and its treatment of women have incited numerous criticisms from governments. After nearly two decades of civil war, the country remains in need of huge amounts of reconstruction assistance, and

Resolution of the Afghanistan war was in part due to the persistent efforts of UN Secretary-General Javier Perez de Cuellar (center right) and his representatives. The United Nations held a pledging conference for humanitarian and economic assistance programs relating to Afghanistan on 12 October 1988 to support Operation Salam. With the secretary-general are (left to right) James Ingram, executive director of the World Food Program; Sadruddin Aga Khan, coordinator for UN Humanitarian and Economic Assistance Program Relating to Afghanistan; and Jean-Pierre Hocké, UN High Commissioner for Refugees. UN/DPI Photo Milton Grant

it is still a land troubled by internal instability, human rights abuses, grinding poverty, and unstable borders.

The wider implication of the Afghanistan situation was that it marked the end of the Soviet Union as a global military power. In the years following its withdrawal from Afghanistan, which had been partially responsible for sapping the Soviet economy, the Soviet Union underwent a major internal revolution, as one socialist republic after another sought and received independence. The collapse of the Soviet Union and of the Communist world could be traced at least in part to the destabilizing effects of its intervention in Afghanistan and in other costly adventures in Africa that bore little political fruit and turned into major drains on Soviet resources. These drains without gains further damaged the Soviet economy, leading to substantial turmoil and eventual economic and political collapse. In the aftermath of its withdrawal and facing major domestic problems of its own, the

Soviet Union disengaged from its aggressive foreign policy posture and began to cooperate with the United States and other Western powers in the United Nations. The end of the Cold War was marked by a frenetic period of international cooperation, and suddenly the United Nations was engaged in dozens of peacekeeping operations made possible by this new-found cooperation between the superpowers.

See also Refugees and Stateless Persons (Debate 4); Terrorism (Debate 28).

FOR FURTHER READING

Anderson, Ewan, and Nancy Dupree, eds. *The Cultural Basis of Afghan Nationalism.* London: Pinter Publishers, 1990.

Cooley, John K. *Unholy Wars: Afghanistan, America and International Terrorism.* London: Pluto Press, 1999.

Cordovez, Diego, and Selig Harrison. *Out of Afghanistan: The Inside Story of the Soviet Withdrawal.* New York: Oxford University Press, 1995.

Kakar, M. Hassan. *Afghanistan: The Soviet Invasion and the Afghan Response, 1979–1982.* Berkeley: University of California Press, 1997.

Maley, William, ed. *Fundamentalism Reborn? Afghanistan and the Taliban.* New York: New York University Press, 1998.

Rubin, Barnett. *The Search for Peace in Afghanistan: From Buffer State to Failed State.* New Haven, CT: Yale University Press, 1995.

UN Yearbooks, 1980–1988.

New International Information
Order (1980)

SIGNIFICANCE OF THE ISSUE

During the 1970s developing countries grew increasingly impatient with the way in which Western news organizations portrayed problems in their countries. Many of these countries practiced various controls on freedom of the press and hoped to place various restrictive and regulative measures on the operation of Western media within their own countries. Many states in the Western world saw this as an attack on the very notion of the freedom of the press, guaranteed in the International Covenant on Civil and Political Rights. The call for a New International Information Order (NIIO) resulted in another series of controversial UN debates.

BACKGROUND TO THE DEBATE

The debate about the NIIO was rooted in essentially two different conceptions of the role and use of the media as understood by the developed democracies of the West and many countries of the developing world. The former view freedom of the press as one of the constituent elements of a democratic society. This view calls for a generally unfettered media, with a right to seek out and publish news stories as they see fit without the prior restraint of governmental bodies or any form of official censorship. Many developing countries during the 1960s, 1970s, and 1980s viewed their own media as an arm of the government, as a means of governmental communication to the people, and as a body with duties and responsibilities to the state. While they might endorse freedom of the press in an abstract sense, in actual practice the print and electronic media in many developing countries, and especially in Communist nations, remained under the control and supervision of the government itself.

Added to these different governmental orientations toward the press and the media was the general approach of the Western media in its coverage of events and trends in the developing world. Developing countries resented what they saw as a Western media only interested in covering the negative stories emanating from the developing world. Indeed, there was a large element of truth in the developing country attitude, because the news generally covered by Western news organizations included revolutions, civil wars, famines, natural disasters, political corruption and inefficiency, coups d'état, government crackdowns, and human rights abuses. All this, developing country governments believed, contributed to a distorted view among public opinion in the West. Ignored were stories of economic development and progress, often achieved at much struggle. Ignored were stories of the Western role in the creation of poverty and instability, according to many developing country governments.

As developing countries gained control of majorities in the United Nations and began to dictate the UN agenda, they came to believe that a restructuring was needed in the way news information was collected and reported. The success the Geneva 77 had achieved in demanding international discussion of the New International Economic Order (NIEO) in previous years led them to seek an extension of the NIEO notion into the realm of the collection and dissemination of information. In 1979, the UN General Assembly called upon the director-general, Amadou Mahtar M'Bow, of the United Nations Educational, Scientific, and Cultural Organization (UNESCO) to undertake a report on his efforts to study the development of an integrated model plan for improving national capacities for mass communication. In a conference at Paris in April 1980, UNESCO identified several principles upon which a new world information and communications order could be based. Consideration of Director-General M'Bow's report stimulated the first major UN debates on the NIIO.

HISTORY OF THE DEBATE

The debate on the NIIO began in the Special Political Committee and in the General Assembly in 1980 and focused on two separate though related issues. The first concerned the need for the development of better systems of communication and information flows within developing countries so as to enhance their efforts at development. Most governments spoke favorably of this initiative, and it excited little opposition. However, related to it was the issue of developing a system for regulating the flow of news among countries and achieving a better representation and balance in news concerning the development of poorer countries. Here some delegations had reservations, because this implied a potential limitation on the notion of the freedom of the press. Many developing countries expressed concern about the inequity in the flow of information concerning developing countries, that Western media did not report news from the developing world objectively, that decisions about news were increasingly monopolistic given the huge technological costs involved in modern news gathering, and that an NIIO should address the problem of prejudicial news by ensuring greater balance. Many also called for developed states to transfer new technologies to them, so that they might more easily develop their own indigenous capacities. Mauritania and Tanzania specifically objected to the bias in favor of conflicts and sensational events and the silence of Western media on positive stories of economic, political, and social progress, whereas several other developing countries deplored the monopolistic features of modern international communication. East bloc nations characterized the current means of information exchange, dominated by the West, as being contrary to the interests of most countries and to the prospects for friendly relations among nations. They emphasized that the freedom of the press carried equally important duties and responsibilities and that freedom of enterprise was not itself constitutive of freedom of the press. Western governments countered that the role of the press in a free society was to report and inform and that to do this they needed to be able to freely criticize and report on both domestic and international issues. The upshot of the debate was Resolution 35/201, which was adopted without vote by the UN General Assembly. It noted with satisfaction UNESCO's initiative to draw up the fundamental principles underlying an NIIO.

Much of the debate on the NIIO shifted to UNESCO. However, in 1981, the General Assembly adopted a Declaration on the Inadmissibility of Intervention and Interference in the Internal Affairs of States, which contained a controversial provision calling upon states to exercise their right and duty to combat the dissemination of false or distorted news that might constitute an unlawful interference in the affairs of another state. The United States and other Western nations saw this principle as an infringement of the Universal Declaration of Human Rights, calling for the right to receive and impart information across borders.

In 1982 the General Assembly called upon governments to contribute to the International Program for the Development of Communication (IPDC), of UNESCO, which was created to help developing countries develop their communications capabilities and to serve as a foundation for the NIIO. Resolutions to this effect were adopted annually in the early 1980s without vote by the UN General Assembly until 1984, when a vote was demanded on the UN resolution supporting UNESCO and the NIIO. The vote was 122 to 6, with 17 abstentions. Several Western governments, including the United Kingdom and the United States, withdrew from UNESCO, considering it to be overly politicized, in part because of the NIIO initiative. Other governments voted no or abstained on the resolution because it failed to treat the NIIO as an "evolving and continuous" process. Still others could not agree to principles agreed upon at regional conferences they had not attended. A similar General Assembly resolution in 1985 received even more opposition, though still passing by a substantial majority. With major countries such as the United States and the United Kingdom having withdrawn from UNESCO General Assembly efforts to support UNESCO, and the "establishment" of an NIIO reached a stalemate in the 1980s. The United States, often alone, voted against resolutions passed in support of UNESCO and NIIO, noting that they routinely contained ideological rhetoric that did not deal with the practical problems of news reporting, communications, and information flows. Many Western governments abstained on such resolutions for similar reasons.

In 1989, UNESCO adopted a new strategy as part of a five-year plan that called for placing communication in the "service of humanity," which for the first time unequivocally affirmed the right of freedom of the press as well as efforts by the United Nations and governments to develop free, independent, and pluralistic media in both the public and private sectors. This new, more positive, and less controversial approach led to much more constructive discussion of the issue of information. The old rancor of the NIIO debate shifted in 1990 to a real effort to understand how rapid changes in communications technology could promote cooperation in international relations. The disintegration of the Communist world in that year, and the increasing awareness that strident ideological confrontations had failed to build international consensus on a range of issues, including that of information, led to a more sober and measured discussion in subsequent years. For the first time in several years, the UN resolution on information issues was adopted without vote, indicating a renewed consensus that no longer called for stricter regulation of the press but, rather, emphasized the need for a free press and a free flow of information.

OUTCOME OF THE DEBATE

Like the calls for an NIEO, the enthusiasm for creating an NIIO only served to divide governments. During the 1990s, UNESCO and UN General Assembly action began to focus on how to protect and defend journalists from attacks on their person, on how to ensure the free flow of information, and on how to strengthen developing country mass communication capacities. The ideological dimension of the debate gave way to more practical issues concerning the acquisition of technology by developing nations to train and develop journalists.

The emergence of the Internet revolutionized the information industry in the late 1990s, raising a whole new set of issues concerning either the desirability or the feasibility of international regulation. Public news agencies and broadcasting systems have lost their monopoly over the flow of information, and the proliferation of news groups, media outlets, and private and public Web sites has provided consumers with many alternative sources of news and information. For developing countries and their peoples to take full advantage of this powerful new technology will require substantial investment in computer technologies. For nongovernmental groups (NGOs) in the developing world, however, who can pool resources or secure funding from outside sources, the Internet has provided them with an increased ability to organize and disseminate information throughout the world. This circumstance has led to an incredible proliferation of NGOs in the developing world.

See also New International Economic Order (Debate 30).

FOR FURTHER READING

Coate, Roger. *Unilateralism, Ideology and U.S. Foreign Policy: The United States In and Out of UNESCO.* Boulder, CO: Lynne Rienner, 1988.

Dutt, Sagarita. *The Politicization of the United Nations Specialized Agencies: A Case Study of UNESCO.* Lewiston, NY: Edwin Mellen Press, 1995.

Hoggart, Richard. *An Idea and Its Servants: UNESCO from Within.* London: Chatto and Windus, 1978.

Spalding, Seth, and Lin Lin. *Historical Dictionary of the United Nations Educational, Scientific and Cultural Organization (UNESCO).* Lanham, MD: Scarecrow Press, 1997.

UN Yearbooks, 1979–1995.

Iran-Iraq War (1980)

SIGNIFICANCE OF THE ISSUE

The Iran-Iraq war, which began in 1980, proved to be one of the bloodiest international conflicts since World War II, with hundreds of thousands of people killed. It was also a ruthless war in which civilian populations, contrary to international law, were specifically targeted in bombing attacks and in which chemical weapons were used by Iraq. Although the United Nations was powerless to prevent the war, and reluctant to take decisive action to stop it in subsequent years, it did play a useful role in resolving the conflict and in deploying peacekeeping forces at its conclusion in order to prevent the conflict from breaking out afresh.

BACKGROUND TO THE DEBATE

Disputes between Iran and Iraq can be traced back to the long-standing problem of the large Kurdish minorities that inhabit primarily northern Iraq but also parts of northwestern Iran. Iran intermittently supported Kurdish rebellion in northern Iraq, especially in the years of open rebellion from 1961 to 1975. In 1974, Iran and Iraq agreed to withdraw troops from along their border until they could resolve their outstanding mutual grievances. After a major offensive by Iraq in 1975, Kurdish resistance largely collapsed. This led to an agreement between Iran and Iraq in March 1975 at meetings of the Organization of Petroleum Exporting Countries (OPEC), at which mutual concessions were made. Iran agreed to cease all support of Kurdish opposition forces in Iraq, and Iraq agreed to abandon a long-asserted claim to the Shatt-al-Arab waterway along its southern border with Iran, a source of ongoing dispute between Iran and Iraq. In 1976, the two governments concluded additional agreements establishing a joint border commission, joint principles for the use and navigation of the Shatt-al-Arab, and rules governing the use of land for common grazing.

Additional sources of strain in the Iran-Iraq relationship include the fact that Iran is populated almost entirely by Shi'ite Muslim sects, whereas a Shi'ite minority in Iraq has been governed by regimes adhering at least nominally to Sunni Islam. Shi'ites composed about 55 percent of the population in the early 1980s, and Sunnis about 45 percent. Since 1958, Iraq has been governed by the secularist-oriented Baathist Party, and Saddam Hussein, Iraq's longtime strongman, was not noted for his religiosity. After the Iranian revolution of 1979, which brought an end to the secular government of Reza Shah Pahlavi, a fundamentalist Shi'ite revival was evident in Iran. The new Iranian regime of Ayatollah Khomeini held the regime of Saddam Hussein in distaste, in part because of its repression of the Shi'ite majority living in Iraq.

In 1979, almost coincident with the fall of the Shah and the rise of the Khomeini regime in Iran, Iraq and Iran engaged in intermittent skirmishes along the Shatt-al-Arab. For ten months these skirmishes continued, until Iraq attacked ten Iranian airfields as well as Teheran airport on 22 September 1980. Iran retaliated by attacking two Iraqi air bases. Iraq also unleashed a ground assault in subsequent days around the cities of Abadan and Khorramshahr, which are located in the oil-rich Iranian province of Khusistan. Iraq seized these areas in October. Thus began the long and bloody Iran-Iraq war.

HISTORY OF THE DEBATE

Within days of the Iraqi attack on Iran, the UN Security Council met on 28 September, deliberated, and unanimously passed a resolution calling for an immediate cessation of hostilities and a withdrawal of forces. The international consensus, however, did little to quell the violence. Secretary-General Kurt Waldheim extended his good offices to the warring parties and appointed Olaf Palme of Sweden as his special representative to mediate between the parties. Iran claimed that Iraq had unilaterally abrogated the 1975 treaty after many violations by its invasion of 22 September. Iran claimed to consider the treaty still in effect despite Iraqi violations. Iraq countercharged that Iranian violations of the agreement left it with no treaty to implement. Iraq charged Israel with sending arms shipments to Iran starting in November 1980. Making little diplomatic headway, the conflict continued through 1981 and into 1982, when Iran successfully counterattacked in May, forcing Iraqi troops to retreat back into Iraq. Not content with this success, Iran pressed its attack against the Iraqi city of Basra, which Iraq was able to defend successfully. By the end of 1982, over 40,000 were dead and over a 100,000 wounded or captured. Following these reverses, Iraq expressed a willingness to comply with UN resolutions, but Iran, sensing an advantage, refused to consider an immediate cease-fire, considering itself the aggrieved party. The Security Council again unani-

Iraqi soldiers and tank engage in operations against Iranian forces at Khorramshahr in 1981. © Francoise de Mulder/CORBIS

mously called for a cessation of hostilities and a withdrawal of forces to internationally recognized boundaries, welcomed Iraq's willingness to comply with its resolutions, and called for ongoing mediation and observation of the dispute. In the General Assembly, a similar resolution was adopted by a vote of 119 to 1, with 15 abstentions. Iran alone voted against the resolution because it was "unbalanced" and failed to note that Iraq had begun the war. Abstaining states had also hoped to see more balance or, like Bangladesh, were active members of the Organization of the Islamic Conference's peace committee and sought to maintain neutrality.

As the military conflict and the propaganda war between Iran and Iraq continued, both countries engaged in bombings of civilian populations, and the threat to navigation in the Persian Gulf became increasingly problematical. The Security Council, in 1983, addressed both problems in a resolution of 31 October, which was adopted by a vote of 12 to 0, with 3 abstentions. It called for a cessation of violations of international humanitarian law and affirmed the right of free navigation and commerce in international waters. In 1984, the war took an ugly turn. Attacks continued on civilian populations, and Iran charged Iraq with the use of chemical weapons, including the use of mustard gas. Investigations by the International Committee of the Red Cross (ICRC) determined that Iraq had indeed engaged in the use of chemical weapons. Through a statement by the Security Council president, the members of the Council resolutely condemned the use of chemical weapons and all other violations of international humanitarian law in March, but Iraq continued to use such weapons. The Council also condemned ongoing interference with and attacks on shipping in the Persian Gulf by Iran. Although Iran and Iraq agreed under UN mediation to refrain from attacking civilian areas, both countries violated the agreement with regularity. Iraq repeatedly raised the issue of the savage treatment of Iraqi prisoners of war (POWs) by Iran in 1984 and 1985. An ICRC mission to both Iran and Iraq found that neither side was guilty of the most outrageous claims made by the other but that in neither case were POWs being accorded anywhere near the standard of treatment expected under the Geneva Convention of 1949.

In 1986, Iran renewed its offensive against Iraq even as bombings of civilians, use of chemical weapons, and attacks on shipping continued. This situation persisted until August 1988 when both parties agreed to a cease-fire. In 1987, the United States announced that it was sending its naval forces into the Persian Gulf to protect international shipping and to protect its allies in the area from attack. Iran and the Soviet Union condemned this action as a case of imperialism and an effort to establish political hegemony in the region. During 1987, the international community grew increasingly insistent that a peaceful resolution to the dispute be sought, a belief expressed in the Security Council's resolution of July 1987 that called for an immediate cease-fire and cooperation by Iran and Iraq with the secretary-general in terms of monitoring the peace. In July 1988, Iran finally accepted Security Council Resolution 598 of 1987 as a basis for a peaceful settlement of the dispute. With the establishment of a cease-fire in August, after tireless negotiations by the secretary-general's office, the openly aggressive phase of the Iran-Iraq war ended.

OUTCOME OF THE DEBATE

On 9 August 1988, the Security Council established, by a unanimous decision, the United Nations Iran-Iraq Military Observer Group (UNIIMOG) to supervise the cease-fire and the subsequent troop withdrawal. The General Assembly rapidly followed with a plan for financing UNIIMOG, which was also adopted unanimously. Over two dozen countries committed troops to the UNIIMOG operation, which successfully oversaw the withdrawal forces and monitored the border until its discontinuance in February 1991. In 1989, the secretary-general's personal representative, Jan Eliasson, made visits to the region to encourage the two parties to directly negotiate the final phases of the peace agreement. In 1990, Iran and Iraq began the direct bilateral phase of peace talks.

With the withdrawal of UNIIMOG forces in 1991, the long and bloody Iran-Iraq war came to an official close. The United Nations had been instrumental in the achievement of peace, but both countries had experienced tremendous loss of life, and civilian populations had been exposed to repeated violations of humanitarian law. Moreover, even before Iraq's aggression with Iran finally ended, Saddam Hussein had unleashed his armies on a much weaker country in 1990, with the invasion of Kuwait. Thus instabilities in the region continued. However, the invasion of Kuwait, unlike the earlier Iraqi invasion of Iran, excited an immediate and forceful response from the international community, which invoked economic sanctions and eventually authorized the use of force to evict Iraq from Kuwait. Nonetheless, Iraq's defeat in 1991 did not end the instability in the region, which continues to be marked by international confrontations with the regime of Saddam Hussein.

See also Persian Gulf War (Debate 44).

FOR FURTHER READING

Banks, Arthur, ed. *Political Handbook of the World: 1977*. New York: McGraw-Hill, 1977.

Farhang, Rajaee. *The Iran-Iraq War: The Politics of Aggression*. Gainesville: University of Florida Press, 1993.

Hiro, Dilip. *The Longest War: The Iran-Iraq Conflict*. London: Routledge, 1991.

Joyner, Christopher. *The Persian Gulf War*. Westport, CT: Greenwood Press, 1990.

Pelletiere, Stephen C. *The Iran-Iraq War*. New York: Praeger, 1990.

UN Chronicles, 1990–1991.

UN Yearbooks, 1980–1991.

Angola Situation (1981)

SIGNIFICANCE OF THE ISSUE

One of the most intractable civil wars facing the international community in the 1980s and 1990s, the Angola situation has defied resolution by the United Nations, which deployed three successive but unsuccessful peace-keeping missions. The United Nations has demonstrated, however, a good deal of perseverance in dealing with the Angola case, and the future prosperity of a country that has promise for economic development simply awaits an agreement between the warring parties.

BACKGROUND TO THE DEBATE

Portugal established a colonial presence in Angola as early as 1575 with the founding of Luanda as a coastal settlement. Dutch settlers contested for the area in the mid-1600s but were eventually driven out by a Portuguese expedition from Brazil intent on opening up the slave trade. The current boundaries of Angola were established by the Berlin Conference of 1884–1885. These boundaries, as in so many other cases in Africa, did not take into account the ethnic and demographic realities of indigenous settlement in the region. Included within the boundaries of Angola were the Ovimbundu (38 percent), the Kimbundu (28 percent), and the Bakongo (13 percent), among others. These ethnic divisions would later prove a source of much instability in Angola at independence. The full-scale colonization of the area did not occur until the twentieth century when some 400,000 Portuguese settlers immigrated into the territory. In 1951, Portugal incorporated Angola as an overseas province. A country with good agricultural lands, excellent marine fisheries, and substantial reserves of oil, diamonds, and iron ore, Angola's potential economic wealth has gone largely unrealized owing to poor development and political instability.

In 1961, Angolan resistance to Portuguese rule broke out in guerrilla war. This resistance continued despite determined efforts by the Portuguese government to eradicate it with military force. During the course of the war for independence, three major resistance groups formed. The Popular Movement for the Liberation of Angola (MPLA) led by Agostinho Neto and backed by the Soviet Union and operated in the central regions of the country. The National Front for the Liberation of Angola (FNLA), led by Holden Roberto and backed by the United States, maintained a government in exile in the Congo from 1963 until independence in 1975, and it operated within the northeast sections of the country. The National Union for the Total Independence of Angola (UNITA), dominated by the Ovimbundu and led by Dr. Jonas Savimbi, operated in the eastern and southern portions of Angola.

When a socialist coup d'état took place in Lisbon in 1974, the new government of Portugal decided to divest itself of its colonial holdings. The three competing movements signed agreements with Portugal stipulating 11 November 1975 as independence day. In the Alvor Agreement with Portugal, all parties agreed to participate in a transition government until formal governmental arrangements could be determined by an electoral process. However, upon the Portuguese departure, the MPLA unilaterally announced the formation of a government with a seat in Luanda, and the FNLA and UNITA followed suit with the formation of a temporary coalition government in Huambo, formerly New Lisbon. Fighting broke out almost immediately, with the MPLA receiving decisive support from over 18,000 Cuban troops. Although about 5,000 South African troops briefly invaded to support the coalition government in Huambo, they later withdrew. In 1976 the MPLA captured the UNITA stronghold of Huambo, forcing it and the FNLA to resort to guerrilla war. The FNLA eventually collapsed, leaving UNITA as the primary threat to the new MPLA regime that was fast gaining international recognition. The MPLA government of Angola took a seat in the Organization of African Unity (OAU) and in the United Nations in 1976. However, UNITA resistance continued, with the support of South Africa and eventually of the United States.

HISTORY OF THE DEBATE

The first occasions on which UN bodies addressed Angolan issues occurred during the 1960s and 1970s when they routinely called for Angola's independence. However, the situation at Angola's independence and the civil war that has persisted ever since excited even more UN Security Council and General Assembly attention. Tensions between Angola and South Africa continued during the late 1970s and into the 1980s, in part because the Marxist-oriented South West Africa People's Organization (SWAPO) national liberation forces from Namibia took refuge in southern

Angola, with the full hospitality of the MPLA. SWAPO and South African forces repeatedly crossed the boundary to conduct attacks on one another, and with each South African action, the Security Council was typically stalemated by a U.S. veto so that formal condemnation of South Africa (and often of the United States) would be undertaken by the General Assembly.

Urgent efforts by Angola to secure a hearing in the Security Council commenced in 1981, when the United States vetoed a draft resolution that otherwise won 13 yes votes and only 1 abstention by the United Kingdom. The draft would have strongly condemned the South African invasion as a violation of Angola's sovereignty, demanded reparations, and called for an immediate withdrawal. The United States explained that its veto resulted from the resolution's silence about the provocative presence of the troops of Cuba and advisers from the Soviet Union and Angola's arming of SWAPO, all of which contributed to the explosively violent conditions of the area. Singling South Africa out for blame was seen as unjust. The United Kingdom expressed a distaste for the overblown rhetoric of the draft. The debate was marked by a dramatic series of charges by Angola and denials by South Africa. The Soviet Union accused the United States of complicity with South Africa in destabilizing the region. This comment reflected its rejection of the recently stated support of President Ronald Reagan for freedom fighters throughout the world, and the new policy of constructive engagement, whereby the United States sought to draw South Africa into negotiated settlements rather than joining the rest of the world in unremitting denunciation of South Africa. China also hinted at the connivance of "a superpower" in the region, a veiled reference to the United States. Developing countries lined up in support of Angola's position. In the General Assembly, the South African invasion was condemned in a resolution dealing with the question of apartheid in South Africa.

In December 1983, Angola was more successful. By this time, South African military actions had become a threat to recently established efforts by the Western Contact Group (Canada, France, the Federal Republic of Germany, the United Kingdom, and the United States), which tried to establish dialogue with South Africa so as to resolve the ongoing Namibia situation. The United States chose to abstain, which allowed the resolution condemning the South African invasion and calling for an unconditional withdrawal to pass with 14 favorable votes. In 1984, with progress being made in negotiating a withdrawal of South African forces, a more strongly worded resolution was passed by the Security Council, as the United States and United Kingdom abstained to permit its passage, while noting that more productive results would be achieved by patient negotiations. In 1985, in a series of five resolutions, each of which was adopted unanimously from June to December, the Council condemned a contemplated South African commando attack against Angola's oil-rich Cabinda enclave. It reiterated previous calls for withdrawal of forces and compensation, and it deployed a fact-finding commission to assess damage. In 1986 Jonas Savimbi met with President Reagan in Washington, D.C. South Africa informed the Council that UNITA was fighting for freedom and that it proudly supported that effort, especially given the Soviet Union's imperialist aims in the area and the presence of Cuban troops. While raids continued in the region, so did negotiations, even as the rhetoric heated up. Both the United States and the United Kingdom vetoed a draft Security Council resolution that would have imposed various extensions of mandatory economic sanctions. While demands for such sanctions continued into 1987, negotiations concerning possible South African withdrawal seemed to make headway. In its unanimously adopted resolution of December 1987, the Security Council took note of this development. In 1988, Contact Group negotiations finally paid off, as South Africa agreed to a phased withdrawal of forces linked to a similar withdrawal of Cuban forces from Angola. In December of the same year the Security Council unanimously approved the deployment of the United Nations Angola Verification Mission (UNAVEM) to monitor the withdrawal of forces. With its job complete, and with the signing of the Bicesse Accords on 31 May by which the MPLA and UNITA agreed to hold free and fair elections for a new government, the Council deployed UNAVEM II to replace UNAMEN I. Its purpose would be to monitor the election process, which eventually took place in September 1992. The MPLA presidential candidate, José Eduardo Dos Santos, carried 49.6 percent of the vote to Savimbi's 40.1 percent. The MPLA also won a majority of seats in the National Assembly. Although the elections were deemed generally free and fair, a second round of elections should have been held for the presidential election, but these were never held as UNITA declared the overall results fraudulent and resumed fighting.

Negotiations to repair the political situation during 1993 continued as the Security Council, in a series of unanimously adopted resolutions, condemned UNITA for continued fighting and extended the UNAVEM II mandate. In September it followed this condemnation with the first ever threat of sanctions against a nonstate entity. Progress in the Lusaka peace talks averted implementation of this threat. The tone of subsequent Council resolutions was supportive of the ongoing talks, although renewed fighting in 1994 drew its strong criticism. In November the Lusaka Protocol was signed by the MPLA and UNITA, by which the parties agreed to a cease-fire; the withdrawal, quartering, and demilitarization of all UNITA forces; the disarming of civilians; the complete formation of a New Angolan Army and police force; a UN mandate to serve as observers of the peace accords; the completion of the electoral process; and a process to achieve total national reconciliation. In February 1995, the Security Council authorized the deployment of UNAVEM III to monitor implementation of the

Among the responsibilities of the United Nations Angola Verification Mission II (UNAVEM II) was the quartering of government and guerrilla army soldiers and the creation of a new Angolan Armed Forces (FAA). Members of the FAA are shown here in training. UNAVEM efforts at resolution of the Angola conflict eventually failed in the late 1990s. UN/DPI Photo Milton Grant

peace accords, to ensure the flow of humanitarian aid, and to withdraw upon the completion of the terms of the Lusaka Accords.

In the two and a half years of the UNAVEM III mission, the situation in Angola substantially improved, incidents of violence ceased, UNITA forces were quartered, and movement toward national reconciliation was achieved. However, in late 1996 and early 1997, instabilities in neighboring Zaire, whose president Mobutu Sese Seko had clandestinely supported UNITA for many years, complicated Angola's situation. Mobutu's fall from power emboldened the MPLA to move against UNITA-occupied diamond-producing areas, ostensibly to protect the border area from radical Hutu refugees and elements of Mobutu's armed forces. The explanation did not satisfy UNITA, despite the fact that the government forces had refrained from an all-out assault on the major diamond center held by UNITA at Luzamba. Still UNITA resisted efforts by the new government to extend administration into areas held by it, and this was a constant source of irritation.

OUTCOME OF THE DEBATE

Because of the ongoing tensions, even though UNAVEM III was phased out, the Security Council decided to deploy a follow-up operation known as the United Nations Observer Mission in Angola (MONUA). On 1 July 1997 MONUA succeeded UNAVEM III, but within weeks the situation in Angola once again deteriorated as UNITA refused to accept the extension of state administration. In resolutions of August and October the Council threatened to apply and later actually applied sanctions against UNITA for failure to comply with the Lusaka Accords. In May 1998, UNITA forces engaged in attacks on MONUA units, calling forth a Security Council condemnation. In late 1998 and early 1999 the situation in Angola continued to deteriorate. All negotiations had broken down; over the course of 1998, 330,000 Angolans had become internally displaced owing to the insecurity. Additional sanctions placed on UNITA evoked only intransigence. MONUA's mandate formally expired with the Security Council's decision to liquidate the mission. The relative calm of four years following the Lusaka Accords was shattered in December 1998, and MONUA's presence no longer served a useful purpose, especially in light of the UNITA attacks on two MONUA chartered aircraft in which over twenty people were killed. These attacks drew an angry response from Secretary-General Kofi Annan, who expressed his outrage at the incidents. In the meantime the number of internally displaced people increased to over 700,000, while thousands of others fled as refugees into the Congo. The Council formally accused UNITA and Savimbi as being the primary cause of the deplorable situation.

To date, the situation in Angola remains in a state of open civil war. The Security Council, lacking the consensus to impose a peace, has chosen simply to deplore and condemn the current state of affairs and to put pressure on UNITA through a series of, to date, largely ineffectual sanctions. The situation illustrates that even during the more robust period of the use of force by nations to intervene in civil conflicts, a determined aggressor, in a country exciting little international attention, can successfully flout Security Council demands where they are not backed up by a real threat of the use of force. Still, the patient involvement of the United Nations throughout the 1990s in endeavors to support locally achieved peace agreements did help give Angolans a four-year reprieve from decades of war. It would appear, at this stage, that the attainment of peace in Angola lies very much within the hands of the new government and its old nemesis Jonas Savimbi and his UNITA compatriots. When these parties grow tired of war, the United Nations will doubtless be ready to lend a hand in the service of peace.

See also Apartheid in South Africa (Debate 14); Decolonization (Debate 18); Southwest Africa (Namibia) Dispute (Debate 3).

FOR FURTHER READING

Anstee, Margaret Joan. *Orphan of the Cold War: The Inside Story of the Collapse of the Angolan Peace Process 1992–1993*. New York: St. Martin's, 1996.

Bender, Gerald J. *Angola under the Portuguese: The Myth and the Reality.* Berkeley: University of California Press, 1978.

Crocker, Chester A. *High Noon in Southern Africa: Making Peace in a Tough Neighborhood.* New York: W. W. Norton, 1993.

Hare, Paul. *Angola's Last Best Chance for Peace: An Insider's Account of the Peace Process.* Washington, DC: U.S. Institute of Peace, 1998.

Henderson, Lawrence W. *Angola: Five Centuries of Conflict.* Ithaca, NY: Cornell University Press, 1979.

UN Yearbooks, 1977–1996.

UN Reforms (1985)

SIGNIFICANCE OF THE ISSUE

From almost its very inception, the United Nations has been criticized by one member state or group of member states or another in regard to its mandates, authorities, administration, and/or budget practices. The means of minor reform are undertaken most often through the supervisory role that governments play since the United Nations is ultimately the servant of the member states collectively. Major reforms require application of the Charter amendment process, in which the permanent members of the Security Council enjoy a huge advantage. Since the 1980s, the United Nations has been under almost constant pressure from the major donors to reform, but calls for reform have also come from nonpermanent members, too, and usually deal with the ongoing complaint over great power dominance of the organization. Reform of the United Nations is ultimately a responsibility of the member states themselves who oversee the Secretariat.

BACKGROUND TO THE DEBATE

Provisions for the amendment of the UN Charter are found in Chapter XVIII of that instrument. Article 108 provides that the Charter may amended when two-thirds of the members of the General Assembly have adopted an amendment that is subsequently ratified through the regular constitutional means by two-thirds of the members of the United Nations, including all of the Security Council permanent members. Article 109 stipulates that amendments may also result from a General Conference of the members of the United Nations, although, as with the regular amendment process, they must secure the support of two-thirds of the Conference members and the ratification of two-thirds of the members of the United Nations, including the concurrence of all permanent members of the Security Council. Reform of the United Nations, then, as long as it is accomplished by the Charter amendment process, ultimately depends upon the consensus of the five permanent members of the Security Council. Not all UN reforms require formal amendment processes. The structure of the UN Secretariat, the size and organization of the staff, the administrative arrangements developed between various UN organizations, and the establishment of committees and commissions are determined by the secretary-general acting under the supervision and direction of the member states.

As the United Nations has grown in membership and as the number and complexity of issues it has addressed have proliferated, governments have created new committees and commissions, enlarged staffs, and created entire new specialized or related agencies. This process has been largely piecemeal in nature, with new mechanisms often being established for new problems. The result over several decades is that the UN bureaucracy grew substantially, and many organizations duplicated one another's work. Inefficiencies abounded, as did jurisdictional disputes. At the same time, developing countries, which eventually constituted a majority of the General Assembly by the 1960s, were not at all shy about creating new organizations and agencies aimed at addressing issues of concern to them. On the other hand, about a dozen countries, mostly Western democratic states, contributed the vast majority of the budgetary resources to pay for these new agencies. The discontinuity between the countries who decided how to spend the money and those who contributed most of the money became more glaring and obvious during the 1970s and 1980s.

Calls for the reform of the United Nations have been made at various times in the life of the organization. The Soviet Union proposed the troika arrangement for reorganization of the Secretariat in the early 1960s after its disenchantment with the way Dag Hammarskjöld managed the position. Such a change would have required a Charter amendment, for which there was inadequate support. From time to time, Western governments considered the wisdom of adopting a weighted voting scheme to deal with the problem of many tiny and poor countries dominating the political agenda while providing only miniscule amounts of the budgetary support. Weighted voting schemes would also have required a Charter amendment.

HISTORY OF THE DEBATE

Much of the bloat in the UN bureaucracy, however, could be addressed through administrative and budgetary reform that did not require Charter amendments. This is what the United States and several European governments sought to do in the 1980s. During the 1980s President Ronald Reagan of the United States, for instance, held back payment of U.S. dues to the United Nations until the Secretariat had responded with various reforms. He insisted on the use of consensus in making budget decisions, not simply majority votes. He demanded a reduction in UN staffing and spending. He insisted that the United Nations reduce the number of Soviet and East bloc members of the Secretariat, since, he argued, a high percentage of these members of the Secretariat were functioning as Communist spies. When a major contributor gets tough like this, the Secretariat is not in a position to simply ignore their demands, and indeed the Secretariat did attempt to address U.S. complaints with a variety of reform measures. Active efforts to consider reform measures were inaugurated in December 1985, when the General Assembly established the "Group of 18" consisting of a high-level group of experts with a mandate to review UN adminsitrative and financial policies and procedures and to make recommendations for reform and for strengthening the effectiveness of UN activities in the political, economic, and social arenas. The Group of 18 produced seventy-one recommendations for reform in August 1986 that were endorsed in December of the same year by the UN General Assembly, thus initiating the first major effort at UN reform since the organization's founding.

The changes that occurred in the world during the 1990s put additional pressure on the United Nations to consider additional reforms, cost cutting, reductions in staff, and reorganization of administrative procedures. In the early 1990s, a cosmetic effort to reorganize the coordination of international humanitarian assistance took place with the establishment in 1991 of the Department of Humanitarian Affairs (DHA), which in turn supervised a Steering Committee of UN agencies involved in the humanitarian assistance field. The proliferation of UN development-related agencies created similar kinds of coordination problems within the UN system. Coordination of funding requests and national development plans was eventually subjected to the oversight, within a developing country of the United Nations Development Program (UNDP) resident representative. In-country development strategy statements were elaborated by developing countries in cooperation with the UNDP resident representative. Appeals by developing countries for development aid packages were in turn coordinated in the Paris Round Table discussions held under the auspices of the World Bank and International Monetary Fund.

The globalization of the world economy in 1990, coupled with the death of global communism and the sudden surge of new member states of the United Nations who were seeking substantial bilateral and multilateral aid, placed additional pressure on the UN system. Civil wars involving UN participation also heavily taxed the humanitarian aid–giving system and the peacekeeping capacities of the United Nations. Hopes were raised for the resuscitation of the collective security provisions of the UN Charter, for the creation of rapid deployment forces at the disposal of the Security Council, and for the more rational financing of peacekeeping operations. Disillusionment set in during the mid-1990s, as UN successes in peacekeeping were matched by glaring failures. Moreover, the huge burst of peacekeeping activity during the early 1990s was very costly, and many governments owed substantial arrears. It was in this climate that the United Nations began seriously, especially after Kofi Annan became secretary-general, to consider how it might streamline and rationalize its operations.

On 16 July 1997, Secretary-General Kofi Annan formally proposed a series of major and fundamental reforms of the United Nations that he saw as addressing the substantial gap existing between the aspirations of UN members and their actual accomplishment. Born out of a desire to promote peace and prosperity, the United Nations still faced devastating wars, although most were now civil wars rather than international ones, and it still faced massive and grinding poverty, even though progress had been made in feeding an expanding population. Human rights instruments had proliferated in the United Nations' first five decades, but human rights abuses were often the norm in many parts of the world, and the huge numbers of refugees and displaced persons worldwide continued to pose challenges to individual countries and to the international community as a whole. The gap between aspiration and accomplishment was very wide. Moreover, Secretary-General Annan noted that over the course of many decades many of the United Nations' "organizational features have tended to become fragmented, duplicative and rigid, in some areas ineffective, in others superfluous." The end of the Cold War opened many new opportunities but also challenges never before faced by the organization. It became involved in a huge expansion of peacekeeping activities, in developing civil society, in supporting national transitions to democracy, in managing market reforms, and in providing huge amounts of humanitarian aid, often in very hostile civil war environments.

Annan proposed several administrative reforms, including the creation of a Senior Management Group and a new Strategic Planning Unit to assist him in the process of identifying and carrying out needed reforms. He announced the establishment of a new deputy secretary-general position to, among other things, serve as a spearhead for UN efforts to attract financing for development. He proposed to revamp a sprawling UN bureaucracy organized into a dozen Secretariat entities or units by collapsing them into five departments, including peace and security, economic and social affairs, development cooperation, humanitarian affairs, and human rights. He called for the decentralization of decision making to the country level and announced that UN agencies would henceforth consolidate their locations and in-country offices under "one flag" rather than maintaining separate facilities. He called for the elimination of 1,000 staff posts, substantial reductions in administrative expenses, and training for UN staff to ensure competence. He announced the formation of a UN Development Group to facilitate and coordinate the far-flung UN development system. He announced the formation of a new United Nations Office for Coordination of

Humanitarian Affairs (UNOCHA) to replace the DHA and more effectively address the growing phenomenon of complex humanitarian emergencies. The failure of many UN agencies to communicate effectively with governments and nongovernmental organizations (NGOs) also concerned the secretary-general. He called for greater transparency, less paranoia about maintaining confidentiality, and more openness in sharing information.

As for the operations of the major organs of the United Nations, Annan proposed—since governments had opposed the formal termination of the Trusteeship Council—to refurbish that UN organ by having it focus on issues of common concern to all nations such as protecting arctic areas, the oceans, outer space, and the environment. He proposed that the General Assembly reorganize its agenda, by dealing with thematic problems, focusing on high-priority issues, and shortening the length of its sessions. He announced the intention to hold a Millennium Assembly in 2000 as well as a People's Assembly to focus attention on how the United Nations can reorient its efforts to face the challenges of a new millennium. He proposed that the collective security provisions of the Charter be revisited to determine how to enhance the rapid reaction capacity of the United Nations to meet threats to peace and security.

The secretary-general's proposals for reform won substantial support from member states, because they proposed to achieve cost savings and improved efficiencies in the United Nations. But the problem of a gap between aspiration and achievement is likely to remain. Fundamental reforms of the United Nations, which would require Charter amendments, will not be easily secured, in part because one country's version of reform is another country's threat. When small or middle powers at the United Nations speak of reform, it is almost always associated with the idea of scrapping the veto privilege in the Security Council. But none of the permanent members is any more likely today than at the United Nations' inauguration to accept such a proposal, and they may use their veto to stop any and all efforts to revoke that privilege. Small and middle powers have always opposed the veto privilege. They resent it, and they are frustrated at their inability to force a change of this magnitude. In 1992, the General Assembly asked the secretary-general to report to it on the question of equitable representation on the Security Council. This report, which contained comments from seventy-six member states, was submitted to the UN General Assembly in 1993, at which time the Assembly decided to establish an Open-ended Working Group to study the matter. Various proposals have been advanced since then to increase the size of the Council to anywhere from twenty to twenty-six members, including several new permanent members. Efforts to dislodge the veto power have made no headway, but efforts to add new permanent members have won broad support. Whether those permanent members should have the veto power is another matter of controversy, however. The United States proposed that Japan, Germany, and three or more countries from the developing world be added as permanent members. Since the elevation of a country to permanent member status is a mark of prestige, competition for that status engenders national jealousies, as does the retention of the veto power by the original permanent members. About the latter, nothing can be done unless the veto-bearing states willingly give up the privilege. There is no indication that they will do so, but this does not preclude other kinds of Security Council reform, including the possibility of establishing a rapid response capability.

There is another kind of reform that UN bureaucrats and many NGO representatives would like to see that involves a wholesale revision of the sovereign state system as we know it. It is not uncommon in UN conferences and debate settings to hear speakers lament the unwillingness of states to sublimate their national interests to the common interest. In this view of reform, the United Nations is the proper place for international decision making that should override the selfish national interests of the member states. This view of reform is unconnected with the fundamental reality that the state system, national sovereignty, and national interests still persist, despite globalization and spreading interdependence. That the latter has occurred is a function of countless decisions by national governments to cooperate within the UN or global setting with other countries. But a decision to cooperate is not tantamount to either a decision or a desire to renounce sovereignty or to ignore national interests. Thus, for most countries, the United Nations remains a place where they can adjust and accommodate their differences with other sovereign states, not a world government that has the right to dictate to states how they must conduct their domestic or foreign policies. The United Nations was clearly not established to eradicate the nation-state but, rather, to serve its needs. Any effort to reorganize the United Nations into something other than an international "civil servant" will no doubt be resisted by most governments.

OUTCOME OF THE DEBATE

In a sense, UN reform is an ongoing process as the organization attempts to adjust itself to changes in the international political and economic environment. Reforms of the sort that Kofi Annan proposed in 1997, and which have been largely implemented, will be welcomed by states. But there is only so far that the United Nations can cut and still do all that its member states call upon it to do. The late 1990s saw the United Nations get into an increasingly difficult cash crunch, as many countries, including most notably the United States, ran up large debts in their mandatory contributions. Although the U.S. Congress finally agreed with the Bill Clinton administration on a deal that allowed it to pay back much of its arrears, the price was that the UN engage in further budget and staff cuts and that the U.S. percentage of contributions be decreased from 25 to 21 percent of the overall UN budget. A conservative U.S. Congress was in no mood to hop on any world government bandwagon, and it continued to believe, despite fifteen years of UN budget cuts and administrative reforms, that the organization could benefit from still more trimming.

In January 2000, Senator Jesse Helms addressed the UN Security Council in an unprecedented event. No national legislator had ever before addressed that body. In subsequent months, the U.S. Congress held hearings at the United Nations related to issues concerning administrative and budgetary reform. Although the U.S. decision to pay its accumulated UN debts eased the immediate financial crisis of the organization, it is clear that the dialogue on UN reforms will continue for some time to come. In all political bodies, whether of a national, local, or international nature, arguments over budgets and administrative reforms are also arguments over politics, not merely technical questions, because where and how money gets spent is really a record of who is winning and losing the battle of ideas and of policy.

Before leaving the matter of UN reforms it is necessary to add an additional observation. While it is true that virtually any bureaucracy can find ways to cut waste and duplication and thus save money, it is also true that some level of resources is essential to the achievement of an organization's goals. The United Nations is the sole truly global body for the maintenance of international peace and security and for a whole range of other cooperative endeavors in support of economic development, humanitarian aid, environmental preservation, and legal development, among many other areas of UN activity. The size of the UN budget and bureaucracy, when compared to the size of the mandates and functions it has been given or asked to perform by member states, is really quite modest. Its regular budget is little more than that of the New York City Fire Department. Even adding all of the specialized agency budgets together, the UN budget is no bigger than that of a medium-sized city budget. Thus, a lot of the wrangling over budgets and reforms is not solely motivated by the desire to ensure budget accountability. A lot of the wrangling is undertaken to produce political messages for and signals to the citizens back home, many of whom may be highly distrustful of the globalization process and of the distant and possibly threatening world of UN diplomacy. This has always been a reality of debates at the United Nations, and it will likely continue to be so for as long as that body functions as a coordinating mechanism of interstate relations.

See also UN Financing Crisis (Debate 20).

FOR FURTHER READING

Boutros-Ghali, Boutros. *An Agenda for Peace*. New York: UN Publications, 1992.
Matthews, Robert O. *United Nations Reform in the 1990s*. New York: Academic Council on the UN System, Reports and Papers, No. 5, 1993.

McDermott, Anthony. *The New Politics of Financing the UN*. New York: St. Martin's, 1999.

Russett, Bruce, ed. *The Once and Future Security Council*. New York: St. Martin's, 1997.

UN Chronicles, 1997–2000.

Persian Gulf War (1990)

SIGNIFICANCE OF THE ISSUE

The invasion and annexation of Kuwait by Iraq in August 1990 constituted a blatant violation of the United Nations (UN) Charter and provoked strong retaliatory action by the UN Security Council, which not only invoked the economic sanctions provisions of Article 41 in Chapter VII but also authorized the use of military force under Article 42 for the first time since the Korean War. Secretary-General Javier Perez de Cuellar stated that the Security Council had never before "reacted with such unanimity to an invasion, occupation and purported annexation." This action to reverse and to punish an act of aggression by one member state against another marked a new willingness on the part of the great powers to cooperate on collective security matters in the wake of the end of the Cold War, and it ushered in a period of frenzied UN peacekeeping and peacemaking activity in the early 1990s.

BACKGROUND TO THE DEBATE

Disputes between Iraq and Kuwait hearken back to Kuwait's independence in 1961, when Iraq refused to recognize it, claiming that the territory belonged to Iraq. Iraq maintained that under Turkish Ottoman rule the administration of Kuwait had been linked to that of Iraq and that Kuwait had been illegally detached from Iraq by the British. However, Kuwait's legal independence could be traced as far back as 1756, when the Kuwaiti people elected their first emir. In 1899, Kuwait ceded its external sovereignty to Great Britain in order to counter harassment by the Ottoman Turk Empire. Britain acknowledged the self-governing status of Kuwait as a protectorate. The modern state of Iraq, by contrast, did not emerge until the 1920s, and it achieved independence in 1932 from Britain. Kuwait acquired complete control of its own affairs in 1961. Eventually Iraq desisted in its claim to own all of Kuwait, with its formal recognition of Kuwait in 1963. A dispute continued over the demarcation of the border, but even the border dispute was largely resolved in 1975. However, in the late 1980s, Iraq began to complain about drilling practices engaged in by Kuwait, specifically a practice known as slant drilling whereby Kuwait could tap into oil reservoirs on the Iraqi side of the border without easily being detected. Kuwait denied the charges, but the dispute continued into 1990.

A complicating factor in this dispute is that Iraq had just finished a bloody war with Iran, which it initiated in 1980. Although Iraq later cast the Iranian government as the aggressor when it refused to bow to an early settlement of that conflict, there was no doubt about who started the war in the first place. With his armies no longer being needed on the eastern front, as peace talks with Iran proceeded, Saddam Hussein could use all of Iraq's substantial military resources against poorly defended Kuwait. With negotiations having failed to produce a settlement over the border dispute, Iraq decided to use force. On 2 August 1990, 140,000 Iraqi troops invaded Kuwait. Within just twelve hours, Iraqi forces effected an almost complete occupation of Kuwait, whose military forces were no match for the infinitely larger and better-armed Iraqi forces. The Iraqi invasion led to an immediate and intense storm of condemnation from countries throughout the world, and the exiled government of Kuwait appealed to the UN Security Council for emergency action.

HISTORY OF THE DEBATE

Within hours the UN Security Council met and adopted a decision sponsored by Canada, Colombia, Côte d'Ivoire, Ethiopia, Finland, France, Malaysia, the United Kingdom, and the United States. By Resolution 660 the Council determined that Iraq's action constituted a breach of the peace, and it decided to invoke Chapter VII of the UN Charter to treat it as an act of aggression. At the session, Kuwait denied Iraq's pretext for invasion as false and unwarranted. Iraq dismissed the Kuwaiti complaint as a completely internal affair that did not involve Iraq, and noted that a new and free provisional government in Kuwait had requested its help to protect it from intervention by the United States. This deceptive representation drew fire from the Big Five. The United States characterized the invasion as an unprovoked and heinous use of military force. France firmly deplored the use of force, while the United Kingdom described Iraq's invasion and its establishment of a "phony" puppet government as an ugly moment in world affairs. China expressed regret and the Soviet Union profound concern and alarm over the invasion.

Over the next several days the Security Council passed several resolutions. On 6 August, it invoked economic sanctions against Iraq for its failure to withdraw forces from Kuwait as required in Resolution 660. This resolution (661), which also called for a freeze on all Iraqi assets in foreign banks, was adopted by a vote of 13 to 0, with 2 abstentions (Cuba and Yemen). On 9 August, the Council unanimously adopted Resolution 662, denying the legality of Iraq's announced annexation of Kuwait. Iraq announced defiantly that its annexation of Kuwait was eternal and irreversible. Member states described such a claim as outrageous. On 18 August, the Council adopted unanimously Resolution 664, calling upon Iraq to cease detaining third-country nationals and to permit consular access to such persons. On 25 August, it took steps in Resolution 665 to impose a naval blockade on Iraq by a vote of 13 to 0, with 2 abstentions (Cuba and Yemen). In Resolution 666 of 13 September it decided to take into account emergency food needs for humanitarian purposes of people in Iraq and Kuwait. In Resolution 667, the Council unanimously adopted a condemnation of Iraqi acts aimed at diplomatic officials and premises in Kuwait. The procession of resolutions continued on 24 September with the Security Council responding to a request from Jordan for relief owing to the negative effects of sanctions on its economy. The resolution provided for appropriate relief to Jordan. On 25 September the Council adopted Resolution 670 by a vote of 14 to 1 (Cuba), in which it called for restrictions of air flights into Iraq, for all states to deny Iraqi aircraft rights of over flight, and for detaining of Iraqi ships. On 29 October, the Council strongly condemned Iraq's ongoing violations of the immunities of diplomatic personnel, the taking and holding of hostages, and the mistreatment of third-country nationals. Finally, in a dramatic resolution (678) of 29 November 1990, the Council authorized, by a vote of 12 to 2 (Cuba and Yemen) and 1 abstention (China), member states to use all necessary means to uphold previous Council resolutions unless Iraq complied with all previous resolutions by 15 January 1991. This language permitted the coalition that had been building up in Saudi Arabia under the designation of "Desert Shield" to use force when deemed necessary after the prescribed date.

The language of diplomacy was largely ignored by Iraq during the months in which the Security Council passed one condemnatory and punitive resolution after another. Economic sanctions failed to dislodge Iraq from Kuwait, and President George Bush of the United States decided not to stand by and wait. After a request by Saudi Arabia for defensive assistance, a massive military buildup began during the fall of 1990, even as the Bush administration slowly built a large military alliance including many fellow member states of the North Atlantic Treaty Organization (NATO), although NATO itself was not directly involved, as well as a number of Middle Eastern countries, including Saudi Arabia, the Gulf States, Egypt, and even Syria. Just two days after the 15 January deadline for action, seeing virtually no movement toward compliance, this coalition unleashed a ferocious aerial bombardment of Iraq, which continued into late February in advance of a ground invasion to evict Iraqi military forces. During this period of coalition bombing, Iraq fired Scud missiles at Israeli cities hoping to provoke a retaliation that might shake the coalition, which included many Arab nations. Israel desisted, and the coalition held. The bombing clearly ravaged Iraqi forces, but no formal move for retreat was begun until a flurry of last-minute diplomatic activity by Mikhail Gorbachev, of the Soviet Union, who extracted concessions from Iraq, but these were too little and too late. After reports reached Washington that Iraqi forces were torching Kuwaiti oil wells prior to their retreat, Bush ordered a ground attack on 24 February that pummeled Iraqi forces in a decisive, sweeping attack that forced Iraq to capitulate to terms in a matter of days. On 2 March, the Security Council in Resolution 686 set terms for Iraq's surrender, namely, that it rescind its annexation of Kuwait, accept liability for reparations to Kuwait and other states, release all Kuwaiti and third-country nationals in detention, return all Kuwaiti property, cease all military action, designate military personnel to arrange the cessation of hostilities, and release prisoners of war (POWs). Only Cuba voted against the resolution, while China, India, and Yemen abstained. Iraq subsequently agreed to the terms of Resolution 686.

A month later, on 3 April, the Security Council adopted an even more sweeping resolution (687) that finalized the terms of peace with Iraq. It de-

Before retreating from Kuwait, Iraqi forces set oil wells on fire. Allied forces authorized by the United Nations to expel Iraq from Kuwait are pictured in the foreground as oil wells at Rumaila blaze in the distance. UN/DPI Photo John Isaac

ployed the United Nations Iraq-Kuwait Observer Mission (UNIKOM) to monitor a demilitarized zone along the Iraq-Kuwait border. It also called upon Iraq to recognize its border with Kuwait, to accept unconditionally the duty to destroy all of its long-range ballistic missiles, as well as its chemical and biological weapons, stocks of agents, and capacity for making such weapons, and to submit to international verification and monitoring. It imposed on Iraq an obligation never to acquire or develop nuclear weapons. Iraq agreed to return all Kuwaiti property pillaged during the illegal occupation and to pay for the costs of repairing the environmental damaged unleashed by its destruction and torching of oil wells in Kuwait. Economic sanctions and an arms embargo were left in place until Iraq complied with other provisions of the resolution. Iraq was obliged to repatriate all Kuwaiti and third-country nationals and to desist from any and all acts of terrorism. Two days later the Council adopted Resolution 688, which condemned continuing Iraqi aggression against its civilian population in various parts of Iraq, especially the Kurds in the north, and called for access by international humanitarian assistance agencies to provide relief in those areas. This resolution was adopted by a vote of 10 to 3 (Cuba, Yemen, Zimbabwe), with 2 abstentions (China and India).

Kuwait gradually returned to normal with the return of its government and citizenry and with the help of teams of firefighters from Western countries that rapidly extinguished the hundreds of oil fires started by Iraqi forces prior to their retreat. Progress was made in repatriation of Kuwaiti and third-country nationals, in the release of POWs, in the return of property to Kuwait, and in payment of compensation for damages. UNIKOM maintained stability along the border, although Iraq later refused to participate in the boundary demarcation discussions and also violated the demilitarized zones by deploying police stations there. However, the situation in Iraq continued to be very difficult. International inspectors began immediately to undertake arrangements for inspections at suspected Iraqi nuclear, chemical, and biological weapons facilities, but Iraqi foot-dragging and delay in these matters began at the outset and continued throughout the 1990s, leading to legendary standoffs and military confrontations. More immediately, however, the humanitarian situation among Kurds in the north and Shi'ites in the southern marshlands was very serious. In 1991 hundreds of thousands of Kurds fled into Iran or Turkey, prompting the latter to close its border. Iraq also undertook military attacks on civilian populations in the South in July 1992, according to reports by a special rapporteur of the Commission on Human Rights, but this was denied by Iraq. The United States, the United Kingdom, and France announced a no-fly zone south of the 32nd parallel to protect civilian populations from Iraqi attacks in August 1992. A similar no-fly zone had been effected in April 1991 in the northern section of Iraq to protect Kurdish civilians from Iraqi attacks.

OUTCOME OF THE DEBATE

Iraqi intransigence on implementing a whole range of commitments it undertook in the cease-fire resolution of the Security Council continued for several years after its defeat in the Persian Gulf War. Inhumane treatment of Shi'ites in the south and Kurds in the north continued into the mid-1990s. Interference with investigations of nuclear, biological, and chemical, weapons sites by the International Atomic Energy Agency and the United Nations Special Commission (UNSCOM) continued intermittently until matters came to a head in summer and fall of 1998, when the United States and the United Kingdom threatened to bomb Iraq if it failed to permit inspections. The issue remained a standoff until 16 December, when, without direct Security Council approval, the United States and the United Kingdom actually did bomb Iraq, claiming they had authorization to do so under previous Security Council resolutions. But this interpretation was challenged by Russia, which accused the United States and the United Kingdom of creating an artificial crisis with Iraq. It did not deny that problems existed between UNSCOM and Iraq, but these were of a negotiable nature and did not justify bombings, which in any case were a violation of the UN Charter. China observed that Iraq had actually made progress in its disputes with UNSCOM in weeks prior to the bombing, so that they represented an unprovoked and groundless military attack. In the wake of the bombings, the United Nations was left with hardly any leverage over Iraq in the weapons inspection area, although Iraq cooperated with the United Nations Monitoring, Verification, and Inspection Commission (UNMOVIC), which replaced UNSCOM in March 2000.

In the meantime, Iraq had made progress since the war's end in compensating individuals for losses owing to the Persian Gulf War. As of 1998, Iraq had paid over $690 million in compensation for claims. In February 1999, the UN Compensation Commission made about $543 million more available for compensation to governments for dispersal to individual claimants, and in September another $481 million was also released. These monies were funded out of oil sales by Iraq permitted by the Security Council as a means of paying compensation debts. In 1997, the Security Council allowed the first shipments of humanitarian aid into Iraq under an Oil-for-Food program in which Iraq was allowed, despite the overall economic boycott, to produce enough oil to purchase emergency food and medical aid. Indeed, especially in the wake of the ineffective bombing by the United States and the United Kingdom in December 1998, Iraq's predicament was finally gaining sympathy from many delegations concerning the humanitarian effect of the long-standing sanctions. Several delegations began to float proposals for ending the sanctions, but these could not succeed without the approval of the United States and the United Kingdom.

Nearly a decade after he unleashed the invasion against Kuwait, Saddam Hussein remains in power; Iraqis continue to suffer under internationally imposed sanctions; Iraq has prevailed against Kurdish separatist groups; and despite the bombings of December 1998, Iraq continues to possess the capacity to develop weapons of mass destruction. In short, many of the provisions of the cease-fire resolution of the Security Council are yet to be fully implemented.

See also Arab-Israeli Dispute (Debate 6); Iran-Iraq War (Debate 41).

FOR FURTHER READING

Bloom, Saul, et al. *Hidden Casualties: Environment, Health and Political Consequences of the Persian Gulf War*. Berkeley, CA: North Atlantic Books, 1994.

Haselkorn, Avigdor. *The Continuing Storm: Iraq, Poisonous Weapons and Deterrence*. New Haven, CT: Yale University Press, 1999.

Newell, Clayton. *Historical Dictionary of the Persian Gulf War, 1990–1991*. Lanham, MD: Scarecrow Press, 1998.

Sciolino, Elaine. *The Outlaw State: Saddam Hussein's Quest for Power and the Gulf Crisis*. New York: John Wiley and Sons, 1991.

UN Chronicles, 1990–1999.

UN Yearbooks, 1990–1996.

Yetiv, Stephen. *The Persian Gulf Crisis*. Westport, CT: Greenwood Press, 1997.

Debate 45

Balkan Civil Wars (1991)

SIGNIFICANCE OF THE ISSUE

The United Nations (UN) response to the crisis in the former Yugoslavia was initially a compromise measure that was symptomatic of the lack of consensus among the great powers to respond aggressively to the deteriorating situation. Unwilling to do more or to totally abandon the region to the logic of its own fratricidal killing, the great powers opted to impose economic sanctions and arms embargoes and to keep a minimal humanitarian presence in the region by establishing the United Nations Protection Force (UNPROFOR), a hopelessly flawed humanitarian mission that was hostage to the civil war being brutally waged in Bosnia-Herzegovina. After the Dayton Accords of 1995, in which the United States finally acted decisively to broker and enforce a peace settlement, the UN undertook several moderately successful operations, but the deep-seated hostilities in the region continue to present an enormous challenge to the international community.

BACKGROUND TO THE DEBATE

The Balkans have been a violent crossroads of invading and competing armies and cultures for at least as far back as the division of the Roman Empire by the Emperor Constantine. It marked the division between the Greek Orthodox Byzantine Empire and the Roman Christendom of the Latin West. It marked the furthest extent of the Muslim advances by the Ottoman Turks into Europe in the fourteenth century. Although populated for more than a millennium mainly by Southern Slavs who speak the Serbo-Croatian language, the peoples are divided by religion: Serbs being Greek Orthodox, Croatians and Slovenians being Roman Catholic, and substantial numbers of Bosnians and Kosovar being Muslims. Coupled with the bloody wars during many centuries of forced migration, plunder, murder, and pillage, deep-seated hostilities among these peoples have fueled one set of upheavals after another. The Balkan Wars of the early twentieth century served as a prelude to the outbreak of World War I. Massive flows of refugees occurred, and ethnic cleansings were perpetrated long before the term *ethnic cleansing* came into use in the 1990s. With the creation of the Kingdom of the Serbs, Croats and Slovenes in 1917, the modern state of Yugoslavia (as it later came to be known) was created.

In 1941, Adolf Hitler's Nazi armies invaded Yugoslavia but met stubborn resistance from the resistance forces of Josip Broz, known as Marshal Tito. Croat collaboration with the Nazis against the Serbs during the occupation deepened resentments between the Serbs and Croats. At war's end, Tito was in control of Yugoslavia and began to pursue creation of a Communist state. In 1948, after a split with the Soviet Union, Tito adopted a distinctive style of Yugoslavian socialism that included flexible approaches to economic development and an elite ruling class gathered from the main ethnic communities. Yugoslavia experienced considerable economic growth and a period of relative political stability under Tito's firm hand. With his death in 1980, however, the country reverted to a collective presidency in which each of the presidents of the major provinces shared in rule. The Serbs during this time, still the largest portion of the population, also controlled the army. A resurgence of nationalism among Serbs as well as other groups eventually led to Slovenia's move to independence in June 1991. Belgrade and the Serbian-dominated army resisted perfunctorily, in part because of the small Serbian population in Slovenia. But Croatia's simultaneous bid for independence activated the Serbs, who constituted about 15 percent of the population in that province. They reacted violently, precipitating a lengthy civil war. The European Community (EC) attempted to mediate the dispute with little success, while Macedonia declared independence in September. When Bosnia, which contained about 35 percent Serbs, declared its independence in October, followed by a rather precipitous decision of Germany and other Western countries to extend it immediate recognition, the Bosnian Serb population rebelled, forming their own government and taking up arms to expand Serbian control. They did so with the help of Belgrade, which did not wish to see yet another large portion of Yugoslavia break away.

HISTORY OF THE DEBATE

Facing a deteriorating situation in the former Yugoslavia, the UN Security Council invoked a blanket arms embargo on delivery of weapons and military equipment to Yugoslavia on 25 September 1991. Unfortunately for the Croats and the non-Serbian Bosnians, this put the Serbian forces at an advantage since they were in control of most of the assets of the former Yugoslavian army. It was not long before this advantage became apparent as the Serbian forces, especially in Bosnia, steadily took more territory. UN

Secretary-General Boutros Boutros-Ghali subsequently engaged in intense negotiations to establish a cease-fire so that UN peacekeeping forces might be safely introduced. Meanwhile, the United Nations High Commissioner for Refugees (UNHCR) coupled with the Word Health Organization (WHO) and United Nations Children's Fund (UNICEF), moved in with humanitarian aid to persons uprooted by the conflict.

On 21 February 1992, the Security Council authorized the creation of the UN Protection Force, for the purpose of patrolling three UN protected areas (UNPAs) in Croatia, namely, Eastern Slavonia, Western Slavonia, and Krajina, where large numbers of Serbs lived. UNPROFOR was to ensure that these areas remained demilitarized as Croatia and Serbia pursued a negotiated settlement. Gradually UNPROFOR's mandate was expanded to include other responsibilities, such as monitoring "pink zones" lying beyond the UNPAs where Serbian forces were active. It was also deployed in June in Bosnia's capital city of Sarajevo, and UNPROFOR was given the authority to protect Sarajevo airport. In August the UNPROFOR mandate under Chapter VII of the Charter was expanded to include the protection of the delivery of humanitarian assistance throughout Bosnia. This protection was later extended to the operations of the UNHCR, which became the lead UN assistance agency in the midst of the civil war. In the meantime the UN General Assembly admitted Bosnia, Croatia, Macedonia, and Slovenia into membership and ruled that Serbia could not simply occupy the former Yugoslavia's seat but would also have to reapply for membership. The EC, United Nations, and Conference on Security and Cooperation in Europe (CSCE), later known as the Organization for Security and Cooperation in Europe (OSCE), jointly sponsored an international conference, which led to the Cyrus Vance–Lord David Owen initiative. The Organization of the Islamic Conference (OIC) was also involved in mediation efforts in a show of support for Bosnia's Muslim majority.

In May 1992, with the situation deteriorating further in both Croatia and Bosnia and with Serb armies advancing, the Security Council placed economic sanctions on Serbia by a vote of 13 to 0, with 2 abstentions (China and Zimbabwe). On several occasions during the year the Council approved the deployment of additional forces to bolster the UNPROFOR operation and expressed increasing concern over the violations of international humanitarian law concerning the treatment of civilians, detainees, and prisoners of war. The General Assembly explicitly condemned the practices of ethnic cleansing in a resolution of 25 August, which was adopted by a vote of 136 to 1 (Yugoslavia), with 5 abstentions (Ghana, Lesotho, Malawi, Namibia, Russian Federation). The Council followed with a vote to prohibit military flights in the airspace of Bosnia, and in December 1992, it extended UNPROFOR protection to the Former Yugoslav Republic of Macedonia (FYROM).

The UN Security Council unanimously adopted Resolution 743 on 21 February 1992 establishing the United Nations Protection Force (UNPROFOR) in Croatia and Bosnia-Herzegovina to establish conditions conducive to a negotiated solution of conflicts in the region. An UNPROFOR military vehicle is seen here traveling through the embattled city of Sarajevo in September 1992. UN/DPI Photo John Isaac

During 1993, negotiation to find support for the Vance-Owen peace plan resulted in a peace plan, but it was rejected by Serb voters in a May referendum. The Council strengthened the sanctions against Yugoslavia to no avail. A further peace plan involving a confederal scheme was floated subsequently, but negotiations proceeded without success. The civil war deepened, with further ethnic cleansing, and the UNPROFOR grew to a force of nearly 27,000 spanning from Croatia across Bosnia and into FYROM. With reports of ethnic cleansing continuing to be made, the UN Security Council established an International Tribunal for the Prosecution of Persons Responsible for Serious Violations of International Humanitarian Law Committed in the Territory of the Former Yugoslavia Since 1991. Its first action to this end was undertaken in February 1993, when it authorized the existence of such a body to investigate, prosecute, and punish war crimes. In later decisions it took further action to initiate the work of the Tribunal.

In early 1993, the Serbian offensive in eastern Bosnia gained ground, putting many people to flight and jeopardizing many cities. The Security Council named several cities protected areas, including the besieged towns of Bihac, Gorazde, Sarajevo, Srebrenica, Tuzla, and Zepa. But these safe havens were anything but safe, as many were subject to Serbian attacks. Dur-

The eleven judges of the International Tribunal for the prosecution of persons responsible for serious violations of international humanitarian law committed in the territory of the former Yugoslavia since 1991, established by Security Council Resolution 827 (1993), meet on 17 November 1993 for the first time at the Peace Palace in The Hague. UN/DPI Photo

ing 1994, the United States began quietly arming Croatia as a means of offsetting the Serbian military advantage. NATO air strikes began in retaliation for Serbian offensive actions, but these often incited Bosnian Serbs to retaliate against UNPROFOR forces and innocent civilians in UNPAs, while endless negotiations failed to produce any real headway. Serbs had little reason to negotiate seriously as long as they continued to advance across Bosnia, while the Council was preoccupied with Serbian violations of the UNPAs throughout Bosnia in 1994.

In 1995, the conflict in Croatia and Bosnia intensified despite the appearance of an agreement for a cease-fire in December 1994. In actuality, the government of Bosnia and the Serbs used the lull as a period of regrouping during the winter, and numerous violations of the cease-fire were reported in March; and by the time the cease-fire had officially expired in April, fighting spread throughout Bosnia and especially in and around the safe areas. Serbian forces shelled and overran Srebinica and Zepa in July, followed by brutal treatment of the Muslim inhabitants. Sarajevo was under almost constant shelling. At the end of August, NATO undertook multiple air strikes. But the decisive factor in the war of 1995 was the success of the now-replenished Croatian army in not only defending against Serb attacks but actually recapturing lost ground. This was especially apparent in the Krajina, where a blistering Croatian offensive in August caused some 200,000 Serbs to flee into northern Bosnia and then into Serbia. In March 1995, the Security Council restructured the UNPROFOR into three separate operations: UNPROFOR proper in Bosnia-Herzegovina; the United Nations Confidence Restoration Operation in Croatia (UNCRO); and the United Nations Preventive Deployment Force (UNPREDEP) in the FYROM. Consonant with the Croatian offensive, the Serbs were pressed to a cease-fire agreement on 5 October, and eventually the negotiation efforts begun in Dayton, Ohio, on 1 November culminated in the Dayton Peace Accords signed in Paris on 14 December 1995. Under this agreement the UN involvement in the security of the region ended, and it was replaced by a multinational Implementation Force (IFOR) to ensure the implementation of the agreements. Ironically, by the terms of the Dayton Accords, the Bosnian Serbs were granted autonomous republic status in federation with Bosnia-Herzegovina, something very close to what they had demanded before the beginning of the war, suggesting that earlier diplomacy and less precipitous recognition of Bosnian independence might well have averted much of the bloodshed. The agreements provided for the disarming of the factions, the return of refugees and displaced persons, the establishment of free elections in each of the two autonomous republics, and the provision of humanitarian and development assistance by various UN agencies and nongovernmental organizations.

OUTCOME OF THE DEBATE

The years since the Dayton Accords have proved to be very calm in contrast to the war years; elections have been held, and relatively stable governments preside over the two autonomous republics. Nevertheless, many problems remain in Bosnia-Herzegovina. Even five years after the settlement, the vast majority of refugees have yet to return to their villages and claim their homes. Serbs are reluctant to return to areas under Muslim rule, as are Muslims to areas of the new Srpska Republic. A kind of de facto partition seems to have evolved despite every effort to avoid this. The Bosnian economy is still in poor shape, and the pace of economic development very slow. Foreign troops, presumably meant to withdraw a year after the settlement, continue to be deployed in Bosnia, illustrating the degree to which foreign powers view their ongoing presence as essential to security. Although a number of Serbs as well as Croats and Bosnian Muslims have been arrested, investigated, and tried for war crimes, many war criminals remain free. In the case of the Serb and Croatian and the Serb and Bosnian wars, the Russian Federation, while not supporting every Security Council resolution or action, never used a veto. This new cooperative spirit between the Western powers and Russia contributed both within and outside of the UN setting to the Dayton process and its aftermath.

In January 1996, the Security Council terminated the mandate for the UNCRO operation in Croatia and subsequently authorized military observers to undertake duties in various parts of Croatia including the UN Mission of Observers in Prevlaka, to oversee the demilitarization of the Prevlaka peninsula, and the UN Transitional Administration for Eastern Slavonia, Baranja and Western Sirmium (UNTAES), to ease the reintegration of Serbs into those regions. UNTAES was withdrawn in January 1998 and followed by the deployment of a UN Civilian Police Support Group to encourage respect for human rights. In Bosnia itself the Security Council authorized the creation of the UN–International Police Task Force and the UN Mission in Bosnia and Herzegovina to assist in the process of policing the country. It also replenished the UNPREDEP in FYROM on several occasions until a Chinese veto in the Council in February 1999 prevented an extension of its reauthorization.

The conflict in neighboring Kosovo, though highlighting the relative stability of Bosnia-Herzegovina, also served as a reminder of the deep-seated hatreds that still persist in this region and that the Dayton Accords and subsequent implementation could not and did not banish. Such scars take longer in the healing than they do in the making. In Kosovo as in Bosnia, it is very likely that a UN and an international presence will likely be needed for many years to come as this region is noted for its long memory of the past misdeeds of others and forgetfulness of the wrongs one's own kin have wrought.

See also Genocide (Debate 9); Human Rights (Debate 10); Kosovo Situation (Debate 50); Refugees and Stateless Persons (Debate 4).

FOR FURTHER READING

Bierman, Wolfgang, and Martin Vadset. *UN Peacekeeping in Trouble: Lessons Learned in the Former Yugoslavia*. London: Avebury, 1998.

Corwin, Phillip. *Dubious Mandate: A Memoir of the UN in Bosnia, Summer 1995*. Durham, NC: Duke University Press, 1999.

Hall, Brian. *The Impossible Country: A Journey through the Last Days of Yugoslavia*. New York: Penguin, 1995.

Udovicki, Jasminka, and James Ridgeway, eds. *Burn This House: The Making and Unmaking of Yugoslavia*. Durham, NC: Duke University Press, 1997.

UN Chronicles, 1997–1999.

UN Yearbooks, 1991–1996.

West, Richard. *Tito and the Rise and Fall of Yugoslavia*. New York: Carroll and Graf, 1996.

Somali Civil War (1991)

SIGNIFICANCE OF THE ISSUE

The UN response to the Somali situation in 1991 represented an innovation in peacekeeping, in the sense that the Security Council decided to intervene in the context of a failed state, with no effective recognized government, in the midst of a civil conflict to ensure the provision of humanitarian aid. The operation succeeded in bringing the famine to a close, but its extension to disarmament of the competing clans ended in failure, raising a series of questions about the circumstances of UN engagement in civil conflicts.

BACKGROUND TO THE DEBATE

Somalia gained its independence in 1960 with the merger of British Somaliland and Italian Somalia. From the standpoint of Somalis, this represented only a partial unification since Somali peoples continued to live under foreign rule in Djibouti, Ethiopia, and Kenya. Traditionally, Somali society is based on nomadic pastoralism and is organized into clans and subclans. The most intense loyalties felt by most Somalis are to their immediate kinship groups and subclans. Through such ties, Somalis historically resolved disputes that arose over the use of pastures and wells in a land that is constantly prone to drought and periodic famine.

During the years of the Cold War, the Horn of Africa was flooded with weaponry. In Somalia, the regime of Mohammed Siad Barre, who assumed power in 1969, sought military aid from the Soviet Union. Neighboring Ethiopia received military assistance from the United States and other Western countries during the Cold War. But the leftist revolution in Ethiopia, begun in 1974 with the forced abdication of Emperor Haile Selassie, gave the Soviet Union an opportunity to extend its influence throughout the Horn of Africa. Somalia had other ideas, however, and undertook to support the Western Somali Liberation Front (WSLF), which was fighting to win independence for Somali peoples in the Ogaden region of Ethiopia. Barre eventually committed Somali regular forces to this fight in 1977 and, a few months later, expelled Soviet diplomats from the country because of their support for Ethiopia. In subsequent months, the Soviet Union and Cuba provided massive military support to Ethiopia, and Somali forces withdrew in defeat in March 1978. The rebel action continued for several more months, precipitating a refugee flow of 1 to 2 million into Somalia.

The defeat of Somali forces was a humiliation to the national aspirations of Somalia. Resistance movements to the government of Mohammed Siad Barre began forming in exile. With Ethiopia having become a client of the Soviet Union, Barre sought and received defensive military assistance and substantial amounts of humanitarian aid to offset the Ethiopian security threat and to meet the needs of the huge refugee population. But groups opposed to Siad Barre continued to operate and grow. In 1988, he joined with the presidents of Ethiopia and Djibouti to prevent the use of their country's territories by rebel groups. One Somali resistance group—the Somali National Movement (SNM)—moved into northwest Somalia, undertaking a destabilizing guerrilla war there. Barre's response was a brutal bombing of the regional capital of Hargeisa, which forced the retreat of the SNM into the countryside. Looting of urban areas in the north by Somali forces increased local resentment to government in Mogadishu.

Dissatisfaction with the Barre regime was not limited to the northwest, which began to contemplate secession from Somalia. Indeed, disaffection with Barre was rising in southern Somalia as well. The Somali Patriotic Movement (SPM), an Ogadeni-based group, and the United Somali Congress (USC), which was Hawiye-based, emerged in the late 1980s and early 1990s as major opponents to the Barre regime. Under constant military pressure, especially from the forces of the USC, Barre's government and army slowly deteriorated as the opposition strengthened. Mogadishu itself became a battleground in 1991, where USC forces openly contested with remnants of Barre's army. Barre fled on 27 January, leaving the country to the rebel factions, although some elements of his army continued to fight in and around the southern city of Kismayo.

Barre's departure did not lead to peace everywhere. Although the north enjoyed relative calm, where Somaliland declared itself independent in May 1991, southern Somalia, especially the country's breadbasket between the Webi Shabbele and Juba Rivers, was subjected to heavy fighting and great insecurity. Flooded with weapons, and divided into more than two dozen clan-related groups, each of which competed for territory and influence, southern Somalia devolved into a vicious struggle among contending forces. In Mogadishu, where the Hawiye clan predominates, two subclans, the Habr Gedir, led by Mohammed Farah Aideed, and the Abgal, led by Ali Mahdi Mohammed, fought for control of the capital. While Aideed was the chief architect of the overthrow of Barre, Ali Mahdi Mohammed was a member of the Manifesto Group, which had unsuccessfully called for Barre's resignation in 1990. Infighting by these subclans and several other clan-based groups severely hampered efforts to ship and transport food aid, especially in Mogadishu, the country's main seaport. During late 1991, the Agbal–Habr Gedir feud intensified in Mogadishu, leading most international relief organizations to leave the country. The International Committee of the Red Cross (ICRC) and a few private agencies who remained were not able to address the growing humanitarian needs. The conflict caused local food shortages and the emergence of severe famine and starvation. This prompted the United Nations to negotiate a cease-fire and to appoint a special coordinator to negotiate the return of relief agencies.

HISTORY OF THE DEBATE

Various problems involving Somalia have found their way onto the UN agenda over the years, commencing with the Ethiopian-Somali war of 1977–1978. Somalia's aggressive actions against Ethiopia, though perhaps having some justification in view of its irredentist claims, were widely condemned by the United Nations and the Organization of African Unity (OAU). The humanitarian dilemmas that resulted from that war, however, saw the international community respond generously to the needs of Somali refugees from Ethiopia. The United Nations High Commissioner for Refugees (UNHCR) took the lead in provision of refugee assistance, and resolutions from the Economic and Social Council (ECOSOC) and the General Assembly expressing support for Somalia's generosity toward reception of the refugees and calling for international assistance to meet their needs were routinely adopted throughout the 1980s without votes. Somalia benefited from substantial refugee aid during the 1980s, but in 1988 and 1989, the civil war in the northwest created a domestic humanitarian problem. UN special missions were fielded to assess the situation in 1989, and response to the disaster situation was placed under the authority of the Special Coordinator for Emergency Relief Operations in Somalia. Humanitarian agencies threatened to withdraw given the insecurity, and UN resolutions pinned most of the blame on the "armed bandits" in the region. However, the human rights abuses of the Siad Barre regime itself were a cause of much of the disruption in the northwest, and both the United Nations, in a report by the secretary-general in 1990, and governments, such as the United States, began to take notice of this as the situation deteriorated. In 1991, as the Barre government collapsed, the United Nations did little except to express its concern that the civil war be brought to a swift resolution and that adequate humanitarian assistance be supplied. But virtually all UN humanitarian agencies evacuated Somalia in January with the collapse of the government, leaving the ICRC and other nongovernmental organizations (NGOs) to undertake the humanitarian work.

UN action in Somalia took form in 1992. As the security situation and the famine began to spread, the Security Council passed a series of unanimous resolutions throughout the year. In January, on the request of Omer Arteh Qhalib, who had been appointed interim prime minister by the various factions that had met in July 1991 in a conference on national reconciliation, appealed to the Security Council to respond to the increasingly difficult security situation and the accompanying humanitarian problems. On 23 January, the Council decided to impose a general and complete embargo on arms deliveries to Somalia and called upon states and international organizations to respond to the humanitarian situation. In March, the Council expressed its support for the sending of a technical team to assess humanitarian needs in Somalia. A cease-fire between Ali Mahdi Mohammed and Mohammed Farah Aideed was effected in subsequent months, with mediation by the Arab League, the OAU and the Organization of the Islamic Conference (OIC). UN Under-Secretary-General James Jonah secured agreements from various factions to allow the supply of humanitarian aid. Security problems persisted, making delivery of such assistance difficult, but without relief assistance, security could not be maintained. The secretary-general urged the Council to act quickly to provide humanitarian aid, even in the absence of fully established security. He asked the Council to establish a United Nations Operation in Somalia (UNOSOM), which would serve as a means for providing delivery of humanitarian aid to the 1.5 million most directly in need of assistance. In Resolution 751 (1992), of April 1992, the Council acted upon this request and formally established UNOSOM. In the same month, Mohammed Sahnoun of Algeria was appointed as special representative to Somalia. Sahnoun indicated, after study of the situation, that the possession of large amounts of weapons by many varied factions posed the most serious threat to the security of food aid. He recommended a comprehensive UN response throughout the country, where problems varied by region.

A technical team was dispatched to explore the possibility of deploying observer forces in the south, of reconstituting the Somali police force, of determining the feasibility of an arms-for-food strategy to secure broader disarmament, and of deploying security forces to protect food supply lines. The Security Council approved the secretary-general's recommendation that the country be divided into four operational zones for the provision of aid, and in subsequent months the World Food Program (WFP) and ICRC, along with a number of NGOs, began to deliver some food assistance, but security remained highly precarious. In August, subsequent to a UN visit, the Mahdi Mohammed and Aideed factions agreed to the deployment of a 500-strong force to monitor food supply and distribution in Mogadishu and for similar forces in other parts of the country. Acting on the secretary-general's recommendation, the Security Council increased the size of UNOSOM forces in August.

In subsequent months, the situation only deteriorated. Pakistani troops serving with UNOSOM were attacked and killed, vehicles were hijacked, factional violence and disagreement prevented delivery of food, large sums of cash were extorted or stolen from donor agencies, humanitarian agency staff members were detained, and food warehouses were looted. Amid this insecurity starvation intensified. By late November, the secretary-general was prepared to ask the Security Council to intervene with a large armed force. U.S. President George Bush stepped forward with a proposal for the deployment of U.S. forces to establish initial security and later to be bolstered by forces from other nations. On 3 December 1992, the Security Council authorized the deployment of 3,500 additional troops for UNOSOM. It also invoked Chapter VII of the Charter in order to establish a secure environment for the provision of humanitarian aid, welcomed the U.S. initiative to establish such an environment, and authorized U.S. forces along with other member states to use all necessary means to promote security. On 4 December, President Bush implemented Operation Restore Hope. On 9 December, the first U.S. Marine units of the Unified Task Force (UNITAF) landed in Somalia. Eventually about 25,000 U.S. troops, bolstered by 10,000 troops from twenty countries, participated in the UNITAF

A U.S. soldier serving in the Unified Task Force (UNITAF) watches as a young Somali woman tries on his sunglasses. UNITAF was later replaced by the unsuccessful United Nations Operation in Somalia II (UNOSOM II) forces. UN/DPI Photo Milton Grant

operation. While UNITAF forces gradually fanned out throughout Somalia, ensuring the delivery of food and medical supplies, the famine was brought under control. At the same time the United Nations called a conference of thirteen competing Somali political organizations in Addis Ababa in order to begin the process of national reconciliation. UNITAF limited its mandate, however, to the securing of transportation lines and food distribution systems for 4.5 million of Somalia's 6 million people, encouraging the return of the 1.5 million internally displaced persons and 1 million refugees. Any expansion of the mandate to include disarmament or other responsibilities would wait until the UNOSOM force was reconstituted.

The process of reconstituting UNOSOM began in the spring of 1993, as UNITAF had met its goals of ensuring a more stable environment for provision of food aid. With the famine in check, the United Nations turned toward the much more difficult and complex task of trying to achieve Somali national reconciliation, rehabilitation, and recovery. On 26 March, the Council authorized the secretary-general to undertake an ambitious program of disarming political factions, rebuilding Somali civil society, investigating violations of international humanitarian law, establishing a mine clearance program, promoting political reconciliation, repatriating refugees, assisting in rehabilitation and development programming, and creating a new UNOSOM II force, which formally took over from UNITAF on 4 May. Although progress in some areas of the UNOSOM II mandate was made, the security situation in Mogadishu deteriorated as Aideed and his followers proved recalcitrant. On 5 June, members of Aideed's United Somali Congress/Somali National Alliance (USC-SNA) attacked and killed twenty-nine Pakistani and Moroccan troops under UNOSOM II command. The Security Council immediately condemned this action, and the UN special representative called for Aideed's arrest and detention on 17 June. An unsuccessful manhunt for Aideed began. Throughout the summer, however, UNOSOM forces continued to sustain casualties, as Aideed eluded capture and as his forces resisted UN efforts to proceed with the disarmament of the political factions.

Efforts to foster political reconciliation and reconstitution of the police force continued, but in September and October, violence against UNOSOM II forces continued, culminating on 3 October in an ambush of U.S. forces in which eighteen soldiers were killed and seventy-five wounded. Under heavy political pressure at home, President Bill Clinton announced his intention to withdraw U.S. forces from UNOSOM II participation by 31 March 1994, largely dooming the operation to failure. Other countries, such as Belgium, France, and Sweden, had previously announced similar intentions and were soon followed by Germany, Italy, Norway, and Turkey. Hosni Mubarak, president of Egypt, and the secretaries-general of the OAU, the Arab League, and the OIC expressed their concern over U.S.

withdrawal, but to no avail. The Security Council's only further action in 1993 was taken on 16 November with the establishment of a Commission of Inquiry to investigate armed attacks on UNOSOM II personnel.

As UNOSOM II troop size declined, especially after the U.S. withdrawal by March 1994, its ability to conduct its mandate was severely handicapped. Political resolution eluded the contending Somali factions despite determined efforts by the United Nations to support a negotiated settlement among the many and diverse parties. The security situation in the country deteriorated throughout 1994. NGO and UN personnel continued to be subject to attack. UNOSOM was muddling through to its eventual withdrawal, although its mandate was renewed periodically for variable lengths of time as the Security Council groped for an appropriate exit strategy. In October 1994, after consultations in New York, the Council sent a mission to Somalia, composed of representatives from China, France, New Zealand, Nigeria, Pakistan, the Russian Federation, and the United States. Its task was to review options for UNOSOM's future. It recommended that 31 March 1995 be the termination date for UNOSOM II. On 4 November 1994, the Council decided to comply with this recommendation. The report of the mission cited several flaws in the UNOSOM II operation, including poor communications between units of different nations, the lack of experience in UN peacekeeping operations, cultural insensitivity to Somalis among senior UNOSOM advisers, failure at UN headquarters to coordinate policy, and a disparity between the large mandate given to UNOSOM II and the actual forces and resources provided to achieve it. It recommended abandoning forced disarmament but continuation of all efforts to promote the political reconciliation process.

The potentially dangerous withdrawal phase of UNOSOM II began with the implementation of a "United Shield" operation in February 1995. Troops from France, India, Italy, Malaysia, Pakistan, the United Kingdom, and the United States participated in the United Shield operation in order to secure the safe withdrawal of UNOSOM II forces, most of which had departed Somalia by 2 March. The last elements of the United Shield forces departed on 28 March, leaving Somalia largely to its own devices insofar as the provision of civic order and security was concerned.

OUTCOME OF THE DEBATE

The withdrawal of UNOSOM II from Somalia initiated an ongoing debate about the wisdom of UN interventions in the context of civil wars. With similar UN operations participating in the precarious Balkan region, member states began to experience reluctance to become involved in other civil war situations. This explains in part the United Nations' and great powers' hesitance to respond to the genocide perpetrated in Rwanda during 1994.

As for the Somalia situation itself, the UNITAF/UNOSOM II operations did in fact help to bring the famine to a halt. For a time they restored a degree of security in the country. But they failed in all of the most important tasks, such as lasting repatriation of refugees, disarmament of hostile clan armies, establishment of a police force, and political reconciliation. The Security Council itself recognized that only a genuinely representative and broad-based approach to national reconciliation could restore peace to Somalia and that this could only be achieved by the Somali people themselves. It could not be forced upon them by UN peacekeepers. The secretary-general continued to make available his good offices toward the end of national reconciliation, and UN agencies such as the United Nations Development Program (UNDP), the UNHCR, the UN Department of Humanitarian Affairs, and the United Nations Educational, Scientific, and Cultural Organization (UNESCO) continued to offer humanitarian and technical assistance to Somalia.

Efforts toward national reconciliation have proved to be difficult, even after the death of Aideed in 1996. Where security was slowly reestablished, degrees of progress were made. In northwest Somalia, which formally declared its independence from Somalia as the new country of Somaliland after affirmation of the clan leaders in the region, much stability and progress were achieved. In 1997, a new constitution was approved and democratic elections held. Somaliland possessed all of the attributes of a sovereign state, but the international community proved reluctant to deal directly with it as a new government, most hoping that a full reconciliation among all Somalis, including those in the northwest, might still be possible. The Somalis of Somaliland decided not to wait indefinitely for such an outcome. Indeed, their instincts may prove correct, as achievement of a political settlement in the south continues to elude the many various competing factions there. Still, other parts of Somalia, including the northeast and even areas of the south, have shown marked improvement, whereas other areas continue to be highly unstable and insecure.

The return of normalcy to Somalia will depend on the patient reconstruction of the traditional systems of the Sharia (Islamic law) courts, the councils of elders, and the traditional conflict resolution mechanisms. Where these have begun to reemerge, life has improved. Where roving bands of armed youth exist, security is continually threatened. The ongoing arms embargo on the country will have some dampening effect on the ability of the factions to sustain their military capacity, although black market trading in arms continues. In the meantime, the slow and tortuous international and regional efforts to support Somali national reconciliation will continue, and it is highly likely that by the end of that process there will still be two Somalias, Somaliland in the north and Somalia in the south. A divided nation will be one legacy of the Somali civil wars of the 1990s. A chastened United Nations will be the other.

See also Rwandan Civil War (Debate 49).

FOR FURTHER READING

Besteman, Catherine, and Lee Cassanelli, eds. *The Struggle for Land in Southern Somalia: The War behind the War*. Boulder, CO: Westview Press, 1996.

Clarke, Walter, and Jeffrey Herbst. *Learning from Somalia: The Lessons of Armed Humanitarian Intervention*. Boulder, CO: Westview Press, 1997.

Drysdale, John. *Whatever Happened to Somalia?* London: Haan, 1994.

Hirsch, John L., and Robert B. Oakley. *Somalia and Operation Restore Hope*. Washington, DC: U.S. Institute of Peace, 1995.

Makinda, Samuel M. *Seeking Peace from Chaos: Humanitarian Intervention in Somalia*. Boulder, CO: Lynne Rienner, 1993.

Sahnoun, Mohammed. *Missed Opportunities*. Washington, DC: U.S. Institute of Peace, 1994.

Sommer, John G. *Hope Restored? Humanitarian Aid in Somalia 1990–1994*. Washington, DC: Refugee Policy Group, 1994.

Mozambique Situation (1992)

SIGNIFICANCE OF THE ISSUE

UN responses to civil wars in the early 1990s produced examples of both failure and success. The Mozambique situation represented a resounding success. UN peacekeeping forces and UN humanitarian agencies contributed significantly to the maintenance of order, the repatriation of refugees, resettlement of displaced persons, rehabilitation of the country, the clearance of mines, the demobilization of the national and guerrilla armies and their reconstitution into a new army, the preparations for and holding of free elections, and the establishment of stable and democratic government in Mozambique after years of debilitating civil war.

BACKGROUND TO THE DEBATE

Mozambique was subject to Portuguese colonial rule from the early 1500s until independence, which was finally achieved in June 1975. Organization and agitation for independence commenced in the early 1960s with the emergence of several national liberation organizations that formed a shaky alliance in 1962 as the Front for the Liberation of Mozambique (FRELIMO). The apartheid situation in South Africa, coupled with white colonial rule by the Portuguese in Angola and Mozambique and the difficult problem of Southern Rhodesia's white minority government, kept Mozambique on the UN General Assembly agenda during most of the 1960s until its independence. The United Nations supported the national liberation struggle in Mozambique, although the decisive factor in the achievement of Mozambican independence was the socialist coup d'état in Lisbon in 1974. The new Portuguese government considered the former government's colonial holdings an embarrassing liability and moved quickly to end the costly military efforts against national liberation groups in Angola, Guinea-Bissau, and Mozambique. Within a year of the coup in Lisbon, Portugal divested itself of these colonies. In Mozambique's case, this was a major relief to Portugal, which had committed 30,000 to 60,000 troops at various times to repress FRELIMO's war for independence.

Independence was a mixed blessing for Mozambique. Most of its white population fled after an unsuccessful bid by the Free Mozambique Movement to challenge FRELIMO in September 1974. The flight of the white population, which had served as the managerial class within the economy, left the national economy in a state of paralysis, while some of the white exiles sought assistance from the white minority regimes in Rhodesia and South Africa to form a military resistance against the FRELIMO government. The adoption by Samora Machel, FRELIMO's president, of Marxist-oriented policies such as a centrally planned economy, collectivization of agriculture, and a military pact with the Soviet Union only reinforced the fears of the white minority regimes in South Africa and Rhodesia about Mozambique's intention to become a source of instability and revolution in the region; so they supported the white Mozambican exile population, which formed the Mozambican National Resistance (RENAMO) in 1977. The civil war in Rhodesia compounded this problem, because Mozambique lent its territory and other support to Robert Mugabe's Zimbabwe African National Union (ZANU) guerrilla forces. Rhodesia attacked ZANU refugee camps in Mozambique on numerous occasions, and the white Rhodesian support for RENAMO could be seen as a further extension of its policy to repress its political opponents abroad. The resolution of the Rhodesian civil war in 1979, and the creation of the new state of Zimbabwe, ironically under Mugabe's leadership, removed this direct threat to Mozambique's stability. However, RENAMO's activities continued with the support of South Africa.

Ongoing and more troublesome guerrilla activities by RENAMO, combined with a severe drought and the collapse of Mozambique's socialist economy, convinced Samora Machel to begin a series of pragmatic reforms. This culminated in 1984 with an agreement between Machel and South Africa, by which Mozambique would desist supporting the African National Congress (ANC), which constituted a threat to the white regime in South Africa, whereas South Africa agreed to desist in support of RENAMO. Known as the Nkomati Accords, this agreement was upheld by Machel, but RENAMO activities continued, owing to covert support from the South African military. In 1984, Machel also sought membership for Mozambique in the World Bank and the International Monetary Fund, signaling his intention to abandon his Marxist orientation and to pursue more liberal economic policies. However, drought combined with intensified RENAMO attacks sent hundreds of thousands of Mozambicans fleeing into neighboring countries during the mid-1980s, while even greater numbers were internally displaced within Mozambique owing to famine and insecurity.

The death of Samora Machel in a plane crash in 1986 was followed by the presidency of Joaquim Chissano, who accelerated Machel's reforms. By 1989, FRELIMO decided to officially abandon its Marxist label and to seek a negotiated settlement with RENAMO, which was led by Alfonso Dhlakama. The battle between FRELIMO and RENAMO had reached a long-term stalemate in which neither side could muster the strength or resources to defeat the other. At about the same time, the new government of F. W. de Klerk took office in South Africa, and movement toward peace in Angola and Namibia was also making progress. In this more favorable climate, through mediation by the Mozambican Catholic Church, the Catholic Community of Sant 'Egidio in Italy, and the Italian government, initial talks between representatives of FRELIMO and RENAMO were painstakingly pursued during 1989. Eventually the flurry of private diplomacy resulted in a meeting in Rome in July 1990 between FRELIMO and RENAMO representatives. Although the negotiations were long and difficult, a partial cease-fire was achieved in December 1990, and this was eventually followed on 4 October 1992 with a peace agreement among the parties that was signed in Rome. The general peace agreement consisted of seven protocols addressing (1) basic principles, (2) criteria and arrangements for the formation and recognition of political parties, (3) principles of the Electoral Act, (4) military questions, (5) guarantees, (6) cease-fire, and (7) donors' conferences. In addition, the parties reaffirmed previously agreed upon statements in which each party promised to work toward a peaceful and stable Mozambique, to maintain the cease-fire, to encourage and protect the delivery of humanitarian assistance, to accept the establishment of a democratic system of government rooted in principles of freedom, and to accept a role for the international community, especially the United Nations as a custodian of the implementation of the peace accords, including the cease-fire and electoral elements. The parties agreed as well to promote the reintegration of refugees, displaced persons, and demobilized soldiers. The demobilization of both forces and their reintegration into a single new national security and police apparatus were seen as necessary preludes to the holding of free and fair elections.

HISTORY OF THE DEBATE

On 13 October 1992, the Security Council took note of a report by the secretary-general in which he recommended that the United Nations undertake responsibilities for oversight of the cease-fire, for the separation, concentration, and demobilization of forces, for monitoring the elections, and for ensuring the provision of humanitarian aid. They named a special representative and dispatched to Mozambique a team of military observers to assess the situation. Two months later, the Council acted on the secretary-general's recommendation to establish a United Nations Operation in

Mozambique (ONUMOZ). The deployment of ONUMOZ was a ticklish matter, because all the modalities of implementing the Rome Peace Accords were not completely agreed upon by FRELIMO and RENAMO, and because occasional violations of the cease-fire were ongoing. Moreover, the resettlement of about 5 to 6 million refugees and displaced persons in a large country that had been subjected to economic disruption and drought and destruction of infrastructure and where the government lacked the capacity to manage all of the elements of the peace agreement would call for a major coordinated effort on the part of the international community. Most of all, no settlement could take place unless the competing forces were committed to peace.

In the first months of its deployment, movement of ONUMOZ forces was inhibited by a lack of agreement on the status of its forces and foot dragging by RENAMO and FRELIMO forces, which delayed the demobilization process. However, humanitarian operations were initiated with the World Food Program (WFP) and the United Nations Children's Fund (UNICEF), supplying food aid and other forms of assistance during the early months of 1993. Spadework proceeded by the Cease-fire Commission established in the General Peace Accords in terms of developing a plan to clear some 2 million mines. Other commissions included a Reintegration Commission and a Joint Commission for the Formation of the Mozambican Defense Force, which initiated their work during 1993, while commissions to establish a new police force, information systems, administrative capacities, and elections were delayed. The UN Office for Humanitarian Assistance Coordination worked within ONUMOZ to prepare a consolidated humanitarian aid package for refugees and displaced persons, while the UNHCR was tasked with repatriation. By midyear about 250,000 refugees in Zimbabwe were readied by UNHCR for repatriation. In October, UNHCR reached an agreement to begin repatriation of 250,000 Mozambican refugees from South Africa. Momentum gathered in the process of refugee return and resettlement of displaced persons by the fall of 1993, as about 400,000 refugees and 1.2 million displaced persons returned to home areas, many spontaneously. The Security Council monitored the situation in Mozambique closely, issuing periodic unanimous resolutions prodding the parties toward implementation of the peace accords. UN General Assembly actions, all adopted without vote, indicating the high degree of consensus, concerned mainly the financing of the ONUMOZ operation.

During 1994, momentum on implementation of the peace accords picked up further steam and concluded in October with free and fair elections, after which ONUMOZ began to withdraw immediately. Demobilization of Mozambican forces moved rapidly, causing some confusion and difficulty. Efforts were redoubled to prepare the majority of the former combatants for civilian life, mine clearance programs were broadened, and

Implementation of the General Peace Agreement between the government of Mozambique and the RENAMO forces involved substantial UN involvement in the political, military, electoral, and humanitarian areas. The United Nations Operation in Mozambique (ONUMOZ), among other things, promoted repatriation of Mozambican refugees from neighboring countries under a UN High Commissioner for Refugees program. This refugee on a train in Boane was one of over a million refugees who repatriated in advance of successful elections leading to the establishment of a democratic government in Mozambique. UN/DPI Photo S. Santimano

efforts to reform RENAMO into a political party were undertaken in advance of the elections. By April a majority of both FRELIMO and RENAMO forces had been garrisoned, most in preparation for decommissioning. The new integrated military force was set at about 65,000, although training of only about 10,000 was accomplished by the elections. Still, about 75,000 troops had been demobilized, and almost 6.4 million voters registered. Massive spontaneous repatriation of refugees prior to the elections demonstrated confidence in the positive direction of the peace process; even a new police force was trained under ONUMOZ supervision. The elections held in October led to a FRELIMO victory, but not by a wide margin. Chissano was elected president over Dhlakama by a margin of 53 to 33 percent. FRELIMO won 44 percent of the popular vote to RENAMO's 33 percent. A large number of smaller parties won votes but failed to win seats in the legislative Assembly. The election ensured that both FRELIMO and RENAMO would have a voice in the governance of the country.

OUTCOME OF THE DEBATE

Little controversy attended UN debates concerning Mozambique. In a climate of newfound international cooperation between the East and the West, the old ideological wars of the past no longer animated UN delegations. Despite the ongoing political antagonisms between FRELIMO and RENAMO, both parties were tired of war and recognized that the time had come for reconciliation and peace. The United Nations was in a mood to act decisively and productively, and the plan of ONUMOZ deployment and its work, though not without flaws, proved to be highly successful. Full cooperation of the major powers in the Security Council, progress toward reform in neighboring South Africa, and the dedication of large amounts of international resources to the peace endeavor in Mozambique and generally capable administration of the ONUMOZ and humanitarian operations clearly set a strong foundation for a long-lasting and stable democratic governance of Mozambique.

ONUMOZ was formally terminated on 31 January 1995, indicating the full and complete implementation of the General Peace Agreement hammered out between FRELIMO and RENAMO in Rome. More than thirty years of revolutionary and guerrilla war, which had wrought havoc on the country, were formally brought to an end. In the years that followed, Mozambique proved to be a relative rock of stability, as compared to the ongoing and debilitating wars in its former sister colony of Angola. International assistance helped with the rehabilitation of the country's infrastructure. Mine clearance programs continued, and perhaps most important, the country survived a second election cycle in 1999 without major destabilizing incidents. In Mozambique, the United Nations participated in the fashioning of a political miracle, a much-needed positive experience for an organization that continued to take lumps in other scenes of conflict where competing parties showed reluctance to achieve genuine resolution of their political differences. In Mozambique the stars aligned, with the combatants convinced that the time had come for peace and with an international community that was ready, willing, and able to dedicate its resources to the effort. This proved to be a winning combination for all concerned. Tragically, these major strides toward economic and political stability were shaken badly by the devastating floods that hit Mozambique in February 2000, causing widespread destruction and displacement. UN humanitarian agencies responded with aid, while Mozambicans began the long task of recovery.

See also Angola Situation (Debate 42); Apartheid in South Africa (Debate 14); Decolonization (Debate 18); Rhodesian Question (Debate 21).

FOR FURTHER READING

Hall, Margaret, and Tom Young. *Confronting Leviathan: Mozambique since Independence.* Athens: Ohio University Press, 1997.

Hanlon, Joseph. *Mozambique: Who Calls the Shots?* London: James Currey, 1991.

Hume, Cameron. *Ending Mozambique's War: The Role of Mediation and Good Offices.* Washington, DC: U.S. Institute of Peace Press, 1994.

Newitt, Malyn. *A History of Mozambique.* Bloomington: Indiana University Press, 1995.

Synge, Richard. *Mozambique: UN Peacekeeping in Action, 1992–94.* Washington, DC: U.S. Institute of Peace Press, 1997.

UN Chronicles, 1990–1995.

UN Yearbooks, 1984–1995.

Vines, Alex. *RENAMO: Terrorism in Mozambique.* Bloomington: Indiana University Press, 1991.

Haiti Situation (1993)

SIGNIFICANCE OF THE ISSUE

UN action in Haiti illustrated the ability of the organization to help resolve a conflict in conjunction with regional peace initiatives, in this case sponsored by the Organization of American States (OAS). Once a major power here, the United States, chose to bring its power to bear, decisive action was finally possible to force a peaceful resolution of the situation. The UN Security Council, using authority vested to it in Chapter VII of the Charter, invoked economic sanctions against the military government of Haiti and later authorized the American military initiative against the refractory regime in order to reinstall a democratically elected government. UN involvement in the development of a coherent and efficient police force contributed to the reemergence of civil society in Haiti and has contributed to its national stability.

BACKGROUND TO THE DEBATE

Haiti has a long and colorful history. Visited by Columbus in 1492, it was colonized by France in the seventeenth century. At the turn of the nineteenth century, however, Haitians grew increasingly restive under French control. Slave revolts began in 1791, and although slavery was outlawed in 1793, Haitian disaffection under French rule continued. A series of rebellions began in which former slave Toussaint-Louverture played an important early role. His capture and death in a French prison did not end the rebellion, which continued under the leadership of other Haitian patriots. Haiti eventually succeeded in winning complete independence in 1804. Political division and instability afflicted the new nation from the outset, however. Except for the period 1820 to 1843 during which Jean Pierre Boyer reunited Haiti and ruled with a firm hand, Haiti was beset by political chaos. From 1843 to 1915 it saw more than twenty rulers come and go. Thus, the country suffered a long history of poverty, deprivation, and political instability. After the outbreak of World War I, the United States intervened to ensure stability on the island. U.S. Marines occupied Haiti from 1915 to 1934, and the country remained under general U.S. fiscal supervision until 1947. Despite the U.S. presence, Haiti became a full member of the League of Nations and was a founding member of the United Nations.

The general instability of Haiti's political system and the widespread poverty on the island established a long tradition of emigration from the country. Haitians who could not find meaningful employment in their own country engaged in both cyclical and long-term migration to the neighboring Dominican Republic and to other island nations in the Caribbean, as well as to the United States. The fact that political corruption and often repressive and or unstable government coexisted with poverty in Haiti has made determinations about whether Haitian flight is rooted primarily in economics or in political persecution difficult.

In 1957 an election was won by François (Papa Doc) Duvalier, who became president. In 1961, Duvalier declared himself reelected, and in 1964 he took the additional step of having himself declared president for life. In the early 1960s, Haiti and the Dominican Republic almost came to blows, but war was averted by the diplomatic intervention of the OAS. Opposition to the Duvalier regime gathered momentum in the mid-1960s, especially among Haitian exiles who attempted an abortive invasion in 1967. When Papa Doc died in 1971, he was succeeded by his son, Jean-Claude (Baby Doc) Duvalier, who continued to rule in the repressive fashion established by his father. Severe drought in Haiti in the late 1970s, followed by the devastation of Hurricane Allen in 1980, added to the economic misery of the country and provoked substantial emigration. Haiti, under the Duvalier dynastic rule, suffered from the distinction of being the Western Hemisphere's poorest country, beleaguered by pervasive squalor and often 50 percent unemployment. In 1986, Baby Doc Duvalier fled the country, seeking asylum in France and ending twenty-eight years of Duvalier rule. But domestic instability continued as voters sought to establish a constitutional democracy in the midst of ongoing instability and under the shadow of military takeover. Elections in January 1988 led to the formation of a short-lived democratic government, which was overthrown in a military coup in June. Daily human rights violations continued during 1988, sometimes attributable to government or police forces but often owing to the incapacity of the police apparatus to prevent uncoordinated violence. This pervasive climate was punctuated in September by brutal attacks on churchgoers that led to numerous deaths and injuries. UN human rights bodies monitored the situation in Haiti during this time and recommended the return to constitutional democracy, begun with the establishment of a democratic constitution in 1987 in the wake of Baby Doc Duvalier's flight from the country. The process of attaining democracy gained momentum in

October 1990. At that time the General Assembly approved the establishment of the United Nations Observer Group for the Verification of the Elections in Haiti (ONUVEH), in which it directed the secretary-general to
oversee and assist Haiti's electoral process. In December 1990, under the
watchful eye of ONUVEH, Haitians elected Jean-Bertrand Aristide as president of Haiti. This tenuous achievement was undertaken in a country with
virtually no tradition of democratic political rule and in a country afflicted
by widespread illiteracy. Still ONUVEH certified the elections as being
generally free and fair, if marred by some irregularities.

Aristide was sworn into office on 7 February 1990 and overthrown by a
military coup d'état on 29 September 1990. The UN Security Council met
without taking action, but the General Assembly condemned the military
takeover and called for the immediate restoration of democracy. It continued to recognize the exiled Aristide government as the legitimate representative of the Haitian people in a resolution adopted by consensus on 11
October 1991. However, the OAS, not the United Nations, proved to be the
central arena in which diplomacy to restore democracy was undertaken to
place sanctions on the new regime and to cooperate with the United Nations High Commissioner for Refugees (UNHCR) in handling the growing
refugee flows from Haiti. The United Nations cooperated in these OAS activities during 1992, and the General Assembly called upon states to join
the OAS nations in refraining from supplying arms, ammunition, or oil to
the military regime.

HISTORY OF THE DEBATE

A direct role for the United Nations in the Haiti crisis began in 1993.
Acting upon a General Assembly recommendation in 1992, the secretary-general presented a report to the General Assembly in March 1993
containing recommendations that the United Nations join the OAS in the
deployment of an international civilian mission in Haiti to monitor the human rights situation. The UN Special Envoy for Haiti, Marc Bazin, whose
position was authorized in December 1992, reported on progress achieved
in negotiations between Aristide and the military regime indicating acceptance of implementation of such a civilian mission. On 20 April 1993, the
General Assembly established the International Civilian Mission to Haiti
(MICIVIH). MICIVIH reports subsequently detailed the human rights
abuses of the Haitian military government.

On 7 June 1993, the Aristide government called upon the Security Council to impose a mandatory embargo on arms, munitions, and oil against the
military regime in order to put international pressure on it to agree to the return of his legitimately elected government. On 16 June in a unanimous action the Security Council invoked such sanctions under Chapter VII of the
Charter, in Resolution 841 sponsored by France, the United States, and Ven-

ezuela. In the meantime, a combined diplomatic initiative by the UN Special Envoy for Haiti and OAS Special Representative Dante Caputo of Argentina led to talks between President Aristide and Commander-in-Chief of the Armed Forces of Haiti, General Raoul Cedrás. These talks eventually led to the Governor's Island Agreement of 3 July, which permitted the return of Aristide as president by 31 October 1993. The New York Pact of 16 July demonstrated further action to resolve the Haitian situation. Under these circumstances, the secretary-general recommended a suspension of the sanctions imposed in June. The Security Council responded on 27 August with a suspension of the sanctions as a means of fostering the ongoing dialogue. This agreement, among other things, provided for the insertion of UN personnel to assist in the modernization of Haiti's army and police forces. The Security Council decided to authorize the deployment of an advance mission to make possible the initiation of the United Nations Mission in Haiti (UNMIH) on 31 August, which in turn would help to pave the way toward the stable return of democratic government to Haiti by providing advice and support to the military and civilian police forces. Fuller deployment of UNMIH was authorized by the Council on 23 September. Advance deployments of UNMIH forces were subsequently made; however, the military government refused to allow the deployment of further UNMIH units on 11 October, and the situation deteriorated, indicating the military regime's reluctance to fully implement the Governor's Island Agreement. On 16 October, the Security Council reinvoked sanctions against Haiti, and the bulk of the UNMIH forces and the MICIVIH were withdrawn.

The situation in Haiti continued to worsen during the early months of 1994, even as the UN Special Representative worked with the Four Friends of the secretary-general—namely, the governments of Canada, France, the United States, and Venezuela—to get the Governor's Island Agreement back on track. MICIVIH returned to Haiti in January 1994 and reported a deterioration of the human rights situation. MICIVIH was briefly withdrawn from Haiti during the summer, owing to the adverse security situation. In May 1994, the Security Council tightened sanctions on the military government of Haiti. This action, of imposing sanctions, like the earlier action, was seen by members of the Security Council as an exceptional case, not to be interpreted as setting a precedent under the UN Charter or international law. China made a statement to this effect after passage of the 6 May Security Council resolution calling for a tightening of sanctions. With the situation in Haiti deteriorating in late July, the Security Council approved, on 31 July, Resolution 940, which authorized member states to form a Multinational Force (MNF) for Haiti under Chapter VII of the Charter, with the right to use all necessary means to facilitate the departure of the military regime. This resolution was adopted by a vote of 12 to 0, with 2 abstentions (Brazil and China). China did not believe that military means could be productively used to solve Haiti's situation, and it viewed the practice of authorizing some member states to take force as setting an inappropriate and dangerous precedent. Brazil noted that defense of democracy did not warrant the use of force.

The United States, operating under the authority of Resolution 940, prepared to use military force against the military regime in September. A flurry of private diplomacy in the early weeks of September allowed U.S. military forces to deploy without military opposition on 19 September, as Cedrás agreed to step down on 18 September. By 22 September about 10,000 U.S. troops were deployed, enhancing the security situation in Haiti. On 29 September, the Council voted to redeploy UNMIH and MICIVIH and to end the economic sanctions upon the return of President Aristide. Brazil and the Russian Federation abstained on the resolution, which otherwise received 13 favorable votes. Both governments expressed doubts in this and subsequent expansions of the UNMIH force about the haste of the deployment and about the terms on which it was being undertaken. On 15 October, President Aristide returned to Haiti, and the Council formally ended the sanctions. With the redeployment of the UNMIH, MNF forces began a gradual transition program involving withdrawal and the handing over of the maintenance of civil order to UNMIH, which began in the spring of 1995. By the fall of 1995, UNMIH forces had reached a level of nearly 6,000 troops, supplemented by several hundred civilian police and other international personnel, with twenty-six countries supplying various contingents.

OUTCOME OF THE DEBATE

With the security situation in Haiti improving in 1996, the UNMIH was terminated and replaced by the United Nations Support Mission in Haiti (UNSMIH) in July. The UNSMIH was in turn replaced in July 1997 with the deployment of a follow-up police training mission known as the UN Transition Mission in Haiti, which was deployed from August to November 1997, and then by the UN Civilian Police Mission in Haiti from December 1997 to the spring of 2000. Gradually the United Nations has been able, through its training of Haitian police forces, to help restore a greater degree of predictability and stability to the maintenance of civil order in Haiti.

The longer-term problem of Haiti, namely, its pervasive poverty, has not been successfully addressed, despite a range of multilateral and bilateral assistance programs. As long as poverty remains so widespread, there is always the possibility that Haiti's violent and unstable past could be reignited. Human rights violations, though reduced compared to the period of military rule, remain a problem in a country whose experience with truly democratic governance is so recent and short-lived. The UN presence, which ended in the spring of 2000, was calculated to support the develop-

UN troops on parade during a ceremony mark the transfer of command from the Multinational Force in Haiti led by U.S. forces to the United Nations Mission in Haiti (UNMIH) on 31 March 1995. UN/DPI Photo E. Schneider

ment of a more reliable and deeply rooted civic culture. But the success of this effort remains tenuous at this early stage, and its long-term success will be secured only by an ongoing commitment of the people of Haiti and its government to democratic principles.

See also Refugees and Stateless Persons (Debate 4).

FOR FURTHER READING

Gibbons, Elizabeth. *Sanctions in Haiti*. Baltimore: Center for Strategic and International Studies, 1999.
Kumar, Chetan. *Building Peace in Haiti*. Boulder, CO: Lynne Rienner, 1998.
Rotberg, Robert I., ed. *Haiti Renewed: Political and Economic Prospects*. Washington, DC: Brookings Institute, 1997.
Shacochis, Bob. *The Immaculate Invasion*. New York: Viking, 1999.

Rwandan Civil War (1993)

SIGNIFICANCE OF THE ISSUE

The international response to the genocide in Rwanda was marked by apathy and tardy action, charges eventually reiterated in a United Nations (UN) report critical of its own sins of omission. The failure was one attributable not only to the United Nations but to the major powers who chose to ignore, rather than respond to, the atrocities unleashed in 1994 by Hutu extremists against the Tutsi minority and Hutu sympathizers. Despite the lukewarm response, the UN Security Council did follow-up reports of the atrocities with the establishment of a War Crimes Tribunal for Rwanda.

BACKGROUND TO THE DEBATE

Rwanda is inhabited by two distinct peoples, the Hutu, who constitute about 90 percent of the population, and the Tutsi, who account for about 10 percent. The latter migrated into Rwanda in the 1400s to 1500s and established themselves as the dominant ruling class. Although Hutus and Tutsis lived among one another for centuries without major conflict, the colonial period tended to exaggerate the wealth and political status of Tutsis at the expense of Hutus, raising the resentment of the latter, especially when at independence the Tutsis pushed to establish a postcolonial system that would perpetuate their influence and political power. Violence between Hutus and Tutsis broke out in 1959, provoking thousands of Tutsis to flee into neighboring countries. Hutus won control of Rwanda at independence in 1962. Violence broke out again in 1963–1964 when Hutus retaliated against Tutsis owing to exiled Tutsi groups undertaking raids into Rwanda. About 20,000 Tutsis were killed, and animosities between the two groups grew, then broke out again in 1972–1973.

The ascension of Juvenal Habyarimana as president ushered in a fifteen-year period of improved Hutu-Tutsi relations, until exiled Tutsis in

Uganda formed the Rwandan Patriotic Front (RPF) and began to make incursions into northern Rwanda in 1990. Habyarimana began to face strong opposition within his own government as right-wing Hutu extremists began to openly call for the extermination of Tutsis. As the RPF rebellion gained steam, Habyarimana was forced to negotiate and conclude a deal with the RPF that instituted a provisional government. Hutu extremists shot down a plane carrying Habyarimana on 6 April 1994, and in the weeks that followed, they unleashed a vicious campaign of extermination against the Tutsi population, in which Tutsis and Hutus who demurred from joining the killing were alike murdered by the hundreds of thousands.

HISTORY OF THE DEBATE

UN involvement inside Rwanda began in the context of the hopeful setting of the Arusha Peace Agreement between RPF leader Paul Kagame and President Habyarimana, in which the two agreed to the establishment of a broad-based transitional government until democratic elections could be held. The RPF had established military control by that time over much of Northeastern Rwanda, and Habyarimana hoped to prevent a total collapse of his government. To supervise and help implement the Arusha Agreement both Kagame and Habyarimana asked that the United Nations deploy forces to assist in the effort. The Security Council established the United Nations Assistance Mission for Rwanda (UNAMIR) on 5 October 1993. In an earlier resolution of 22 June 1993, the Security Council had deployed a United Nations Observer Mission Uganda-Rwanda (UNOMUR) on the Ugandan side of its border with Rwanda to ensure that no military assistance reached Rwanda from Uganda. Although the UNAMIR forces were deployed, mainly in Kigali, Rwanda's capital, when the genocide broke out in April and May, it remained largely confined to barracks as the slaughter occurred all around. UN Secretary-General Boutros Boutros-Ghali called for a cease-fire as the RPF resumed operations in face of the genocide under way. The UN effort to call for a cease-fire, as though both the RPF and the Hutu extremists left in control of the Rwandan government were responsible for the unfolding slaughter, eventually convinced the RPF to make a determined assault on Kigali and to seize the entire country, as it became clear that neither UNAMIR nor any other outside force would do anything to stop the carnage. The Security Council on 21 April reduced the size of the UNAMIR force and simultaneously called for an end to the "senseless" violence, as though words rather than troops could do anything to halt the genocide. Actions such as these convinced the RPF that the United Nations was totally unreliable, that it must take matters into its own hand to stop the genocide. On 17 May the Council decided to expand UNAMIR in order to protect refugees and civilians. The UN Human Rights Commission subsequently undertook investigative missions into Rwanda. The Security Council later undertook to investigate human rights violations on 1 July.

France, acting under Security Council authorization, did send a force known as Operation Turquoise on 22 June, as RPF armies advanced against retreating Rwandan government forces. Operation Turquoise took up positions in the south and eastern portions of Rwanda where the RPF had yet to advance. Hutu refugees fled into these areas fearing reprisals by the Tutsi-dominated RPF, and Operation Turquoise was able to provide some humanitarian relief. However, among those receiving relief were Hutus who had perpetrated the genocide. Where French troops were deployed, massacres did cease over time, but the situation in Rwanda was highly fluid, and eventually over 800,000 Hutus fled into neighboring Zaire, or to Tanzania, fearing RPF reprisals. In July the RPF had succeeded in controlling virtually all of Rwanda and the humanitarian problems now shifted to the neighboring countries. A UN relief assessment mission visited Rwanda in late July, but by this time the world was paying more attention to the massive flows of Hutus out of Rwanda and the desperate conditions in the refugee camps. International response to the Hutu situation consisted principally of humanitarian assistance to the camps, which nonetheless remained a security nightmare, especially in Zaire (Congo) where the Hutu militias and government officials responsible for the genocide maintained

Young Rwandan refugee children cry for their mothers at Ndosha camp in Goma, Zaire (Congo). UN/DPI Photo John Isaac

control of the camps. Thus the international community, though helping many innocent Hutus, also aided and abetted the ongoing programs and intentions of the most murderous elements of Rwandan society. The security conditions in the camps where armed Hutu militias ruled by intimidation eventually destabilized the political situation in Zaire and provoked an armed uprising by Banyamulenge Tutsis of the eastern Congo who resented the destabilization of their regions by militant Hutu refugees.

In November 1994, the UN Security Council established an international tribunal for war crimes in Rwanda, by a vote of 13 to 1 (Rwanda), with 1 abstention (China). In the meantime, attention turned to how conditions inside Rwanda could be improved so as to permit the repatriation of refugees, who languished in insecure camps along the border. The security situation was so bad that many nongovernmental organizations(NGOs) had withdrawn their operations. In November 1996, Tanzania closed the refugee camps, forcing the inhabitants to return to Rwanda. In Zaire, the chaos caused by the Hutu refugees, and the undisciplined troops of President Mobutu Sese Seko, Zaire's longtime strongman, provoked an open rebellion, which eventually overthrew the Mobutu regime. Banyamulenge support for Laurent Kabila contributed to his successful effort against Mobutu, but in time Kabila also alienated his Banyamulenge supporters, who undertook yet another rebellion to overthrow him. By failing to deal effectively with the Rwandan crisis the international community unwittingly contributed to further instabilities in the Great Lakes region and in all of Central Africa. In the meantime, faced with military pressure and virtually forced to quit the refugee camps in the Goma area, hundreds of thousands of Hutus reluctantly decided to repatriate, while tens of thousands of others fled deep into the jungles of the Congo, creating a further nightmare for themselves and for the humanitarian agencies that still endeavored to help them.

OUTCOME OF THE DEBATE

The violence of Rwanda in 1994 spilled over into Zaire in 1995 to 1996, leading eventually to the overthrow of Mobutu's rule in 1997 and to an ongoing civil war that became continental in scope as one African nation after another joined the fray in the Congo. This is but one legacy of the United Nations' and international community's largely botched response to the Rwandan civil war and genocide. A report undertaken under the auspices of the United Nations to examine its own role in the Rwandan dispute found that the United Nations had been tardy in its response and woefully inadequate. Secretary-General Kofi Annan, who was in charge of the peacekeeping aspects of the United Nations at the time, came in for heavy criticism. As secretary-general he has apologized to the Rwandan people and has indicated his regrets that he and the United Nations had not done more to respond to the suffering of the Rwandan people. However, the major powers were equally if not more responsible, for they are the only ones who could have provided sufficient force quickly enough to stop the carnage. The administration of Bill Clinton, having just extricated itself from the disastrous Somalia operation, decided simply to ignore the Rwanda agony as a politically inexpedient and inopportune situation to address. Clinton, too, has apologized for his acts of omission.

The war crimes tribunals both inside and outside of Rwanda continue to prosecute many accused of violations of international humanitarian law. Slowly, Rwanda recovers from the trauma of war and genocide, but the scars are deep, and its government continues to chastise the world for its glaring apathy in the face of the humanitarian enormities it was forced to endure. The death of Laurent Kabilah in January 2001 and the accession of his son Joseph as president of the Congo gives rise to new hope for the prospect of implementing the July 1999 peace agreement.

See also Genocide (Debate 9); Human Rights (Debate 10); Refugees and Stateless Persons (Debate 4).

FOR FURTHER READING

Adelman, Howard, and Astri Suhrke. *The Rwanda Crisis from Uganda to Zaire*. New Brunswick, NJ: Transaction Publications, 1999.
Boutros-Ghali, Boutros. *The United Nations in Rwanda 1993–1996*. New York: UN Publications, 1996.
Klinghoffer, Arthur Jay. *The International Dimensions of Genocide in Rwanda*. New York: New York University Press, 1998.
Prunier, Gerard. *The Rwanda Crisis: History of a Genocide*. New York: Columbia University Press, 1995.
UN Chronicles, 1993–1999.

Kosovo Situation (1998)

SIGNIFICANCE OF THE ISSUE

International action on Kosovo represented the first time that the North Atlantic Treaty Organization (NATO) had formally undertaken war against a nonmember state without authorization by the United Nations (UN) Security Council. The action, justified on humanitarian grounds, precipitated a Serbian ethnic cleansing, and a huge flow of refugees ensued. Russian and Chinese opposition to the NATO action illustrated that the UN Security Council, though more active in the wake of the end of the Cold War, was still liable to the veto. Where great power interests are at stake, as they were in Kosovo, the whole episode illustrated that such powers would act to protect them, regardless of apparent inconsistencies with the UN Charter.

BACKGROUND TO THE DEBATE

The conflict in Kosovo has roots that extend back for several centuries. The original inhabitants of the area were Illyrians, today known as Albanians. However, in the twelfth century, Serbs began to settle in and to dominate the region. In the fourteenth century, Ottoman Turks moved into the Balkan peninsula to expand their conquests beyond the Byzantine empire. Serbian forces met them in battle in 1389 in northern Kosovo and were defeated. The long-term presence of the Turks led to a substantial adherence of the Illyrian population to Islam, though the Serbs, now an increasingly small minority of the population, clung to Greek Orthodoxy. Instability in the entire Balkans continued into the early part of the twentieth century and were a chief cause of the outbreak of World War I. With the defeat of the Ottoman Turks, Ottoman colonial holdings were divided up among various members of the League of Nations after World War I. Kosovo was awarded to the newly formed Kingdom of Yugoslavia. During World War II, the rise of the Yugoslavian resistance to Nazi occupation propelled Josip

Broz, later known as Tito, to power. Tito took the helm of Yugoslavia after the war. His strong-handed regime ruled on the basis of ethnic consensus, and during this time Kosovo was granted autonomous provincial status in 1974 within the Yugoslav Federation. By that time, Albanians constituted about 85 percent of the population, with Serbs making up most of the other 15 percent.

While Tito ruled, the natural divisiveness of the Balkans was moderated and suppressed. However, with his death in 1980, the country reverted to a collective presidency in which leaders of each of the federated republics and autonomous provinces rotated in succession. This arrangement proved unworkable, however, and gradually the separatist tendencies of the region manifested themselves. In the early 1990s, Slovenia, Croatia, and then Bosnia-Herzegovina sought and achieved independence, in the case of Croatia and Bosnia-Herzegovina only after extensive and bloody wars with the government in Belgrade, which was dominated by the Serbs, as was the military. In the context of the dismemberment of Yugoslavia, Serbian nationalist sentiments grew as fears spread that it might become a landlocked state. The Former Yugoslav Republic of Macedonia (FYROM) bolted from Yugoslavia in 1993. Yugoslavia consisted of only Serbia, Montenegro, and Kosovo, and the latter provinces enjoyed a degree of autonomy.

President Slobodan Milosevic assured Serbian Kosovar in the late 1980s that he would never retreat from Kosovo, and he revoked the province's autonomous status in 1989, provoking widespread opposition among Kosovar Albanians. During the 1995 Dayton Peace Talks, the issue of Kosovo was not discussed, owing in part to Milosevic's insistence that its status was nonnegotiable. Western powers deferred to this, hoping to win a settlement to the bloody and protracted civil war in Bosnia, where eventually the Serbian population was granted autonomous republic status.

The move by Serbia to deny Kosovar Albanians a capacity to provide their own education and other social services further excited popular resentment. In 1996, a variety of armed resistance groups began to oppose Serbian police and military repression by unleashing terrorist attacks on government installations and forces. This evoked even more repression on the part of Serbia. Tens of thousands of Kosovar Albanians fled as refugees, as the civil instability and conflict spread. Worries mounted in the international community that Kosovo could become the next Bosnia. In this context the UN Security Council began to take notice of the issue.

HISTORY OF THE DEBATE

Given the growing violence in Kosovo, the UN Security Council decided on 31 March 1998 to impose an arms embargo on the Federal Republic of Yugoslavia (FRY) under Chapter VII of the Charter. The prohibitions included an obligation by governments not to arm terrorist groups including the various factions of the Kosovar Liberation Army (KLA) or to foster terrorist acts. The Resolution (1160) was adopted by a vote of 14 to 0, with 1 abstention (China). The resolution also called upon the FRY and the Kosovar Albanian community to peacefully resolve their differences, and in regard to the latter it asked for an explicit condemnation of terrorist actions by KLA factions in the hopes that Kosovo might eventually qualify for enhanced status with a larger degree of autonomy and self-administration. It called upon the FRY to engage in real dialogue with Kosovar Albanian leaders to resolve the situation peacefully, to withdraw the special police units and security forces that had terrorized the civilian population, and to allow access by humanitarian agencies.

In subsequent months, it became clear that the KLA was being armed through ties to Albania. President Boris Yeltsin of Russia attempted to initiate a diplomatic solution to the problem, but the situation deteriorated. The FRY insisted that Kosovo was an integral part of its territory and that it had a right to suppress the terrorist acts of the KLA. The problem was that the special police and security forces were engaging in a policy of reprisals against the civilian Kosovar Albanian population as a form of collective punishment to convince them not to support the KLA. Thus, on 24 October, the Security Council took further steps to cope with the deepening crisis in Kosovo in passing Resolution 1203 by a vote of 13 to 0, with 2 abstentions (China and Russia). By this decision, the Security Council called for the FRY and the Kosovar Albanians to comply with its previous resolution, to agree to an immediate cease-fire, and to withdraw FRY security forces. The Council supported the Organization for Security and Cooperation in Europe (OSCE) mission to introduce human rights monitors and, with the NATO air surveillance program, to verify compliance with Security Council resolutions. The Council demanded that the Kosovar Albanian leadership immediately condemn all acts of terrorism. The Chinese abstention was based on its opposition to the Council's invocation of Chapter VII of the Charter, which China believed was unnecessary, while the Russian representative pointed out that there was not consensus that the Kosovar situation constituted an international threat to peace, being contained to a province of Serbia. While the security situation in Kosovo seemed to improve, several thousand people had been displaced, and some evidence of FRY security forces reprisals against civilians was still in evidence. The OSCE and NATO missions that were agreed to in October promised to monitor the situation, in the case of the OSCE by deploying 2,000 human rights monitors throughout Kosovo. Efforts by the international Contact Group, including France, Germany, Italy, Russia, the United Kingdom, and the United States, to pursue negotiations was commended, and the Council, by an earlier resolution, had urged all parties to undertake humanitarian assistance to the displaced populations.

In the early months of 1999, despite the deployment of the OSCE verification mission in Kosovo, evidence of ongoing KLA fighting and reprisals by the FRY continued. Belgrade declared the head of the OSCE Mission persona non grata, and OSCE Verification Mission personnel were attacked in January. In late January the Contact Group met in London to establish a political framework for the peace talks, which were initiated by the Contact Group at Rambouillet, France. There they attempted to impose a settlement on Serbia and the KLA, calling on both to immediately permit the imposition of NATO ground forces and calling on Serbia to withdraw from Kosovo, permitting it to resume its autonomous status, revoked by the FRY in 1989. KLA elements initially refused to agree to this arrangement owing to the fact that they sought complete independence from Serbia, but they eventually agreed to it, realizing that Serbia, in refusing, would suffer bombing by NATO. Serbia, despite being threatened with bombing by the NATO countries, refused to sign the agreement under that form of duress, arguing that Kosovo was under its jurisdiction and that its status as part of Yugoslavia was nobody else's business. It flatly rejected the idea of NATO troops on its soil as an infringement of its national sovereignty. With this Serbian refusal to agree to the ultimatum delivered by NATO powers at Rambouillet, NATO was left with following through with its bombing threat or appearing to lose credibility. Russia implored the NATO countries to desist from bombing, but these pleas were ignored, and NATO, without authorization of the Security Council, commenced bombing on 24 March. This sidestepping of the only world body authorized legally to conduct such a collective security action took place because NATO countries knew full well that Russia and China would veto any such action by the Security Council itself.

In the wake of the bombing, which was declared necessary to prevent a humanitarian catastrophe in Kosovo by NATO powers, one of the worst humanitarian catastrophes in Europe since World War II unfolded. As the bombing took its own toll in lives and property, the Serbian security forces began a campaign of reprisals against the local Kosovar Albanian population, which was now possible owing to the fact that OSCE human rights monitors were evacuated prior to the bombing. Moreover, Serbia could blame the deaths and refugee exodus on the bombing itself. This ploy did not deceive much of the world, even though evidence did exist that some Kosovar Albanians were killed in various NATO bombing incidents. The Serbian effort to terrorize the Albanian population, appears to have been a selective effort to scare them so that they would flee out of the country, thereby achieving an ethnic cleansing of the region. About 10,000 Kosovar Albanians were brutally murdered by Serbian forces to this end, although NATO spokespersons exaggerated the carnage as a justification for continued bombing. Within a few months 850,000 Kosovar Albanians had fled into neighboring countries, mainly Albania, where an unprepared international community struggled to meet their needs.

The bombing by NATO was opposed by both Russia and China, and China's embassy in Belgrade was destroyed by a NATO attack, giving rise to angry protests, which NATO apologies did little to soften. Russia and China sought a Security Council decision to condemn and cease the bombing, but because the NATO initiative was well under way, they could not muster adequate support on the Council for such a measure, despite the misgivings of many UN delegations about the manner in which the NATO powers had ignored the UN Charter. A Yugoslavian suit before the International Court of Justice (ICJ) seeking to obtain orders for a halt to the bombing was rejected by the ICJ on the grounds that it lacked jurisdiction to entertain them. However, the Court stressed that all countries were obliged to abide by international law and were responsible for their actions in contravention of treaties and customary international law, including humani-

The International Court of Justice (ICJ) meets in chambers at The Hague, Netherlands. In 1999 the ICJ ruled that it did not have jurisdiction to hear cases brought by the Former Republic of Yugoslav against NATO members for commission of aggression against Serbian territory in connection with the Kosovo conflict. UN/DPI Photo A. Brizzi

tarian law, and it also stressed that the peaceful settlement of disputes and collective action against aggression were the special purview of the Security Council under Chapter VII of the UN Charter. Thus the Court aimed sharp language at both Yugoslavia and the NATO powers.

After weeks of bombing, in which not only Kosovo but much of the infrastructure of Serbia was targeted, Slobodon Milosevic agreed on 3 June to withdraw Serbian forces from Kosovo and to submit to a NATO occupation of the region that would enforce a demobilization of KLA forces. On 10 June, the Security Council welcomed the end of the violence and the Serbian agreement to a political resolution of the dispute; and acting under Chapter VII of the Charter, it decided to deploy both a civilian and a military force to the region, under the United Nations Interim Administration Mission in Kosovo (UNMIK). A force consisting of NATO allies and Russian troops (International Force in Kosovo [KFOR]) would bear the initial brunt of the peacekeeping activity. The resolution was adopted by a vote of 14 to 0, with 1 abstention (China). During the course of the debate a number of countries expressed concern about the way in which NATO had proceeded in the use of force. Brazil, Cuba, Mexico, and Russia expressed reservations about NATO's marginalization of the United Nations and its ignoring of the Security Council role under the Charter. China observed that NATO, though proclaiming to avoid a humanitarian crisis, had actually provoked one. Gambia and Namibia regretted that violence had been necessary. The United States and the West European governments placed the blame squarely on Yugoslavia's intransigence.

OUTCOME OF THE DEBATE

With the arrival of KFOR units in Kosovo to ensure security, the refugee populations in neighboring countries began to stream back into Kosovo almost as rapidly as they had left, especially when it became clear that the Serbians were making good on their promise to withdraw forces. The first UNMIK units also began arriving on 13 June, and within a month UNMIK had finalized a comprehensive operation to rebuild civil administration including the judicial and police systems, to provide humanitarian assistance, to rebuild local institutions, and to reconstruct the physical infrastructure. Various UN or regional bodies took the lead in performing these functions. UNHCR took the lead in humanitarian assistance, the UNMIK representatives took the lead in rebuilding civil administration, whereas the OSCE took responsibility for rebuilding local institutions, and the European Union took the lead in reconstruction and development aid.

With the massive return of the Kosovar Albanians, there commenced a massive exodus of some 130,000 Serbian Kosovars fearing reprisals, fears that were not unjustified. As KLA forces resisted disarmament in the early stages of the international deployment in Kosovo, the KFOR seemed helpless to stop KLA attacks against civilian Serbs, provoking even more of the latter to flee. In the meantime, evidence of the Serbian ethnic cleansing was discovered by KFOR units, and the International War Crimes Tribunal began gathering evidence for legal action against the perpetrators. Milosevic himself was indicted in late May on war crimes, along with other members of his government.

The sad legacy of the Kosovo affair is that one form of ethnic cleansing has been replaced by another, despite the presence of KFOR and of UNMIK. The length of time that will be necessary to achieve any lasting peace in Kosovo is unknown, nor is there any real limit on the extension of the international mandates, although in theory elections will be held to determine the future status of the region within Serbia. The reality is that Kosovar Albanians still desire independence, which remains unacceptable to Serbia and unpalatable to other countries in the region with large Albanian minorities.

The long legacy of hatred and ethnic animosity that afflicts this region is unlikely to be genuinely resolved any time soon by international involvement. Indeed, the legacy of violence, including the NATO bombing, will no doubt linger for a very long time in a region where grudges and feuds last for centuries. For now, the UNMIK operation attempts to cope with the here and now in a country where once and future animosities are easily ignited.

See also Balkan Civil Wars (Debate 45); Genocide (Debate 9); Human Rights (Debate 10); Refugees and Stateless Persons (Debate 4).

FOR FURTHER READING

Anzulovic, Branimer. *Heavenly Serbia: From Myth to Genocide*. New York: New York University Press, 1999.

Banac, Ivo. *The National Question in Yugoslavia: Origins, History, Politics*. Ithaca, NY: Cornell University Press, 1984.

Campbell, Greg. *The Road to Kosovo: A Balkan Diary*. Boulder, CO: Westview Press, 1999.

Gow, James. *Triumph of the Lack of Will: International Diplomacy and the Yugoslav War*. New York: Columbia University Press, 1997.

Malcolm, Noel. *Kosovo: A Short History*. New York: HarperPerennial, 1999.

UN Chronicles, 1998–1999.

APPENDIXES

Appendix 1

UN Structure

THE UNITED NATIONS SYSTEM

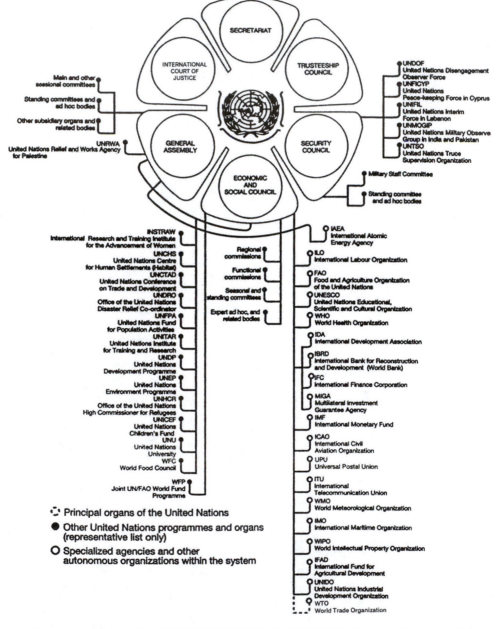

Source: Bennett, A. LeRoy, INTERNATIONAL ORGANIZATIONS: Principles & Issues 6/e ©
1995. Adapted by permission of Prentice-Hall, Inc., Upper Saddle River, NJ.

Appendix 2

Member States by Year of Admission

1945   Founding Members: Argentina, Australia, Byelorussia (Belarus), Belgium, Bolivia, Brazil, Canada, Chile, China, Colombia, Costa Rica, Cuba, Czechoslovakia (since 1993 the Czech Republic and the Slovak Republic), Denmark, Dominican Republic, Ecuador, Egypt, El Salvador, Ethiopia, France, Greece, Guatemala, Haiti, Honduras, India, Iran, Iraq, Lebanon, Liberia, Luxembourg, Mexico, Netherlands, New Zealand, Nicaragua, Norway, Panama, Paraguay, Peru, Philippines, Poland, Russian Federation (formerly the Soviet Union), Saudi Arabia, South Africa (formerly the Union of South Africa), Syria, Turkey, Ukraine, United Kingdom, United States, Uruguay, Venezuela, Yugoslavia (now the Former Republic of Yugoslavia)

1946   Afghanistan, Iceland, Sweden, Thailand

1947   Pakistan, Yemen

1948   Myanmar (formerly Burma)

1949   Israel

1950   Indonesia

1955   Albania, Austria, Bulgaria, Cambodia, Finland, Hungary, Ireland, Italy, Jordan, Lao People's Democratic Republic (Laos), Libyan Arab Jamahiriya (Libya), Nepal, Portugal, Romania, Spain, Sri Lanka (formerly Ceylon)

1956   Japan, Morocco, Sudan, Tunisia

1957   Ghana, Malaysia

1958   Guinea

1960   Benin (formerly Dahomey), Burkina Faso (formerly Upper Volta), Cameroon, Central African Republic, Chad, Congo (Brazzaville), Côte d'Ivoire (Ivory Coast), Cyprus, Democratic Republic of the Congo (formerly the Congo [Leopoldville] and then Zaire), Gabon, Madagascar, Mali, Niger, Nigeria, Senegal, Somalia, Togo

1961	Mauritania, Mongolia, Sierra Leone, United Republic of Tanzania
1962	Algeria, Burundi, Jamaica, Rwanda, Trinidad and Tobago, Uganda
1963	Kenya, Kuwait
1964	Malawi, Malta, Zambia
1965	Gambia, Maldives, Singapore
1966	Barbados, Botswana, Guyana, Lesotho
1968	Equatorial Guinea, Mauritius, Swaziland
1970	Fiji
1971	Bahrain, Bhutan, Oman, Qatar, United Arab Emirates
1973	Bahamas, Germany (originally admitted as the Federal Republic of Germany and the German Democratic Republic and now united as Germany)
1974	Bangladesh, Grenada, Guinea-Bissau
1975	Cape Verde, Comoros, Mozambique, Papua New Guinea, Sao Tome and Principe, Suriname
1976	Angola, Samoa, Seychelles
1977	Djibouti, Vietnam
1978	Dominica, Solomon Islands
1979	Saint Lucia
1980	Saint Vincent and the Grenadines, Zimbabwe
1981	Antigua and Barbuda, Belize, Vanuatu
1983	Saint Kitts and Nevis
1984	Brunei Darussalam
1990	Liechtenstein, Namibia
1991	Democratic People's Republic of Korea, Estonia, Latvia, Lithuania, Marshall Islands, Micronesia (Federated States of), Republic of Korea
1992	Armenia, Azerbaijan, Bosnia and Herzegovina, Croatia, Georgia, Kazakhstan, Kyrgyzstan, Republic of Moldova, San Marino, Slovenia, Tajikistan, Turkmenistan, Uzbekistan
1993	Andorra, Czech Republic, Eritrea, Monaco, Slovak Republic, The Former Republic of Macedonia
1994	Pulau
1999	Kiribati, Nauru, Tonga

Source: *UN Chronicle.*

Appendix 3

General Assembly Special and Emergency Sessions

1947	Special Session on Palestine (28 Apr.–15 May)
1948	Special Session on Palestine (16 Apr.–14 May)
1956	Emergency Session on the Suez Crisis (1–10 Nov.)
1956	Emergency Session on the Crisis in Hungary (4–11 Nov.)
1958	Emergency Session on Lebanon (8–21 Aug.)
1960	Emergency Session on the Congo (17–19 Sept.)
1961	Special Session on the Crisis in Tunisia (21–25 Aug.)
1963	Special Session on the UN financial crisis (14–27 June)
1967	Special Session on Namibia (21 Apr.–13 June)
1967	Emergency Session on the Middle East Crisis (17 June – 27 July)
1974	Special Session on Raw Materials and Development (9 Apr.–2 May)
1975	Special Session on the Development of International Economic Cooperation (1–16 Sept.)
1978	Special Session on Disarmament (23 May– 30 June)
1978	Special Session on Financing the UN Interim Force in Lebanon (20–21 Apr.)
1978	Special Session on Namibia (24 Apr.–3 May)
1980	Emergency Session on Afghanistan (10–14 Jan.)
1980	Special Session on International Economic Cooperation (7 Aug.–5 Sept.)
1980	Emergency Session on Palestine (22–29 July)
1981	Emergency Session on Namibia (3–14 Sept.)
1982	Emergency Session on the Occupied Arab Territories (29 Jan.–5 Feb.)

1982   Special Session on Disarmament (26 Apr.–14 May)

1986   Special Session on the Critical Economic Situation in Africa (27 May–1
            June)

1986   Special Session on Namibia (17–20 Sept.)

1988   Special Session on Disarmament (31 May–25 June)

1989   Special Session on Apartheid (12–14 Dec.)

1990   Special Session on Drug Problems (20–23 Feb.)

1990   Special Session on International Economic Cooperation (23 Apr.–1
            May)

1997   Special Session on Earth Summit + 5 (23–27 June)

1998   Special Session on Countering the World Drug Problem (8–10 June)

1999   Special Session on Population and Development (30 June–2 July)

1999   Special Session on Small Island Developing States (27–28 Sept.)

2000   Special Session on Social Development (26 June–1 July)

2000   Special Session on Women 2000: Gender Equality and Peace (5–9 June)

Sources: *UN Yearbooks*; *UN Chronicle.*

Appendix 4 ———————

World Years

1950	UN Demographic Year
1957	UN Geophysical Year
1959–1960	World Refugee Year
1964–1965	International Year of the Quiet Sun
1965	International Year of Cooperation
1968	International Year for Human Rights
1970	International Year of Education International
1971	International Year against Racism and Discrimination
1973	International Copernicus Year
1975	International Year of Women
1982	International Year of Mobilization of Sanctions against South Africa
1983	World Year of Communication
1985–1986	International Year of Peace
1990	International Literacy Year
1992	International Space Year
1993	International Year for the World's Indigenous People
1994	International Year of the Family
1995	United Nations Year for Tolerance
1998	International Year of the Ocean
1999	International Year of Older Persons

Sources: UN Yearbooks; UN Chronicle.

Peacekeeping Operations

UN Truce Supervision Organization (UNTSO), Middle East, June 1948–present

UN Military Observer Group in India and Pakistan (UNMOGIP), Jan. 1949–present

UN Emergency Force I (UNEF I), Middle East, Nov. 1956–June 1967

UN Observation Group in Lebanon (UNOGIL), June 1958–Dec. 1958

UN Operation in the Congo (ONUC), July 1960–June 1964

UN Security Force in West New Guinea [West Irian] (UNSF), Oct. 1962–Apr. 1963

UN Yemen Observation Mission (UNYOM), July 1963–Sept. 1964

UN Peacekeeping Force in Cyprus (UNFICYP), Mar. 1964–present

Mission of the Secretary-General in the Dominican Republic (DOMREP), May 1965–Oct. 1966

UN India-Pakistan Observation Mission (UNIPOM), Sept. 1965–Mar. 1966

UN Emergency Force II (UNEF II), Middle East, Oct. 1973–July 1979

UN Disengagement Observer Force (UNDOF), Golan Heights, June 1974–present

UN Interim Force in Lebanon (UNIFIL), Mar. 1978–present

UN Good Offices Mission in Afghanistan and Pakistan (UNGOMAP), May 1988–Mar. 1990

UN Iran-Iraq Military Observer Group (UNIIMOG), Aug. 1988–Feb. 1991

UN Angola Verification Mission I (UNAVEM I), Jan. 1989–June 1991

UN Transition Assistance Group (UNTAG), Namibia, Apr. 1989–Mar. 1990

UN Observer Group in Central America (ONUCA), Nov. 1989– Jan. 1992

UN Iraq-Kuwait Observation Mission (UNIKOM), Apr. 1991–present

UN Mission for the Referendum in the Western Sahara (MINURSO), Apr. 1991–present

UN Angola Verification Mission II (UNAVEM II), June 1991–Feb. 1995

UN Observer Mission in El Salvador (ONUSAL), July 1991–Apr. 1995

UN Advance Mission in Cambodia (UNAMIC), Oct. 1991–Mar. 1992

UN Protection Force (UNPROFOR), Former Yugoslavia, Mar. 1992–Dec. 1995

UN Transitional Authority in Cambodia (UNTAC), Mar. 1992–Sept. 1993

UN Operation in Somalia I (UNOSOM I), Apr. 1992–Mar. 1993

UN Operation in Mozambique (ONUMOZ), Dec. 1992–Dec. 1994

UN Operation in Somalia II (UNOSOM II), Mar. 1993–Mar. 1995

UN Observer Mission Uganda–Rwanda (UNOMUR), June 1993–Sept. 1994

UN Observer Mission in Georgia (UNOMIG), Aug. 1993–present

UN Observer Mission in Liberia (UNOMIL), Sept. 1993–Sept. 1997

UN Mission in Haiti (UNMIH), Sept. 1993–June 1996

UN Assistance Mission for Rwanda (UNAMIR), Oct. 1993–Mar. 1996

UN Aozou Strip Observer Group (UNASOG), Chad/Libya, May–June 1994

UN Mission of Observers in Tajikistan (UNMOT), Dec. 1994–present

UN Angola Verification Mission III (UNAVEM III), Feb. 1995–June 1997

UN Confidence Restoration Operation in Croatia (UNCRO), Mar. 1995–Jan. 1996

UN Preventive Deployment Force (UNPREDEP), Former Yugoslav Republic of Macedonia, Mar. 1995–Feb. 1999

UN Mission in Bosnia and Herzegovina (UNMIBH), Dec. 1995–present

UN Transitional Administration for Eastern Slavonia, Baranja and Western Sirmium (UNTAES) Croatia, Jan. 1996–Jan. 1998

UN Mission of Observers in Prevlaka (UNMOP), Croatia, Jan. 1996–present

UN Support Mission in Haiti (UNSMIH), July 1996–July 1997

UN Verification Mission in Guatemala (MINUGUA), Jan. 1997–May 1997

UN Observer Mission in Angola (MONUA), July 1997–Feb. 1999

UN Transition Mission in Haiti (UNTMIH), Aug. 1997–Nov. 1997

UN Civilian Police Mission in Haiti (MIPONUH), Dec. 1997–Mar. 2000

UN Civilian Police Support Group (UNCPSG), Croatia, Jan. 1998–present

UN Mission in Central African Republic (MINURCA), Mar. 1998–present

UN Observer Mission in Sierra Leone (UNOMSIL), July 1998–present

UN Interim Administration Mission in Kosovo (UNMIK), June 1999–present

UN Assessment Mission in East Timor (UNAMET), June 1999–Mar. 2000

International Force in East Timor (INTERFET), Sept. 1999–Mar. 2000

UN Transitional Administration in East Timor (UNTAET), Mar. 2000–present

Source: *UN Chronicles*.

Secretaries-General of the United Nations

Trygvie Lie	Finland	1945–1953
Dag Hammarskjöld	Sweden	1953–1961
U Thant	Burma (now Myanmar)	1961–1971
Kurt Waldheim	Austria	1972–1981
Javier Perez de Cuellar	Peru	1982–1991
Boutros Boutros-Ghali	Egypt	1992–1996
Kofi Annan	Ghana	1997–

Appendix 7

Presidents of the General Assembly

Session President	Nationality	Year
1. Paul-Henri Spaak	Belgium	1946
2. Oswaldo Aranha	Brazil	1947
3. H. V. Evatt	Australia	1948
4. Carlos P. Romulo	Philippines	1949
5. Nasrollah Entezam	Iran	1950
6. Luis Padilla Nervo	Mexico	1951
7. Lester B. Pearson	Canada	1952
8. Vijaya Lakshmi Pandit	India	1953
9. Eelco N. van Kleffens	Netherlands	1954
10. José Maza	Chile	1955
11. Prince Wan Waithayakon	Thailand	1956
12. Sir Leslie Munro	New Zealand	1957
13. Charles Malik	Lebanon	1958
14. Víctor Andrés Balaúnde	Peru	1959
15. Frederick H. Boland	Ireland	1960
16. Mongi Slim	Tunisia	1961
17. Sir Muhammad Zafrulla Khan	Pakistan	1962
18. Carlos Sosa Rodríguez	Venezuela	1963
19. Alex Quaison-Sackey	Ghana	1964
20. Amintore Fanfani	Italy	1965
21. Abdul Rahman Pazhwak	Afghanistan	1966
22. Corneliu Manescu	Romania	1967
23. Emilio Arenales Catalán	Guatemala	1968
24. Angie E. Brooks	Liberia	1969

25. Edvard Hambro	Norway	1970
26. Adam Malik	Indonesia	1971
27. Stanislaw Trepczynski	Poland	1972
28. Leopoldo Benites	Ecuador	1973
29. Abdelaziz Bouteflika	Algeria	1974
30. Gaston Thorn	Luxembourg	1975
31. H. S. Amerasinghe	Sri Lanka	1976
32. Lazar Mojsov	Yugoslavia	1977
33. Indalecio Liévano	Colombia	1978
34. Salim A. Salim	United Republic of Tanzania	1979
35. Rüdiger von Wechmar	Federal Republic of Germany	1980
36. Ismat T. Kittani	Iraq	1981
37. Imre Hollai	Hungary	1982
38. Jorge E. Illueca	Panama	1983
39. Paul J. F. Lusaka	Zambia	1984
40. Jaime de Piniés	Spain	1985
41. Humayun Rasheed Choudhury	Bangladesh	1986
42. Peter Florin	German Democratic Republic	1987
43. Dante M. Caputo	Argentina	1988
44. Joseph Nanven Garba	Nigeria	1989
45. Guido de Marco	Malta	1990
46. Samir S. Shihabi	Saudi Arabia	1991
47. Stoyan Ganev	Bulgaria	1992
48. Samuel R. Insanally	Guyana	1993
49. Amara Essy	Côte d'Ivoire	1994
50. Diogo Freitas do Amaral	Portugal	1995
51. Ismail Razali	Malaysia	1996
52. Hennadiy Udovenko	Ukraine	1997
53. Didier Opertii	Uruguay	1998
54. Dr. Theo-Ben Gurirab	Namibia	1999
55. Harri Holkeri	Finland	2000

Source: *UN Chronicles*, 1995–1999.

Appendix 8

Sample Resolutions

UN SECURITY COUNCIL RESOLUTION 242 (1967)

Concerning the Middle East Dispute and the Seven Days War
Adopted unanimously on November 22 at the 1382nd meeting

The Security Council,

Expressing its continuing concern with the grave situation in the Middle East,

Emphasizing the inadmissibility of the acquisition of territory by war and the need to work for a just and lasting peace in which every State in the area can live in security,

Emphasizing further that all Member States in their acceptance of the Charter of the United Nations have undertaken a commitment to act in accordance with Article 2 of the Charter,

1. *Affirms* that the fulfillment of Charter principles requires the establishment of a just and lasting peace in the Middle East which should include the application of both the following principles:

> (i) Withdrawal of Israel armed forces from territories occupied in the recent conflict;
> (ii) Termination of all claims or states of belligerency and respect for and acknowledgment of the sovereignty, territorial integrity and political independence of every State in the area and their right to live in peace within secure and recognized boundaries free from threats or acts of force;

2. *Affirms further* the necessity

> (a) For guaranteeing freedom of navigation through international waterways in the area;
> (b) For achieving a just settlement of the refugee problem;
> (c) For guaranteeing the territorial inviolability and political independence of every State in the area, through measures including the establishment of demilitarized zones;

3. *Requests* the Secretary-General to designate a special representative to proceed to the Middle East to establish and maintain contacts with the States concerned in order to promote agreement and assist efforts to achieve a peaceful and accepted settlement in accordance with the provisions and principles in this resolution;

4. *Requests* the Secretary-General to report to the Security Council on the progress of the efforts of the special representative as soon as possible.

UN GENERAL ASSEMBLY RESOLUTION 377(V): UNITING FOR PEACE 3 NOVEMBER 1950

A

The General Assembly,
Recognizing that the first two stated Purposes of the United Nations are:

"To maintain international peace and security, and to that end: to take effective collective measures for the prevention and removal of threat to the peace, and for the suppression of acts of aggression or other breaches of the peace, and to bring about by peaceful means, and in conformity with the principles of justice and international law, adjustment or settlement of international disputes or situations which might lead to a breach of the peace", and

"To develop friendly relations among nations based on respect for the principle of equal rights and self-determination of peoples, and to take other appropriate measures to strengthen universal peace,"

Reaffirming that it remains the primary duty of all Members of the United Nations, when involved in an international dispute, to seek settlement of such a dispute by peaceful means through the procedures laid down in Chapter VI of the Charter, and recalling the successful achievements of the United Nations in this regard on a number of previous occasions,

Finding that international tension exists on a dangerous scale,

Recalling its resolution 290 (IV) entitled "Essentials of Peace", which states that disregard of the Principles of the Charter of the United Nations is primarily responsible for the continuance of international tension, and desiring to contribute further to the objectives of that resolution,

Reaffirming the importance of the exercise by the Security Council of its primary responsibility for the maintenance of international peace and security, and the duty of the permanent members to seek unanimity and to exercise restraint in the use of the veto,

Reaffirming that the initiative in negotiating the agreements for armed forces provided for in Article 43 of the Charter belongs to the Security Council, and desiring to ensure that, pending the conclusion of such agreements, the United Nations has at its disposal means for maintaining international peace and security,

Conscious that failure of the Security Council to discharge its responsibilities on behalf of all the Member States, particularly those responsibilities referred to in the two preceding paragraphs, does not relieve Member States of their obligations or the United Nations of its responsibility under the Charter to maintain international peace and security,

Recognizing in particular that such failure does not deprive the General Assembly of its rights or relieve it of its responsibilities under the Charter in regard to the maintenance of international peace and security,

Recognizing that discharge by the General Assembly of its responsibilities in these respects calls for possibilities of observation which would ascertain the facts and expose aggressors; for the existence of armed forces which could be used collectively; and for the possibility of timely recommendation by the General Assembly to Members of the United Nations for collective action which, to be effective, should be prompt,

A

1. *Resolves* that if the Security Council, because of lack of unanimity of the permanent members, fails to exercise its primary responsibility for the maintenance of international peace and security in any case where there appears to be a threat to the peace, breach of the peace, or act of aggression, the General Assembly shall consider the matter immediately with a view to making appropriate recommendations to Members for collective measures, including in the case of a breach of the peace or act of aggression the use of armed force when necessary, to maintain or restore international peace and security. If not in session at the time, the General Assembly may meet in emergency special session within twenty-four hours of the request therefor. Such emergency special session shall be called if requested by the Security Council on the vote of any seven members, or by a majority of the Members of the United Nations:

2. *Adopts* for this purpose the amendments to its rules of procedure set forth in the annex to the present resolution;

B

3. *Establishes* a Peace Observation Commission which, for the calendar years 1951 and 1952, shall be composed of fourteen Members, namely: China, Colombia, Czechoslovakia, France, India, Iraq, Israel, New Zealand, Pakistan, Sweden, the Union of Soviet Socialist Republics, the United Kingdom of Great Britain and Northern Ireland, the United States of America and Uruguay, and which could observe and report on the situation in any area where there exists international tension the continuance of which is likely to endanger the maintenance of international peace and security. Upon the invitation or with the consent of the State into whose territory the Commission would go, the General Assembly, or the Interim Committee when the Assembly is not in session, may utilize the Commission if the Security Council is not exercising the functions assigned to it by the Charter with respect to the matter in question. Decisions to utilize the Commission shall be made on the affirmative vote of two-thirds of the members present and voting. The Security Council may also utilize the Commission in accordance with its authority under the Charter;

4. *Decides* that the Commission shall have authority in its discretion to appoint sub-commissions and to utilize the services of observers to assist it in the performance of its functions;

5. *Recommends* to all governments and authorities that they co-operate with the Commission and assist it in the performance of its functions;

6. *Requests* the Secretary-General to provide the necessary staff and facilities, utilizing, where directed by the Commission, the United Nations Panel of Field Observers envisaged in General Assembly resolution 297 B (IV);

C

7. *Invites* each Member of the United Nations to survey its resources in order to determine the nature and scope of the assistance it may be in a position to render in support of any recommendations of the Security Council or of the General Assembly for the restoration of international peace and security;

8. *Recommends* to the States Members of the United Nations that each Member maintain within its national armed forces elements so trained, organized and equipped that they could promptly be made available, in accordance with its constitutional processes, for service as a United Nations unit or units, upon recommendation by the Security Council of the General Assembly, without prejudice to the use of such elements in exercise of the right of individual or collective self-defence recognized in Article 51 of the Charter;

9. *Invites* the Members of the United Nations to inform the Collective Measures Committee provided for in paragraph 11 as soon as possible of the measures taken in implementation of the preceding paragraph;

10. *Requests* the Secretary-General to appoint, with the approval of the Committee provided for in paragraph 11, a panel of military experts who could be made available, on request, to Member States wishing to obtain technical advice regarding the organization, training, and equipment for prompt service as United Nations units of the elements referred to in paragraph 8;

D

11. *Establishes* a Collective Measures Committee consisting of fourteen Members, namely: Australia, Belgium, Brazil, Burma, Canada, Egypt, France, Mexico, Philippines, Turkey, the United Kingdom of Great Britain and Northern Ireland, the United States of America, Venezuela and Yugoslavia, and directs the Committee, in consultation with the Secretary-General and with such Member States as the Committee finds appropriate, to study and make a report to the Security Council and the General Assembly, not later than 1 September 1951, on methods, including those in section C of the present resolution, which might be used to maintain and strengthen international peace and security in accordance with the Purposes and Principles of the Charter, taking account of collective self-defence and regional arrangements (Articles 51 and 52 of the Charter);

12. *Recommends* to all Member States that they co-operate with the Committee and assist it in the performance of its functions;

13. *Requests* the Secretary-General to furnish the staff and facilities necessary for the effective accomplishment of the purposes set forth in sections C and D of the present resolution;

E

14. *Is fully conscious* that, in adopting the proposals set forth above, enduring peace will not be secured solely by collective security arrangements against breaches of international peace and acts of aggression, but that a genuine and lasting peace depends also upon the observance of all the Principles and Purposes established in the Charter of the United Nations, upon the implementation of the resolutions of the Security Council, the General Assembly and other principal organs of the United Nations intended to achieve the maintenance of international peace and security, and especially upon respect for and observance of human rights and fundamental freedoms for all and on the establishment and maintenance of conditions of economic and social well-being in all countries; and accordingly

15. *Urges* Member States to respect fully, and to intensify, joint action, in co-operation with the United Nations, to develop and stimulate universal respect for and observance of human rights and fundamental freedoms, and to intensify individual and collective efforts to achieve conditions of economic stability and social progress, particularly through the development of underdeveloped countries and areas.

B

For the purpose of maintaining international peace and security, in accordance with the Charter of the United Nations, and, in particular, with Chapters, V, VI, and VII of the Charter,

The General Assembly

Recommends to the Security Council:

That it should take the necessary steps to ensure that the action provided for under the Charter is taken with respect to threats to the peace, breaches of the peace or acts of aggression and with respect to the peaceful settlement of disputes or situations likely to endanger the maintenance of international peace and security;

That it should devise measures for the earliest application of Articles 43, 45, 46, and 47 of the Charter of the United Nations regarding the placing of armed forces at the disposal of the Security Council by the States Members of the United Nations and the effective functioning of the Military Staff Committee;

The above dispositions should in no manner prevent the General Assembly from fulfilling its functions under resolution 377 A (V).

C

The General Assembly

Recognizing that the primary function of the United Nations Organization is to maintain and promote peace, security and justice among all nations,

Recognizing the responsibility of all Member States to promote the cause of international peace in accordance with their obligations as provided in the Charter,

Recognizing that the Charter charges the Security Council with the primary responsibility for maintaining international peace and security,

Reaffirming the importance of unanimity among the permanent members of the Security Council on all problems which are likely to threaten world peace,

Recalling General Assembly resolution 190 (III) entitled "Appeal to the Great Powers to renew their efforts to compose their differences and establish a lasting peace",

Recommends to the permanent members of the Security Council that:

(a) They meet and discuss, collectively or otherwise, and, if necessary, with other States concerned, all problems which are likely to threaten international peace and hamper the activities of the United Nations, with a view to their resolving fundamental differences, and reaching agreement in accordance with the spirit and letter of the Charter;

(b) They advise the General Assembly and, when it is not in session, the Members of the United Nations, as soon as appropriate, of the results of their consultations.

---------------------------------- *Appendix 9* ----------------------------------

United Nations Charter

WE THE PEOPLES OF THE UNITED NATIONS determined

to save succeeding generations from the scourge of war, which twice in our lifetime has brought untold sorrow to mankind, and

to reaffirm faith in fundamental human rights, in the dignity and worth of the human person, in the equal rights of men and women and of nations large and small, and

to establish conditions under which justice and respect for the obligations arising from treaties and other sources of international law can be maintained, and

to promote social progress and better standards of life in larger freedom, and for these ends

to practice tolerance and live together in peace with one another as good neighbors, and

to unite our strength to maintain international peace and security, and

to ensure, by the acceptance of principles and the institution of methods, that armed force shall not be used, save in the common interest, and

to employ international machinery for the promotion of the economic and social advancement of all peoples,

have resolved to combine our efforts

to accomplish these aims

Accordingly, our respective Governments, through representatives assembled in the city of San Francisco, who have exhibited their full powers found to be in good and due form, have agreed to the present Charter of the United Nations and do hereby establish an international organization to be known as the United Nations.

CHAPTER I
PURPOSES AND PRINCIPLES

Article 1

The Purposes of the United Nations are:

1. To maintain international peace and security, and to that end: to take effective collective measures for the prevention and removal of threats to the peace, and for the suppression of acts of aggression or other breaches of the peace, and to bring about by peaceful means, and in conformity with the principles of justice and international law, adjustment or settlement of international disputes or situations which might lead to a breach of the peace;

2. To develop friendly relations among nations based on respect for the principle of equal rights and self-determination of peoples, and to take other appropriate measures to strengthen universal peace;

3. To achieve international co-operation in solving international problems of an economic, social, cultural, or humanitarian character, and in promoting and encouraging respect for human rights and for fundamental freedoms for all without distinction as to race, sex, language, or religion; and

4. To be a centre for harmonizing the actions of nations in the attainment of these common ends.

Article 2

The Organization and its members, in pursuit of the Purposes stated in Article 1, shall act in accordance with the following Principles:

1. The Organization is based on the principle of the sovereign equality of all its Members.

2. All Members, in order to ensure to all of them the rights and benefits resulting from membership, shall fulfil in good faith the obligations assumed by them in accordance with the present Charter.

3. All Members shall settle their international disputes by peaceful means in such a manner that international peace and security, and justice, are not endangered.

4. All Members shall refrain in their international relations from the threat or use of force against the territorial integrity or political independence of any state, or in any other manner inconsistent with the Purposes of the United Nations.

5. All Members shall give the United Nations every assistance in any action it takes in accordance with the present Charter, and shall refrain from giving assistance to any state against which the United Nations is taking preventive or enforcement action.

6. The Organization shall ensure that states which are not Members of the United Nations act in accordance with these Principles so far as may be necessary for the maintenance of international peace and security.

7. Nothing contained in the present Charter shall authorize the United Nations to intervene in matters which are essentially within the domestic jurisdiction of any state or shall require the Members to submit such matters to settlement under the present Charter; but this principle shall not prejudice the application of enforcement measures under Chapter VII.

CHAPTER II
MEMBERSHIP

Article 3

The original Members of the United Nations shall be the states which, having participated in the United Nations Conference on International Organization at San Francisco, or having previously signed the Declaration by United Nations of 1 January 1942, sign the present Charter and ratify it in accordance with Article 110.

Article 4

1. Membership in the United Nations is open to all other peace-loving states which accept the obligations contained in the present Charter and, in the judgment of the Organization, are able and willing to carry out these obligations.

2. The admission of any such state to membership in the United Nations will be effected by a decision of the General Assembly upon the recommendation of the Security Council.

Article 5

A Member of the United Nations against which preventive or enforcement action has been taken by the Security Council may be suspended from the exercise of the rights and privileges of membership by the General Assembly upon the recommendation of the Security Council. The exercise of these rights and privileges may be restored by the Security Council.

Article 6

A Member of the United Nations which has persistently violated the Principles contained in the present Charter may be expelled from the Organization by the General Assembly upon the recommendation of the Security Council.

CHAPTER III
ORGANS

Article 7

1. There are established as the principal organs of the United Nations: a General Assembly, a Security Council, an Economic and Social Council, a Trusteeship Council, an International Court of Justice and a Secretariat.

2. Such subsidiary organs as may be found necessary may be established in accordance with the present Charter.

Article 8

The United Nations shall place no restrictions on the eligibility of men and women to participate in any capacity and under conditions of equality in its principal and subsidiary organs.

CHAPTER IV
THE GENERAL ASSEMBLY

COMPOSITION

Article 9

1. The General Assembly shall consist of all the Members of the United Nations.

2. Each Member shall have not more than five representatives in the General Assembly.

FUNCTIONS AND POWERS

Article 10

The General Assembly may discuss any questions or any matters within the scope of the present charter or relating to the powers and functions of any organs provided for in the present Charter, and, except as provided in Article 12, may make recommendations to the Members of the United Nations or to the Security Council or to both on any such questions or matters.

Article 11

1. The General Assembly may consider the general principles of co-operation in the maintenance of international peace and security, including the principles governing disarmament and the regulation of armaments, and may make recommendations with regard to such principles to the Members or to the Security Council or to both.

2. The General Assembly may discuss any questions relating to the maintenance of international peace and security brought before it by any Member of the United Nations, or by the Security Council, or by a state which is not a Member of the United Nations in accordance with Article 35, paragraph 2, and, except as provided in Article 12, may make recommendations with regard to any such questions to the state or states concerned or to the Security Council or to both. Any such question on which action is necessary shall be referred to the Security Council by the General Assembly either before or after discussion.

3. The General Assembly may call the attention of the Security Council to situations which are likely to endanger international peace and security.

4. The powers of the General Assembly set forth in this Article shall not limit the general scope of Article 10.

Article 12

1. While the Security Council is exercising in respect of any dispute or situation the functions assigned to it in the present Charter, the General Assembly shall not make any recommendations with regard to that dispute or situation unless the Security Council so requests.

2. The Secretary-General, with the consent of the Security Council, shall notify the General Assembly at each session of any matters relative to the maintenance of international peace and security which are being dealt with by the Security Council

and shall similarly notify the General Assembly, or the Members of the United Nations if the General Assembly is not in session, immediately the Security Council ceases to deal with such matters.

Article 13

1. The General Assembly shall initiate studies and make recommendations for the purpose of:

a. promoting international co-operation in the political field and encouraging the progressive development of international law and its codification;
b. promoting international co-operation in the economic, social, cultural, educational, and health fields, and assisting in the realization of human rights and fundamental freedoms for all without distinction as to race, sex, language, or religion.

2. The further responsibilities, functions and powers of the General Assembly with respect to matters mentioned in paragraph 1(b) above are set forth in Chapters IX and X.

Article 14

Subject to the provisions of Article 12, the General Assembly may recommend measures for the peaceful adjustment of any situation, regardless of origin, which it deems likely to impair the general welfare or friendly relations among nations, including situations resulting from a violation of the provisions of the present Charter setting forth the Purposes and Principles of the United Nations.

Article 15

1. The General Assembly shall receive and consider annual and special reports from the Security Council; these reports shall include an account of the measures that the Security Council has decided upon or taken to maintain international peace and security.
2. The General Assembly shall receive and consider reports from the other organs of the United Nations.

Article 16

The General Assembly shall perform such functions with respect to the international trusteeship system as are assigned to it under Chapters XII and XIII, including the approval of the trusteeship agreements for areas not designated as strategic.

Article 17

1. The General Assembly shall consider and approve the budget of the Organization.
2. The expenses of the Organization shall be borne by the Members as apportioned by the General Assembly.

3. The General Assembly shall consider and approve any financial and budgetary arrangements with specialized agencies referred to in Article 57 and shall examine the administrative budgets of such specialized agencies with a view to making recommendations to the agencies concerned.

VOTING

Article 18

1. Each member of the General Assembly shall have one vote.

2. Decisions of the General Assembly on important questions shall be made by a two-thirds majority of the members present and voting. These questions shall include: recommendations with respect to the maintenance of international peace and security, the election of the non-permanent members of the Security Council, the election of the members of the Economic and Social Council, the election of members of the Trusteeship Council in accordance with paragraph 1(c) of Article 86, the admission of new Members to the United Nations, the suspension of the rights and privileges of membership, the expulsion of Members, questions relating to the operation of the trusteeship system, and budgetary questions.

3. Decisions on other questions, including the determination of additional categories of questions to be decided by a two-thirds majority, shall be made by a majority of the members present and voting.

Article 19

A Member of the United Nations which is in arrears in the payment of its financial contributions to the Organization shall have no vote in the General Assembly if the amount of its arrears equals or exceeds the amount of the contributions due from it for the preceding two full years. The General Assembly may nevertheless permit such a member to vote if it is satisfied that the failure to pay is due to conditions beyond the control of the Member.

PROCEDURE

Article 20

The General Assembly shall meet in regular annual sessions and in such special sessions as occasion may require. Special sessions shall be convoked by the Secretary-General at the request of the Security Council or of a majority of the Members of the United Nations.

Article 21

The General Assembly shall adopt its own rules of procedure. It shall elect its President for each session.

Article 22

The General Assembly may establish such subsidiary organs as it deems necessary for the performance of its functions.

CHAPTER V
THE SECURITY COUNCIL

COMPOSITION

Article 23

1. The Security Council shall consist of fifteen Members of the United Nations. The Republic of China, France, the Union of Soviet Socialist Republics, the United Kingdom of Great Britain and Northern Ireland, and the United States of America shall be permanent members of the Security Council. The General Assembly shall elect ten other Members of the United Nations to be non-permanent members of the Security Council, due regard being specially paid, in the first instance to the contribution of Members of the United Nations to the maintenance of international peace and security and to the other purposes of the Organization, and also to equitable geographical distribution.

2. The non-permanent members of the Security Council shall be elected for a term of two years. In the first election of the non-permanent members after the increase of the membership of the Security Council from eleven to fifteen, two of the four additional members shall be chosen for a term of one year. A retiring member shall not be eligible for immediate reelection.

3. Each member of the Security Council shall have one representative.

FUNCTIONS AND POWERS

Article 24

1. In order to ensure prompt and effective action by the United Nations, its Members confer on the Security Council primary responsibility for the maintenance of international peace and security, and agree that in carrying out its duties under this responsibility the Security Council acts on their behalf.

2. In discharging these duties the Security Council shall act in accordance with the Purposes and Principles of the United Nations. The specific powers granted to the Security Council for the discharge of these duties are laid down in Chapters VI, VII, VIII, and XII.

3. The Security Council shall submit annual and, when necessary, special reports to the General Assembly for its consideration.

Article 25

The Members of the United Nations agree to accept and carry out the decisions of the Security Council in accordance with the present Charter.

Article 26

In order to promote the establishment and maintenance of international peace and security with the least diversion for armaments of the world's human and economic resources, the Security Council shall be responsible for formulating, with the assistance of the Military Staff Committee referred to in Article 47, plans to be sub-

mitted to the Members of the United Nations for the establishment of a system for
the regulation of armaments.

VOTING

Article 27

1. Each member of the Security Council shall have one vote.
2. Decisions of the Security Council on procedural matters shall be made by an
affirmative vote of nine members.
3. Decisions of the Security Council on all other matters shall be made by an affirmative vote of nine members including the concurring votes of the permanent
members; provided that, in decisions under Chapter VI, and under paragraph 3 of
Article 52, a party to a dispute shall abstain from voting.

PROCEDURE

Article 28

1. The Security Council shall be so organized as to be able to function continu-
ously. Each member of the Security Council shall for this purpose be represented at
all times at the seat of the Organization.
2. The Security Council shall hold periodic meetings at which each of its members may, if it so desires, be represented by a member of the government or by some
other specially designated representative.
3. The Security Council may hold meetings at such places other than the seat of
the Organization as in its judgment will best facilitate its work.

Article 29

The Security Council may establish such subsidiary organs as its deems necessary for the performance of its functions.

Article 30

The Security Council shall adopt its own rules of procedure, including the
method of selecting its president.

Article 31

Any Member of the United Nations which is not a member of the Security Council may participate, without vote, in the discussion of any question brought before
the Security Council whenever the latter considers that the interests of that Member
are specially affected.

Article 32

Any Member of the United Nations which is not a member of the Security Council or any state which is not a Member of the United Nations, if it is a party to a dispute under consideration by the Security Council, shall be invited to participate,
without vote, in the discussion relating to the dispute. The Security Council shall

lay down such conditions as it deems just for the participation of a state which is not a Member of the United Nations.

CHAPTER VI
PACIFIC SETTLEMENT OF DISPUTES

Article 33

1. The parties to any dispute, the continuance of which is likely to endanger the maintenance of international peace and security, shall, first of all, seek a solution by negotiation, enquiry, mediation, conciliation, arbitration, judicial settlement, resort to regional agencies or arrangements, or other peaceful means of their own choice.

2. The Security Council shall, when it deems necessary, call upon the parties to settle their dispute by such means.

Article 34

The Security Council may investigate any dispute, or any situation which might lead to international friction or give rise to a dispute, in order to determine whether the continuance of the dispute or situation is likely to endanger the maintenance of international peace and security.

Article 35

1. Any Member of the United Nations may bring any dispute, or any situation of the nature referred to in Article 34, to the attention of the Security Council or of the General Assembly.

2. A state which is not a Member of the United Nations may bring to the attention of the Security Council or of the General Assembly any dispute to which it is a party if it accepts in advance, for the purposes of the dispute, the obligations of pacific settlement provided in the present Charter.

3. The proceedings of the General Assembly in respect of matters brought to its attention under this Article will be subject to the provisions of Articles 11 and 12.

Article 36

1. The Security Council may, at any stage of a dispute of the nature referred to in Article 33 or of a situation of like nature, recommend appropriate procedures or methods of adjustment.

2. The Security Council should take into consideration any procedures for the settlement of the dispute which have already been adopted by the parties.

3. In making recommendations under this Article the Security Council should also take into consideration that legal disputes should as a general rule be referred by the parties to the International Court of Justice in accordance with the provisions of the Statute of the Court.

Article 37

1. Should the parties to a dispute of the nature referred to in Article 33 fail to settle it by the means indicated in that Article, they shall refer it to the Security Council.

2. If the Security Council deems that the continuance of the dispute is in fact likely to endanger the maintenance of international peace and security, it shall decide whether to take action under Article 36 or to recommend such terms of settlement as it may consider appropriate.

Article 38

Without prejudice to the provisions of Articles 33 to 37, the Security Council may, if all the parties to any dispute so request, make recommendations to the parties with a view to a pacific settlement of the dispute.

CHAPTER VII
ACTION WITH RESPECT TO THREATS TO THE PEACE, BREACHES OF THE PEACE, AND ACTS OF AGGRESSION

Article 39

The Security Council shall determine the existence of any threat to the peace, breach of the peace, or act of aggression and shall make recommendations, or decide what measures shall be taken in accordance with Articles 41 and 42, to maintain or restore international peace and security.

Article 40

In order to prevent an aggravation of the situation, the Security Council may, before making the recommendations or deciding upon the measures provided for in Article 39, call upon the parties concerned to comply with such provisional measures as it deems necessary or desirable. Such provisional measures shall be without prejudice to the rights, claims, or position of the parties concerned. The Security Council shall duly take account of failure to comply with such provisional measures.

Article 41

The Security Council may decide what measures not involving the use of armed force are to be employed to give effect to its decisions, and it may call upon the Members of the United Nations to apply such measures. These may include complete or partial interruption of economic relations and of rail, sea, air, postal, telegraphic, radio, and other means of communication, and the severance of diplomatic relations.

Article 42

Should the Security Council consider that measures provided for in Article 41 would be inadequate or have proved to be inadequate, it may take such action by air, sea, or land forces as may be necessary to maintain or restore international peace and security. Such action may include demonstrations, blockade, and other operations by air, sea, or land forces of Members of the United Nations.

Article 43

1. All Members of the United Nations, in order to contribute to the maintenance of international peace and security, undertake to make available to the Security Council, on its call and in accordance with a special agreement or agreements, armed forces, assistance and facilities, including rights of passage, necessary for the purpose of maintaining international peace and security.

2. Such agreement or agreements shall govern the numbers and types of forces, their degree of readiness and general location, and the nature of the facilities and assistance to be provided.

3. The agreement or agreements shall be negotiated as soon as possible on the initiative of the Security Council. They shall be concluded between the Security Council and Members or between the Security Council and groups of Members and shall be subject to ratification by the signatory states in accordance with their respective constitutional processes.

Article 44

When the Security Council has decided to use force it shall, before calling upon a Member not represented on it to provide armed forces in fulfillment of the obligations assumed under Article 43, invite that Member, if the Member so desires, to participate in the decisions of the Security Council concerning the employment of contingents of that Member's armed forces.

Article 45

In order to enable the United Nations to take urgent military measures, Members shall hold immediately available national air-force contingents for combined international enforcement action. The strength and degree of readiness of these contingents and plans for their combined action shall be determined, within the limits laid down in the special agreement or agreements referred to in Article 43, by the Security Council with the assistance of the Military Staff Committee.

Article 46

Plans for the application of armed force shall be made by the Security Council with the assistance of the Military Staff Committee.

Article 47

1. There shall be established a Military Staff Committee to advise and assist the Security Council on all questions relating to the Security Council's military requirements for the maintenance of international peace and security, the employment and command of forces placed at its disposal, the regulation of armaments, and possible disarmament.

2. The Military Staff Committee shall consist of the Chiefs of Staff of the permanent members of the Security Council or their representatives. Any Member of the United Nations not permanently represented on the Committee shall be invited by the Committee to be associated with it when the efficient discharge of the Committee's responsibilities requires the participation of that Member in its work.

3. The Military Staff Committee shall be responsible under the Security Council for the strategic direction of any armed forces placed at the disposal of the Security Council. Questions relating to the command of such forces shall be worked out subsequently.

4. The Military Staff Committee, with the authorization of the Security Council and after consultation with appropriate regional agencies, may establish regional sub-committees.

Article 48

1. The action required to carry out the decisions of the Security Council for the maintenance of international peace and security shall be taken by all the Members of the United Nations or by some of them, as the Security Council may determine.

2. Such decisions shall be carried out by the Members of the United Nations directly and through their action in the appropriate international agencies of which they are members.

Article 49

The Members of the United Nations shall join in affording mutual assistance in carrying out the measures decided upon by the Security Council.

Article 50

If preventive or enforcement measures against any state are taken by the Security Council, any other state, whether a Member of the United Nations or not, which finds itself confronted with special economic problems arising from the carrying out of those measures shall have the right to consult the Security Council with regard to a solution of those problems.

Article 51

Nothing in the present Charter shall impair the inherent right of individual or collective self-defence if an armed attack occurs against a Member of the United Nations, until the Security Council has taken measures necessary to maintain international peace and security. Measures taken by Members in the exercise of this right of self-defence shall be immediately reported to the Security Council and shall not in any way affect the authority and responsibility of the Security Council under the present Charter to take at any time such action as it deems necessary in order to maintain or restore international peace and security.

CHAPTER VIII
REGIONAL ARRANGEMENTS

Article 52

1. Nothing in the present Charter precludes the existence of regional arrangements or agencies for dealing with such matters relating to the maintenance of international peace and security as are appropriate for regional action, provided that such arrangements or agencies and their activities are consistent with the Purposes and Principles of the United Nations.

2. The Members of the United Nations entering into such arrangements or constituting such agencies shall make every effort to achieve pacific settlement of local disputes through such regional arrangements or by such regional agencies before referring them to the Security Council.

3. The Security Council shall encourage the development of pacific settlement of local disputes through such regional arrangements or by such regional agencies either on the initiative of the states concerned or by reference from the Security Council.

4. This Article in no way impairs the application of Articles 34 and 35.

Article 53

1. The Security Council shall, where appropriate, utilize such regional arrangements or agencies for enforcement action under its authority. But no enforcement action shall be taken under regional arrangements or by regional agencies without the authorization of the Security Council, with the exception of measures against any enemy state, as defined in paragraph 2 of this Article, provided for pursuant to Article 107 or in regional arrangements directed against renewal of aggressive policy on the part of any such state, until such time as the Organization may, on request of the Governments concerned, be charged with the responsibility for preventing further aggression by such a state.

2. The term enemy state as used in paragraph 1 of this Article applies to any state which during the Second World War has been an enemy of any signatory of the present Charter.

Article 54

The Security Council shall at all times be kept fully informed of activities undertaken or in contemplation under regional arrangements or by regional agencies for the maintenance of international peace and security.

CHAPTER IX
INTERNATIONAL ECONOMIC AND SOCIAL
CO-OPERATION

Article 55

With a view to the creation of conditions of stability and well-being which are necessary for peaceful and friendly relations among nations based on respect for the principle of equal rights and self-determination of peoples, the United Nations shall promote:

a. higher standards of living, full employment, and conditions of economic and so-
    cial progress and development;
b. solutions of international economic, social, health, and related problems; and in-
    ternational cultural and educational co-operation; and
c. universal respect for, and observance of, human rights and fundamental free-
    doms for all without distinction as to race, sex, language, or religion.

Article 56

All members pledge themselves to take joint and separate action in cooperation
with the Organization for the achievement of the purposes set forth in Article 55.

Article 57

1. The various specialized agencies, established by intergovernmental agreement and having wide international responsibilities, as defined in their basic instruments, in economic, social, cultural, educational, health, and related fields, shall be
brought into relationship with the United Nations in accordance with the provisions of Article 63.

2. Such agencies thus brought into relationship with the United Nations are
hereinafter referred to as specialized agencies.

Article 58

The Organization shall make recommendations for the coordination of the policies and activities of the specialized agencies.

Article 59

The Organization shall, where appropriate, initiate negotiations among the
states concerned for the creation of any new specialized agencies required for the
accomplishment of the purposes set forth in Article 55.

Article 60

Responsibility for the discharge of the functions of the Organization set forth in
this Chapter shall be vested in the General Assembly and, under the authority of the
General Assembly, in the Economic and Social Council, which shall have for this
purpose the powers set forth in Chapter X.

CHAPTER X
THE ECONOMIC AND SOCIAL COUNCIL

COMPOSITION

Article 61

1. The Economic and Social Council shall consist of fifty-four Members of the
United Nations elected by the General Assembly.

2. Subject to the provisions of paragraph 3, eighteen members of the Economic and Social Council shall be elected each year for a term of three years. A retiring member shall be eligible for immediate re-election.

3. At the first election after the increase in the membership of the Economic and Social Council from twenty-seven to fifty-four members, in addition to the members elected in place of the nine members whose term of office expires at the end of that year, twenty-seven additional members shall be elected. Of these twenty-seven additional members, the term of office of nine members so elected shall expire at the end of one year, and of nine other members at the end of two years, in accordance with arrangements made by the General Assembly.

4. Each member of the Economic and Social Council shall have one representative.

FUNCTIONS AND POWERS

Article 62

1. The Economic and Social Council may make or initiate studies and reports with respect to international economic, social, cultural, educational, health, and related matters and may make recommendations with respect to any such matters to the General Assembly, to the Members of the United Nations, and to the specialized agencies concerned.

2. It may make recommendations for the purpose of promoting respect for, and observance of, human rights and fundamental freedoms for all.

3. It may prepare draft conventions for submission to the General Assembly, with respect to matters falling within its competence.

4. It may call, in accordance with the rules prescribed by the United Nations, international conferences on matters falling within its competence.

Article 63

1. The Economic and Social Council may enter into agreements with any of the agencies referred to in Article 57, defining the terms on which the agency concerned shall be brought into relationship with the United Nations. Such agreements shall be subject to approval by the General Assembly.

2. It may co-ordinate the activities of the specialized agencies through consultation with and recommendations to such agencies and through recommendations to the General Assembly and to the members of the United Nations.

Article 64

1. The Economic and Social Council may take appropriate steps to obtain regular reports from the specialized agencies. It may make arrangements with the Members of the United Nations and with the specialized agencies to obtain reports on the steps taken to give effect to its own recommendations and to recommendations on matters falling within its competence made by the General Assembly.

2. It may communicate its observations on these reports to the General Assembly.

Article 65

The Economic and Social Council may furnish information to the Security Council and shall assist the Security Council upon its request.

Article 66

1. The Economic and Social Council shall perform such functions as fall within its competence in connexion with the carrying out of the recommendations of the General Assembly.

2. It may, with the approval of the General Assembly, perform services at the request of Members of the United Nations and at the request of specialized agencies.

3. It shall perform such other functions as are specified elsewhere in the present Charter or as may be assigned to it by the General Assembly.

VOTING

Article 67

1. Each Member of the Economic and Social Council shall have one vote.

2. Decisions of the Economic and Social Council shall be made by a majority of the members present and voting.

PROCEDURE

Article 68

The Economic and Social Council shall set up commissions in economic and social fields and for the promotion of human rights, and such other commissions as may be required for the performance of its functions.

Article 69

The Economic and Social Council shall invite any Member of the United Nations to participate, without vote, in its deliberations on any matter of particular concern to that Member.

Article 70

The Economic and Social Council may make arrangements for representatives of the specialized agencies to participate, without vote, in its deliberations and in those of the commissions established by it, and for its representatives to participate in the deliberations of the specialized agencies.

Article 71

The Economic and Social Council may make suitable arrangements for consultation with non-governmental organizations which are concerned with matters within its competence. Such arrangements may be made with international organizations and, where appropriate, with national organizations after consultation with the member of the United Nations concerned.

Article 72

1. The Economic and Social Council shall adopt its own rules of procedure, including the method of selecting its President.

2. The Economic and Social Council shall meet as required in accordance with its rules, which shall include provision for the convening of meetings on the request of a majority of its members.

CHAPTER XI
DECLARATION REGARDING NON-SELF-GOVERNING TERRITORIES

Article 73

Members of the United Nations which have or assume responsibilities for the administration of territories whose peoples have not yet attained a full measure of self-government recognize the principle that the interests of the inhabitants of these territories are paramount, and accept as a sacred trust the obligation to promote to the utmost, within the system of international peace and security established by the present Charter, the well-being of the inhabitants of these territories, and, to this end:

a. to ensure, with due respect for the culture of the peoples concerned, their political, economic, social, and educational advancement, their just treatment, and their protection against abuses;
b. to develop self-government, to take due account of the political aspirations of the peoples, and to assist them in the progressive development of their free political institutions, according to the particular circumstances of each territory and its peoples and their varying stages of advancement;
c. to further international peace and security;
d. to promote constructive measures of development, to encourage research, and to co-operate with one another and, when and where appropriate, with specialized international bodies with a view to the practical achievement of the social, economic, and scientific purposes set forth in this Article; and
e. to transmit regularly to the Secretary-General for information purposes, subject to such limitation as security and constitutional considerations may require, statistical and other information of a technical nature relating to economic, social, and educational conditions in the territories for which they are respectively responsible other than those territories to which Chapters XII and XIII apply.

Article 74

Members of the United Nations also agree that their policy in respect of the territories to which this Chapter applies, no less than in respect of their metropolitan areas, must be based on the general principle of good-neighborliness, due account being taken of the interests and well-being of the rest of the world, in social, economic, and commercial matters.

CHAPTER XII
INTERNATIONAL TRUSTEESHIP SYSTEM

Article 75

The United Nations shall establish under its authority an international trustee-ship system for the administration and supervision of such territories as may be placed thereunder by subsequent individual agreements. These territories are here-inafter referred to as trust territories.

Article 76

The basic objectives of the trusteeship system, in accordance with the Purposes of the United Nations laid down in Article 1 of the present Charter, shall be:

a. to further international peace and security;
b. to promote the political, economic, social, and educational advancement of the inhabitants of the trust territories, and their progressive development towards self-government or independence as may be appropriate to the particular cir-cumstances of each territory and its peoples and the freely expressed wishes of the peoples concerned, and as may be provided by the terms of each trusteeship agreement;
c. to encourage respect for human rights and for fundamental freedoms for all without distinction as to race, sex, language, or religion, and to encourage recog-nition of the interdependence of the peoples of the world; and
d. to ensure equal treatment in social, economic, and commercial matters for all Members of the United Nations and their nationals, and also equal treatment for the latter in the administration of justice, without prejudice to the attainment of the foregoing objectives and subject to the provisions of Article 80.

Article 77

1. The trusteeship system shall apply to such territories in the following catego-ries as may be placed thereunder by means of trusteeship agreements:

a. territories now held under mandate;
b. territories which may be detached from enemy states as a result of the Second World War; and
c. territories voluntarily placed under the system by states responsible for their ad-ministration.

2. It will be a matter for subsequent agreement as to which territories in the fore-going categories will be brought under the trusteeship system and upon what terms.

Article 78

The trusteeship system shall not apply to territories which have become Members of the United Nations, relationship among which shall be based on respect for the principle of sovereign equality.

Article 79

The terms of trusteeship for each territory to be placed under the trusteeship system, including any alteration or amendment, shall be agreed upon by the states directly concerned, including the mandatory power in the case of territories held under mandate by a Member of the United Nations, and shall be approved as provided for in Articles 83 and 85.

Article 80

1. Except as may be agreed upon in individual trusteeship agreements, made under Articles 77, 79, and 81, placing each territory under the trusteeship system, and until such agreements have been concluded, nothing in this Chapter shall be construed in or of itself to alter in any manner the rights whatsoever of any states or any peoples or the terms of existing international instruments to which Members of the United Nations may respectively be parties.

2. Paragraph 1 of the Article shall not be interpreted as giving grounds for delay or postponement of the negotiations and conclusion of agreements for placing mandated and other territories under the trusteeship system as provided for in Article 77.

Article 81

The trusteeship agreement shall in each case include the terms under which the trust territory will be administered and designate the authority which will exercise the administration of the trust territory. Such authority, hereinafter called the administering authority, may be one or more states or the Organization itself.

Article 82

There may be designated, in any trusteeship agreement, a strategic area or areas which may include part or all of the trust territory to which the agreement applies, without prejudice to any special agreement or agreements made under Article 43.

Article 83

1. All functions of the United Nations relating to strategic areas, including the approval of the terms of the trusteeship agreements and of their alteration or amendment, shall be exercised by the Security Council.

2. The basic objectives set forth in Article 76 shall be applicable to the people of each strategic area.

3. The Security Council shall, subject to the provisions of the trusteeship agreements and without prejudice to security considerations, avail itself of the assistance of the Trusteeship Council to perform those functions of the United Nations under

the trusteeship system relating to political, economic, social, and educational matters in the strategic areas.

Article 84

It shall be the duty of the administering authority to ensure that the trust territory shall play its part in the maintenance of international peace and security. To this end the administering authority may make use of volunteer forces, facilities, and assistance from the trust territory in carrying out the obligations towards the Security Council undertaken in this regard by the administering authority, as well as for local defence and the maintenance of law and order within the trust territory.

Article 85

1. The functions of the United Nations with regard to trusteeship agreements for all areas not designated as strategic, including the approval of the terms of the trusteeship agreements and of their alteration or amendment, shall be exercised by the General Assembly.
2. The Trusteeship Council, operating under the authority of the General Assembly, shall assist the General Assembly in carrying out these functions.

CHAPTER XIII
THE TRUSTEESHIP COUNCIL

COMPOSITION

Article 86

1. The Trusteeship Council shall consist of the following Members of the United Nations:

a. those Members administering trust territories;
b. such of those Members mentioned by name in Article 23 as are not administering trust territories; and
c. as many other Members elected for three-year terms by the General Assembly as may be necessary to ensure that the total number of members of the Trusteeship Council is equally divided between those Members of the United Nations which administer trust territories and those which do not.

2. Each member of the Trusteeship Council shall designate one specially qualified person to represent it therein.

FUNCTIONS AND POWERS

Article 87

The General Assembly and, under its authority, the Trusteeship Council, in carrying out their functions, may:

a. consider reports submitted by the administering authority;

b. accept petitions and examine them in consultation with the administering authority;

c. provide for periodic visits to the respective trust territories at times agreed upon with the administering authority; and

d. take these and other actions in conformity with the terms of the trusteeship agreements.

Article 88

The Trusteeship Council shall formulate a questionnaire on the political, economic, social, and educational advancement of the inhabitants of each trust territory, and the administering authority for each trust territory within the competence of the General Assembly shall make an annual report to the General Assembly upon the basis of such questionnaire.

VOTING

Article 89

1. Each member of the Trusteeship Council shall have one vote.
2. Decisions of the Trusteeship Council shall be made by a majority of the members present and voting.

PROCEDURE

Article 90

1. The Trusteeship Council shall adopt its own rules of procedure, including the method of selecting its President.
2. The Trusteeship Council shall meet as required in accordance with its rules, which shall include provisions for the convening of meetings on the request of a majority of its members.

Article 91

The Trusteeship Council shall, when appropriate, avail itself of the assistance of the Economic and Social Council and of the specialized agencies in regard to matters with which they are respectively concerned.

CHAPTER XIV
THE INTERNATIONAL COURT OF JUSTICE

Article 92

The International Court of Justice shall be the principal judicial organ of the United Nations. It shall function in accordance with the annexed Statute, which is based upon the Statute of the Permanent Court of International Justice and forms an integral part of the present Charter.

Article 93

1. All Members of the United Nations are ipso facto parties to the Statute of the International Court of Justice.

2. A state which is not a Member of the United Nations may become a party to the Statute of the International Court of Justice on conditions to be determined in each case by the General Assembly upon the recommendation of the Security Council.

Article 94

1. Each Member of the United Nations undertakes to comply with the decision of the International Court of Justice in any case to which it is a party.

2. If any party to a case fails to perform the obligations incumbent upon it under a judgment rendered by the Court, the other party may have recourse to the Security Council, which may, if it deems necessary, make recommendations or decide upon measures to be taken to give effect to the judgment.

Article 95

Nothing in the present Charter shall prevent Members of the United Nations from entrusting the solution of their differences to other tribunals by virtue of agreements already in existence or which may be concluded in the future.

Article 96

1. The General Assembly or the Security Council may request the International Court of Justice to give an advisory opinion on any legal question.

2. Other organs of the United Nations and specialized agencies, which may at any time be so authorized by the General Assembly, may also request advisory opinions of the Court on legal questions arising within the scope of their activities.

CHAPTER XV
THE SECRETARIAT

Article 97

The Secretariat shall comprise a Secretary-General and such staff as the organization may require. The Secretary-General shall be appointed by the General Assembly upon the recommendation of the Security Council. He shall be the chief administrative officer of the Organization.

Article 98

The Secretary-General shall act in that capacity in all meetings of the General Assembly, of the Security Council, of the Economic and Social Council, and of the Trusteeship Council, and shall perform such other functions as are entrusted to him by these organs. The Secretary-General shall make an annual report to the General Assembly on the work of the Organization.

Article 99

The Secretary-General may bring to the attention of the Security Council any matter which in his opinion may threaten the maintenance of international peace and security.

Article 100

1. In the performance of their duties the Secretary-General and the staff shall not seek or receive instructions from any government or from any other authority external to the Organization. They shall refrain from any action which might reflect on their position as international officials responsible only to the Organization.

2. Each member of the United Nations undertakes to respect the exclusively international character of the responsibilities of the Secretary-General and the staff and not to seek to influence them in the discharge of their responsibilities.

Article 101

1. The staff shall be appointed by the Secretary-General under regulations established by the General Assembly.

2. Appropriate staffs shall be permanently assigned to the Economic and Social Council, the Trusteeship Council, and, as required, to other organs of the United Nations. These staffs shall form a part of the Secretariat.

3. The paramount consideration in the employment of the staff and in the determination of the conditions of service shall be the necessity of securing the highest standards of efficiency, competence, and integrity. Due regard shall be paid to the importance of recruiting the staff on as wide a geographical basis as possible.

CHAPTER XVI
MISCELLANEOUS PROVISIONS

Article 102

1. Every treaty and every international agreement entered into by any Member of the United Nations after the present Charter comes into force shall as soon as possible be registered with the Secretariat and published by it.

2. No party to any such treaty or international agreement which has not been registered in accordance with the provisions of paragraph 1 of this Article may invoke that treaty or agreement before any organ of the United Nations.

Article 103

In the event of a conflict between the obligations of the Members of the United Nations under the present Charter and their obligations under any other international agreement, their obligations under the present Charter shall prevail.

Article 104

The Organization shall enjoy in the territory of each of its Members such legal capacity as may be necessary for the exercise of its functions and the fulfillment of its purposes.

Article 105

1. The Organization shall enjoy in the territory of each of its Members such privileges and immunities as are necessary for the fulfillment of its purposes.

2. Representatives of the Members of the United Nations and officials of the Organization shall similarly enjoy such privileges and immunities as are necessary for the independent exercise of their functions in connexion with the Organization.

3. The General Assembly may make recommendations with a view to determining the details of the application of paragraphs 1 and 2 of this Article or may propose conventions to the Members of the United Nations for this purpose.

CHAPTER XVII
TRANSITIONAL SECURITY ARRANGEMENTS

Article 106

Pending the coming into force of such special agreements referred to in Article 43 as in the opinion of the Security Council enable it to begin the exercise of its responsibilities under Article 42, the parties to the Four Nations Declaration, signed at Moscow, 30 October 1943, and France, shall, in accordance with the provisions of paragraph 5 of that Declaration, consult with one another and as occasion requires with other Members of the United Nations with a view to such joint action on behalf of the Organization as may be necessary for the purpose of maintaining international peace and security.

Article 107

Nothing in the present Charter shall invalidate or preclude action, in relation to any state which during the Second World War has been an enemy of any signatory to the present Charter, taken or authorized as a result of that war by the Governments having responsibility for such action.

CHAPTER XVIII
AMENDMENTS

Article 108

Amendments to the present Charter shall come into force for all Members of the United Nations when they have been adopted by a vote of two thirds of the members of the General Assembly and ratified in accordance with their respective constitutional processes by two-thirds of the Members of the United Nations, including all the permanent members of the Security Council.

Article 109

1. A General Conference of the Members of the United Nations for the purpose of reviewing the present Charter may be held at a date and place to be fixed by a two-thirds vote of the members of the General Assembly and by a vote of any nine members of the Security Council. Each Member of the United Nations shall have one vote in the conference.

2. Any alteration of the present Charter recommended by a two-thirds vote of the conference shall take effect when ratified in accordance with their respective constitutional processes by two-thirds of the Members of the United Nations including all the permanent members of the Security Council.

3. If such a conference has not been held before the tenth annual session of the General Assembly following the coming into force of the present Charter, the proposal to call such a conference shall be placed on the agenda of that session of the General Assembly, and the conference shall be held if so decided by a majority vote of the members of the General Assembly and by a vote of any seven members of the Security Council.

CHAPTER XIX
RATIFICATION AND SIGNATURE

Article 110

1. The present Charter shall be ratified by the signatory states in accordance with their respective constitutional processes.

2. The ratifications shall be deposited with the Government of the United States of America, which shall notify all the signatory states of each deposit as well as the Secretary-General of the Organization when he has been appointed.

3. The present Charter shall come into force upon the deposit of ratifications by the Republic of China, France, the Union of Soviet Socialist Republics, the United Kingdom of Great Britain and Northern Ireland, and the United States of America, and by a majority of the other signatory states. A protocol of the ratification deposited shall thereupon be drawn up by the Government of the United States of America which shall communicate copies thereof to all the signatory states.

4. The states signatory to the present Charter which ratify it after it has come into force will become original Members of the United Nations on the date of the deposit of their respective ratifications.

Article 111

The present Charter of which the Chinese, French, Russian, English, and Spanish texts are equally authentic, shall remain deposited in the archives of the Government of the United States of America. Duly certified copies thereof shall be transmitted by that Government to the Governments of the other signatory states.

IN FAITH WHEREOF the representatives of the Governments of the United Nations have signed the present Charter.

DONE at the city of San Francisco the twenty-sixth day of June, one thousand nine hundred and forty-five.

Glossary

Adjudication. The settlement of international disputes by recourse to international courts.

Advisory opinion. A legal opinion offered by the International Court of Justice following a nonadversarial request by a UN agency or government.

Aggression. An illegal use of force by one country or group of countries against another. In the UN system, acts of aggression are determined by the Security Council.

All necessary means. A phrase used in UN Security Council resolutions to indicate the invocation of Chapter VII, Article 43, permitting the use of military force.

Apartheid. An Afrikaaner term meaning "apartness," this policy was employed by the government of South Africa from the late 1940s until 1992 to segregate races. It was opposed in a host of UN forums.

Applicant. A country bringing suit against another state before an international court.

Arbitration. A mechanism by which states agree to submit disputes for binding and final resolution to an ad hoc or permanent panel of their choosing.

Arms control. Measures taken by governments to slow down the pace of an arms race by placing limits or ceilings on their development or acquisition of weapons.

Arrearages. Accumulated unpaid mandatory dues owed to international organizations by governments.

Basic needs. Access by persons to food, water, clothing, shelter, health care, and other fundamental necessities of life.

Belligerent. Any country at war with any other country or group of countries.

Bloc politics. The process by which groups of countries that share common historical, ideological, political, cultural, economic, or religious affinities and interests and that meet periodically to consider how to advance their common interests in international organizations.

Bretton Woods system. Principles and institutions, such as the World Bank and International Monetary Fund, which were established after World War II, along with trade-regulating bodies to enhance international economic stability.

Caucus. A meeting of a group or bloc of states to discuss strategy and policy regarding issues debated in official meetings of intergovernmental organizations.

Civil society. Institutions and processes by which decisions are made through democratic and peaceful means.

Cold War. The ideological, political, and military competition existing between the East and West blocs after World War II until about 1990.

Collective security. Principle by which governments agree as members of an international organization to refrain from the use of force to resolve disputes and to punish any member state that fails to abide by the principle of the nonuse of force.

Commodity cartel. A group of countries producing a similar commodity that attempts to control international supplies, thereby affecting international prices.

Communiqué. A diplomatic message, bulletin, or statement made public by one country or a group of countries.

Complex emergency. A humanitarian emergency in the context of ongoing civil war calling for assistance to refugees and displaced persons, rehabilitation and reconstruction of infrastructure, deployment of peacekeeping or peacemaking forces, and the negotiation and implementation of peace agreements.

Compulsory jurisdiction. The state of affairs by which a country is compelled to submit to adjudication when taken to court by another country. Most international courts lack full compulsory jurisdiction as governments are reluctant in advance to submit to it.

Concert of Europe. A precursor to modern conference diplomacy, this involved diplomatic consultations undertaken by European countries during the nineteenth century to maintain the stability of Europe.

Conciliation. A means by which third parties attempt through nonbinding means to help solve a dispute between two countries.

Conditionality. Terms established by the World Bank and International Monetary Fund that must be met by governments before loans to them are approved.

Countermeasure. A response taken by a state or an intergovernmental organization (IGO) to an action or to inaction of other states.

Declaration. A legally nonbinding statement of principles or aspirations of governments.

Decolonization. A process whereby non-self-governing territories gain independence as sovereign states.

Démarche. A diplomatic term referring to an initiative or proposal made by a government or group of governments to resolve a dispute often through a change in policy.

Détente. A relaxation of tensions among countries previously in confrontation or dispute.

Developing country. A nonindustrialized country with low per capita gross national product that relies primarily on agricultural or commodity-based economic activity.

Development. A process whereby a country improves its capacity to ensure economic growth and prosperity, to provide infrastructure for attainment of basic needs, and to ensure stable and democratic political interaction.

Disarmament. A process whereby countries reduce stockpiles of weapons or eliminate various weapons systems.

Displaced person. A person who has been involuntarily uprooted from their home or habitual place of residence without crossing international boundaries.

Earmarked funds. Funds contributed by countries to intergovernmental organizations with the requirement that they be spent on specific activities.

Emergency. Any situation in which massive assistance is needed to avoid substantial loss of life.

Fact-finding. A diplomatic process whereby a country or intergovernmental organization conducts a mission to assess the facts of and report on a situation or dispute among nations.

Functionalism. The belief that by separating political from technical and practical matters of economic and social cooperation in international relations, states can better achieve peace. Many UN specialized agencies follow functionalist principles.

Geneva 77. *See* **Group of Seventy-seven (G-77).**

Globalization. Deepening interdependence among nations in international economic, monetary, cultural, and social cooperation and through global communications in ways that undermine national control of borders.

Good offices. An offer made by a government or intergovernmental organization to make its services available to countries desiring to resolve a dispute peacefully.

Group of Seven (G-7). A group of seven wealthy industrialized nations whose leaders meet regularly to discuss global economic policy.

Group of Seventy-seven (G-77). A group of countries numbering about 125 that have pressed for reforms of the global economy.

Guerrilla forces. Irregular military forces usually engaged in civil wars against established and recognized governments. Such forces may gain belligerent status provided that they observe the international law of war.

Human development. As a complement to economic development, human development measures the quality of human life in terms of life expectancy, literacy, nutritional levels, and access to health care.

Humanitarian intervention. A qualified right of governments, the UN, or other collective security organizations to intercede on behalf of populations whose mistreatment by their government shocks the conscience of humanity.

Human rights. Civil, political, economic, social, and cultural rights and fundamental freedoms that governments acknowledge they are bound to promote and respect in their dealing with all persons, citizens and aliens alike.

Incommunicado. Persons or officials who are confined in such a way as to lack means of communications.

Independence. One of the characteristics and rights of sovereign states in which they enjoy a full freedom to develop their own domestic and foreign policies without external dictate.

Indicative planning. Planning undertaken by UN bodies, in regular cycles, such as a five-year planning cycle.

Indigenous peoples. Descendants of the original inhabitants of colonized lands or lands occupied and governed by later arrivals.

Inquiry. A process whereby governments, UN bodies, or other intergovernmental organizations may be called upon by parties to investigate a specific dispute or question.

Integration. A process whereby formerly independent and separate national states seek to form new and unified economic or political systems.

Interdependence. The process whereby independent states gradually increase cooperative relations with one another, especially in the economic and trade areas in such a way as to become mutually dependent on one another.

Intergovernmental organizations (IGOs). Established by governments through treaties, IGOs carry out the wishes of member governments in order to enhance their mutual interrelations and common interests.

Interim. A time between periods, events, or regular changes in office. A temporary or partial measure undertaken in response to a problem in advance of its full and complete resolution. A position or office held temporarily until filled by regular means.

International law. Customs and treaties entered into by states creating obligations among them.

Irredentism. A claim by one country or people to the territory of a neighboring country based on past historical ownership or ethnic similarity of the local population.

Less-developed countries (LDCs). Countries whose per capita gross national products are very low and require special assistance from other governments and multilateral agencies.

Mandate system. Established under the League of Nations, the mandate system stripped Axis powers of their colonial holdings and placed them under the legal trusteeship of other governments until their independence was achieved.

Matériel. Supplies, transport, weapons, and other materials used by the civilian or military forces of governments or intergovernmental organizations.

Mediation. A conflict resolution process by which a third party makes active proposals to disputing parties concerning the resolution of the dispute.

Most-favored nation (MFN). A clause included in commercial trade agreements whereby a country is automatically guaranteed the most favorable tariff rates extended subsequently by its trade partner on commodities imported from any third party.

Most seriously affected countries (MSAs). Countries most hurt by the oil price increases that took place during the 1970s.

Multinational corporations. *See* **Transnational corporations.**

Negotiation. A peaceful process whereby governments attempt through bilateral, multilateral, or third party means to resolve a dispute or conflict.

New International Economic Order (NIEO). A program of global economic reform advanced by the G-77.

Newly industrializing countries (NICs). Former less-developed countries (LDCs) that successfully initiated programs for industrialization, thereby enhancing their economic growth.

Nonalignment. A policy of neutralism pursued by many developing countries so as to avoid ideological entanglement between the East and the West during the Cold War.

Nongovernmental organizations (NGOs). These private, voluntary, nonprofit agencies provide resources, information, and advice to governments and intergovernmental organizations.

Nonintervention. A duty of states, under normal circumstances, to refrain from interfering in the domestic affairs of other states.

Non-self-governing territory. Any area of land lacking self-rule and independence.

Nuclear, chemical, and bacteriological (NBC) weapons. *See* **Weapons of mass destruction.**

Nuclear proliferation. The process by which the capacity to make nuclear weapon spreads from one country to another.

Observer status. A status conferred by UN bodies on nonmember states or nonstate bodies giving them the right to attend meetings without membership or voting rights.

Optional clause. A clause in the Statute of the International Court of Justice whereby a ratifying member state may choose to accept the court's compulsory jurisdiction.

Pacific settlement of disputes. Means by which governments resolve conflicts by peaceful means.

Pacta sunt servanda. A customary norm of international law whereby states acknowledge their duty to keep good faith in treaties.

Peace-building. The process whereby governments seek to ensure the implementation of peace settlements via elections, human rights monitoring, development of civil administration, and the infusion of economic assistance.

Peacekeeping. The deployment of forces to separate warring parties, to observe and monitor cease-fire lines, and on occasion, to provide humanitarian aid, in order to allow time for the negotiation of a lasting settlement of the dispute.

Peacemaking. The deployment of armed forces to punish aggression or a violation of the UN Charter.

Plebiscite. An popular referendum, usually to determine the desire of a local population for independence or self-determination.

Plenary debate. Discussions undertaken in the primary body of an intergovernmental organization or international conference where all member governments are fully represented.

Preferential access. The granting of special trade rights, especially in regard to LDCs; the right of coastal states to regulate and exploit fishery resources within their economic zones.

Preventive diplomacy. Efforts by the international community to monitor potential conflicts and avoid their outbreak by diplomatic means.

Proportionality. A principle of international law whereby states retaliating against prior wrongdoing must do so in a way commensurate with the prior wrongful action.

Protectionism. The policy of placing tariffs and other barriers on imported goods to confer advantages on domestic producers.

Rapporteur. A person who submits a main committee, subcommittee, or working group report to a plenary body of an intergovernmental organization or international conference.

Rapprochement. A restoration of cordial relations between any two states previously in conflict with one another.

Ratification. An act by the head of state of a country whereby is indicated the government's intention to adhere to the terms of a treaty.

Reciprocity. Any mutual exchange of benefits or privileges, most often associated with international trade policies whereby trade partners confer tariff reductions on one another.

Recognition. The process whereby existing sovereign states and governments acknowledge the legal existence of new states, governments, or some other legal entity.

Refoulement. The forced and usually illegal return of a refugee to their country of origin or nationality.

Refugee. Any person who, owing to a well-founded fear of persecution, has fled from or fears to return to their country of origin or nationality.

Regime. Any set or body of institutions, rules, norms, procedures, and policies established by governments to regulate and harmonize an aspect of their interrelations.

Regional organizations. Intergovernmental bodies established by states to deal with problems and issues affecting a particular geographical region. Under Chapter VIII of the UN Charter such bodies may carry out collective security functions.

Reprisal. A normally illegal act that may be legal if undertaken against and in proportion to a prior illegal act.

Resolutions. Recommendations and decisions of intergovernmental organizations and UN bodies.

Respondent. A government against whom legal action is being brought by another state before an international court.

Retaliation. Any act, whether by retorsion or reprisal, whereby one country or group of countries takes action against a prior hostile act by another country or group of countries.

Retorsion. An unfriendly or hostile but legal act undertaken by one country or group of countries in response to a prior legal but hostile act by another country or group of countries.

Roll call. A calling of a membership roll to determine the existence of a quorum; a form of voting whereby each member country of an organization announces verbally its support of, opposition to, or abstention upon a proposal.

Sanctions. Punishments involving severance of diplomatic relations, trade relations, communications, or transportation up to and including the use of armed forces by one group of states against another state or group of states for violations of the UN Charter or customary international law.

Secretariat. The administrative staff of an international organization.

Secretary-general. The chief executive officer of the United Nations.

Self-determination. The right of a people or nation to seek independence and recognition as a sovereign state.

Separatism. The desire of a particular people to secede from an existing state to establish a government of their own.

Sovereignty. A state's capacity and supreme authority to conduct its domestic and foreign affairs.

Special drawing right (SDR). A form of international currency established under International Monetary Fund auspices to help states resolve short-term deficits in their balance of payments accounts.

Specialized agencies. Organizations within the UN system established by governments to perform special functions or tasks.

Special session. Called by the General Assembly of the United Nations outside of its regular annual session to discuss a particular issue or concern of nations.

State. An entity composed of an independent government possessing international recognition of its sovereign legal authority over a specific population and territory.

Terms of trade. The relative value of a country's imports in relation to its exports.

Territorial integrity. The right of a sovereign state to exclusive jurisdiction and control over its own territory and to be free of external interference or intervention.

Terrorism. The illegal use of violence against innocent people for purposes of political extortion, coercion, or publicity in the advancement of a political cause.

Third World country. A term applied to developing countries relying primarily on commodities and agricultural resources for their economic welfare.

Transnational corporations. Large business enterprises having operations, investments, or sales activities in more than one country.

Trusteeship. The UN system's successor to the League of Nations mandate system whereby non-self-governing territories were placed by administrating nations under the supervision of the UN Trusteeship Council with a view to their attainment of eventual independence.

Uniting for Peace Resolution. A UN Resolution permitting the General Assembly to make recommendations regarding threats to international peace and security when the Security Council has reached stalemate.

Veto. The legal power granted to the five permanent members of the Security Council under the UN Charter by which their negative vote prevents passage of a recommendation or decision.

War. The declared or undeclared outbreak of hostilities between two or more countries involving the deployment and use of military force.

Weapons of mass destruction. Refers to weapons such as nuclear and thermonuclear bombs as well as chemical and bacteriological agents that may be used indiscriminately against the civilian populations of countries.

Westphalian system. The modern state system of national sovereignty, territorial jurisdiction and integrity, independence, and equality originating with the Peace of Westphalia in 1648.

Bibliographic Essay

Students of United Nations (UN) debates have multiple avenues for research on issues facing the UN system. In the fifty-five years of its existence, the United Nations has been the subject of numerous scholarly studies. Moreover, the UN has generated a mountain of information on its own. These include verbatim records, of meetings, summaries of debates, reports, background records, and resolutions. The United Nations has designated over 350 libraries throughout the world as depositories for its Official Records. The UN Department of Public Information, in turn, publishes a number of very useful research tools. Available at most libraries is the *UN Chronicle* (formerly the *UN Monthly Chronicle*), which is published on a quarterly basis. The *UN Chronicle* is a digest of important decisions, events, and conferences. Its March issue regularly provides summaries of UN General Assembly plenary debate speeches by member state representatives. The *UN Chronicle* is a good place to start basic research, especially when more recent information is needed. For more detailed summaries of debates and decisions, one may then consult the *UN Yearbooks*, although publication of this resource typically lags about four years behind the current date. However, it contains texts of all resolutions adopted by the Security Council, the Economic and Social Council, UN Main Committees, and the UN General Assembly, along with summaries of discussion and debate on these resolutions.

For the student who wishes to have an even more detailed understanding of an issue or to consult the full text of debates, then the General Assembly Official Records (GAOR) may be consulted if a UN depository library is at hand. GAOR Records take the form of Plenary Documents (a record of discussion and votes in the General Assembly itself), Main Committee Records and Documents, Annexes, and Supplements, which contain copies of all correspondence, background documents, reports, administrative memorandums, and, in the last supplement, a record of all decisions taken during a particular session. Issues reach the UN agenda through requests of governments, through recommendations, requests, and reports of various UN organs, and sometimes through the request of the secretary-general. The secretary-general keeps track of all such requests and reports them to the General Committee of the General Assembly, which makes a recommendation to the General Assembly on which items should be placed on the agenda, and to which committee they should be referred. The General Assembly routinely accepts the recommendations of the General Committee but may and sometimes does revise them. Debate on issues then takes place within the relevant committee, which reports back any recommendations to the General Assembly, where final action is taken. The agenda of the UN Security Council, is more ad hoc in nature, as it must be prepared to convene on a moment's notice in the face of a crisis.

With the advent of the Internet, access to UN data and documents has been greatly enhanced. A student may now find free of charge copies of the very latest UN resolutions, databases, documents, publications, and reports at the UN home page (www.un.org) and related links. A list of Web sites is provided at the end of this essay. The UN home page includes late-breaking news, daily highlights, press releases, fact sheets, and periodicals. Information on upcoming conferences and events is provided. Databases provide the latest statistical information collected by the UN Statistical Division. One may find data on registry and status on international treaties, and a full collection of UN official documents and resolutions. Under the heading of General Information, students may find a wide array of basic data on the functions, duties, and roles of the United Nations, and the UN CyberSchool Bus page (www.un.org/Pubs/CyberSchoolBus) provides a variety of useful learning tools. The UN Dag Hammarskjöld Library is also available via Internet, and a large collection of photographs may be accessed through the UN Photo Library. The UN home page contains an extensive list of UN specialized agency links, along with links to other intergovernmental organizations. Following the prompts from the Humanitarian Affairs Office, the student may gain access to the Relief Web with latest information, journalistic and agency reports, documents, and statistics on refugee and humanitarian emergencies throughout the world. This site also contains a directory of nongovernmental organizations working in humanitarian relief operations throughout the world. In short, once one gets into cyperspace at the United Nations, a whole world of data and information lies at one's very fingertips.

In the introduction to this encyclopedia and in the individual entries, the academic and scholarly literature regarding the UN activities and particular issues addressed by UN bodies has been cited to provide readers with sources for further information. A number of classic works, however, deserve special attention here. Two very fine histories of the early decades of the United Nations include Inis L. Claude's *Swords into Plowshares: The Problems and Progress of International Organization*, 4th ed. (New York: Random House, 1984) and Evan Luard's *A History of the United Nations: The Years of Western Domination, 1945–1955* (New York: St. Martin's, 1982). Philip E. Jacob, Alexine L. Atherton, and Arthur M. Wallenstein collaborated to produce a comprehensive treatment of a range of issues dealt with by the United Nations and various other intergovernmental organizations in *The Dynamics of International Organization* (Homewood, IL: Dorsey Press, 1972). A. LeRoy Bennett's *International Organization: Principles and Issues* (Englewood Cliffs, NJ: Prentice-Hall, 1995) is a solid basic text on the United Nations with several chapters devoted to its genesis, development, and key issues, as is Harold K. Jacobson's *Networks of Interdependence* (New York: Alfred A. Knopf, 1984). Robert E. Riggs and Jack C. Plano offer another comprehensive overview of the United Nations in *The United Nations: International Organization and World Politics* (Belmont, CA: Wadsworth, 1994). Two more recent texts taking into account post–Cold War developments include Thomas G. Weiss, David P. Forsythe, and Roger A. Coate's *The United Nations and Changing*

World Politics (Boulder, CO: Westview Press, 1997) and Karen A. Mingst and Margaret P. Karns's *The United Nations in the Post–Cold War Era*, 2nd ed. (Boulder, CO: Westview Press, 2000). Other useful treatments on multilateral debate and diplomacy in the UN system include: James P. Muldoon, Jr. et al., eds., *Multilateral Diplomacy and the United Nations Today* (Boulder, CO: Westview Press, 1999); and Chadwick Alger, *The Future of the United Nations System: Potential for the Twenty-first Century* (Tokyo: United Nations University Press, 1998). A classical work on bloc politics in the UN system is Thomas Hovet, Jr., *Bloc Politics in the United Nations* (Cambridge, MA: Harvard University Press, 1960). Voting procedures in UN organs are examined by Sydney D. Bailey's *The General Assembly of the United Nations: A Study of Procedure and Practice* (New York: Praeger, 1964), and a new third edition of Bailey's classic, with Sam Daws, *The Procedure of the UN Security Council* (Oxford: Oxford University Press, 1999), similarly examines Security Council practice. A related recent work is Miguel Marin-Bosch's *Votes in the UN General Assembly* (The Hague: Kluwer Law International, 1998).

Works on the legal development of the UN system and the UN Charter include: Leland Goodrich, Edvard Hambro, and Anne P. Simons, *Charter of the United Nations: Commentary and Documents*, 3rd rev. ed. (New York: Columbia University Press, 1969), which provides an article-by-article analysis of the Charter and early UN practice; D. W. Bowett, *The Law of International Institutions* (London: Stevens, 1970); Rosalyn Higgins, *The Development of International Law through the Political Organs of the United Nations* (New York: Oxford University Press, 1963); and Edward McWhinney, *United Nations Law Making* (New York: Holmes and Meier, 1984). For specific information on cases heard before the International Court of Justice, see the *International Court of Justice Yearbook* (The Hague: UN Publications, annual).

An explosion in recent literature on the peacekeeping aspects of UN activity has occurred since the demise of the Cold War. A few of the many excellent new treatments on this subject include: Frances Kofi Abiew, *The Evolution of the Doctrine and Practice of Humanitarian Intervention* (The Hague: Kluwer Law International, 1999); Boutros Boutros-Ghali, *An Agenda for Peace*, 2nd ed. (New York: United Nations, 1995); Paul Diehl, *International Peacekeeping* (Baltimore: Johns Hopkins University Press, 1993); Michael Doyle and Olara Otunnu, eds., *Peacemaking and Peacekeeping for the New Century* (Lanham, MD: Rowman & Littlefield, 1998); William J. Durch, ed., *The Evolution of UN Peacekeeping: Case Studies and Comparative Analysis* (New York: St. Martin's, 1993); and Steven R. Ratner, *The New UN Peacekeeping: Building Peace in Lands of Conflict After the Cold War* (New York: St. Martin's, 1996). An equally wide and growing literature exists concerning the humanitarian dimension of civil conflicts where UN peacekeepers and relief agencies work often simultaneously to meet security and assistance needs. Examples of this increasingly large literature include: Mary Anderson, *Do No Harm: How Aid Can Support Peace—or War* (Boulder, CO: Lynne Rienner, 1999); Thomas G. Weiss and Cindy Collins, *Humanitarian Challenges and Intervention: World Politics and the Dilemmas of Help* (Boulder, CO: Westview Press, 1996); and Thomas G. Weiss and Larry Minear, eds., *Humanitarianism across Borders: Sustaining Civilians in Times of War* (Boulder, CO: Lynne Rienner, 1993). The UN Blue Book series includes a number of volumes on various UN peacekeeping and peacemaking activities.

UN activities in the area of human rights have always drawn attention. More recent treatments on this subject include: Philip Alston, ed., *The United Nations and*

Human Rights: A Critical Appraisal (Oxford: Clarendon, 1992); Jack Donnelly, *International Human Rights* (Boulder, CO: Westview Press, 1998); and United Nations, *The United Nations and Human Rights, 1945–1995*, Blue Book vol. VII (New York: United Nations, 1996). For a comprehensive resource book on the subject see Robert F. Gorman and Ed Mihalkanin, *Historical Dictionary of Human Rights and Humanitarian Organizations* (Lanham, MD: Scarecrow Press, 1997).

The work of the United Nations in promotion of economic development has been extensive, and the literature detailing it is equally extensive. See Javed Ansari, *The Political Economy of International Economic Organization* (Boulder, CO: Lynne Rienner, 1986); Boutros Boutros-Ghali, *An Agenda for Development* (New York: United Nations, 1995); Richard Goode, *Economic Assistance to Developing Nations through the IMF* (Washington, DC: Brookings Institution, 1985); Bernard M. Hoekman, *The Political Economy of the World Trading System: From GATT to WTO* (Oxford: Oxford University Press, 1995); Mahbub Ul Haq et al., eds., *The UN and the Bretton Woods Institutions* (New York: St. Martin's, 1995); and Douglas Williams, *The Specialized Agencies and the United Nations* (New York: St. Martin's, 1987).

A range of scholarly and academic journals deal with UN-related issues. The United Nations Association publishes a bimonthly journal, *The Interdependent*, that assesses U.S. involvement in the UN system. Frank Cass and Company of London publishes a fine specialized journal, *International Peacekeeping*, that deals with UN peacekeeping activities, while Lynne Rienner Press of Boulder publishes a journal of international policy, *Global Governance: A Review of Multilateralism and International Organizations*.

Other journals containing scholarly and policy-related treatments on UN activities and policy issues include: *Foreign Affairs, Foreign Policy, International Journal, International Journal of Refugee Law, International Organization, Journal of International Affairs, Journal of Refugee Studies, Orbis, World Affairs, World Policy Journal,* and *World Politics.*

Most UN specialized and related agencies publish newsletters or periodicals relating to the work they undertake within the UN system. Links to such publications are often available online. See the Web site list below for Web site addresses. In addition, a variety of useful reference works are available to students seeking detailed information on the UN system. A range of such sources are listed below.

Bennett, A. LeRoy. *Historical Dictionary of the United Nations.* Lanham, MD: Scarecrow Press, 1997.

Everyman's United Nations. New York: United Nations Office of Public Information, various editions.

Everyone's United Nations. New York: United Nations Office of Public Information, 1986.

Hovet, Thomas Jr., Erika Hovet, and Waldo Chamberlain. *Chronology and Factbook of the United Nations.* Dobbs Ferry, NY: Oceana, 1979.

Matsuura, Kumiko, Joachim Müller, and Karl Sauvant, eds. *Annual Review of United Nations Affairs.* 2 vols. Dobbs Ferry, NY: Oceana, 1993.

———. *Chronology and Factbook of the United Nations.* Dobbs Ferry, NY: Oceana, 1992.

Osmańczyk, Edmund Jan. *Encyclopedia of the United Nations and International Agreements.* London: Taylor and Francis, 1985 and 1990.

Schivone, Giuseppe. *International Organizations: A Dictionary and Directory*. Chicago: St. James Press, 1983.

Union of International Associations. *Yearbook of International Organizations*. Munich: K. G. Saur, 1998.

WEB SITES

Main UN Web Sites

UN home page: www.un.org

UN System of Organizations (alphabetical list): www.unsystem.org

Related UN Sites

Crime Prevention and Criminal Justice Branch Information Network (UNCJIN): www.ifs.univie.ac.at/uncjin/uncjin.html

Dag Hammarskjöld Library (DHL): www.un.org/Depts/dhl

Databases: www.un.org/databases

Department and Offices: www.un.org/Depts

Department for Policy Coordination and Sustainable Development (DPCSD): www.un.org/dpcsd

Department for Political Affairs (DPA): www.un.org/Depts/dpa

Department of Peace-Keeping Operations (DPKO): www.un.org/Depts/dpko

Division for Ocean Affairs and the Law of the Sea: www.un.org/Depts/los

Division for the Advancement of Women: www.un.org/womenwatch

Economic and Social Commission for Asia and the Pacific (ESCAP): www.un.org/Depts/escap

Economic and Social Development: www.un.org/ecosocdev

Economic Commission for Africa (ECA): www.un.org/Depts/eca

Economic Commission for Europe (ECE): www.unece.org

Economic Commission for Latin America and the Caribbean (ECLAC): www.eclac.cl

Executive Office of the Secretary-General: www.un.org/Docs/SG

Food and Agriculture Organization (FAO): www.fao.org

Humanitarian Affairs: www.un.org.ha or www.unocha.org

Human Rights: www.un.org/rights

International Atomic Energy Agency (IAEA): www.iaea.or.at

International Civil Aviation Organization (ICAO): www.cam.org/icao

International Court of Justice (ICJ): www.icj-cij.org

International Criminal Tribunal for the Former Yugoslavia: www.un.org/icty

International Fund for Agricultural Development (IFAD): www.unicc.org/ifad

International Labor Organization (ILO): www.ilo.org

International Law: www.un.org/law

International Maritime Organization (IMO): www.imo.org

International Monetary Fund (IMF): www.imf.org

International Organization for Migration (IOM): www.iom.int

International Telecommunication Union (ITU): www.un.itu.ch

Nongovernmental Organization (NGO) links: www.un.org/MoreInfo/ngolink/welcome.htm

Office for Outerspace Affairs: www.or.at/OOSA_Kiosk/index.html

Office of the Spokesman for the Secretary-General: www.un.org/New/ossg

Office of the UN High Commissioner for Human Rights (UNHCHR): www.unhchr.ch

Office of the UN High Commissioner for Refugees (UNHCR): www.unhcr.ch

Peace and Security: www.un.org/peace

Publications and Sales: www.un.org/Pubs

Relief Web: www.reliefweb.int

Statistics Division: www.un.org/Depts/unsd

UN Children's Fund (UNICEF): www.unicef.org

UN Conference on Trade and Development (UNCTAD): www.unicc.org/unctad

UN CyberSchoolBus: www.un.org/Pubs/CyberSchoolBus

UN Development Programme (UNDP): www.undp.org

UN Educational, Scientific, and Cultural Organization (UNESCO): www.unesco.org

UN Environment Programme (UNEP): www.unep.org

UN Fund for Population Activities (UNFPA): www.unfpa.org

UN Industrial Development Organization (UNIDO): www.unido.org

UN Institute for Training and Research (UNITAR): www.rio.net/unitar/home.htm

UN International Drug Control Programme (UNDCP): www.undcp.org

UN News: www.un.org/News

UN Office at Geneva: www.unog.ch

UN Office at Vienna: www.un.or.at

UN Office for Project Services: www.unops.org

UN University (UNU): www.unu.edu

UN Volunteers (UNV): www.unv.org

War-Torn Societies Project (WSP): www.unicc.org/unrisd/wsp

World Bank: www.worldbank.org

World Food Programme (WFP): www.wfp.org

World Health Organization (WHO): www.who.ch

World Intellectual Property Organization (WIPO): www.wipo.int

World Meteorological Organization (WMO): www.wmo.ch

World Trade Organization (WTO): www.wto.org

Web Sites of Other Intergovernmental Organizations

Asia-Pacific Economic Cooperation (APEC): www.apecsec.org.sg/

Association of Southeast Asian Nations (ASEAN): www.aseansec.org/

Council of Europe: www.coe.fr/index.asp

European Union (EU): www.europa.eu.int

G-7 Information Center: www.g7.utoronto.ca/

G-77 Home Page: www.g77.org/

North Atlantic Treaty Organization (NATO): www.nato.int/

Organization for Economic Cooperation and Development (OECD): www.oecd/org

Organization of African Unity (OAU): www.oau-oua.org/

Organization of American States (OAS): www.oas.org

Web Sites of Important Nongovernmental Organizations

Academic Council on the United Nations System (ACUNS): www.yale.edu/acuns

American Society of International Law (ASIL): www.asil.org

Amnesty International: www.amnesty.org

CARE: www.care.org

CARITAS: www.caritas.org

Earthaction: www.earthaction.org

Human Rights Watch: www.hrw.org

Interaction (U.S. NGO umbrella body): www.interaction.org

International Committee of the Red Cross (ICRC): www.icrc.org

International Council of Voluntary Agencies (ICVA): www.icva.ch

International Federation of Red Cross and Red Crescent Societies (IFRC): www.ifrc.org

OXFAM (United Kingdom): www.oxfam.org.uk

Stockholm International Peace Research Institute (SIPRI): www.sipri.org

United Nations Association (UNA): www.unausa.org

UN Reform Home Page: www.un.og/reform

U.S. Committee for Refugees (USCR): www.refugees.org

World Council of Churches (WCC): wccx.wcc-coe.org

World Federalist Association: www.wfa.org

World Vision International: www.worldvision.org

World Wide Fund for Nature: www.panda.org

Index

About the Author

ROBERT F. GORMAN is Distinguished Teaching Professor of Humanities and Professor of Political Science at Southwest Texas State University. He served as a Council on Foreign Relations Fellow in the U.S. Department of State's Bureau for Refugee Programs, working on African refugee issues, and was also a visiting scholar at Africare, an American private voluntary organization. He is the author of numerous articles on refugee affairs, African politics, foreign affairs, and international relations. He is also the author of many books, including *Historical Dictionary of Refugee and Disaster Relief Organizations* (2000), *Historical Dictionary of Human Rights and Humanitarian Organizations* (1997), and *Refugee Aid and Development: Theory and Practice* (Greenwood Press, 1993).